CRITICAL RESPONSES TO *HAMLET* 1600-1900

◆ Volume 4: 1850-1900 ◆

Part One

The Hamlet Collection

General Editor: John Manning

ISSN 1078-7909

Titles in this series:

I. *New Essays on Hamlet*, eds. Mark Thornton Burnett and John Manning.

II. *'Hamlet' and Japan*, ed. Yoshiko Uéno.

III. *Critical Responses to 'Hamlet' 1600-1900*:
Vol. 1. 1600-1790, ed. David Farley-Hills.

IV. *Critical Responses to 'Hamlet' 1600-1900*:
Vol. 2. 1790-1838, ed. David Farley-Hills.

V. *Critical Responses to 'Hamlet' 1600-1900*:
Vol. 3. 1839-1854, ed. David Farley-Hills.

VI. *Critical Responses to 'Hamlet' 1600-1900*:
Vol. 4 (2 parts). 1850-1900, eds. John Manning, David Farley-Hills, and Johanna Procter.

THE HAMLET COLLECTION

CRITICAL RESPONSES TO *HAMLET* 1600-1900
✧ Volume 4: 1850-1900 ✧

Part One

Edited by

David Farley-Hills, John Manning,
and Johanna Procter

AMS Press
New York

Library of Congress Cataloging-in-Publication Data

Critical responses to Hamlet. 1600-1900 / edited by
  David Farley-Hills and John Manning.
    (The Hamlet collection; no. VI, part 1, part 2)
    Includes bibliographical references and index.
    Contents: – v. 4, parts 1 and 2: 1850-1900.
    Set ISBN 0-404-62316-6
    Part 1: ISBN 0-404-62271-2
    Part 2: ISBN 0-404-62272-0
    1. Shakespeare, William, 1564-1616. Hamlet. I.
    Farley-Hills, David. II. Series.
PR2807.C75 2006
822.3'3–dc20   94-44316
                                                              CIP

All AMS Books are printed on acid-free paper that meets the guidelines for performance and durability of the Committee on Production Guidelines for Book Longevity of the Council on Library Resources.

Copyright © 2006 by AMS Press, Inc.
All Rights reserved.

AMS Press, Inc.
Brooklyn Navy Yard, 63 Flushing Ave. – Unit #221
Brooklyn, NY 11205-1005, USA

MANUFACTURED IN THE UNITED STATES OF AMERICA

Contents

Textual Note	xiii
Acknowledgments	xv
Introduction	xvii
Selective Bibliography	
(i) Editions of *Hamlet*, 1850–1900	lxiii
(ii) Critical, Bibliographical and Textual Studies, 1850–1900	lxvii
(iii) Critical and Textual Studies in German, 1850–1900	lxx
(iv) Critical and Textual Studies in French and French Translations, 1850–1900	lxxiii
(v) Medical, Psychological and Critical Studies of Hamlet's Insanity, 1850–1900	lxxiii
(vi) Stage History	lxxiv
(vii) Modern Discussions	lxxv
1. George Henry Lewes	
(a) 'Charles Kean's Hamlet'	1
(b) '*Hamlet* and the German actors'	5
(c) From *The Life of Goethe*	
(i) *Hamlet* and *Wilhelm Meister*	10
(ii) *Hamlet* and *Faust*	10
(a) From 'Fechter in *Hamlet* and *Othello*'	12
(b) From 'First Impressions of Salvini'	18
2. Richard Grant White	
(a) Comments on *Hamlet*, III, i	22
(i) *Hamlet*	22
(ii) *Ophelia*	23
(b) Comment on *Hamlet*, III, iii	24

	(c) Comment on *Hamlet*, IV, iv	25
	(d) Note on the available texts	26
	(e) From introductory remarks to *Hamlet*	27
	(f) From 'The case of Hamlet the Younger'	
	(i) Ophelia	27
	(ii) Did Hamlet see the ghost in the closet scene?	28
	(iii) Hamlet's sanity or insanity	28
	(iv) The moral lesson of Hamlet	28
	(v) Hamlet's appearance on the stage, and the text	29
	(g) Stage Traditions: The Closet Scene	30
3.	William Watkiss Lloyd	
	(a) From 'Critical Essay on *Hamlet*'	31
	(b) Comment on 'How all occasions do inform against me'	48
4.	Henry Hope Reed	
	(a) From 'Four Lectures on Tragic Poetry: *Hamlet*'	49
	(b) Hamlet's inaction	54
5.	Walt Whitman: From 'Shakespeare Born'	58
6.	John Charles Bucknill	
	(a) Hamlet	60
	(b) Ophelia	118
7.	Charles Dickens: 'Mr Wopsle plays Hamlet'	129
8.	George Eliot: From *The Mill on the Floss*	135
9.	Samuel Timmins	136
10.	The *Times* Review of Fechter's Hamlet	139

11. Charles Cowden Clarke   142

12. Hippolyte Adolphe Taine
    (a) Shakespeare's style   165
    (b) Hamlet   168

13. Victor Hugo   174

14. Thomas Kenny
    (a) From 'The Men and Women of Shakespeare'   180
    (b) *'Hamlet'*   181

15. The Hamlet Controversy
    1. James Smith   188
    2. 'John Brown' (James Neild)   194
    3. 'Thomas Jones' (Charles Bright)   199
    4. 'Jack Robinson' (Archibald Michie)   203
    5. 'Jack Robinson (Jun.)' (David Blair)   208
    6. James Smith   209
    7. 'R.H.H.' (R.H. Horne)   216

16. James Russell Lowell   221

17. George Henry Miles   239

18. Alfred Lord Tennyson
    (a) *Maud* as a nineteenth-century *Hamlet*   298
    (b) Tennyson's letter to Dr Mann   299
    (c) Two theater visits 1873, 1874   299

19. 'Mr Irving's Hamlet'   301

20. Henry Irving's first night as Hamlet   308

Contents

21. The *Times* Review of Irving's Hamlet	312
22. Edward Dowden	
(a) From *Shakspere: His Mind and Art*	318
(b) From the introduction to the edition of *Hamlet*, 1899	345
23. Frank Marshall: From the Preface	350
24. Anthony Trollope	411
25. A.W. Ward	
(a) The First Quarto	413
(b) Shakespere's Power of Characterization	414
26. F.J. Furnivall	
(a) From his 'Introduction' to 'Hamlet' in the Leopold Shakespeare	416
(b) From *Measure for Measure*	428
27. John Weiss	
(a) The Gravediggers	431
(b) 'Antic disposition' and comedy	432
(c) Polonius	432
(d) 'Antic disposition' and irony	432
28. George Wilkes	444
29. Henry Irving	
(a) 'Hamlet and Ophelia. Act III, scene i'	447
(b) The opening of Irving's lecture, 1890	455
30. Mary Cowden Clarke: From 'Ophelia; the Rose of Elsinore'	457
31. Edmund Falconer	470

32. Margaret Oliphant	474
33. Helena Faucit, Lady Martin	501
34. Algernon Charles Swinburne	519
35. Joseph Knight	525
36. Matthew Arnold	528
37. The *Times* Review of Wilson Barrett's Hamlet	532
38. Ernesto Rossi	538
39. William Moy Thomas	544
40. George MacDonald	
(a) From the 'Preface' to his edition of *Hamlet* (1885)	549
(b) *Hamlet*, I, ii, 129ff.	550
(c) *Hamlet*, I, v, 108–9	551
(d) *Hamlet*, I, v, 121–2	551
(e) *Hamlet*, I, v, 151	551
(f) *Hamlet*, I, v, 173	552
(g) *Hamlet*, II, i, 3–4	552
(h) *Hamlet*, II, i, 88f.	553
(i) Summary at end of Act II	554
(j) *Hamlet*, III, i, 105	558
(k) *Hamlet*, III, iii, 73f.	559
(l) *Hamlet*, III, iv, 23	560
(m) *Hamlet*, III, iv, 25	560
(n) *Hamlet* Q2 IV, iv, 221–2	560
(o) *Hamlet* Q1 IV, v, 21 s.d.	561
(p) *Hamlet*, IV, v, 145f.	561
(q) *Hamlet*, V, ii, 357. End note	563

41. F. G. Fleay	
(a) Shakespeare's Public Career	564
(b) Shakespeare's ... Personal Connections with other Poets	565
(c) The Chronological Succession of Shakespeare's Plays	565
42. Julia Wedgwood	570
43. Hiram Corson: Hamlet	581
44. Fredericka Beardsley Gilchrist	600
45. Sinclair Korner	606
46. William Ward Crane	609
47. Mowbray Morris	613
48. The *Times* Review of Beerbohm Tree's Hamlet	627
49. Master Jack Howison (aged 12)	631
50. Barrett Wendell	634
51. John Corbin	642
52. George Bernard Shaw	
(a) From 'The Old Acting and the New'	657
(b) From 'Michael and his Lost Angel'	658
(c) From a letter to Ellen Terry	659
(d) Review of Forbes Robertson's production	659

53. Sir Herbert Beerbohm Tree	667
54. Frederick S. Boas	687
55. Ella Adams Moore	712
56. Ivan Turgeniev	719
57. Kate Terry Gielgud	
(a) *Hamlet*. Lyceum Theatre, 25 September, 1897	733
(b) *Hamlet*. Adelphi Theatre. A Translation from the French. 21 June, 1899	735
58. John M. Robertson	737
59. Georg Brandes	768
(a) *Hamlet* . . . Trails of Danish Manners	768
(b) The Psychology of Hamlet	771
(c) *Hamlet* as a Drama	780
(d) Hamlet and Ophelia	786
(e) *Hamlet*'s Influence on later Times	789
60. Sir Sidney Lee	794
61. Max Beerbohm	797
Index	801

Textual Note

All references to Shakespeare's plays and poems are to Stanley Wells and Gary Taylor, eds., *The Complete Works of William Shakespeare* (Oxford, 1988). Textual quotations are as given by the individual critics included in this volume. No attempt has been made to normalize the spelling of Shakespeare's name. The dates given in the headnotes refer in most cases to the date of first publication, with the exception of correspondence, in which the reference is to the date of writing. Authorial footnotes are cited within square brackets.

Acknowledgments

I have to thank a number of people for their help in compiling this anthology of criticism. First, I owe to my co-editors, David Farley-Hills and Johanna Procter, a huge debt of gratitude, in their suggestions for the inclusion of particular items, and the scanning and keying in of text. Particular thanks are due to the inter-library loan librarians at University of Wales, Swansea and University of Wales, Lampeter, who have been tireless and hugely efficient in their assistance to this project. Every effort has been made to trace the holder of copyright material. This does not apply to the earlier entries in this anthology, and many of the later items are in the public domain.

I have an enormous debt of gratitude to Gabe Hornstein for his continued commitment to the series, and to the team at AMS Press who have typeset and assisted with the proofreading of the volume. Particular mention should be given to Ashlie Sponenberg for her attention to this project.

John Manning
January, 2006

Introduction

Sir, we would see Hamlet

Covering the years 1850 to 1900, this fourth volume of *Critical Responses to Hamlet 1600–1900* bulks by far the largest.[1] Although it is often said that 'size does not matter', we can honestly say in this case the mass of material here presented points to the play's unprecedented popularity at this time not only in Britain, Europe, and America, but throughout the globe, from as far afield as Russia to the gold fields of Ballarat. During this period 'Hic et ubique' might with equal justice be exclaimed of the play as of its famous Ghost. *Hamlet*'s reputation was at its apogee. If no one suspected during the first century and a half after *Hamlet*'s first appearance that this play was in any way exceptional,[2] it most certainly was regarded as such in the period with which we are here concerned. Shakespeare without the Prince was unthinkable. Any other work from the received canon might possibly be lost, but not this. *Hamlet* was indispensable. Hamlet *was* Shakespeare.

Excerpts from contemporary documents in this present volume of *CRH* range from literary history, professional literary criticism, academic textual studies, critical commentaries, and psychoanalytic and other metafictions, and also include reviews, and familiar letters, and accounts of adaptations of the play for the theatre and for the general reading public. These confirm that Shakespeare was the literary darling of the age, and that *Hamlet* was his most glorious creation, the best-loved offspring of

1 This actually understates the importance of *Hamlet* for the period 1850–1900. It should be borne in mind that the present anthology of critical opinion does not include everything that was written between these dates. Also, three of the essays in *CRH* iii properly belong to our period. Gervinus (*CRH*, iii, 242–78) was translated in 1863 and reprinted in 1875, 1877, and 1892. The extract from H.N. Hudson's *Shakespeare: His Life, Art and Characters* (1871), that appeared in *CRH*, iii, 226–41, chronologically belongs to our present volume. Strongly influenced by the work of Karl Werder, it should be read in the context of the critical debate in this current volume.

2 See Thomas Kenny below, pp. 181–2. On the sparseness of early comment on *Hamlet*, see David Farley-Hills' 'Introduction' to *CRH*, i, xi.

his genius. During this period, this poetic 'child' was, it must be admitted, in grave danger of being over-indulged, and almost certainly somewhat spoilt. 'We revere even its irregularities,' John Charles Bucknill unashamedly enthused.[3] *Hamlet* was 'the great lyric of the nation' and 'Shakespeare . . . for aye its great dramatist'.[4] Such was its pressure and weight, the great literary minds of this generation could not ignore it: Alfred Lord Tennyson, Charles Dickens, George Eliot, Walt Whitman, Algernon Charles Swinburne, George Bernard Shaw, Max Beerbohm, Victor Hugo, and others, all had to find ways of dealing with it. The play formed part of the major discourses of the age: literary, historical, psychoanalytical, religious, and political.[5] It was inescapable. It provoked literary debate across Europe, and from the Old World to the New. Its cultural footprint extended beyond the literary and theatrical to embrace music, art, fashion, and popular culture. Around 1890, Houbigant, the French cosmetics firm, named a new face-powder, 'Poudre Ophélia',[6] because, presumably, they thought the association with the world's most famous madwoman might make the wearer of their product more alluring, or perhaps 'more attractive' (*Hamlet*, III, ii, 105) to *un beau tenebreux*, a young man dedicated to the current Hamletesque style, an up-to-the-minute fashionable melancholic.

Even setting aside what Kenny referred to as the play's uniquely 'strange and dark' fascination, this was the season of full-blown bardolatry. Shakespeare, and in particular *Hamlet*, was big box office in even the provincial theatres, but especially in London during the last quarter of the century. The year 1864 saw the celebration of the tercentenary of Shakespeare's birth; not in this year alone but throughout the last half of the nineteenth century there was a jubilee of celebration of the poet's fame. Shakespeare was not simply an English Renaissance actor-dramatist, he was a cultural icon, a national treasure.

---

[3] See below, p. 61.

[4] See Bucknill, p. 114 below.

[5] See also Marjorie Garber, *Shakespeare's Ghost Writers: Literature as Uncanny Causality* (New York and London: Methuen, 1987).

[6] See Bram Dijkstra, *Idols of Perversity: Fantasies of Feminine Evil in Fin-de-Siècle Culture* (New York and Oxford: Oxford University Press, 1986), p. 46.

The Victorian Reputation of *Hamlet*

The Victorians could only describe *Hamlet* with superlatives. William Watkiss Lloyd provides an extensive list: it is the 'longest', the 'most popular', 'the most effective . . . on the stage'. It produces the highest body count of all Shakespeare's tragedies. It is the most written about, and the quality of that writing is 'excellent'.[7] Samuel Timmins in 1860 could only affirm that *Hamlet* was 'the most popular of Shakespeare's plays' and 'one of the greatest works of dramatic art yet given to the world'.[8] Charles Cowden Clarke, discussing the state of the hero's mind, added: Hamlet was 'the most mysterious of all the characters in Shakespeare', while *Hamlet* was 'the giant of philosophical dramas'.[9] Thomas Kenny prolongs the list of mosts: '*Hamlet* is the most universally interesting of all the dramas of Shakespeare. It . . . unites the greatest diversity of thought and feeling in its central figure'. It was for him 'the most remarkable and the most enthralling of all the works of mortal hands'.[10] It was also the 'most quoted from' of all Shakespeare's plays.[11] The American, George Henry Miles, simply considered the play 'the supreme masterpiece of human genius'.[12]

If the play attracted superlatives, so did its hero. 'Of all Shakspeare's male characters Hamlet is the most fascinating, the most perplexing, the most various, and the most thoroughly identified in the national mind with the creator's genius.' Thus wrote George Henry Lewes in 1850. The qualifier, 'male', is almost certainly a tautology, for how could anyone looking at the Shakespearean canon at this time propose a 'fascinating' or 'perplexing' female as a serious rival?[13]

---

7   See below, pp. 43–4. On the popularity of *Hamlet*, see also Frank Marshall, p. 352 below; Edmund Falconer, pp. 470f. below; and Margaret Oliphant, pp. 474f. below.

8   See below, p. 136.

9   See below, pp. 145 and 164.

10 See below, pp. 181 and 187.

11 See below, p. 352.

12 See below, p. 280.

13 See below, p. 1. Others of this time would bestow the accolade of 'genius' on this production of Shakespeare: see Charles Cowden Clarke (p. 152 below).

Two years later Lewes could only affirm that 'no play is so popular as *Hamlet*. It amuses thousands annually. It stimulates the minds of millions'.[14] He attributes its attraction for even the lowest and most ignorant audiences to its 'profundity and sublimity', for 'the human soul can *feel* a grandeur that it cannot understand'. So attuned to the play was the popular Victorian taste that Thomas Kenny could go even further and claim that 'every mind of ordinary sensibility and intelligence' could not only 'feel' but comprehend both Hamlet's amazement at the discovery of hidden crimes, that involve those that are nearest and dearest, and his repugnance at the 'uncongenial mission', which he is called upon to perform. Frank Marshall claimed that, while the fiercer passions of Lear, Othello and Macbeth may be beyond most people, everyone could identify with Hamlet.[15]

Henry Hope Reed believed that the play reflected 'the constitution of Shakespeare's own mind', for it incorporates 'the habits of his intellect'.[16] To read it, is to be closer to the genius of the bard himself. Any notion of a Keatsian 'negative capability' are out of the question in this climate. John Charles Bucknill adds his considerable weight to Reed's views: 'Never does Shakespeare seem to have found a character so suited to give noble utterance to his own most profound meditations as in Hamlet.... [W]e unconsciously personify Shakespeare in this character'.[17] Bucknill saw Hamlet as a representation of Shakespeare no less surely than he regarded Childe Harold as a personification of Byron.[18] The study of Hamlet thus was held to shed light on Shakespeare's own opinions. 'Shakespeare has here ... reflected the depth of his own great soul; has set up a glass in which the ages will read the inmost part of him; how

---

14 See below, p. 6. The same point is repeated on p. 11.

15 See below, p. 352,

16 See below, pp. 49ff. The Shakespeare=Hamlet equation will be found not infrequently in this volume. But, as in Victorian society at large, there were dissenters. Thomas Kenny took it for granted that Shakespeare does not 'appear ... in his own personal character' in this play. See below, p. 186.

17 See below, p. 103.

18 See below, p. 103.

he thought of death and suicide; how he doubted of the future, and felt the present'.[19]

The Airbrushing of Hamlet

To Richard Grant White and to John Charles Bucknill, Hamlet was 'a dear and intimate personal friend'. Indeed, an 'interesting and ever-eloquent friend'. 'If he came back from the grave, like his father, I should be very happy to make his acquaintance,' opined one young gentleman in the afterglow of Henry Irving's brilliant performance of the part.[20] The Prince's 'humour and sensibility, wit and philosophy'[21] would surely make him welcome in any *salon*, Victorian dinner party, or drawing room. While we might smile at the critical naïveté of these comments, the gullible belief in a character as an actual person with a life beyond the play, some of the best criticism of the time was, in fact, character based. For the Victorians Shakespeare's supreme gift as a dramatist lay in his powers of characterization.[22] It was Edward Dowden's belief that the play sprang from 'Shakespeare's profound sympathy with an individual soul and a personal life'. The play 'deals not with a problem, but with a life'. Because the play is like real life, 'there is much to elude and baffle enquiry'.[23] It is true that *Hamlet* was more heard than understood at this period.

To produce a 'Hamlet as our fireside friend' the character has had to have been extensively air-brushed and bears little relation to Shakespeare's Revenge-Tragedy protagonist, and even less to Saxo's Danish original. Charles Cowden Clarke unblushingly acknowledges the fact: 'we make the handsomest excuses for him; and, in short, elevate him in our esteem'.[24] His character, for Henry Hope Reed, was at once 'gentle

---

19   Bucknill again. See below, p. 118.
20   See below, p. 304.
21   See below, pp. 27 and 116.
22   See particularly A.W. Ward, below, p. 414.
23   See below, pp. 320–1.
24   See below, p. 164.

and noble and thoughtful'.[25] To Charles Cowden Clarke he was a thorough gentleman. Even in the scene with Ophelia (III, i) Hamlet's 'rudeness' is only 'apparent', and his underlying disposition is, somewhat surprisingly, characterized by 'truth and gentleness'.[26] 'Get thee to a nunnery' becomes 'a loving admonition, springing ... from the conviction that there she would find a haven of security and repose ... '.[27] No one in the Victorian period seemed prepared to acknowledge that a 'nunnery' was in current Elizabethan canting terms nothing more or less than a house of ill-fame.[28]

In performance the 'apparent' harshness of his language and behaviour was 'mitigated' by the introduction of some stage business, which indicates that Hamlet was aware that the King and Polonius were eavesdropping on his conversation.[29] Frank Marshall assures his audience that had it not been for his suspicions that he was being watched, Hamlet 'would have spoken to Ophelia with the greatest affection'.[30] And, as a

25 See below, p. 50.

26 See below, p. 53.

27 See below, p. 192. The reviewer is quick to add: 'There is nothing either in the text or the stage directions to warrant it'. George Henry Miles, p. 266 below, also sees the 'nunnery' as a place of refuge. Dowden is closer to the mark, though his reading of the outburst still favours the Prince. For him, the 'nunnery' becomes a bitter satiric jibe at the missal she holds and her sham show of piety (pp. 337–8 below).

28 In *Christs Teares over Iervsalem* (1593) Thomas Nashe refers to 'a Colledge of Curtizans' as a 'Nunnery' (*The Works of Thomas Nashe*, ed. Ronald B. McKerrow, reprinted .. . with ... supplementary notes ... by F. P. Wilson, 5 vols [Oxford: Basil Blackwell, 1966], ii, 151–2). Henry VIII's dissolution of the monasteries had rendered obsolete a congregation of females for religious purposes; in the 1590s a house gathering a number of women together, as Nashe indicates, must arouse at least the suspicion of immoral practices. Shakespeare's Globe was in the suburbs of London, and 'nunneries', in the shape of the stews of Bankside, were not far from its door. Ophelia's journey would be but a short and simple step.

29 For example in Montgomery's 1867 performance. See below, pp. 191–2. Frank Marshall describes the business and presents it, probably inadvertently, as grotesquely ludicrous: 'Polonius, who had previously been fidgeting behind the arras, pops his head out to see what is going on, and in so doing drops his staff.' See below, pp. 365–6. Furnivall (see below, p. 423) rules this piece of clownage out of court, and sees no evidence for it in the text.

30 See below, p. 366.

Victorian, Marshall was an intimate of Hamlet's most private thoughts, and could communicate them to us. Though Bucknill was prepared to admit that Hamlet was 'not a perfect character', like most of his contemporaries he could not bring himself to believe that the 'noble and sensitive' Prince's love for the 'beautiful and virtuous' Ophelia was other than 'sincere'.[31] This became the Fortieth of the Thirty-Nine Articles, an act of faith and a point of national piety. To Frank Marshall the notion that Hamlet had been guilty of the 'ruin' of Ophelia was altogether monstrous, a 'foul stain on Hamlet's character, based on 'ignorance of the play itself'.[32] As we will later see, his airbrushed notion of 'the play itself' may not in every particular have corresponded with the text of the Clarendon edition.

Hamlet's 'apology' to Laertes, in Act V, scene ii, must appear to any modern reader as little more than a piece of verbal shuffling, whether sincerely meant or not. But for Charles Cowden Clarke it was 'conceived in the very highest sense of magnanimity and gentle bearing:—"gentle" in every sense:— a perfect gentleman'.[33]

The King-at-prayer scene (Act III, Scene iii), which gave Dr Johnson such problems—the sentiments were 'too horrible to be read or uttered' or, as Coleridge embroiders it, 'so atrocious and horrible, as to be unfit to be put into the mouth of a human being'—[34], were, according to Richard Grant White, 'altogether omitted in the stage copy'.[35] Frank Marshall later in the century refers to it as 'a scene rarely, if ever, represented on the stage'. When Marshall does consider Hamlet's soliloquy, he has to agree with Johnson and Coleridge that such sentiments are 'revolting to our feelings' as well as to theirs, but, unlike them, he cannot believe that Shakespeare 'intend[ed] us to believe that these horrid sentiments were

---

31 See below, pp. 71–2.

32 See below, pp. 363–4.

33 See below, p. 163.

34 See *CRH*, i, 190 and *CRH*, ii, 58.

35 See below, p. 24. Henry Irving restored the soliloquy in his production of 1874, though the whole scene was apparently cut from the 1878 performance (see Margaret Oliphant, p. 497 below).

entertained with any seriousness by the mind of Hamlet'.[36] Once again we find that the Victorians felt they had greater insight into the mind of Shakespeare and Hamlet (they were one and the same, after all) than all previous generations.

Lewes points to the fact that actors always omitted Hamlet's 'irreverent words' spoken to and about his father (I, v, 120–66). Rather than confront the difficulty of an irreverent Hamlet, it was easier and safer to cut Shakespeare's text.[37] Similarly, Hamlet's coarse address to the body of Polonius at the end of Act III, scene iv, was never presented upon the stage.[38] The closet scene, that scene of passion between Hamlet and his mother, was often 'lopped and cut . . . in deference to modern modesties'.[39] Actors did not usually portray Hamlet's over-the-top reaction to the King's response to the performance of the *Murder of Gonzago* (III, ii, 249–81), according to Lewes, 'for fear of seeming comic'.[40] And this, presumably, is the root cause of the actors' reluctance to represent Hamlet as mad.[41] Thus Walter Montgomery in his 1867 Melbourne performance 'cut whole passages which are . . . demonstrative of a disordered intellect'.[42]

Charles Cowden Clark viewed theatrical versions of the play as 'so notoriously abridged, that it is impossible to judge . . . the poet's delineation of character', citing the fact that Act IV, scene iv, in which Hamlet

---

36 See below, pp. 377 and 379.

37 See below, p. 26. In this tradition, William Montgomery's Melbourne performance of 1867 omitted 'the unfilial and scoffing language [Hamlet] employs towards his father' (see below, pp. 196–7).

38 See Frank Marshall, pp. 382–3 below. Henry Irving abbreviated the address to the corpse, p. 495 below.

39 Margaret Oliphant (p. 494 below), referring specifically to Henry Irving's production. But her comment applies to nineteenth-century stage traditions in general, of which she seems to approve as 'necessary'.

40 See below, p. 18. Henry Irving's 1874 Hamlet did portray this. For its effectiveness, see p. 310 below.

41 See below, p. 20.

42 See below, p. 191. The lines omitted are III, ii, 263–72.

meets the forces of Fortinbras, 'is never represented upon the stage'.[43] Indeed, it was only towards the end of the century that Forbes Robertson allowed Fortinbras to sweep in at the end of the play to upstage the deceased Prince and to claim the throne of Denmark.

The critics, too, were inclined to cut some of the more objectionable lines assigned to the Prince. Thomas Bowdler's expurgated *Family Shakespeare* was, after all, reprinted in the same period. In quoting from Act III, Scene ii, George Henry Miles, possibly following contemporary stage practice, passes over Hamlet's bawdily indecent lines to Ophelia. Kemble, of course, had famously refused to speak them.[44] Frank Marshall believed that 'all the offensive portion of [this scene] can be omitted from representation without any injury to the interest of the play' and, therefore, 'we need not dwell any further upon it'.[45] This is what might be termed the 'ostrich' school of criticism. Edward Dowden in 1875 is the first critic in this collection to refer to Hamlet's 'intolerably improper' 'half-ambiguous obscenities', but he declines to explicate in detail. It is sufficient that 'Ophelia understands his words'.[46] Later, Frank Marshall would only mention in passing this portion of dialogue with the sole purpose of abhorring it. He does not fail to record its 'filthiness', its 'outrage on decency', its 'impure allusions', and its 'foul innuendoes'. Where for some, the passage of time might blunt the force of obscene innuendo as the dialect of another age, Marshall records his present outrage, and for him, time has not dulled the edge of these utterances. His references to these verbal lubricities may well have aroused the interest of his original, young, Catholic audience, but he does not elaborate. In fact, he could only with difficulty bring himself to believe that the 'pure-minded' Shakespeare could possibly have written this part of the text: 'some of [Hamlet's] most offensive lines were inserted by the players to suit the depraved taste of their audience'. In deploring this 'depraved taste' of Shakespeare's audience, he commended by implication the great

43 See below, pp. 146–7.
44 See *CRH*, ii, xvif.
45 See below, p. 375.
46 See below, p. 340.

advance in moral and literary decency of his own Victorian cultural moment. Nevertheless, Marshall had to execute a double take on this by admitting that Shakespeare must have at least approved this filth, even if he did not write it. The implication here is that if Shakespeare had written in the last half of the nineteenth century, and been a beneficiary of Marshall's high Victorian literary and moral values, he certainly would not have sullied his page with such gross indecency. Of course, that also meant that Shakespeare would not have written *Hamlet*. The editors of the Oxford edition, however, failed to endorse Marshall's moral position. They not only printed the indecencies, but gave them the Clarendon *imprimatur*. This discredited and undermined Marshall's moral stance and textual suppositions. Marshall could offer no scholarly rebuttal, but simply consigned the edition 'to the library', where presumably he hoped it would remain safely unread.[48] Marshall's position might be referred to the non-Darwinian monkey posture of neither 'seeing nor hearing'. If, however, Shakespeare needed a defense, we might note that if the gross dunghill of Elizabethan popular culture brought forth *Hamlet*, the nice moral sensibility of Marshall's age could claim no work of literary genius to rival it. All critics such as Marshall could do would be to seek to gag and geld it.

On the stage, the simple expedient of rendering the Prince morally acceptable was achieved by cutting and lopping. The merest suspicion of an offending phrase or line, any affront to public decency, no matter what authority it might have in Quarto, Folio, or other provenance, was cut on the stage without benefit of clergy. Any distractions from the Prince's absolute moral integrity were eliminated in advance of the performance: Fortinbras was 'taken out' before he could upstage the dying Hamlet at the play's conclusion. Any suggestion that the *beau idéal* of the *beau monde* might have been, shall we say, 'beside himself', were excised, and never appeared on the public stage. Irreverence to his father (alive or dead) was simply unthinkable. And a Victorian gentleman could never speak harsh words to father, mother, and, I pause, because, who is Ophelia? What is she—beloved, intended wife; treacherous decoy;

---

47 See below, p. 369. For Marshall's discussion of the scene, which is found in an appendix, see pp. 368–70. Later, p. 375 below, he condones the practice of omitting the offending passages in performance.

Critical Responses to Hamlet   xxvii

deluded simpleton, fallen strumpet? Yet all the Victorian critical swains seem to commend her. We will return to this character later.

While actors cut, critics added and embroidered. Frank Marshall begins his account of the play, not as Shakespeare does on the chilly battlements of the Danish Royal Castle, but at the University, where Hamlet first receives the news of his father's death. There follows a frenzied ride not from Ghent to Aix, but from Wittenberg to Elsinore.[48] As far as we know, such a scene in Quarto, Folio or *Ur*-format, was never penned until the Victorian period. If we ever needed it—Shakespeare with better judgment thought we did not—the Victorians provide us with a touching rendition of the girlhood of Ophelia, happily dandled on her eminently low-class nanny's knee, the while regaled with bawdy songs, which remained in some half-forgotten place in her memory until they were unfortunately recalled in her adult distracted state.[49] We gain access to Hamlet's inmost thoughts, things Shakespeare never seems to have known, or saw fit to write. Yes, the Victorians' boast that no previous period in history knew as much about Hamlet as they did is herein vindicated.[50] Perhaps it was because he was their fireside friend.

Amidst all the adulation of Hamlet's exemplary character, F. J. Furnivall's doubly agnostic take on the Prince is refreshing. He is clearly impatient with all those who refuse to admit any imperfection in Hamlet. He determinedly argues that, in his view, Hamlet is no hero. In fact, Hamlet is a disgrace to his lineage of Scandinavian warrior kings, who would not have thought twice about exacting revenge and would have done the deed without hesitation. It is not Hamlet's superior intellect and wit, nor his exceptional sufferings that should commend him to us. It is his very weakness, his reluctance to embrace the duties that are thrust upon him, his utter disgust at female sexuality. These things, Furnivall

---

48   See below, p. 357.

49   See below, pp. 363–4. The point does not originate with Marshall. Anna Jameson first introduced the nurse to the discussion of this scene. See *CRH*, ii, 226–7. Mary Cowden Clarke indulges herself with a fictionalized girlhood of Ophelia, which enshrines the critical fantasies of Jameson and Marshall. See extract 30 in this volume.

50   See below, p. 302.

tells us, make Hamlet our kinsman, our *semblable*, our *frère*. Perhaps it was Furnivall's agnosticism that freed him from the moral and theological baggage that caused Johnson, Coleridge and others to gag when discussing the infamous king-at-prayer scene. Whatever difficulties previous commentators had with the scene, Furnivall approaches it with evident enjoyment:

> On his road to his mother [Hamlet] finds the king at that pathetic prayer of his ... and has an easy chance of performing his vow. He will do it; but then he thinks, and then he won't do it. His former uncertainties about heaven and hell have been cleard up, he knows all about the conditions of entry to both, and if he kills the murderer on his knees he'll send him to heaven .... So, to avoid this, he keeps him for hell: a mere excuse of course for delay. His mind is full of his mother. The duty of revenge is a bore to him, and has almost died out of his mind; any excuse will do to be rid of it.[51]

Furnivall exacts some humour at Hamlet's and the Church's expense. Not only does he cock a snook at previous generations of critics, he also manages to score some palpable hits against established Christianity. 'Prayer' is 'pathetic'—and we can be fairly certain that Furnivall does not wish to suggest that this is the pathos that uplifts the human spirit. It is 'pathetic' in its most degraded sense. Hamlet then bandies about the theological mysteries of 'heaven' and 'hell', but in a way which Furnivall encourages us to regard as self-serving and self-deceived. Salvation and damnation, the soul's future state in eternity, are stripped of any higher Christian tincture. These notions are no more than a further instance of present time-serving, another 'excuse for delay'. Hamlet is therefore seen as deluded concerning both this life and the next. 'Heaven' and 'Hell' are mere subterfuges to justify a failure to perform his duty to revenge. This has become a 'bore' to him. Furnivall unashamedly implies that 'heaven' and 'hell' are equally boring concepts.

If Goethe's famous 'acorn-in-a-vase' metaphor epitomized the earlier, Romantic attitude to Hamlet, can we discern any distinctive, shared Victorian characterization of the Prince? Such a view would seem to emerge in the latter half of the period with which we are here concerned. William

---

51   See below, p. 424.

Watkiss Lloyd sees the issue as 'the predominance of the contemplative over the practical in a mind of the highest order, both intellectually and morally.'[52] Bucknill comments on the 'contrast between [Hamlet's] vivid intellectual activity, and the inertness of his conduct'.[53] The whole plot of the tragedy, according to Charles Cowden Clarke, turns upon 'the conflict between determination and irresolution, arising from over-reflectiveness'. Had it been otherwise we might have dismissed the hero as unworthy of our attention. As it is, we esteem the character as having a mind superior to the task which is imposed upon him.[54] To James Russell Lowell, it was an excess of imagination that paralyzed Hamlet's power to act.[55] Margaret Oliphant compellingly states that his principal trait is 'disenchantment'. All the things that had previously sustained his existence—his father's honour, his belief in his mother's love and virtue, his affection for Ophelia, his delight in his schoolfellows—are shown up to be no more than illusions, which are progressively torn away. This process of *désillusionment* results in a new painful vision of life, which paralyzes the will and renders all action futile, for the world can never be put back into the same shape that it was, can never be 'put right'. The revenge on his father's murderer is nothing more than a paltry anodyne.

The Victorians and Hamlet
Only a fool would come to this fourth volume of *Critical Responses to Hamlet* looking for the 'right' reading of Shakespeare's play. When a new generation of actors, audiences, critics, and readers takes over the responsibility of interpreting any Shakespearean text, it will inevitably reject the findings of those who went before. And this, as we will see, the contributors to this volume did in respect of *Hamlet*. But, while the Victorians believed they knew more about *Hamlet* than their predecessors, they were not, however much they believed they were, getting nearer the truth. They were simply shifting points of view and offering different

---

52   See below, p. 31.
53   See below, p. 112.
54   See below, p. 164.
55   See below, p. 128.

perspectives on the play. Clearly, the Victorian psyche felt passionately about *Hamlet* and believed that there was something rattling around inside its profound verbal music that was worthy of attention. The tragedy, in the words of Thomas Kenny, excited 'perplexity', 'wonder and bewilderment'.[56] But in the responses to the play included in this volume we often see more of these Victorian authors and their times than we do of Shakespeare's *Hamlet*.

Hamlet sets out to hold a mirror up to human nature, and the Victorians were delighted to see their own cherished views and visages reflected therein. 'It is *we* who are Hamlet', they could say, with even greater conviction than Hazlitt had done in the previous generation.[57] Tennyson saw, with whatever degree of self-conceit, his *Maud* as 'a little *Hamlet*'.[58] The Victorian sages are cited in nodding assent to the effects of the play. Charles Cowden Clarke cites Carlyle on the majesty of silence in connection with *Hamlet*, I, i.[59] Others were pleased to find in the play prescient echoes of the great Victorian poets, Tennyson and Longfellow.[60] Bucknill found remarkable 'points of resemblance between *Hamlet* and *In Memoriam*'.[61] A modern reader might also describe these as 'remarkable', but only because they are so far-fetched and improbable, that they draw attention to themselves.

In *Hamlet* Victorians could find their cherished belief systems affirmed. The play 'warmed [their] wiser and holier thoughts'.[62] In it 'Faith in the existence of a God, and of a future state of existence', is expressed so powerfully that it invalidates and refutes any sceptical materialist philosophy the Prince might have imbibed at Wittenburg.[63] In this play

---

56   See below, p. 182.

57   Bucknill cites Hazlitt's assertion on p. 116 below. For Hazlitt's 1817 comment, see *CRH*, ii, 114. The italics in the quotation are mine.

58   See below, pp. 298 and 299.

59   See below, pp. 150–1.

60   See below, pp. 68, 106, 115.

61   See below, p. 115.

62   See below, p. 164.

63   According to Bucknill. See below, p. 86.

Shakespeare exhibits a 'breadth of wisdom' and the 'beauty of morality'. Shakespeare's 'wisdom' and 'morality' uncannily anticipated that of the Victorian age. Any suspicion of the 'immorality of Shakespeare' must be attributed only to the ignorant, the thoughtless, or the hypocritical, and can be refuted by pointing to any of the Prince's great speeches, especially that on Providence (V, ii, 156–68).[64] The efficacy of prayer is exhibited in Hamlet's soliloquy as he watches his uncle praying. Even the arch-hypocrite, Claudius, expresses a belief in the power of prayer, although he cannot avail himself of its benefits.[65]

To see the play in this way, it was necessary for the Victorian reader to identify its excerpted 'beauties', its so-called 'purple passages', taken out of dramatic context, and to relate them to various kinds of morally uplifting reading, which found favour at this time: the homily, the adage, the essay, the epitome, the lecture, the epitaph, the 'advice' to young persons. In Hamlet's speech to Horatio in Act Three, Scene Two 'Shakespeare has almost exceeded himself; a more beautiful epitome of the character of a true friend does not exist, nor a better guide for those who wish to find this treasure'.[66] Hamlet's thoughts on Providence at V, ii, 134–8 are 'a beautiful little homily upon resignation and reliance'.[67] His meditation on Yorick's skull (V, i, 180–90) is 'an epitaph to [the jester's] fame, and a lecture upon vanity'.[68] Ophelia's sharp retort to her brother concerning the 'primrose path of dalliance' (I, iii, 46–51) becomes a miniature sermon. For Charles Cowden Clarke 'no one dispenses sounder advice, or speaks more practical axioms' than Polonius. His 'advice to his son . . . is as fine as an essay in Bacon', a 'string of axioms that would make a perfect gentleman'.[69]

Dowden believed that Hamlet's mission in the closet scene was to save 'a human soul from the bondage of corruption'. In the hands of George

---

64 The opinion of Charles Cowden Clarke. See below, pp. 162–3.
65 See below, p. 93.
66 The sentiments of Marshall. See below, p. 374.
67 See below, pp. 162–3.
68 See below, p. 164.
69 See below, p. 153.

Henry Miles the Prince becomes a Spurgeon before Spurgeon, a contemporary revivalist, soul-saving preacher: 'H[amlet] labours giant-like to save [Gertrude's] "fighting" soul, reaching down a redeeming hand through the darkness of deep abysses, dragging her half willing, half reluctant, bruised, trembling, bleeding, into the full daylight of God's holy summits'![70] If Hamlet is here the preacher, Gertrude is the archetypal Victorian 'fallen' woman.

It may strike readers of Shakespeare's text as odd, but the churchyard scene for the Victorian play-goer embodied a certain faith in the afterlife: Hamlet's declaration of love, 'whose echoes ringing down the aisles of death, must have conveyed to [Ophelia's] ransomed soul and reillumined mind the dearest tribute of mortality to perfect the chalice of spiritual bliss. That sweet face on the threshold of another sphere, must have turned earthward awhile to catch those noble, jealous words'.[71] At this point we have abandoned any text of *Hamlet* (Quarto, Folio, or *Ur*). This is not a flight of angels, but a flight of fantasy. Under the influence of such gushing sentimentality one wonders whether Claudius's ordered the 'living monument' to be erected over Ophelia's tomb from Highgate cemetery rather than from a local, medieval Danish monumental mason.

How aptly would the Ghost's 'revelations from the spirit-world', as Bucknill styled them,[72] strike a chord with the table-rapping, séance culture of the Victorians! Only a Victorian fantasy, imbued with a spiritualist faith, could construe the Ghost's strict instructions to his son not to 'contrive against thy mother aught' as inspired by 'yearning emotion on the part of the spirit', 'the idea of love in that life beyond life, still hovering with angelic tenderness . . . over his weak and repentant partner in the flesh'.[73] One wonders what evidence can be found in Shakespeare's play of Gertrude's 'repentance' or, for that matter, of the Ghost's 'yearning' for his former partner, or, even more extraordinarily, of his 'angelic tenderness'? Hamlet *père*, however besotted he may have once

---

70 For Dowden, see below, pp. 341–2. For Miles, see below, p. 272.
71 Miles, again. See below, p. 286.
72 See below, p. 74.
73 See below, pp. 151f.

been during his mortal life, now knows more about the character of his former 'partner in the flesh' than ever he did during his corporeal existence.

It should come as no surprise that Victorian prejudices necessarily emerge in the contemporary writings on the play. For example, it is hard for a twenty-first-century reader to judge the virulence of anti-Catholic sentiment during this time. To provide a context we might turn to 'Pisanus Fraxi' (a.k.a. H. S. Ashbee):

> Every reflecting mind must find it difficult to understand how, in the present nineteenth century, a system so false, prurient, and polluted can still be believed in, can find devotees ready to lay down their lives in its support, and even make converts of men of knowledge, experience, and bright parts. For, whether we consider the absurd miracles which are even today being palmed off upon the credulous, the blunders, crimes and follies of the infallible popes, the vices and hypocrisy of many of the clergy, . . . the duplicity, lax teaching, infamous doctrines, and dishonest commercial dealings . . . [74]

I break off only to spare the reader more. And there is much, much more. Against this background we can place Edward Dowden's words on the maimed funeral rites accorded Ophelia:

> There is no Friar Laurence in this play. To him the Catholic children of Verona carried their troubles . . . . Hamlet is hardly a man to seek for wisdom or for succour from a priest. Let them resolve his doubts about the soul, about immortality, about God first. But Shakspere has taken care to show us . . . what religion is. To Ophelia's funeral the Church reluctantly sends her representative. All that the occasion suggests of harsh, formal, and essentially inhuman dogmatics is uttered by the Priest. The distracted girl has by untimely accident met her death, and therefore, instead of charitable prayers, 'Shards, flints, and pebbles should be thrown on her'. . . .

Hamlet's superior intellectual independence is here contrasted with the implied gullibility of 'the Catholic children of Verona'. Dowden then

---

[74] Pisanus Fraxi, *Centuria Librorum Absconditorum: Notes Bio—Biblio—Iconographical and Critical on Curious and Uncommon Books* (London: Privately printed, 1879), pp. xxi–xli. Ian Gibson, *The Erotomaniac: The Secret Life of Henry Spencer Ashbee* (London: Faber and Faber, 2001), p. 208, tells of Ashbee's low estimate of Irving's *Hamlet* and of his knowledge of the play from reading it many times (see also, pp. 11–12).

proceeds to make the circumstances of Ophelia's death much more clearcut than Shakespeare ever did, and suggests that her corpse is subjected to some religiously motivated, uncharitable rite of ritualistic stoning. Finally, Dowden's anti-Catholic scorn (it should be remembered that he was Professor of English in the Protestant ascendancy enclave of Trinity College, Dublin) is vigorously pointed up (just in case we missed his heavy-handed irony) by the succession of exclamation marks and the final alliterative plosives of the next quoted passage: 'These are the sacred words of truth, of peace, of consolation which Religion has to whisper to wounded hearts! . . . Better to consort in Denmark with players than with priests!'[75] Dowden's almost Hamletesque parenthetical 'in Denmark' (cf. I, v, 110) suggests that this is not so in Britain. Yes, Hamlet's *alma mater* was not the Sorbonne but Wittenberg, 'a name honoured in the Protestant hearts of England'.[76]

Frank Marshall would probably agree that anti-Catholic sentiments had left their mark on the play, though he comes from the other side of the sectarian divide. His *Study of Hamlet* (1875) had its origins in two lectures presented to the Catholic Young Men's Association. The sermonizing and moralistic tone that often intrudes on his commentary must surely stem from this provenance. Nor, given this, should we be altogether surprised that Marshall passes over in total silence the officiating priest at Ophelia's funeral, whose inflexible, uncharitable dogmatism so outraged Dowden. But Dowden and Marshall both agree on Hamlet's exceptional intellectual capacity. Yet where in Dowden's mind Hamlet's scepticism and reasoning independence are signs of intellectual superiority, in Marshall's eyes these are symptoms of his weakness, his moral fault, and his lack of humility. For Marshall it is no accident that the play was written in the shadow cast by his country's historical breach with the Church of Rome. The abandonment of unquestioning obedience to the old Faith caused many minds 'to be tossed upon a fathomless sea of doubt, hopelessly uncertain which way to steer, no longer believing in their compass,

---

75 See below, pp. 339–40.

76 The phrase is Gervinus's. See *CRH*, iii, 262. The translation of Gervinus' highly influential *Shakespeare Commentaries* was issued several times within our period (1862, 1875, 1877, 1892).

and distrustful of the very stars by which otherwise they might have directed their course . . . Nothing in this world seemed certain or secure, and the very foundations of Christianity were shaken beyond repair. . . . Of such minds Hamlet is a striking type', and one which Marshall recognized in his contemporaries. Marshall regards Hamlet with something more like pity than admiration, because he lacks 'the sweet hope, and humble trust, of a true Christian'.[77] By 'Christian', he almost certainly means 'Catholic'.

Marshall's attempt to contextualize the play within broad brush-strokes of sixteenth-century religious and intellectual history is potentially interesting. Had he taken these views back to the text he would have found many details to support him. The Ghost's present residence in Purgatory, a future state utterly discredited by the Protestants, suggests that Hamlet *père* belongs to the old religious order. The younger Hamlet's education at Wittenberg, founded in 1501 and the centre of Luther's stand against Rome, places him in the new Protestant way of thinking and may indicate where he picked up his taste for vehement, foul-mouthed invective and bawdy innuendo. The Protestant reformers, after all, had something of a reputation in these matters. Théodore de Bèze was more famous in his lifetime for the salacious epigrams of his youth than for his pastoral care of Calvin's flock in Geneva; Simon Lemnius' epigrams, published while still a student at Wittenberg, shocked even Luther, which is surprising since Luther's *Table-Talk* is full of scatological obscenity. The fact, too, that Shakespeare chose to portray Claudius' new régime in Elsinore as tainted not by murder alone but by sexual transgression places the play in precisely the social and religious context Marshall generally invoked. The opprobrium that Marshall heaps upon the sexuality of the 'shameless' Gertrude and the way this colours Hamlet's whole perception of women and the world at large probably stems from his Catholic perspective. The Protestant monarchs, Elizabeth I and James I, were both anathematized as illegitimate by the Catholic Church. Their right to rule was questioned because of their respective mothers' sexual sins. Marshall also shows his disgust towards Polonius, when the old man presses a missal into service as part of his political scheming against Hamlet: new uses are found for

---

77   See below, pp. 410 and 406.

old devotional practices. Marshall makes little or nothing of any of these things explicitly, because he is not really interested in the historical context of the play. His interpretation grows not from his sense of the past, but from a Newmanesque crisis of faith that he saw around him in his Victorian present. This is what colours his reading.

The Victorian academic mind was nurtured by an education system grounded upon the Greek and Roman classics. Not surprisingly, therefore, do we find comparisons between Shakespeare and Aeschylus, Hamlet and Orestes or Prometheus. The cultural status of Shakespeare and his hero is enhanced by such comparisons. But what threw *Hamlet* into relief for the Victorians was that they conceived it as a *Christian* play, that could, indeed must, be judged by the standards of *their* day. George Henry Miles could talk of the 'deep spirituality' of the play, and the 'religious mystery' it embraced.[78] Voltaire, of course, would have scoffed: to have made 'Christians of the Danes three centuries too soon' was in his view one of Shakespeare's *niaiseries*.[79] But for most Victorians, Hamlet's tragedy turned on a matter of faith. From a paganized point of view, Hamlet should have got on with the business of revenge without dwelling over-precisely upon the event. Classical heroics were defined by the manner of the hero's death and his stance towards immovable destiny and the will of the gods. *Hamlet*, however, moves 'in the dark passes between time and eternity'. This is the only tragedy of Shakespeare's where we are called upon to follow the hero's trajectory from death into the life to come. For the Victorians, Hamlet was a drama of free will, and on the exercise of that will depended the eternal fate of the human soul, whether it should be saved or damned. Delay, therefore, becomes not a sign of weakness, as Goethe and the Romantic critics would have it, but of theological circumspection.[80]

But if the Victorians honestly resonated to anything in this play, it was not so much to questions of faith as the Prince's state of doubt. 'He is incapable of certitude', concluded Dowden.[81] Their Hamlet was Hamlet

---

78   See below, p. 297.

79   See below, p. 222. For Voltaire, see *CRH*, i, 76.

80   Miles, p. 262 below. For Miles' Christian reading, see pp. 259–62.

81   See below, p. 325 (and preceding discussion).

the cynic, Hamlet the satirist, Hamlet the sceptic, a Hamlet preoccupied by Montaigne's overwhelming question, 'Que sçais-je?': 'Hamlet doubts everything. He doubts the immortality of the soul ... He doubts Horatio ..., and swears him to secrecy on the cross of his sword, though probably he himself has no assured belief in the sacredness of the symbol. He doubts Ophelia.... He doubts the ghost ...'.[82] 'L'Amleto c'è il dubbio', remarked the great Italian exponent of the role, Salvini.[83] In this state of agnosticism, Hamlet poses profound questions: 'the contention between his religious sentiments and his sceptical philosophy ... between belief and unbelief, between confidence in an overruling Providence ... and scepticism which sees in man so much animated dust, and looks upon death as annihilation'.[84] He refuses to take a leap in the dark, and demands 'grounds more relative'. Frank Marshall sees the play as a contest between doubt and faith. Hamlet's final words, 'The rest is silence' sum up his doubting creed: 'Neither hope, nor despair ... his religion is a resigned uncertainty'.[85] From these perspectives *Hamlet* is played out not on the battlements of Elsinore but on Dover Beach.

The Problems of *Hamlet*
Hamlet, no less than the Ghost of his father, comes down to the Victorians in 'questionable shape'. Notwithstanding the universal agreement on the popularity of the character and the play in this period, Margaret Oliphant could rightly exclaim, 'there is ... no dramatic creation in the world about which there has been so much difference of opinion'.[86]

Matthew Arnold could not suppress his irritation with this state of affairs. '*Hamlet* is a piece which opens, indeed, simply and admirably, and then: the rest is puzzle! ... *Hamlet* ... [is] a problem soliciting interpretation and solution. It will never, therefore, be a piece to be seen with pure satisfaction ...'.[87] For Arnold, the aim of criticism was 'to see the

82   James Russell Lowell. See below, p. 231.
83   Reported by Frank Marshall. See below, p. 408.
84   See below, p. 114.
85   See below, pp. 407 and 406.
86   See below, p. 478.
87   See below, p. 530.

object as in itself it really is'. But in the case of *Hamlet* it is impossible to see the object as it 'really is', because it is fundamentally shifting and indeterminate. Leaving aside the larger metaphysical issues which the play invokes, there are even on a narrative level many unresolved questions: How old is Hamlet? Is he nineteen or thirty? Is he insane or only feigning madness? Does he love Ophelia, and if he did, how far did they go in that relationship? Was the Queen an accessory to the murder of her first husband? When did her relationship with Claudius commence? How long was it between the funeral and her re-marriage? Indeed, what is the duration of the play itself? Is Hamlet's delay inordinate? Do these uncertainties matter? These are only a few of the questions Shakespeare leaves unanswered, but which critics and actors found themselves compelled to address.

If these unanswered questions suggest that the Victorians did not know enough about *Hamlet*, in other respects they knew too much. To complicate matters further, the Victorians had in their possession three texts of Hamlet from the seventeenth century (the two quartos, and the folio version). The texts differed substantially. There was no agreement on their respective authority, or indeed, their priority. Although it seems obvious to common sense that the version printed in 1604 must have chronologically followed that printed in 1603, it was suspected that the text of the second quarto might well have pre-dated that of the first, Q1 being a subsequent, imperfect abridgment of Q2, but printed first. To compound their confusion the Victorians could have for their delectation facsimile reprints of the Quartos of 1605 and 1611.[88] There were also in existence many Victorian 'acting versions' of the play with substantial cuts, and added stage-directions that were of modern invention. *Hamlet* in the theatre was not the *Hamlet* in the library. One wonders just what *Hamlet* was to the ordinary play-goer. What text, if any, would they have reached for in order to assess the authenticity of the performance they had earlier witnessed? Bowdler's *Family Shakespeare*, perhaps. But to whom did Hamlet belong to after all: the actor, who had a freedom to recreate the role in the image he wished to project of himself as a worthy tragedian? the theatre-goer, who had a capacity to choose his or her

---

88 See the Selective Bibliography below, (i) Editions of Shakespeare's *Hamlet*, 1850–1900.

favourite Hamlet of the hour? the scholar, who could construct the Prince on historical or textual principles? or the world, which viewed the hero through nationalistically constructed spectacles?

Hamlet and the Mad Doctors
The science of psychiatry burgeoned in the nineteenth century. The newly-fledged subject felt it imperative to establish not only its authenticity but its infallibility. The increasing involvement of psychiatrists as expert witnesses in criminal trials meant that their opinions could and often did mitigate or determine the sentence of the accused: medical opinion often overruled the law as framed in statute and legal precedent. Wearing the mantle of superior 'scientific' expertise, these medics occupied the professional high ground vis-à-vis their judicial counterparts. The legal profession did not like this, and sought to reassert its precedence by attempting to undermine the credibility of the 'mad doctors', as they became known. The psychiatrists, on the other hand, daringly offered to resolve issues that other professions found beyond their capacities, and pretended to provide clarity in cases where there was none before.[89]

It is in this context that the psychiatrists intervened in the literary sphere, and offered to give a clinical, professional answer to a question which had eluded literary scholars: Was Hamlet mad? Their expert opinion was to be had at only a nominal fee, the price of their published pamphlet. In offering to diagnose the world's most famous lunatic, they sought to gain maximum publicity, to enhance the reputation of both their subject and their own 'scientific' infallibility. In so doing they would establish the superiority of their methods over the more subjective, and therefore unreliable, field of literary scholarship.

John Charles Bucknill, from 1862 to 1876 the Lord Chancellor's medical visitor of lunatics, boldly claimed the subject of Shakespeare's Hamlet as his own. At first sight, it appears to Bucknill's credit that he recognized, as many of his contemporaries did not, that *Hamlet* 'invites and evades criticism'; it teases by its profundity, while evading neat conclusions by its evasiveness and double meanings. But, this is merely to show that the arts that hitherto applied to the problem had been insufficient to

---

89 See Vernon A. Rosario, *The Erotic Imagination: French Histories of Perversity* (New York and Oxford: Oxford University Press, 1997), pp. 56ff.

the task. Evasive and teasing to some, maybe, but not to the psychiatrist. He rapidly insisted that 'all critical study of Hamlet must be psychological'. In fact, 'Hamlet's character becomes one of the most interesting and complicated subjects *of psychological study* anywhere to be met with'.[90] Hamlet is a fly swallowed whole by the predatory doctor. Hamlet accordingly was judged mad beyond reasonable doubt, fit to be kept behind the asylum walls, where the doctors could have the indubitable pleasure of long interviews with their famous patient. Theatre-goers were furious. If the psychiatrists incarcerated Hamlet, his companionship was denied to those who looked upon him as their 'fire-side friend'. In all of this it is apparent that both the psychiatrists and the theatre-goers looked on Hamlet as a real-life character.

Bucknill and his fellow psychiatrist, John Conolly, the superintendent of Hanwell lunatic asylum, anticipated by half a century Freud's and Ernest Jones' interest in the play. Conolly quickly and perceptively saw that Hamlet's 'Get thee to a nunnery' is motivated not by Hamlet's feelings for Ophelia, but for his mother.[91] Bucknill, however, differed from Jones in his conclusions and in his open-mindedness.[92] And while Shakespeare conveys most skillfully 'Hamlet's profound affection for' his mother, there is no suspicion of any Oedipal attraction. To the Victorians, in their pre-Freudian innocence, Hamlet may have been cruel, but certainly not 'unnatural'.[93]

Literary critics and the actors tended to resist the magisterial diagnoses of the medical men. Many are at pains to make clear that Hamlet was only 'feigning' madness, and that, though acting, he was in his perfect senses all the time. The nub of the issue was, that if Hamlet was judged

---

90   See below, p. 76. The italics in this quotation are mine.

91   John Conolly, *A Study of Hamlet* (London: E. Moxon & Co., 1863), pp. 117–18, cited below, p. 193.

92   For Bucknill see entry 6 below (pp. 60ff.). Jones's Freudian reading was first published as 'The Oedipus-Complex as an Explanation of Hamlet's Mystery: A Study in Motive', *American Journal of Psychology*, 21 (1910), 72–113. His views were expanded into a ninety-eight-page monograph, *A Psychological Study of Hamlet*, in 1922.

93   See below, p. 95.

clinically mad, he was therefore irresponsible for his actions, and there could be no tragedy in the depiction of such a character. Actors, as we have seen, ducked the problem by omitting any suggestion that the Prince was not in his right mind.

'The Real Hamlet': Hamlet on the Stage
Lewes characterized Hamlet as 'a part in which no man thoroughly succeeds, and few men altogether fail'.[94] Any actor who sought to make his name had to perform Hamlet. It was a theatrical *rite de passage*, but the tradition was not altogether welcome.

James Edward Neild, the principal theatre critic for *The Australasian*, in 1877 gave a thumb-nail sketch of the traditional stage presentation of the role: ' . . . a gloomy person in black velvet, who wore a long coat and had tall ostrich feathers in his hat. He walked with a measured pace, did not sit down much, spoke in a sepulchral tone and wept at intervals. His hair was black and curly and upon his breast there was a decoration of St George and the Dragon'.[95] This representation of the role was largely drawn from Neild's recollections of the London theatre of the 1840s. It was about to change.

Charles Kean, Lewes asserted in 1850, 'was far the best now on the English stage'.[96] But Lewes' review of the performance is not enthusiastic. It left him dissatisfied. Kean had 'no mastery over emotion'. The performance was simply (or over-simply) characterized by a 'settled melancholy'. He did not represent the changing emotions that overtake the hero. Thomas Kenny would agree that this was a weakness. Though his criticism is not specifically aimed at Kean, but at any 'great actor'. 'It would be a mistake,' he affirms, 'to attempt to elaborate [the character's] multiform details into any distinctly harmonious unity'. What Kenny perceives as the play's and the protagonist's 'order' is their common 'disordered energy'.[97]

94 See below, p. 5

95 Quoted below, p. 188. For Neild, see below, p. 194 n.11 and Harold Love, *James Edward Neild, Victorian Virtuoso* (Carlton, Vic.: Melbourne University Press, 1989).

96 See below, p. 1.

97 See below, p. 187.

The Germans had a reputation for being the superior interpreters of *Hamlet*. Thus Emil Devrient's 1852 visit to London to perform the leading role was eagerly anticipated and received high praise. But George Henry Lewes was unimpressed. He dismissed Devrient's interpretation of the role as 'indifferent'. The Prince's meditative nature was 'more like dyspepsia than sorrow'. Confronted by the Ghost, he was 'like a frightened school-boy'. There was 'no trace of superior intelligence' in the interpretation of the part. It was 'careless, superficial'. Lewes required 'an appreciation of intellect' from any actor undertaking the part. But this was altogether missing from Devrient's performance. 'Whatever else there may be in his acting, there is not intense mental vigour.'[98]

Charles Fechter in 1861 played Hamlet at the Princess's Theatre for seventy consecutive nights. And the reception he received was rapturous. Some of this success, George Henry Lewes remarked, could be put down 'to the curiosity of seeing a Frenchman play Shakespeare in English'. Although it is conceded that 'Fechter pronounces English very well for a Frenchman', Lewes with anglophone superiority eagerly pointed out 'the foreigner's accent and the foreigner's mistakes in emphasis'. The review in the *Times* of 22 March, 1861, noted 'we cannot forget that the part is played by a Frenchman' and recorded the fact that in this performance 'the physical force' of Shakespeare's words is entirely lacking. This, the reviewer opined, 'seems to be beyond the reach of an alien'.[99] While 'Shakespeare never has been ... played so well by a *foreign* artist', (my italics) the reviewer concludes, 'it would be wholly incorrect to measure him by an English standard'.[100]

The reviewer's obvious xenophobic prejudices mask the fact that in Fechter's performance he was confronted by something even more obnoxiously 'alien': a new interpretation of the role, which dispensed with the time-honoured conventions that had surrounded the part as interpreted on the English stage. Fechter had the temerity not only to play the part in a foreign accent, but in a blonde wig as well! It must be remembered that at this time Shakespeare was decidedly, in Charles Cowden Clarke's

---

98   See below, pp. 8–10.

99   See below, p. 140.

100 See below, p. 141.

near-contemporary phrase, not only '*our* ... Shakespeare' (my italics)—a national treasure—, but 'our *beloved* Shakespeare' (my italics).[101] Any attempt at foreign annexation of this cultural property was almost certainly going to be doubly resented, both consciously and subliminally.

Lewes, however, was quick to recognize the merits of Fechter's performance. 'I think his Hamlet one of the very best'. No small praise, since, we must remember, Lewes had seen all the great Hamlets of his time.[102] The key to Fechter's success was naturalism. His delivery was 'as far away as possible from the conventional declamatory style'.[103] Fechter *acted* rather than declaimed the part. 'We feel we have Hamlet the Dane before us.' What impressed Lewes was the rendition of a Romantic Hamlet, following the reading of the character laid down by Goethe in *Wilhelm Meister*: 'that there is a burden laid upon Hamlet too heavy for his soul to bear'. And perhaps it is from this, rather than the fact that the role was assayed by a Frenchman, that the *Times* review commented on a lack of 'physical force'. This 'physical force' was discerned not only by the English, but by Fechter's contemporary compatriot, Hippolyte Taine, who was astounded by the violence of Shakespeare's language: 'it seems ... he never writes a word without shouting it'.[104] Fechter's rendition of the role was based upon an earlier generation's interpretation of the role; he was out of step with contemporary British and continental *readers* of the play. On the other hand, there can be no doubt that his performance, conceived in theatrical terms, was altogether innovative. His popular success at the time is evidence of that. But by 1879 Margaret Oliphant could only note that 'Fechter had fallen out of fashion',[105] an indication that the reading of the play and its performance had come into some species of alignment, to the disadvantage of Fechter's reputation.

In 1867 Walter Montgomery, the London-based actor, played Hamlet in Melbourne, Australia, as did James Anderson. In the event Montgomery's performance sparked a lively exchange of views in the magazine,

101   See below, p. 163.
102   See below, p. 12.
103   See below, p. 13.
104   See below, p. 166.
105   See below, p. 476.

The Argus.[106] James Smith, widely recognized as the leading literary figure in the Melbourne of his day, initiated proceedings with an unfavourable verdict on Montgomery's 'eminently agreeable and thoroughly artistic' Hamlet: 'vacillating, wayward, irresolute, and half-hearted'.[107] Montgomery had obviously attempted to bring Fechter's new Hamlet to the Antipodes. He could not have anticipated Smith's ultra-conservative cultural reaction. Smith's problem was that Montgomery's rendition of the part lacked authenticity, in that it departed both from canonical critical readings of the role by 'nearly all the great critics, English, German, and French' and from a theatrical tradition that went back through Garrick to Burbage himself, who was instructed in the role by the author. Montgomery's 'innovations' in the role 'have nothing to recommend them beyond the fact of their novelty'.[108] Smith's approach in the review was an altogether conservative one, but one based upon a strong theatrical tradition. It was usual, in London as well as the Antipodes, to measure any performance of Hamlet by what had gone before. There was an expectation that certain 'points' would be included in any rendition of the role. Judged by these standards, Montgomery's departures from this traditional interpretation could only be seen as faults.

James Neild, a medical man and Melbourne's chief theatre critic at this time, took issue with Smith's evaluation of Montgomery's attempt at the part. But however much Montgomery may have occasioned the ensuing debate, the real issues at stake were far larger. As more and more contributors to the argument joined in, it did not seem to matter whether one had actually seen Montgomery's Hamlet or not. The question turned on whether, as in Smith's view, performance should be underpinned by critical authority and by (at this time) two and a half centuries of stage tradition, or whether, as Neild would state, the actor should interpret 'Shakespeare unclogged by tradition, and guided only by the light of nature and a fine intelligence'.[109] Throwing his hand in with Neild,

---

106   For the letters, see below, pp. 188–220.
107   See below, p. 189.
108   See below, p. 190.
109   See below, p. 199.

Archibald Michie would rhetorically, and possibly irreverently, ask, 'What is it ... to Mr. Montgomery how Garrick played Hamlet ... ?' One might retort, 'What is it to Michie, how Montgomery played Hamlet?', for he was one of those who cheerfully admitted, 'I have not seen his Hamlet'.[110] David Blair would go even further and argue that it was a positive advantage that he had never seen Montgomery's Hamlet. That, he claims, with tongue firmly in cheek, did away with any notion that he was tainted by any prejudice and secured his impartiality in the argument. But to Michie, uncluttered as his mind was with the material circumstances of the performance, the general issue was plain: either we settle for a mechanical, waxwork rendition of the role as set down by stage tradition and by 'the critics', or we have an innovative performance that arises from the actor's close study of the part, illuminated by his observation of human nature. Michie strongly argues for the latter.

It was a Victorian debate conducted in Arcadia. The lines of engagement were drawn between 'ancients' and 'moderns', traditionalists and innovators, between a constructed vision of the past and a new willingness to rethink received opinions. This exchange exposed a growing gap between Shakespeare's plays as living theatre, and the closet study of the text and histories of performance. Some of the debate is myopically silly, and perhaps deliberately so. Lopping 'tall poppies', when the occasion arises, is still to this day an Antipodean sport. Those that opposed Smith seem almost deliberately to miss his main point: that the performance must be consistent with the text of the play. They knew that this should not involve questions concerning the presence or absence of 'stage directions'. Equally, they knew that this was not what Smith was really talking about. No one in their right mind would want to elevate 'stage directions', whether absent or present, above the speeches spoken by the characters in the play. But the nub of the argument—and it goes beyond merely trying to take Smith down a notch or two—involves tradition as against innovation. And, interestingly enough, this Antipodean debate anticipated by a decade the arguments that surrounded Henry Irving's new interpretation of the role in London some years further on. In matters of innovation and originality Irving's claims would powerfully outweigh

---

110   See below, p. 204.

Montgomery's. In mentioning both in the same breath, we compare great things with small, to paraphrase Virgil. But the matters of principle underpinning the debate remain much the same whether conducted in Melbourne or London. In this, the new world ran in advance of the old.

It is perhaps appropriate to indicate here the trajectory of this debate. Towards the end of the period under discussion in this volume of *CRH*, the American scholar, John Corbin, at the conclusion of his groundbreaking contextualization of the mad scenes in *Hamlet* within Elizabethan and Jacobean theatrical culture, surprisingly seems to turn his back on his whole historical endeavour. He writes:

> Hamlet ... still lives and grows in beauty. ... Each actor and critic has divined new traits of beauty, and the generations have so loved the gentleness of the Prince, that in the light of their love the brutal facts of many of the scenes in which he moves are glorified. The modern Hamlet is the real Hamlet. In the truest sense of the word he is the Shaksperean Hamlet: and will continue so, until new ages shall add new beauties to our interpretation.[111]

While there is a continuum that links theatrical tradition with modern individual talent, in Corbin's view Hamlet is bettered 'with each passing century'. In an almost poetic strain he asserts that the hand of a modern master can elicit new melodies upon an ancient instrument; 'the Cathedral softens its sharp outlines with each century that steals over it'. The argument for modern innovation over slavish adherence to precedent would seem to have been made by a literary historian, who was a lover of the modern Hamlet. Hamlet *was* living at his hour.

The decisive turning point in this debate between ancients and moderns, and which would allow Corbin to make the point he did, would seem to have occurred in 1874, when Henry Irving undertook the role of the Prince at London's Lyceum Theatre. There was excited anticipation of this theatrical event. On the afternoon of 31 October, queues began to form in the Strand to await the performance. The demand for tickets exceeded the supply, and many were turned away. Irving's playing did

---

111 John Corbin, *The Elizabethan Hamlet: A Study of the Sources, and of Shakspere's Environment, to show that the Mad Scenes had a Comic Aspect now Ignored* (London: Elkin Mathews, and New York: Charles Scribner's Sons, 1895), p. 87, *CRH*, iv, 656. For Corbin, see entry 51 below (pp. 642–56).

not disappoint. It was a theatrical triumph, a display of genius. The applause was rapturous. This was shown at the unkenneling of the King's guilt at the performance of the 'Murder of Gonzago', during which Hamlet taunts the King to his face. After Claudius exits, Hamlet flings himself into the King's chair. Whereupon the reviewer, Frederic Wedmore, reported:

> all this wrought so plainly upon the audience that it forgot to cheer. It hardly knew its own mind for a minute. . . . But when somebody began to applaud, the contagion spread. Clapping of hands got louder and louder, but the audience was not content. It rose to its feet and fairly satisfied itself at last with a great roar in recognition of this power.[112]

The initial stunned silence was, of course, a result of the breath-taking theatricality of the performance. But it also must have stemmed in part from the fact that Hamlet's over-the-top reaction to the King's guilt was usually cut in performances of the play. The audience were confronted by an aspect of Hamlet they had never seen before.

Tennyson was present at the first night, and fully appreciated the power of this performance of what he considered 'the greatest creation in literature'.[113] Although Tennyson did not think Irving was 'a perfect Hamlet', his was better, in the Laureate's view, than Macready's. He said to the actor, '*Hamlet* is a multi-faceted gem, and you have given more facets than anyone I have seen'. When Irving commented on his presentation of the role (see extract 29 below), it was precisely this 'multi-faceted' quality that he sought to bring out. In the interview with Ophelia (Act III, scene i), he perceived 'the conflict of motive and the variety of passion' united 'in a credible and vivid personality'. This interpretation was arrived at, not by slavish adherence to any stage tradition, that might or might not derive from Shakespeare himself, but from close and detailed study of the text.[114]

---

112   For this quotation and Wedmore account of Irving's rendition of the scene, see below, pp. 309–10. For notices of Irving's performance see entries 18, 19, 20, and 21 below.

113   See below, p. 300.

114   See below, p. 455. In Irving's discussion of the play, one might discern the influence of Frank Marshall, in much the same way that in the twentieth century one can discern the influence of Ernest Jones on Olivier's Hamlet.

Irving's interpretation of the role was regarded as innovative. Not only did he restore parts of the original text that had been previously deleted from the 'acting copies', but the style of his playing was also different. He was thought to be the only Hamlet in history who did not rant. Indeed, his delivery was thought to be almost colloquial, giving rise to the opinion that he could not speak blank verse. But in order to understand fully just how different he was from other Hamlets, we must consider the acting conventions and theatre criticism of the time. These were dominated by a strong sense of theatrical tradition. In the case of a classic such as *Hamlet*, these became codified into a series of 'points', theatrical effects that were rehearsed by the actors and expected by the audience: Hamlet would thus turn pale in Act I, scene v *à la Betterton*; a chair would be overturned in the closet scene at the appearance of the Ghost, *à la Garrick*;[115] and so on. The parts between these theatrical tricks were filled up by a heavily declamatory style of delivery, that inclined towards the tedious. The play was performed mechanically according to prescribed rules, and for this reason several commentators had begun to talk of *Hamlet* as 'boring'. But Irving's reputation promised something different: a *new* Hamlet. And the amazing thing was, that the theatre-going public were ready for such a thing. Irving did not disappoint.

Irving made the interpretation of the character as a whole the focus of the performance. The 'points' became subservient, or could be dispensed with, if they conflicted with the psychological consistency of the character. Hamlet thus became a person, rather than a role. For Irving the dominant cast of Hamlet's mind was one of settled sadness. His spirit has been crushed by the tragic circumstances that surround him. This 'sadness', however, differed substantially from the traditional 'melancholy' of previous actors, the monotone of Charles Kean, for example. Such 'sadness' as Irving portrayed was not inconsistent with a naturally cheerful, genial temperament, which breaks through on occasions, as does a quick and fiery temper. Throughout the role Irving conveyed a nervous excitement, an agitated irritability, which was marked, as the *Times*' reviewer noted, by 'frequent changes from sitting to standing, his fitful walks up and down the stage, the frequent visits of his hand to his

---

115 See *CRH*, i, xxiv and 287.

forehead... The words seemed to be flung about at random, and the facial movements corresponded to the recklessness of the words'. Margaret Oliphant, though she did not altogether approve of it, recorded the excitement of the spectacle, the sheer physical force of Irving's performance, that could do no other than fix the attention of those that saw it.[116]

Irving introduced several unusual innovations into the production. In Act Three the eavesdropping Polonius and Claudius were visible to the audience. The hero's soliloquy during the King-at-prayer scene was restored to the stage. The 'counterfeit presentment of two brothers' during the closet scene was bodied forth in an eloquent piece of purely verbal painting, fired by Hamlet's vivid imagination. Two life-sized portraits were part of the traditional furniture of the Queen's closet, or, by 1794 it was more usual for Hamlet to point to two contrasting miniatures.[117] In this, as in other matters, one can see Irving's willingness to rethink the role unfettered by any slavish adherence to stage convention.

When Irving's production opened it was anticipated it would run for eighty nights. In the event it exceeded the hopes of actor and manager and ran for two hundred. It was revived on several occasions. Later in the century Beerbohm Tree and Forbes Robertson would continue theatrically innovative approaches to the role. Reviews and assessments of their performances may be found in the pages below; Forbes Robertson's main 'innovation', of course, was to reintroduce the part of Fortinbras to the stage, from which he had been absent for nearly two hundred years.

The Ghost
Although the play requires a supernatural frisson to surround this character, reviewers exact some mirth from the all-too-corporeal renditions of the role: the 'heavy footed' presence that made the stage-boards creak. Fechter circumvented such physical inconveniences by a piece of modern technological ghost-raising; for the Ghost's first and last appearances he projected the form by means of a 'transparency' into the scene. This device was also used by Wilson Barrett with some success.

---

116 See below, pp. 477f.

117 Seee Walter Whiter, 'The Two Portraits', in *CRH*, ii, 14–15.

The stage direction in the first Quarto that has the Ghost appear in the closet scene 'in his night gowne' could do nothing but provoke unfortunate mirth when it was adopted on the Victorian stage, for it must have seemed that this was no Shakespearean ghost, but Wee Willie Winkie. Margaret Oliphant derisively describes the apparition in Henry Irving's production: 'with a rush, a venerable gentleman in familiar domestic costume came on the stage, shaking it with substantial footsteps . . . and it was impossible to avoid the natural idea that the lady's husband hearing an unaccountable commotion in the next room, had jumped out of bed, seized his dressing-gown, and rushed in to see what was the matter'.[118]

Gertrude

'How old is Hamlet?' is a question that pedantically recurs in essays in this volume. Let us leave that, for the moment, to the bibliographers. After all, Fredson Bowers was hazardous enough to propose that all questions of literary interpretation could ultimately be resolved by the science of bibliography. We still await their answers. But a more pertinent, if more indelicate question is, 'How old is the Queen?' This question rapidly transmutes from twenty-first century hindsight into the more worrying question, 'How old is "old"?'

One should never inquire after a woman's age, but the Victorians, it seems, had no such qualms. Indeed, they were highly curious over the matter. 'When,' they asked, 'does the "heydey in the blood" begin to "wait upon the judgment"?' If we were honest, we would also like to know the answer. But the question as put by Moy Thomas, and probably as originally implied by Hamlet, relates specifically to female sexuality.[119]

For the Victorians, it seems, a Gertrude of 'fifty-two' is different from a Gertrude of 'forty-two'. Victorian proprieties probably exaggerated these upper and lower limits in their constructions of a Renaissance Gertrude, for she may well have been married to her first husband at the age of fourteen. But Hamlet was, we know, the Victorians' fireside friend, and Gertrude was his scandalous mother to be gossiped about behind the lace curtains. In the Victorians' eyes 'fifty-two' made her a 'matron',

---

118   See below, p. 495.
119   See below, pp. 546f.

whereas 'forty-two' gave her realistic prospects of a sexually active remarriage. These distinctions look silly from our perspective. But it is enormously useful to have an indication of any such time scheme, if we want to enter into any sort of understanding of nineteenth-century [male?] views on female sexuality.

Whether the upper or lower range of this transitional decade in a Victorian woman's life is being invoked, the stage presentation of the Queen's 'mutually passionate relations with her second husband'—together with allusions in the text of the closet scene to their public physical intimacies, wanton pinchings on the cheek, etc.—either becomes interestingly plausible or plainly disgusting, 'ludicrous and absurd' in Moy Thomas's words, in the eyes of the audience. Of course, at whatever age the Queen assumes on stage the audience would be expected to take the moral high ground and deplore this adulterous, incestuous second marriage. This is why the role of Gertrude was for actresses an unpopular and difficult one. In Hamlet's case, whether we think of him as an adolescent or a young thirty-something, he would probably be in a state of shock that his mother was ever a sexually active being. Late nineteenth-century productions played upon a similar state of shock being translated to their audiences. The horror that the play confronts is not so much death and murder, but sex. The Queen, as George MacDonald sternly reminds us, 'is living in habitual incest'.[120]

To Dowden, though, the Queen is 'soft and sensual, a lover of ease, withal a little sentimental, and therefore incapable of genuine passion'. Thus Dowden avoids the problem of her sexuality, whatever her age, and all the references in the text to her physical intimacies with Claudius. *Supressio veri, suggestio falsi*. To Dowden, she is essentially a superficial woman: 'For thirty years she had given the appearance, the simulacrum of true love to her husband'.[121] Any suggestion that she was unfaithful to Hamlet's father during his lifetime or was an accessory to his murder is ruled completely out of the question. The critic knows things the dramatist never told us.

Frank Marshall takes a tougher line. He is the first critic in this volume to ask whether or not the Queen was an accessory to her first husband's

120   See below, p. 550.
121   See below, pp. 324 and 326.

murder, though he quickly dismisses the charge.[122] For Marshall, her crime is against her husband's honour. Gertrude's o'er-hasty marriage is a revolting and hideous affront to the memory of her noble and loving husband of thirty years. If Dowden gives the impression that he knew Gertrude, Marshall was obviously an intimate of the older Hamlet for even longer. 'Even the most abandoned woman might have shrunk from dishonouring *him*'.[123] That immediately places her in the forefront of the ranks of 'abandoned' women, and her deceased husband on a pedestal. It is this behaviour that causes Hamlet to lose all faith in womankind and brought about his tragedy.

Furnivall had no desire to mince words. He saw Hamlet's life blighted by the Queen's incestuous lust. This idea was taken up in Wilson Barrett's 1884 production of the play. Here, at every opportunity, the 'amorous toyings' of the royal newlyweds take place under Hamlet's, the court's, and the audience's collective noses, and strongly suggest that 'the guilty *liaison* dates . . . from . . . the late king's lifetime'. This was, as the *Times* reviewer remarks, a 'novel rendering' on the stage, but it had formed part of the libidinous speculations of more than one critic, even if they desired to quickly suppress the suggestion.[124] But now it was bodied forth upon the stage! We are, let us admit, at this date within the penumbra of the 'naughty' 90s.

Women tend to judge their own sex more harshly than men do, and so it is the case with Margaret Oliphant's view of the Queen. At her feet Oliphant lays the source of all Hamlet's woes. It is not his father's death that plunges him into melancholic sadness at the start of the play, but 'the monstrous inconstancy and wantonness of his mother'. Gertrude has sinned against the exalted Victorian station of 'motherhood', 'the one original type of faithful affection which cannot be doubted, even if heaven and earth were melting and dissolving'. Her 'unnatural' re-marriage, her 'monstrous bridehood', has polluted all that is honorable, all that is sacred. The impression Hamlet may once have had of his mother as a devoted and loving wife is stripped away. But for Oliphant, the dishonour

---

122   See below, pp. 379 and 381–2.
123   See below, p. 362. My italics.
124   See below, pp. 533f.

is not principally Gertrude's. Nor is it against Hamlet's deceased father. It is against Hamlet himself. The revelation of her degradation, whether this is a result of her wantonness or merely a case of her moral insensitivity, kills his very soul. It sickens him with disgust and loathing, the horror of which infects his whole world. It may be no injustice to the Victorians' perceptions of the play if we were to appropriate with some slight adjustment Laertes' declaration in Act V. scene ii, and exclaim, 'The Queen, the Queen's to blame'.[125]

The 'revolting nature of her crime', her 'crime' in Frank Marshall's eyes being her inconsiderate 'o'er hasty' remarriage, is used to justify Hamlet's total lack of respect for his mother in the closet scene. Her unexamined 'criminality' is coupled with her 'utter want of contrition'. This he implicitly juxtaposes to Claudius' false contrition in the previous scene, implying that Claudius has at least an inkling of moral conscience, where Gertrude has none. This serves to condemn her even further.[126] From a Victorian patriarchal perspective, perhaps, it was no more than a son's duty to awaken the mother's conscience to the 'outrage' she had committed against his father's memory. Hamlet's, therefore justifiable, indignation here 'overpowers his courtesy'. But his commission, for Marshall, comes not just from the visitation of his father's spirit, but from the 'Deity' himself! Shakespeare does not credit Hamlet with that authority, but for Marshall it is entirely appropriate that the Prince should 'show no scruple or delicacy in laying bare the hideousness of the double crime committed against his father'. In all of this Marshall is outraged by Gertrude's utter indifference to matters of right and wrong. But unfortunately she comes from a 'rude and disadvantaged' background, lacking the Victorians' discernment in these things. Oh how we yearn for such clearcut judgments between right and wrong. Victorians laid claim to this moral territory. They know about these things. Ages before and since have not been so certain.

As might be expected Furnivall treats the closet scene with a sense of irony and it is difficult to pin down his precise viewpoint. He inveighs

---

125   *Hamlet*, V, ii, 273. The original text reads 'King' for 'Queen'. For Oliphant's reading, see below, pp. 478–80 and 482.

126   See below, p. 379. For Marshall's development of these themes, see pp. 379ff.

against Gertrude's 'disgraceful adultery and incest'. He deplores her 'treason' against her first husband's memory. From that point of view Hamlet's reproaches are entirely justified. Yet Furnivall's description of Hamlet's obvious relish in the vigorous verbal castigation of his mother is contrasted with the Prince's manifest lack of enthusiasm in avenging his father's murder. For Furnivall Hamlet's priorities are wrong and from that point of view Hamlet is nothing more than a moral prig and a bully.

Claudius
On the Victorian stage Claudius is portrayed as an out and out rotter. In spite of Shakespeare, he becomes a caricatured villain that would grace any Victorian melodrama. Some critics reluctantly acknowledge his intellectual parts—he is, after all, related to Hamlet. And in the eyes of his court, for four-and-a-half acts and slightly more, he just about gets away with murder, incest and various other treacheries by way of his eloquence and conviviality. Yet, even if intellectually gifted, for the Victorians he is usually described as utterly drowned in drink and sensual indulgence. His stage presentation influenced the way he is represented in print.

Frank Marshall saw, however, the possibility of a more subtle rendition of the character, closer perhaps to Shakespeare's own: Claudius is no reeling drunkard. He carries on the business of state, dispatching ambassadors and carrying on the day-to-day administration of the country. 'Instead of representing the seducer of Gertrude as a beetle-browed villain', the theatre should give us a plausible politician, a 'smiling villain . . . with features . . . expanded by conviviality', and who, in spite of all his governmental responsibilities, indulgently tolerates the ingratitude of his brother's son, until his nephew's outrages can be no longer borne. That is a stage Claudius that would carry conviction. Unfortunately, in Marshall's day, such a performance had not been theatrically realized.[127]

Marshall picks up well on the fact that Claudius always has moral sentiments in his mouth, if not in his heart. He 'overflows with nice morality'. He professes not enmity but so great a 'love' for his nephew that it blinded his judgment.[128] He breaks his villainous plot to Laertes,

---

127   See below, p. 386.
128   See below, p. 386, and *Hamlet*, IV, i, 18ff.

and at the same time regales the youth with 'unctuous lectures on the heavenly nature of filial love, and of "goodness" in general'.[129] In this, one perceives a recognition of contemporary double-standards and hypocrisies.

Polonius
The stage continued to portray Polonius as a drivelling, moralizing dotard. The part was milked for laughs. But the Victorian critics on the whole distanced themselves from this stage tradition. At times his morality was elevated to almost sublime proportions, but more often than not he was seen as duplicitous and self-serving, always on the look-out for the advancement of himself and his family.

Ophelia
The Polonius family as a whole does not have a good press from the critics. Even Ophelia comes in for her share of censure. To Dowden she was superficial, totally unworthy as a partner for the noble Hamlet. She elevates mere proprieties into the status of moral law.[130] The propensity of a woman to judge a member of her own sex more harshly than would any man is once again seen in Margaret Oliphant's dismissive opinion of Ophelia. 'Simple and submissive', she is the 'most shallow of all Shakespeare's women'. She thinks more of her father's approval than of any loyalty she might owe to Hamlet. 'It is manifest that this soft submissive creature . . . is in no way a possible mate for Hamlet'. Oliphant can barely conceal her impatience with 'the great part of the public, who [are] soft-hearted to the soft Ophelia'.[131] Oliphant rejects out of hand any notion that the relationship between Hamlet and Ophelia could be based on 'love'. She brings an insightful female perspective to the issue. If we disagree with her, we must side with the opinion of the ambitiously motivated fool, Polonius.

As remarked above, it was an article of faith that 'Hamlet's love for Ophelia was pure and honourable'. Ophelia is 'sweetly innocent'. For

---

129 See below, p. 395.

130 See below, p. 340.

131 See below, pp. 484f. and 487.

George Henry Miles, she is an 'unblemished innocent'.[132] Although she evidently understands Hamlet's bawdy allusions as they watch the play, her 'outraged modesty' is proof enough, at least for Frank Marshall, of her 'spotless chastity'.[133] In her madness she repeats the words of a bawdy song 'with simple child-like ignorance of their meaning, the verses which probably she had never heard since she was being dandled on her nurse's knee, and which, in her right senses, she might never have remembered'.[134]

For Bucknill, her character excites the 'intense pity' which was necessary to make the play a tragedy. She seizes upon our sympathy.[135] Bucknill's eulogy on Ophelia's death is entirely moving: 'singing her life away, she passes from the melody of madness to the silence of the grave'.[136] This affecting rendition of her death goes some way to explain the popularity of Ophelia in Victorian art. Indeed, she would seem to have become irresistible, for artists seemed ineluctably drawn to her, ever since John Everett Millais established the iconographic tradition in mid-century, as she floats on her flowery bier in passive submission to her fate. Arthur Hughes in 1852 produced a sweet, child-like Ophelia, standing on the edge of a stream. Richard Redgrave, William Waterhouse, Henrietta Rae and Louise Jopling followed in this tradition. The latter based her image on Mrs Tree's crazed, emaciated stage performance.

On the Continent the pictorial renditions of Ophelia were less innocent. Madeleine Lemaire in the 1880 shows her precariously balanced on the edge of the stream, her gown slipping from her shoulders to reveal her naked breast. The implication is that her morals, like her gown, have also slipped. Others were drawn to her insanity, and her physical debility. The mixture of beauty and morbidity seemed irresistible.[137]

132 See below, p. 279.
133 See below, p. 370.
134 The opinion of Frank Marshall. See below, pp. 363–4.
135 See below, p. 119.
136 See below, p. 128.
137 On the Ophelia theme in nineteenth-century art, see Dijkstra, *Idols of Perversity*, pp. 42–51.

Hamlet around the World
By the end of the century there existed translations of *Hamlet* in almost all the world's languages: French, German, Italian, Bengali, Catalan, Danish, Dutch, Modern Greek, Hungarian, Icelandic, Polish, Portuguees, Roumanian, Russian, Serbocroatian, Spanish, Swedish, Ukrainian, and Welsh. The first translation of Shakespeare into Japanese was Hamlet's 'To be or not to be' soliloquy, and a complete translation of the play followed.[138] Hamlet by this time was truly a world-wide phenomenon.

This polyglot enrichment of *Hamlet* was demonstrated on the London stage. Sarah Bernhardt performed Hamlet in French translation, much to Max Beerbohm's amusement. More successfully Tomasso Salvini performed the title role of Shakespeare's play in Italian at Drury Lane in 1875. His rendition of the part was received with considerable enthusiasm. Frank Marshall was impressed by his 'charming grace and melodious elocution'. The actor laboured under the disadvantage of performing the role in a language very few of his paying audience could understand. Yet George Henry Lewes was particularly struck with his Hamlet. After disparagingly remarking that this was 'not Shakespeare's Hamlet', the play, he explains, 'had been cut down to suit Italian tastes,' he goes on to surprise us by announcing: 'Of all the Hamlets I have seen, Salvini's is the least disappointing.' He then adds: 'Of all that I have seen,'—and he had seen the best Hamlets of his generation—'it has the greatest excellencies.'[139] Rare praise indeed! And particularly when we consider that such praise was given to a foreigner. Lewes was particularly struck by his rendition of the scene with Ophelia. 'Salvini is strange, enigmatical, but always tender; and his "To a nunnery go" is the mournful advice of a broken-hearted lover, not the advice of a bully'. What convinces Lewes is 'the growing intensity of emotion', and the 'truthful expression of powerful emotion'. 'The close was magnificent', Lewes goes on, and concludes, 'Salvini is the greatest speaker I have heard.'

---

138 See Takeshi Murakami, 'Shakespeare and *Hamlet* in Japan: A Chronological Overview' in Yoshiko Uéno, ed., *Hamlet and Japan* (New York: AMS Press, 1995), pp. 245–7.

139 See below, pp. 20f.

The French

There may possibly be a difference between a Continental or European interpretation of the play, and its current interpretation within the United Kingdom. Hippolyte Taine acknowledged that his reading of Hamlet's character was largely shaped by Goethe.[140] And this may well have been generally still the case on the Continent of Europe. Similarly, neo-classical canons of taste still left their mark on European approaches to the play. The introduction of humour into the tragedy was always going to prove difficult for them. Frank Marshall presses to defend Shakespeare on this point and assures us that this was a mark of the author's undoubed genius. It was, however, 'contrary to all the canons of foreign criticism'. He recalls a production of *Hamlet* he saw in Naples, where all the actors were at pains to remove any taint of comedy. The two gravediggers became one, and the humorous ballad sung by Shakespeare's First Clown was replaced by 'a pretty little song'.[141]

But the popularity of Hamlet in France during this period was unquestioned. The French poet, Jules Laforgue, made a pilgrimage to Elsinore on New Year's Day, 1886, where he conducted an imaginary interview with the Prince. The play and its hero seem to have been held in almost religious veneration, and provided a point of identification for the decadent generation of the *fin-de-siècle*. Victor Hugo had affirmed during the first belated blush of French Romanticism: 'Other works of the human mind equal *Hamlet*, none surpasses it. . . . *Hamlet*, is to our mind, Shakespeare's chief work'.[142] This was a marvelously satisfying (from a British point-of-view) rejection of Voltaire's superior neo-classically inspired gibes of the previous century against the play and its author.

The identification between Shakespeare and Hamlet was also made on the other side of the English Channel by Hippolyte Taine: 'The truth is that Hamlet . . . is Shakspeare'. Yet his Hamlet/Shakespeare is an altogether different being than the one we find at home by the Victorian fireside. Far from a comfortable companion and friend, his 'Shakspeare

---

140   See below pp. 168ff.
141   See below, p. 396.
142   See below, p. 177.

dazzles, repels, terrifies, disgusts, oppresses . . . offends our ears'.[143] His Hamlet is hardly a gentleman, given as he is to 'strange ideas, . . . incoherencies . . . exaggerations . . . sarcasms . . . his thought sullies whatever it touches. He rails bitterly . . . against marriage and love. . . . He jeers lugubriously. . . . His thoughts inhabit a churchyard'. His philosophy is 'hopeless'.[144] Taine's aesthetic distance—unlike contemporary British critics he accepts that Hamlet is a man of the sixteenth century—comes closer to an appreciation of Shakespeare's dramatic genius and his creation, than does the Victorians' comfortable assumption that the dramatist and the character were one of them.

But many Frenchmen of this generation saw Hamlet as very much their contemporary. Baudelaire saw his melancholy self reflected in Hamlet. Delacroix caught the melancholy sensitivity of Shakespeare's hero. Mallarmé responded to the hero's disillusionment, and identified with it. Hamlet is both genius and clown, paralyzed by doubt into inaction. He is beset by unanswered and seemingly unanswerable questions. For Mallarmé he becomes the type of contemporary impotence. Laforgue catches and mocks the Prince's self-pity.

The play may well have been the perfect mirror to reflect the medical, moral and social preoccupations of *fin-de-siècle* France: the demoralization that followed defeat in the Franco-Prussian War, concerns about immorality, effeminacy, mental illness, declining French fertility, not to mention a growing tendencies towards suicide.[145]

The Germans
The Germans might have still continued to believe that *Hamlet* was *their* property. But the British now knew better, and they were prepared to

---

143 See below, pp. 167f. Taine repeats the identification of Hamlet and Shakespeare on p. 173 below.

144 See below, pp. 171–2.

145 On these see Rosario, *The Erotic Imagination*, p. 89 and Robert A. Nye, *Crime, Madness and Politics in Modern France: The Medical Concept of National Decline* (Princeton, N.J.: Princeton University Press, 1984). I am indebted to Martin Scofield, *The Ghosts of Hamlet: The Play and Modern Writers* and to Helen Bailey, *Hamlet in France* for many of the points in this discussion. For more detailed discussion of the play's influence in France, see these works.

shed light upon 'points in Hamlet's soul / Unseized by the Germans'.[146] Teutonic claims on this national treasure were not only disputed, but soundly beaten off. Goethe and Schlegel, the critical gods of the Romantic generation, if not totally dethroned, were subjected to severe questioning.

The Romantic interpretation of the role was now, if not under attack, already subject to debate. Kenny regarded the interpretative subtleties of Goethe, Schlegel, and Coleridge, the high priests of the previous generation of Romantic Shakespearean critics, as 'elongated' and unnecessary.[147] Apparently, by 1864 their conclusions had become trite, obvious, and possibly otiose. James Russell Lowell characterizes these bulky contributions to the understanding of the play as 'over-subtile'. Edward Dowden thought the Germans' readings 'misleading' and that they had over-influenced the criticism of the play.[148] Bucknill questioned the character that the Romantic generation had foisted upon the Prince, of a mind too feeble to accomplish the great task that had been thrust upon it. 'Hamlet the lover, Hamlet the dawdling dreamy *fainéant*, Hamlet the *debonnaire*, Hamlet with a large infusion of Werther'. What was lacking was roughness and violence, 'Hamlet the moody, with a wildness that is half false, and a madness that is half real, the misanthopical, the vindictive, with a thin crust of courtly culture, overlying the fundamental coarseness'.[149] George Henry Miles, and others, argued for a strong Hamlet, rather than Goethe's weakling. The notorious metaphor of the oak planted in a costly jar, which Goethe famously used to sustain his interpretation of the character,[150] came under scathing scrutiny. Although A.W. Ward in his *History of English Literature* (1875) quotes the metaphor of the

---

146 Robert Browning, 'Bishop Blougram's Apology', ll. 946–7, cited pp. 284 and 519 below.
147 See below, p. 182.
148 For Lowell, see below, p. 221. For Dowden, see below, pp. 321–3.
149 John Smith. See below, pp. 193–4.
150 See *CRH*, ii, 25.

vase and the oak with approval, it was more usual to find it being questioned by the Victorians as over-sentimental or simply misleading.[151]

Even the Germans in our period questioned the 'subjective' nature of Hamlet's tragedy as read by Goethe. For the Romantics, Hamlet's tragedy came from within, from the incapacity of his own nature to sustain the role that had been thrust upon him. But for Karl Werder the roots of the tragedy were 'objective'. How could the Prince slay his uncle in cold blood without some material proof to justify his action. His delay in executing his revenge, if delay it is, is simply caused by the fact that the hero does not have sufficient evidence to convince the court and the country that Claudius is the guilty party. The views of Werder, as they were presented in translation by Furness's Variorum *Hamlet*, seem to have exerted some degree of influence, particularly in the United States, and served further to undermine the authority of Goethe.

Other aspects of Goethe's interpretation of the play, particularly those related to the character of Ophelia, also came under question. Charles Cowden Clarke thought of them as the product of a prurient mind, wholly given over to the catching of suggestive innuendo. In defence of Ophelia's honour Clarke did not spare Goethe's own character, which he imputed 'was not wholly untainted with the leaven of grossness'.[152] For British writers of our period, there could be no question of Ophelia's corruption. Yet the subtlety and indeterminate nature of the play tended to attract much German academic writing, as will be seen from the Selective Bibliography below.

The Russians and the Slavonic World
It is to Georg Brandes that we owe the most comprehensive evidence that in our period Hamlet had indeed become a citizen of the world.[153]

151 For A. W. Ward's citation of Goethe's simile, see below, p. 415. For Bucknill's criticism of Goethe's interpretation of Hamlet's character and Goethe's oak and vase metaphor, see below, p. 114. See also James Russell Lowell, p. 234 below, George Henry Miles, p. 239 below, and Edward Dowden, pp. 321ff. For Goethe's influential comment, see *CRH*, ii, 24–5.

152 See below, p. 157. On Goethe's reading of Ophelia's character in *Wilhelm Meisters Lehrjahre*, see *CRH*, ii, 25–9. On the songs, see particularly, pp. 27–9.

153 See extract 59 below, and in particular 'Hamlet's Influence on Later Times', *CRH*, iv, 789–93. On this, see also R. A. Foakes, *Hamlet versus Lear: Cultural Politics*

He discusses the influence of Hamlet in France and Germany, as well as Russia (Pushkin, Gogol, Gontscharoff, Tolstoy and Turgeniev), and Poland (Mickiewicz, Slowacki and Krassinski). Brandes concludes movingly:

> [N]early two centuries and a half after the figure of Hamlet was conceived in Shakespeare's imagination, we find it living in English and French literature, and reappearing as a dominant type in German and two Slavonic languages. And now, three hundred years after his creation, Hamlet is still the confidant friend of sad and thoughtful souls in every land. There is something unique in this.[154]

Conclusion

At the outset of this introduction I indicated that during the period covered by *CRH* iv, the reputation of *Hamlet* was at its apogee. Towards the end of the volume we might see signs of the beginning of its decline. This might perhaps be detected in extract 56, Turgeniev's delightfully perceptive comparison of Hamlet and Don Quixote, which comes down decidedly in favour of the latter. Or, perhaps, equally, in Max Beerbohm's review of Sarah Bernhardt's rendition of the title role, at which he can barely restrain his mirth. Hamlet's stage reputation for effeminacy is rendered risible as Hamlet appears as 'très grande dame'.

These perhaps are no more than straws in the wind of the play's ever so slight decline. It is worth reminding ourselves, however, that we are only five years away from George Bernard Shaw's attack on Shakespeare in which he affirmed that the author's characters have 'no religion, no politics, no conscience, no hope, no convictions of any sort', a sign of the author's 'deficiency in th[e] highest sphere of thought'. One year further on Tolstoy would seek to free the world from 'the false glorification of Shakespeare'. But that story must wait for the next volume of *CRH*.

---

and Shakespeare's Art (Cambridge: Cambridge University Press, 1993), in particular chapter 2: 'Hamlet and Hamletism'.

154 See below, p. 793.

Selective Bibliography

(i) Editions of *Hamlet*, 1850–1900:

The Tragicall Historie of Hamlet . . . (1603). A facsimile executed by the direction of the Duke of Devonshire (London: Privately printed, 1858)

The Tragicall Historie of Hamlet . . . Newly imprinted and enlarged to almost as much againe as it was . . . (1604). A facsimile executed by the direction of the Duke of Devonshire (London: Privately printed, 1859)

Allen, Josiah, *The Devonshire 'Hamlets': Hamlet by William Shakespeare, 1603; Hamlet by William Shakespeare, 1604: Being exact Reprints of the First and Second Editions of Shakespeare's great Drama, from the very rare Originals in the possessions of his Grace the Duke of Devonshire; with the two texts printed on opposite pages, and so arranged that the parallel passages face each other, And a Bibliographical Preface by Samuel Timmins* (London: Sampson Low, Son, and Co., 1860)

Ashbee, Edmund William, *Shakespeare's Hamlet, facsimiled from the Edition printed at London in the year 1603* (London: for private circulation, 1866)

———, *Shakespeare's Hamlet, facsimiled from the Edition printed at London in the year 1604* (London: for private circulation, 1867)

———, *Shakespeare's Hamlet, facsimiled from the Edition printed at London in the year 1605* (London: for private circulation, 1868)

———, *Shakespeare's Hamlet, facsimiled from the Edition printed at London in the year 1611* (London: for private circulation, 1870)

Bentley, Walter, *Hamlet, Prince of Denmark . . . Arranged for Stage Representation from the 'Famous Folio of 1623'* (Belfast: D. Allen & Sons, 1888)

Booth, Edwin and Henry L. Hinton, *Shakespeare's Tragedy of Hamlet*, Booth's Series of Acting Plays, No. 1 (New York: S. French, 1866)

Bowdler, Thomas, ed., *The Family Shakspeare, in which Nothing is added to the Original Text, but those Words and Expressions are omitted which cannot with Propriety be read aloud in a Family*, 6 vols. (London: Longman, Brown, Green, and Longmans, 1853)

Clark, William George and William Aldis Wright, eds., 'Hamlet' in *The Works of William Shakespeare*, The Globe Edition (New York: Grosset & Dunlap, 1866)
——— *Hamlet*,. The Cambridge Shakespeare, vol. 8 (Cambridge: Macmillan, 1866)
——— *Hamlet*, The Clarendon Press Shakespeare (Oxford: Clarendon Press, 1872)
Collier, John Payne, ed., 'Hamlet' in *The Plays and Poems of William Shakespeare: With the Purest Text, and the Briefest Notes*, vol. 6 (London: Privately printed for the subscribers, 1878)
Delius, N., ed., *Hamlet, Prince of Denmark* (Elberfeld: R. L. Friderich, 1865)
Dowden, Edward, ed., *Hamlet*, The Arden Shakespeare (s.l.: Methuen, 1899)
Dyce, Alexander, ed., 'Hamlet' in *The Works of William Shakespeare*, vol. 5 (London: E. Moxon, 1857)
———, 'Hamlet' in *The Works of William Shakespeare*, 2nd edn, vol. 7 (London: Chapman & Hall, 1867)
Elze, K., ed., *Shakespeares Hamlet* (Leipzig: G. Mayer, 1857)
———, *Shakespeare's Tragedy of Hamlet* (Halle: M. Niemeyer, 1882)
Fechter, Charles Albert, *Hamlet . . . Performed at the Royal Lyceum Theatre under the Management of Mr. Fechter* (London: Thomas Hailes Lacy, 1864)
Fiebig, O., *Hamlet, Prince of Denmark . . . In which . . . those Words and Expressions are omitted which cannot with Propriety be read before Young Students. With copious English Explanatory Notes*, The College Shakespeare 1 (Leipzig: T. Thomas, 1857)
Forbes-Robertson, J., *Hamlet . . . as arranged for the Stage by Forbes Robertson . . . With Illustrations by Hawes Craven* (London: Nassau Press, 1897)
Fritsche, *Hamlet, Prince of Denmark . . . Mit Einleitung und Anmerkungen . . .* (Berlin: Weidmann, 1880)
Furness, Horace Howard, ed., *A New Variorum Edition of Shakespeare, Vols III and IV: Hamlet*, 2 vols (Philadelphia: J.B. Lippincott, 1877)
Furnivall, F. J., *Shakspere's Hamlet: The First Quarto, 1603: A Facsimile in Photolithography by W. Griggs . . . With a Fore-words by F.J.*

Furnivall, Shakspere-Quarto Facsimiles, No. 1 (London: W. Griggs, [1880])

Furnivall, F. J., *Shakspere's Hamlet: The Second Quarto, 1604: A Facsimile in Photolithography by W. Griggs . . . With a Fore-words by F.J. Furnivall*, Shakspere-Quarto Facsimiles, No. 2 (London: W. Griggs, [1880])

Halliwell-Phillipps, James O., ed., 'Hamlet' in *The Works of William Shakespeare*, vol. 14 (London: Printed for the editor by J.E. Adlard, 1865)

———, *Fac-simile Copies from the Edition of Hamlet dated 1605, made for the Purpose of Showing that it is the same Impression as that of 1604, the Date only being altered* (London: Printed for Private Circulation, 1860)

Herford, C.H., ed., 'Hamlet' in *The Works of Shakespeare*, The Eversley Edition, vol. 8 (London and New York: Macmillan, 1899)

Heussi, Jakob, ed., *Hamlet* (Leipzig: Paul Frohberg, 1872)

Hudson, H. N., ed., 'Hamlet' in *The Works of William Shakespeare*, The Harvard Edition, vol. 14 (Boston: Ginn, 1881)

Kean, Charles, *Hamlet; With Portrait of Mr. C. Kean as Hamlet and Memoir*, Tallis's Acting Edition of Shakespere, 1 (1851)

———, *Hamlet . . . arranged for Representation at the Royal Princess's Theatre, as First Performed on Monday, January 10th, 1859* (London: Bradbury and Evans, 1859)

Keightley, Thomas, ed., 'Hamlet' in *The Plays of William Shakespeare*, vol. 5 (London: Bell and Daldy, 1864)

Knight, Charles, ed., 'Hamlet' in *The Comedies, Histories, Tragedies and Poems of William Shakspere: The Pictorial Shakspere*, vol. 5 (London: Charles Knight, 1852)

Lacy, T. H., *Hamlet, Prince of Denmark . . .* , Lacy's Acting Edition of Plays, 23 (London: T. H. Lacy, 1850)

MacDonald, George, ed., *Hamlet, Prince of Denmarke: A Study with the Text of the Folio of 1623* (London: Allen & Unwin, 1885)

Maclachlan, D., ed., *The Tragedy of Hamlet . . . With Introduction, Emendations, Notes, and Appendix . . .* (London: Reeves and Turner, 1888)

[Marshall, Francis Albert], ed., *Hamlet . . . as arranged for the Stage by Henry Irving and presented at the Lyceum Theatre on Monday, December 30th, 1878*, revised edn (London: Chiswick Press, 1880)

Moberly. C. E., ed., *Shakespeare's Tragedy of Hamlet . . . [With introduction and notes.] For the Use of Rugby School* (Rugby: W. Billington, 1870)
Neill, S., ed., *Shakespeare's Tragedy of Hamlet . . . with Introductory Remarks, Notes, etc. . . .* , Collins's School and College Classics (London: W. Collins, 1873)
Ribton-Turner, C. J., *Shakespeare's Tragedy of Hamlet, as arranged for the Stage by Wilson Barrett . . . With Notes and an Introduction by C.J. Ribton-Turner* (London: J. S. Virtue & Co., [1886])
Rolfe, W. J., ed., *Shakespeare's Tragedy of Hamlet, Prince of Denmark* (New York: Harper & Brothers, 1890)
Rooney, M. W., *Hamlet. First Edition (1603). The Last Leaf of the Lately Discovered Copy, carefully reprinted, with a Narrative of its Discovery . . .* (Dublin: M. W. Rooney, 1856)
Salvini, Tommaso Cesare, *Hamlet . . . The Italian Version as Performed by Signior Salvini and his Italian Company, at Drury Lane Theatre . . .* (London: Clayton & Co., 1875)
Singer, Samuel Weller, ed., 'Hamlet' in *The Dramatic Works of William Shakespeare. The Text . . . revised with Notes by Samuel Weller Singer. The Life of the Poet . . . by William Watkiss Lloyd*, vol. 9 (London: George Bell, 1856)
Stratmann, F. H., ed., *The Tragicall Historie of Hamlet, Prince of Denmarke . . . edited according to the first printed copies with the various readings and critical notes . . .* (London: N. Trübner & Co., 1869)
Staunton, Howard, ed., 'Hamlet' in *The Plays of Shakespeare*, vol. 3 (London: G. Routledge, 1860)
Timmins, Samuel, *Hamlet . . . 1603; Hamlet . . . 1604: Being exact Reprints of the First and Second Editions of Shakespeare's great Drama, from the very rare Originals in the possession of his Grace the Duke of Devonshire; with the two texts printed on opposite pages, . . . and a Bibliographical Preface by Samuel Timmins* (London: Sampson Low, Son & Co., 1860)
Tschischwitz, Benno, ed., *Shakspeares Hamlet, Prince of Denmark. Englischer Text, berichtigt und erklärt . . . Nebst einer historisch-kritischen Einleitung*, Shakespere sämmtliche Werke, 1 (Halle: Barthel, 1868)

Viëtor, Wilhelm, ed., *Shakespeare Reprints, II. Hamlet. Parallel Texts of the First and Second Quartos and the First Folio* (Marburg: N.G. Elwert, 1891)

Vining, Edward P., *Hamlet, Prince of Denmarke: The Players text of 1603, with the Heminges and Condell Text of 1623*, The Bankside Shakespeare, 11 (New York: The Shakespeare Society of New York, 1890)

White, Richard Grant, ed., 'Hamlet' in *The Works of William Shakespeare*, vol. 11 (Boston: Little, Brown & Co., 1861)

Wright, William Aldis, ed., 'Hamlet' in *The Works of William Shakespeare*, The Cambridge Shakespeare, revised edn, vol. 7 (Cambridge: Macmillan, 1892)

(ii) Critical, Biographical and Textual Studies in English 1850–1900:

Anon. *Hamlet: An Attempt to ascertain whether the Queen were an Accessory, Before the Fact, in the Murder of her First Husband* (London: John Russell Smith, 1856)

Arnold, Matthew, '*Hamlet* Once More', *Pall Mall Gazette*, 23 October, 1884

Blake, E.V., 'The Impediment of Adipose: A Celebrated Case', *Popular Science Monthly*, May (1880), 60–71

Boas, F. S., *Shakspere and his Predecessors* (London: J. Murray, 1896)

Brandes, Georg, *William Shakespeare* (1898; London: William Heinemann, 1920)

Calvert, G. H., *Shakespeare. A Biographic Aesthetic Study* (Boston: Lee and Shepard, and New York: Dillingham, 1879)

Cartwright, N., 'Hamlet's Philosophy' in *The Prince and the Offered Crown* (London and Manchester: John Heywood, 1879), pp. 9–45

Clarke, Charles Cowden, *Shakespeare-Characters: Chiefly Those Subordinate* (London: Smith, Elder & Co., 1863)

Cohn, Albert, *Shakespeare in Germany in the Sixteenth and Seventeenth Centuries: An Account of English Actors in Germany and the Netherlands, and of the Plays Performed by them during the same Period* (London and Berlin: Asher & Co., 1865)

Cooke, Martin W., *The Human Mystery in Hamlet* (New York: Fords, Howard & Hulbert, 1888)

Corbin, John, *The Elizabethan Hamlet: A Study of the Sources, and of Shakspere's Environment, to show that the Mad Scenes had a Comic Aspect now Ignored* (London: Elkin Matthews, and New York: Charles Scribner's Sons, 1895)

Corson, Hiram, *Jottings on the Text of Hamlet* (Ithaca: Privately printed, 1874)

——, 'Hamlet', *Shakespeariana*, 3 (1886), 337–52. An earlier version of the argument of the following.

——, 'Hamlet' in *An Introduction to the Study of Shakespeare* (Boston: D. C. Heath & Co., 1889), pp. 194–222

Crane, William Ward, 'The Allegory of *Hamlet*', *Poet-Lore*, 3 (16 November, 1891), 565–9

Cunliffe, J. W., *The Influence of Seneca on Elizabethan Tragedy* (London: Macmillan, 1893)

Dowden, Edward, *Shakspere: A Critical Study of His Mind and Art* (London: Henry S. King & Co., 1875)

Feis, J., *Shakspere and Montaigne: An Endeavour to Explain the Tendency of 'Hamlet' from Allusions in Contemporary Works* (London: K. Paul, Trench, & Co., 1884)

Fleay, F. G., *A Chronicle History of the Life and Work of William Shakespeare: Player, Poet, and Playmaker* (London: John C. Nimmo, 1886)

——, 'Neglected Facts on *Hamlet*', *Englische Studien*, 7 (1884), 87–97

Ford, Harold, *Shakespeare's Hamlet: A New Theory, or, What was the Poet's Intention in the Play?* (London: E. Stock, 1900)

Gilchrist, Fredericka B., *The True Story of Hamlet and Ophelia* (Boston and Cambridge, Mass: Little, Brown & Co., 1889)

Grinfield, Thomas, *The Moral Influence of Shakespeare's Plays with Illustrations from Hamlet* (London: Longman, Brown & Co., 1850)

Guernsey, Rocellus S., 'Ecclesiastical Law in *Hamlet*: The Burial of Ophelia', *Papers of the New York Shakespeare Society*, 1 (1885)

Haddon, F.W., ed., *The Hamlet Controversy, Was Hamlet Mad? or, The Lucubrations of Messrs. Smith, Brown, Jones and Robinson. With a Preface by the Editor of the* Argus (Melbourne: H.T. Dwight, 1867). See also s.v. Horne, R. H.

Halliwell-Phillipps, J. O., *Memoranda on the Tragedy of Hamlet* (Brighton: Fleet and Bishop, 1879)

Horne, R. H., *Was Hamlet Mad?: Being a Series of Critiques on the Acting of the Late Walter Montgomery* (London: Lacy, 1871)

Howison, Jack, *Hamlet. A Descriptive Account of its Performance witnessed by Jack Howison, aged 12* (Philadelphia, 1894)

Hudson, Henry Norman, *Shakespeare: His Life, Art and Characters...*, 2 vols (1872; Boston: Ginn Brothers, 1888)

Jacox, Francis, *Shakspeare Diversions: Second Series, from Dogberry to Hamlet* (London: Daldy, Isbister, & Co., 1877)

Johnson, Charles F., 'Ophelia', *The New Englander and Yale Review*, n.s. 9 (August, 1886), 679–91

Kenny, Thomas, *The Life and Genius of Shakespeare* (London: Longman, Green, Longman, Roberts, and Green, 1864)

Korner, Sinclair, '*Hamlet* as a Solar Myth', *Poet-Lore*, 3 (15 April, 1891), 214–16

Latham, R. G., *Two Dissertations on the Hamlet of Saxo Grammaticus and of Shakespear* (London: Williams and Norgate, 1872)

Lewes, George Henry, *The Life of Goethe*, rev. edn (1855; London: Smith, Elder & Co., 1864)

Lloyd, William Watkiss, *Essays on the Life and Plays of Shakespeare, contributed to the Edition of the Poet by S.W. Singer, 1856* (London: C. Whittingham, 1858)

Lowell, James Russell, 'Shakespeare Once More', in *Among my Books* (London: Macmillan, 1870), pp. 196–217

Marshall, Francis Albert, *A Study of Hamlet* (London: Longmans, Green, & Co., 1875)

Martin, Helena Faucit, Lady, *On Some of Shakespeare's Female Characters, by One Who Has Personated Them* (Edinburgh and London: for private circulation, 1885). Her essay on Ophelia first appeared in *Blackwood's Magazine*, 129 (1881), 66–77. Later published in a German translation by Karl August Lantzner in 1890.

Meadows, Arthur, *Hamlet: An Essay* (Edinburgh: MacLachan & Stewart, 1871)

Miles, George Henry, *A Review of Hamlet*, 2nd edn (1870; New York: Longmans, Green, 1907)

Moore, Ella Adams, 'Moral Proportion and Fatalism in *Hamlet*', *Poet-Lore*, 7 (1895), 191–7

Owen, John, 'Shakespeare's *Hamlet*' in *The Five Great Skeptical Dramas of History* (London: Sonnenschein & Co., 1896), pp. 277–348

Reed, Henry Hope, *Lectures on English History and Tragic Poetry, as illustrated by Shakespeare* (Philadelphia: Parry & McMillan, 1855)

Robertson, John, *Montaigne and Shakspere* (London: The University Press, 1897)

Swinburne, Algernon Charles, 'Hamlet' in *A Study of Shakespeare* (London: Chatto & Windus, 1880), pp. 160–9

Tree, Herbert Beerbohm, Sir, *Hamlet from an Actor's Prompt Book. The Substance of a Lecture* . . . (London: Nassau Press, 1897)

Turgeniev, Ivan Sergeevich, 'Hamlet and Don Quixote', *The Fortnightly Review*, n.s. 56 (1894), 191–205

Vining, Edward P., *The Mystery of Hamlet* (Philadelphia: J. P. Lippincott & Co., 1881)

Walker, William S., *A Critical Examination of the Text of Shakespeare*, 3 vols (London: J.R. Smith, 1860)

Wedgwood, Frances Julia, 'Aeschylus and Shakespeare: The *Eumenides* and *Hamlet*', *Contemporary Review*, 49 (1886), 82–91. This essay also appeared in *Shakespeariana*, 3 (1886), 65–74

Weiss, John, 'Hamlet' in *Wit, Humor, and Shakspeare. Twelve Essays* (Boston: Roberts Brothers, 1876)

Wendell, Barrett, 'Hamlet' in *William Shakspere: A Study in Elizabethan Literature* (New York: C. Scribner & Sons, 1894), pp. 250–62

Wenley, R.M., 'Hamlet' in *Aspects of Pessimism* (Edinburgh: W. Blackwood, 1894)

White, Richard Grant, *Shakespeare's Scholar: Being Historical and Critical Studies of his Text, Characters, and Commentators, with an Examination of Mr Collier's Folio of 1632* (New York: D. Appleton & Co., 1854)

———, 'The Two Hamlets', *Atlantic Monthly*, 48 (1881), 467–79

——, 'The Case of Hamlet the Younger' in *Studies in Shakespeare* (London: Sampson Low, Marston, Searle & Rivington, 1885)

Wilkes, George, *Shakespeare from an American Point of View*, 3rd rev. and corr. edn (1877; New York: D. Appleton & Co., 1881)

(iii) Critical and Textual Studies in German 1850–1900:

Anon., 'Die Charakterzüge Hamlets, nachgezeichnet von einem Nichtphilosophen', *Jahrbuch der Deutschen Shakspeare-Gesellschaft*, 2 (1867), 16–36

Becque, Henri, 'Der wahre Hamlet', *Magazin für Literatur*, 37 (12 September, 1891), 587–91

Besser, H., *Zur Hamletfrage: Versuch einer Erklärung des Stücke* (Dresden: Pierson, 1882)

Büchler, Hermann, *Shakespeare's Dramen in ihrem Verhältnisse zur griechischen Tragödie* ... (Nuremberg, 1856)

Conrad, H., *Shaksperes Selbstbekenntnisse: Hamlet und sein Urbild* (Stuttgart: J.B. Metzler, 1897)

Dehlen, A., *Shakespeare's Hamlet, Prinz von Dänemark Besprochen* (Göttingen: Vandenhoeck & Ruprecht, 1883)

Döring, August, *Hamlet seinem Grundgedanken und Inhalte nach erläutert* (Hamm: G. Grote, 1865)

———, *Hamlet. Ein neuer Versuch zur ästhetischen Erklärung der Tragödie* (Berlin: R. Gaertner and H. Heyfelder, 1898)

Eckhardt, Ludwig, 'Ueber Shakspeares Hamlet', *Archiv für das Studium der neueren Sprachen und Literaturen*, 31 (1853), 93–112

———, *Vorlesungen über Shakspeares Hamlet: Versuch einer psychologischen Entwicklung* (Aarau: Sauerland, 1853)

Feist, Leopold, *Ueber das Verhältniss Hamlets und Ophelias: Eine ästhetische Untersuchung* (Bingen am Rhein: Verlagsgesellschaft und Drückerei, 1877)

Flathe, J. L. F., *Shakspeare in seiner Wirklichkeit* (Leipzig: Dyk'sche, 1863)

Flir, Alois, *Briefe über Shakespeares Hamlet* (Innsbruck: Wagner, 1865)

Fischer, Kuno, *Shakespeares Hamlet* (Heidelberg: C. Winter, 1896)

Friedrich, Gustav (pseud.), *Hamlet und seine Gemüthskrankheit* (Heidelberg: G. Weiss, 1899)

Friesen, H. von, *Briefe über Shakespeares Hamlet* (Leipzig: B. G. Teubner, 1864)

Gelber, Adolf, *Shakespeare'sche Probleme. Plan und Einheit im Hamlet* (Vienna: C. Konegen, 1891)

Gervinus, G. G., *Shakespeare Commentaries*, tr. F. E. Bunnett, 2 vols (London: Smith, Elder and Co., 1863)

Goethe, J. W. von, *Wilhelm Meister's Apprenticeship and Travels*, tr. T. Carlyle (London: Chapman & Hall, 1899)

Gregori, Ferdinand, *Shakespeares Hamlet im Lichte einer neuen Darstellung. Vortrag* (Barmen, 1894)

Hirschfeld, Jakob, *Ophelia, ein poetisches Lebensbild von Shakespeare, zur ersten Male im Lichte ärtlicher Wissenschaft, zugleich als Beitrag zur ästhetischen Kritik der Tragödie 'Hamlet'. Ein Monographie* (Danzig and Leipzig: E. Grühn, 1881)
Klein, J. L., 'Ueber Hamlet', *Berliner Modenspiegel* (1846), translated in Furness, ii, 296–9.
Paulsen, Friedrich, 'Hamlet' in *Schopenhauer, Hamlet, Mephistopheles. Drei Aufsätze zur Naturgeschichte des Pessimismus* (Berlin: W. Hertz, 1900), pp. 95–173
Schmidt, Alexander, *Lexicon zu Shakespeares Werken*, 2 vols (Berlin: G. Reimer, and London: Williams & Norgate, 1874)
Semler, Christian, *Shakespeares Hamlet. Die Weltanschauung und der Styl des Dichters* (Leipzig: Wartig, 1879)
Stedefeld, G. F., *Hamlet, ein Tendenzdrama Shakespeares gegen die skeptische und kosmopolitische Weltanschauung des Montaigne* (Berlin: Gebr. Paetel, 1871)
Traut, Hugo, *Die Hamlet-Kontroverse im Umrisse bearbeitet* (Leipzig: Dr Seele & Co., 1899)
Tschischwitz, Benno, *Shakespeare Forschungen. I. Hamlet vorzugsweise nach historischen Gesichtspuncten erläutert* (Halle: Waisenhaus, 1868)
Türck, Hermann, *Das Wesen des Genies. Faust und Hamlet: Eine philosophische Studie* (Reudnitz-Leipzig: M. Hoffmann, 1888)
———, *Das psychologische Problem in der Hamlet-Tragödie* (Reudnitz-Leipzig: M. Hoffmann, 1890)
———, *Faust-Hamlet-Christus* (Berlin: Borngraber, 1900)
Vischer, Friedrich Theodor, *Kritische Gänge* (Stuttgart: J. G. Cotta, 1860)
Wagner, Gustav, see above s.v. Friedrich, Gustav.
Werder, K., *Vorlesungen über Shakespeares Hamlet* (Berlin: Hertz, 1875)
———, *The Heart of Hamlet's Mystery*, tr. E. Wilder (New York and London: Putnam, 1907)
Werner, H. A., 'Ueber das Dunkel in der Hamlet-Tragödie', *Jahrbuch der Deutschen Shakspeare Gesellschaft*, 5 (1870)

(iv) Critical and Textual Studies in French and French Translations 1850–1900

Chasles, Philarète, *Etudes sur William Shakespeare, Marie Stuart, et L'Arétin: Le drame, les moeurs, et la religion au XVIe siècle* (Paris: Amyot, 1852)

Davis, William John, *Explication philosophique sur la tragédie d'Hamlet* (1864) translated into English by Frederick John Millard as *Philosophical Explanation of Shakespeare's Hamlet with some Observations on F.V. Hugo's French translation*... (Amsterdam: Jan D. Brouwer, 1867)

Delacroix, Ferdinand Victor Eugène, *Hamlet. Seize sujets dessinés et lithographiés* (Paris: Dusacq & Cie, 1864)

Ducis, Jean-François, *Hamlet: Tragédie en cinq actes, imitée de l'anglais* (Paris: Firmin Didot, 1855)

Dugit, Ernest, 'Oreste et Hamlet', *Annales de l'enseignement supérieur de Grenoble*, I (Grenoble: F. Allier père et fils, 1889), 143–86

Dumas, Alexandre, Benjamin Laroche and Paul Meurice, tr., *Hamlet, Prince de Danemark, En vers* (Paris: Calman Lévy, 1852)

Dumas, Alexandre, the Elder, *Etude sur Hamlet* (1867)

Guizot, F., *Shakspeare et son Temps* (Paris, 1852)

Hugo, Victor-Marie, *William Shakespeare*, authorized English translation by A. Baillot (London: Hurst & Blackett, 1864)

Montégut, Emile, 'Hamlet et de quelques éléments du génie poétique', in *Types littéraires* (Paris: Hachette, 1882), pp. 93–126

Morand, Eugène, and Marcel Schwob, tr., *La tragique histoire d'Hamlet, prince de Danemark* (Paris: Charpentier et Fasquelle, 1900)

Taine, Hippolyte Adolphe, *History of English Literature*, 4 vols tr. H. Van Laun (1873–74; London: Chatto & Windus, 1899)

(v) Medical, Psychological and Critical Studies of Hamlet's 'Insanity' 1850–1900

Biaute, Alcée, *Etude médico-psychologique sur Shakespeare et ses oeuvres, sur Hamlet en particulier* (Nantes, 1889)

Bigelow, Horatio R., 'Hamlet's Insanity', *Chicago Medical Journal* (1873)

Bucknill, John Charles, *The Psychology of Shakespeare* (London: Longman, Brown, Green, Longmans & Roberts, 1859).
——, *The Mad Folk of Shakespeare* (1867). Not a separate work, but a second edition of the above under a different title.
Conolly, John, *A Study of Hamlet* (London: E. Moxon & Co., 1863)
Cox, Edward William, 'The Psychology of Hamlet', *Papers of the Psychological Society of Great Britain*, 17 (London, 1879)
Delbrück, Anton, *Ueber Hamlets Wahnsinn*, Sammlung gemeinverständlicher wissenschaftlicher Vorträge, N.F. No. 172 (Hamburg, 1893)
Kellogg, A.O., *Delineation of Insanity, Imbecility and Suicide* (New York: Hurd & Houghton, 1866). [These essays first appeared in *The American Journal of Insanity* between 1859 and 1864.]
Maudsley, Henry, 'Hamlet' in *Body and Mind* (New York: D. Appleton & Co., 1874), p. 123
Nicholson, Brinsley, 'Was Hamlet Mad?', *New Shakspere Society Transactions*, Part II (1880–85), 341–69
Ray, Isaac, 'Shakespeare's Delineation of Insanity', *The American Journal of Insanity*, (April, 1847)
Schröder, Christoph von, *Wille und Nervosität in Shakespeares Hamlet: Ein Versuch, Hamlets Naturell vom medizinischen Standpunkte zu beleuchten* (Riga, 1893)
Winslow, F.L.S., 'The Psychology of Hamlet', *Journal of Psychological Medicine*, n.s. 5 (1879), 123–7

(vi) Stage History
Arnold, Matthew, *Letters of an Old Playgoer*, ed. Brander Matthews (New York: Dramatic Museum of Columbia University, 1919)
Ball, Robert Hamilton, *Shakespeare on Silent Film* (London: Allen and Unwin, 1968)
Beerbohm, Max, 'Hamlet, Princess of Denmark', *Saturday Review*, 17 June, 1899
Brereton, Austin, *Some Famous Hamlets: From Burbage to Fechter* (London: D. Bogue, 1884)
Gielgud, Kate Terry, *A Victorian Playgoer*, ed. Muriel St. Clare Byrne (London: Heinemann Educational Books, 1980)
Grebanier, Bernard, *Then Came Each Actor* (New York: David McKay, 1975)

Gregori, Ferdinand, 'Die Bühnendarstellung der Hamlet-Rolle' in *Das Schaffen des Schauspielers* (Berlin, 1899)

Hewitt, B., *Theatre U.S.A. 1665 to 1957* (New York: McGraw-Hill, 1959)

Hutton, Lawrence, 'A Century of Hamlet', *Harper's Magazine*, 79 (November, 1889), 866–84

Irving, Henry, 'An Actor's Notes on Shakespeare', *Nineteenth Century Review* (May, 1877)

———, *Four Favourite Parts: Hamlet, Richard III, Iago and King Lear* (London: Macmillan, 1893)

[Lewes, George Henry], 'Charles Kean's Hamlet', *The Leader*, October, 1850

———, 'Hamlet and the German Actors', *The Leader*, 19 June, 1852

Mander, Raymond and Joe Mitchenson, *Hamlet through the Ages* (London: Rockliff, 1952)

Morris, Mowbray Walter, '*Hamlet* and the Modern Stage', *Macmillan's Magazine*, 65 (March, 1892)

Odell, George C. D., *Shakespeare from Betterton to Irving*, 2 vols (London: Constable, 1921)

Scott, Clement, *Some Notable Hamlets of the Present Time: Sarah Bernhardt, Henry Irving, Wilson Barrett, Beerbohm Tree, and Forbes Robertson* (London: Greening, 1900)

Shattuck, Charles H., *Shakespeare and the American Stage*, 2 vols (Washington: Folger Shakespeare Library, 1976 and 1987)

Weilen, A. von, *Hamlet auf der deutschen Bühne bis zur Gegenwart*, Schriften der Deutschen Shakespeare Gesellschaft, 3 (Berlin: G. Reimer, 1908)

Williams, Simon, *Shakespeare on the German Stage, 1586–1914* (Cambridge: Cambridge University Press, 1990)

Winter, William, *Shakespeare on the Stage* (New York: Moffatt, Yard & Co., 1911)

Zabel, Eugen, 'Weibliche Hamlets', *Jahrbuch der deutschen Shakespeare Gesellschaft*, 36 (1900), 249–55

(vii) Modern discussions

Bailey, H.B., *Hamlet in France from Voltaire to Laforgue* (Geneva: Droz, 1964)

Clayton, Thomas, ed., Hamlet *First Published (Q1, 1603): Origins, Form, Intertextualities* (Newark: University of Delaware Press, 1992)
Dijkstra, Bram, *Idols of Perversity: Fantasies of Feminine Evil in Fin-de-Siècle Culture* (New York and Oxford: Oxford University Press, 1986)
Dunn, E. C., *Shakespeare in America* (New York: The Macmillan Company, 1939)
Foakes, R. A., *Hamlet versus Lear: Cultural Politics and Shakespeare's Art* (Cambridge: Cambridge University Press, 1993)
Garber, Marjorie, *Shakespeare's Ghost Writers: Literature as Uncanny Causality* (New York and London: Methuen, 1987)
Haines, C. M., *Shakespeare in France: Criticism, Voltaire to Victor Hugo* (London: Oxford University Press, 1925)
Lamont, Rosette, 'The Hamlet Myth', *Yale French Studies*, 33 (1964), 80–91.
Love, Harold, *James Edward Neild, Victorian Virtuoso* (Carlton, Vic.: Melbourne University Press, 1989)
Ralli, Augustus, *A History of Shakespearian Criticism*, 2 vols (London: Oxford University Press, 1932)
Raven, Anton Adolph, Hamlet *Bibliography and Reference Guide 1877–1935* (Chicago: University of Chicago Press, 1936)
Scofield, Martin, *The Ghosts of Hamlet: The Play and Modern Writers* (Cambridge: Cambridge University Press, 1980)
Spencer, T. J. B., 'The Decline of Hamlet', *Stratford-On-Avon Studies*, vol. 5, ed. J.R. Brown and B. Harris (London, 1963)
Taupin, René, 'The Myth of Hamlet in France in Mallarmé's Generation', *Modern Language Quarterly*, 14.
Taylor, Gary, *Reinventing Shakespeare: A Cultural History from the Restoration to the Present* (London: Hogarth, 1990)
Williamson, Claude H., *Readings on the Character of Hamlet 1661–1947* (London: Allen and Unwin, 1950)

1. George Henry Lewes

1850, 1852, 1861, 1864, 1875

Journalist, critic, writer on science and the arts, author of an influential *Life of Goethe*, partner of George Eliot, Lewes (1817–78), the grandson of a talented comic actor, had a lifelong interest in the theater. His earliest dramatic criticism was written for *The Leader*, of which he was the literary editor. His review 'Charles Kean's Hamlet' appeared there (unsigned; October 1850); parts of '*Hamlet* and the German Actors' (written under the pseudonym of Vivian, *The Leader*, June 19, 1852) were reproduced in the *Life of Goethe* (1st edn. 1855). Extracts from the *Life* are from the second revised edition of 1864. Lewes's review of Fechter appeared in *Blackwood's Edinburgh Magazine*, Vol. 90, December 1861. His assessment of Salvini's 1875 performance of Hamlet was included in Ch. XV in the revised edition of *On Actors and Acting* of that year.

a) 'Charles Kean's Hamlet'[1]

Of all Shakspeare's male characters Hamlet is the most fascinating, the most perplexing, the most various, and the most thoroughly identified in the national mind with its creator's genius. No wonder, therefore, if it has at all times been the ambition of actors to represent it; no wonder if actors, one and all, have failed to personate it in a thoroughly satisfactory manner. We have seen many Hamlets, both in England and in Germany: one played this scene well, another uttered that soliloquy to perfection, but they all, without exception, impressed us with a sense of incompleteness, and, to some extent, of misconception.

This by way of preface to a consideration of Charles Kean's Hamlet—by far the best now on the English stage. Twice within the week we

---

1   Charles Kean (1811–1868), son of Edmund Kean; actor manager; acclaimed less for his skill as an actor than for his use of authentic costume and scenery and innovations in stage lighting.

have watched it carefully, and all that follows will be understood as the expression of a deliberately formed opinion. Charles Kean has, by arduous labour and constant practice in a very few parts, secured for himself all that stage practice can give a man, and it may well be supposed that he has not studied and played Hamlet many hundred nights without having by this time settled, in his own mind, the meaning of every passage, and the effect which he is capable of giving to it.[2] Some years ago we thought his Hamlet a very poor performance. It has become great in comparison, but it still falls short of that standard which is set up in our minds, it does not 'body forth' the poet's creation, it does not throw light upon the dark because profound passages of the text, it does not leave us satisfied. At the opening of the play Hamlet is grave with the gloom of a father's sudden death, and the gloom is deepened and embittered by the indelicate marriage of his mother with his uncle. The world has become weary, flat, stale and unprofitable to him. Woman has, in the person of his mother, been smitten from the pedestal whereon his love had placed her, to fall down and worship, and her name has become the synonym of Frailty. Were it not that God had 'set'[3] his canon 'gainst self-slaughter', this gloom and bitterness would seek an issue in death; but he resolves to suffer all in silence. In the representation of this settled sorrow Charles Kean is unsurpassed. The tones of his voice in which he answers, 'Ay, madam, it is common', and 'I prithee do not mock me, fellow-student; I think it was to see my mother's wedding' (I, ii, 74; 176–7), together with the look of painful disbelief of Horatio—as if his soul, throwing off its load for awhile to interest itself in friendship, was suddenly checked, and flung back again upon the woe it tried to escape—were most effective touches. But this state of Hamlet's mind is only preparatory. It bears the same relation in the subsequent acts as the solemn, ghostly opening scenes, with their awful revelations, bear to the scenes of madness and crime which follow. The play opens on the platform of the castle at Elsinore. It is the depth of midnight; the sentinel pacing to and fro is nipped with cold, and shivering with vague terrors: not a mouse stirring! The silence is broken only by the regular footstep on the platform, and

2   Charles Kean's first major London success was the role of Hamlet in 1838.
3   A mistake for 'fix'd.'

the hoarse sullen murmurs of the Baltic raving below. On this scene appears the Ghost. He reveals the crime which sent him from the world, and then the storm and terror of the play begins [sic]; then come the madness of Hamlet, the conviction of the King, the murder of Polonius, the ravings of Ophelia, the gravediggers casting skulls upon the stage and desecrating the graveyard with their jesting, Ophelia's funeral interrupted and disgraced by a hideous quarrel, and, finally, the general massacre of the last scene! The same ascension from settled gloom to wild and whirling horror and madness may be seen in Hamlet. After the visitation of the Ghost, Hamlet is a *changed man*. His sorrowing nature has been ploughed to its depths by a horror so great that his distended brain refuses every alternate moment to credit it: the shock has unsettled his reason. If he is not mad, he is at any rate in such a state of irrepressible excitement that to feign madness seems the only possible relief to him. This is the point where our differences from Charles Kean's version take their rise. He may not agree with us that Hamlet was really mad; though, unless Shakspeare is to be set down as a bungler, we think that we could bring a mass of evidence wholly irresistible to prove that Hamlet was in a state of cerebral excitement not distinguishable from insanity; but we waive the point, and admit that he was perfectly sane, and still the fact remains that, *after* the revelations of the Ghost, Hamlet must be in a totally different condition of mind from what he was before. That difference Charles Kean does not represent. The *same* gloom overshadows him when alone; the *same* expression of face accompanies him. Instead of the agonized soul of a son in presence of an adulterous mother and a murderous uncle, he exhibits the concentrated sorrow of the first act, diversified only by the outbreaks of assumed madness. He does not depict the hurrying agitation of thoughts that dare not settle on the one horror which, nevertheless, they cannot escape. The excitement, even as simple excitement, is not represented; and thus neither the meaning of the assumed madness, nor the effects of the Ghost's revelations are apparent in his acting. Indeed, Charles Kean seems to have no *mastery* over emotion. He can pourtray a fixed condition of mind, but not its fluctuations. He can be passionate, sorrowful, but he cannot let the emotions *play* in his face and tones. There are flashes, but no fusion. All the early portions of Hamlet he plays with a subdued melancholy which is perfectly in place and very effective; but one detail will explain our objections, and it shall be taken from the very scene where the *change* is most imperative. The Ghost having narrated his terrible story vanishes, leaving Hamlet in a state of bewildering horror. To show how completely unsettled Hamlet's reason is by the apparition, we need not refer to his incoherent ramblings which draw forth Horatio's remark, we will refer to his language in addressing the Ghost as 'old truepenny'! 'old mole'! and the 'fellow in the cellarage',—imagine Hamlet sane, and speaking thus! The language indicates a bewilderment and distraction which the actor should make apparent in his manner; but so far from this, Charles Kean kneels to the Ghost as he departs; remains sobbing with his hands covering his face for a few seconds, as if grief, not horror, were the feeling of the time, and makes a *literal* application of the words—

> Hold, hold my heart;
> And you my sinews grow not instant old
> But bear me stiffly up!
>
> (I, v, 93–5)

rising at the last line. All which we hold to be a misconception of the situation. Throughout the rest of his performance we miss the one essential element of a changed condition (madness or not, it matters little) consequent upon the revelations of the ghost. It is *vehement* enough—sometimes too vehement—but not *wild* enough—an important distinction. Nor is this wildness the only omission. Hamlet's subsequent career should be impregnated with the horror, the feverish desire for revenge, and the alternations of doubt as to whether, after all, he is not the plaything of his own imagination, whether the ghost's story is *true* or not: thus his tone of thought should not only be agitated, it should be intensified. Charles Kean is not mad enough, nor sceptical enough, nor intense enough. There is one 'point' which he makes, and is applauded for, which we cannot understand. In the famous outburst, 'O what a rogue and peasant slave am I', he delivers the words—

> Bloody, bawdy villain!
> Remorseless, treacherous, lecherous, kindless villain,
>
> (II, ii, 581–2)

with great vehemence until he comes to the word 'kindless', and then, pausing, sobs it forth into his handkerchief, as if his uncle's unkindness had then, for the first moment, occurred to him. But, surely, Hamlet is in no mood for tears: his sorrow lies too deep for that; and, moreover, the word 'kindless' here, we take it, means not 'unkind', but 'inhuman'. *Kind* is frequently used by the old writers in the sense of *nature*, thus in *Ferrex and Porrex*:-

> In kinde a father, not in kindliness[4].

Our space forbids entering upon the other details we had noted both for approval and dissent; but we will say, generally, that we not only miss in the performance the psychological modifications above noted, but also the princely courtesy and grave gaiety, like a smile on a sad face, of Shakspeare's Hamlet when he unbends. The scene with Ophelia is the best, after the opening scenes, and plainly indicates the heart that is breaking underneath the harshness; there is also more *wildness* in this interview than elsewhere. On the whole, Charles Kean's Hamlet, though not the Hamlet of Shakspeare, as *we* understand him, is a far more satisfactory performance than Macready's:[5] it lies very open to criticism as a conception, no less than in its details of execution; but it is an elaborate and in many places effective representation of a part in which no man thoroughly succeeds, and few men altogether fail.

b) '*Hamlet* and the German actors'

I once had a maternal uncle (had, alas! *vixit!*[6]), whose views on the drama were freely communicated to me in the high and buoyant days when five act tragedies in swelling verse were the dream and occupation of my life. He resided in Bungay, where he adorned a large domestic circle with all the virtues of a citizen, and earned the eternal gratitude of mankind by his improvements in soap!

In soap! Imagine Vivian in connection with saponaceous commerce! But biography has no delicacy, and facts are shattering to all illusions;

---

4 Thomas Norton and Thomas Sackville, *Gorboduc, or Ferrex and Porrex*, I, i, 18.
5 See *CRH*, iii, 15–36.
6 *vixit*: he lived [and is no more].

and the fact is as I state. This free-spoken uncle was an anticipation of the Fast School of Critics. He snored at five act dramas, and was merciless to mine. Shakspeare was his personal enemy. I think I see him now, rubbing his fat fingers through his scanty hair, as he authoritatively delivered himself of this favourite remark: 'Hamlet, sir? If *Hamlet* were produced to-morrow *Hamlet* would be d-d, sir'. After uttering that he would relapse into his chair, complacent, authoritative, obese.

I have since heard the remark from others, especially from actors, although, in *fact*, no play is so popular as *Hamlet*. It amuses thousands annually. It stimulates the minds of millions. Performed in barns, in minor theatres, and theatres royal, it always attracts. The lowest and most ignorant audiences delight in it; partly, no doubt, because of its profundity and sublimity—for the human soul can *feel* a grandeur which it cannot understand, and the dullest will listen with hushed awe and sympathy to those outpourings of a great meditative mind obstinately questioning fate and existence; to the lowest as the highest it is, *To be or not to be!* But *Hamlet* mainly delights the crowd by its wondrous dramatic and theatric art.

Consider for a moment the variety of its effects. The Ghost—the tyrannous murderer—the faithless wife and queen—the melancholy hero doomed to such an awful fate—the poor Ophelia, brokenhearted, and dying mad—the play within a play, entrapping the conscience of the King—the grave-diggers in ghastly mirth—the funeral of Ophelia, and the quarrel over her grave—and finally, the hurried bloody *dénouement*. Here are elements for several Fast dramas. Let us add thereto the passion and the poetry—let us note how Shakspeare by his art has made intensely interesting that which in other hands would have been insufferably tedious—I mean *Reverie. Hamlet* is a tragedy of Thought; there is as much reflection as action in it. It is the representation of a great *meditative* soul struggling against circumstance; and in this respect it is a theatrical paradox, for it makes Scepticism, Reverie, Reflection, *dramatic*. Here the *activity* of thought supplies the place of action, and hurries the audience along with it.

The peculiarity of *Hamlet* is its indissoluble union of refinement with horrors, of thought with tumult, of high and delicate poetry with gross theatrical effects. Only pause for a moment to consider the machinery of this play. What a tissue of horrors it is! the ghostly apparitions—the incestuous adultery and murder—Hamlet half mad—Ophelia raving mad—Polonius killed like a rat behind the arras—grave-diggers casting skulls upon the stage, and desecrating the churchyard with their ribaldry—a funeral interrupted by a furious quarrel between the two who loved the dead most dearly—murder planned—poisonings and stabbings to close this history,—and all these as the machinery for the most thoughtful and philosophic of poems! In this respect, as in so many others, it resembles *Faust*: that, also, is a poem wild, fantastic, brutal in its machinery; lofty, refined, and impassioned in its spirit.

I think, then, there is a good reason for siding with fact against avuncular dogmatisms, and for declaring that *Hamlet* is not only a marvellous poem, but a great play. And this great play was performed here in London by the 'great Germans', who discovered Shakspeare, and who have taken out a patent for the correct appreciation of him. I have much to say on this hypothetical superiority of German appreciation; but for the present my business is with Herr Devrient, as the acknowledged Hamlet of Germany at this moment[7]. The expectation raised was immense. Before venturing an opinion on the performance, it will be well to fix the point of view.

There are three capital aspects in the representation of Hamlet—1st. The princely elegance of a sorrowing profoundly meditative man. 2nd. The fitful wildness of madness only half assumed. 3rd. The lover of Ophelia. On the first point there is no dispute. On the second and third points critics are not agreed. Now, did the occasion warrant it, I could prove Hamlet to be in such a state of cerebral excitement, that its outward manifestations should be those of madness, whether we consider him really mad or not; so that, as regards the actor, it matters very little what view he takes of this vexed question, he must depict the wildness and fitfulness proper to the scene, and not, as Charles Kean does, preserve the same settled gloom and contemplative quiet *after* the interview with the Ghost which served to express his mental condition *before* the interview. On this point I shall venture to repeat what two years ago I said when noticing Charles Kean's *Hamlet*:

7   In 1852 Emil Devrient (1803–1872) led the first company of German actors to play in London; he performed Hamlet, his most celebrated role, at the St James's Theatre. Popular and critical acclaim led to the return of Devrient's company and their *Hamlet* in 1853.

[Quotes from a) above: 'At the opening of the play Hamlet is grave with the gloom of a father's sudden death . . . ' to ' . . . and thus neither the meaning of the assumed madness, nor the effects of the Ghost's revelations are apparent in his acting', omitting the discussion of Kean's playing of the early scenes, and the divergence of interpretations of Hamlet's (in)sanity.]

According to the view taken of Hamlet's madness, his demeanour towards Ophelia will be somewhat modified. That he loved her is clear enough; his treatment of her is not so clear if he were sane, though explicable upon the assumption of his derangement. At any rate, in their great scene there is a mingled tenderness and bitterness which affords the actor great scope: he should always *look* the contrary of what he utters, and his ferocity should have that restless wildness in it which would excuse it in her eyes. If he is assuming madness, he would wish her to believe him mad, and *so* interpret his harshness; if he is really mad, the wildness is natural.

I have thus established, as it were, some definite grounds of philosophic criticism on the representation of Hamlet. Setting details aside, I call your attention to the three central points in the character: if the actor rightly seize them, we may pass over imperfections of detail; if he miss them, no excellence of detail will compensate. And now I am prepared to answer the question, How did Emil Devrient succeed in *Hamlet*? Indifferently. The princely elegance was never represented; indeed I thought him ungainly, but those around me thought him graceful, so let him have the benefit of their admiration. The sorrowing of a profoundly meditative nature I caught no glimpse of; it was more like dyspepsia than sorrow, and as unlike meditation as it was unlike reality. In fact, the first scene was very inferior to that played by Charles Kean, who does represent the settled sorrow of Hamlet, if he represent little else. While, in his interview with the Ghost, Herr Devrient had more the demeanour of a frightened school-boy than of the sceptical student and affectionate son. Let me say, once for all, that I see no trace of superior intelligence in Emil Devrient's reading of his part, but very many evidences of careless, superficial interpretation, such as will bear no examination. There is too much of what may be called *haphazard emotion—i.e.,* emotion not following a thorough study of identification with the character, but arising from a sort of guess at what should be the feeling of the moment. To give an example: He asks the players if they can perform a certain piece which he has in his eye, and moreover, if they will insert some dozen lines that he will write. I am ashamed to be forced into such an obvious remark as that Hamlet must be thoroughly aware of the peculiar *bearing* of the play he has chosen, and has already determined upon the use he will make of it to catch the conscience of the King; but I am forced to make the remark, because Herr Devrient, in the soliloquy which followed—

'O what a rogue and peasant slave am I,' etc.,

made a great point of suddenly conceiving this idea of using the play as a means of testing the King; he smacked his forehead, paused a long while, tried to throw speculation into his eyes, and in low, mysterious accents announced to himself this very determination. Now this is what I call haphazard emotion. The slightest consideration of the character as a *whole* will serve to exhibit repeated instances of the same kind. Of all characters on the stage, Hamlet most demands from its performer a subtle sympathy and an appreciation of intellect, which certainly are not with Herr Devrient's nature. Whatever else there may be in his acting, there is not intense mental vigour. Were it not that space and time are wanting, I would undertake to go through any scene, and point out proofs of what I say. Having, however, expressed my opinion with a frankness demanded by the occasion, and by the enormous praise which has greeted Herr Devrient, with more hospitality than discernment, let me now turn to what was excellent in his performance.

The second aspect which the character presents—viz., that of Hamlet half-mad, was forcibly given. Herr Devrient—probably according to German tradition—preserves the significant phrases addressed to the Ghost, 'How now, old mole! dost work i' the earth so fast', etc., and taking the plain hint given in such language, he represents the reason of Hamlet as completely unsettled by the revelations of the Ghost—he *is* the madman he affects to be. This one scene was sufficient to show that a new version of Hamlet, more consistent with the text, would be far more effective than our English versions. Herr Devrient was wild, fitful, and impressive. The change from the earlier manner was complete. Perhaps in the subsequent scenes a more intelligent actor would have been less monotonous in his wildness; but, at any rate, it was something to see the mad view of the part seriously taken up. As Ophelia's lover—the third aspect of the part—Herr Devrient wanted tenderness altogether (he always does), but he played without the harshness which usually spoils this scene; and, indeed, it only wanted a little tenderness to make it perfect. The elegance, the pathos, the fluctuating passion, and the thought of Hamlet, were but poorly represented; but, on the other hand, the madness was thoroughly grasped; and very many of the speeches which one has been accustomed to hear ranted and mouthed, were spoken with a naturalness far more effective. To sum up in a phrase: Herr Devrient has not a spark of *genius*, but he is a practised actor, capable of giving effect to certain passages; and his Hamlet has some scenes one can honestly praise, though not one passage that roused any enthusiasm in me.

The Polonius of Herr Limbach, on the contrary, was a fine piece of acting. He conceived Polonius rather as a stupid than a senile man, and in so far he erred, I think; nevertheless, this is almost hypercriticism on his excellent performance, which was admirable within its own limits. He was 'made up' like a Van Dyke; and the unconscious garrulity and feebleness of intellect were naively and quietly hit off.

(c) From: *The Life of Goethe,*
(i) Book VI, Ch. 2 [*Hamlet* and *Wilhelm Meister*]:
The criticism on *Hamlet*, which Wilhelm makes, still remains the best criticism we have on that wonderful play[8]. Very artfully is *Hamlet* made as it were a part of the novel; and Rosenkrantz praises its introduction not only because it illustrates the affinity between Hamlet and Wilhelm, both of whom are reflective, vacillating characters, but because Hamlet is further allied to Wilhelm in making the Play a touchstone, whereby to detect the truth, and determine his own actions.

(ii) Book VI, Ch. 7 [*Hamlet* and *Faust*]
In *Faust* we see, as in a mirror, the eternal problem of our intellectual existence; and, beside it, varied lineaments of our social existence. It is at once a problem and a picture. Therein lies its fascination. The problem

---

8   For Goethe's *Wilhelm Meister*, see *CRH*, ii,19–42.

embraces questions of vital importance; the picture represents opinions, sentiments, classes, moving on the stage of life. The great problem is stated in all its nudity; the picture is painted in all its variety.

This twofold nature of the work explains its popularity; and, what is more to our purpose, gives the clue to its secret of composition; a clue which all the critics I am acquainted with have overlooked; and although I cannot but feel that considerable suspicion must attach itself to any opinion claiming novelty on so old a subject, I hope the contents of this chapter will furnish sufficient evidence to justify its acceptance. The conviction first arose in my mind as the result of an inquiry into the causes of the popularity of *Hamlet*. The two works are so allied, and so associated together in every mind, that the criticism of the one will be certain to throw light on the other.

Hamlet, in spite of a prejudice current in certain circles that if now produced for the first time it would fail, is the most popular play in our language.[9] It *amuses* thousands annually, and it stimulates the minds of millions. Performed in barns and minor theatres oftener than in Theatres Royal, it is always and everywhere attractive. The lowest and most ignorant audiences delight in it. The source of the delight is twofold: First, its reach of thought on topics the most profound; for the dullest soul can *feel* a grandeur that it cannot *understand*, and will listen with hushed awe to the outpourings of a great meditative mind obstinately questioning fate; Secondly, its wondrous dramatic irony. Only consider for a moment the striking effects it has in the Ghost; the tyrant murderer; the terrible adulterous queen; the melancholy hero, doomed to so awful a fate; the poor Ophelia, broken-hearted and dying in madness; the play within a play, entrapping the conscience of the King; the ghastly mirth of gravediggers; the funeral of Ophelia interrupted by a quarrel over her grave betwixt her brother and her lover; and finally, the hurried bloody *dénouement*. Such are the figures woven in the tapestry by passion and poetry. Add thereto the absorbing fascination of profound thoughts. It may indeed be called the tragedy of thought, for there is as much reflection as action in it; but the reflection itself is made dramatic, and hurries

---

9 From this point to the end of the paragraph, Lewes largely reproduces the substance of part of '*Hamlet* and the German Actors'.

the breathless audience along, with an interest which knows no pause. Strange it is to notice in this work the indissoluble union of refinement with horrors, of reflection with tumult, of high and delicate poetry with broad, palpable, theatrical effects. The machinery is a machinery of horrors, physical and mental: ghostly apparitions—hideous revelations of incestuous adultery and murder—madness—Polonius killed like a rat while listening behind the arras—gravediggers casting skulls upon the stage and desecrating the churchyard with their mirth—these and other horrors form the machinery by which moves the highest, the grandest, and the most philosophic of tragedies.

It is not difficult to see how a work so various should become so popular. *Faust*, which rivals it in popularity, rivals it also in prodigality.

(d) From 'Fechter in *Hamlet* and *Othello*'

In the present deplorable state of the drama and the stage, every lover of the art must rejoice at the surprising success achieved by the remarkable Frenchman who has undertaken to give a new aspect to Shakespearian tragedy, and who has drawn all London to witness two of the greatest dramatic works ever written. No man ever before played Hamlet for seventy consecutive nights; no man, since the great Kean, ever excited so much discussion. That much of this success is owing to the curiosity of seeing a Frenchman play Shakespeare in English, no one will doubt. But whatever the cause, the success is a fact which must have its influence; and now that a second part has been added to Fechter's Shakespearian repertory, the discussion becomes more animated, and the questions involved become more capable of solution.

To express my own opinion in a sentence—I think his Hamlet one of the very best, and his Othello one of the very worst I have ever seen; and I have seen all the good actors, and many of the bad actors, from Kean downwards. On leaving the theatre after *Hamlet*, I felt once more what a great play it was, with all its faults, and they are gross and numerous. On leaving the theatre after *Othello*, I felt as if my old admiration for this supreme masterpiece of the art had been an exaggeration; all the faults of the play stood out so glaringly, all its beauties were so dimmed and distorted by the acting of every one concerned. It was necessary to recur to Shakespeare's pages to recover the old feeling.

Reflecting on the contrast offered by these two performances, it seemed to me that a good lesson on the philosophy of acting was to be read there. Two cardinal points were illustrated by it. First, the very general confusion which exists in men's minds respecting naturalism and idealism in art; secondly, the essential limitation of an actor's sphere, as determined by his personality. Both in *Hamlet* and *Othello*, Fechter attempts to be *natural*, and keeps as far away as possible from the conventional declamatory style, which is by many mistaken for idealism only because it is unlike reality. His physique enabled him to represent Hamlet, and his naturalism was artistic. His physique wholly incapacitated him from representing Othello; and his naturalism, being mainly determined by his personality, became utter feebleness. I do not mean that the whole cause of his failure rests with his physical incapacity, for as will presently be shown, his intellectual conception of the part is as false as his execution is feeble; but he might have had a wrong conception of the part, and yet have been ten times more effective, had nature endowed him with a physique of more weight and intensity. Twenty Othellos I have seen, with far less intelligence, but with more effective representative qualities, whose performances have stirred the very depths of the soul; whereas I cannot imagine any amount of intelligence enabling Fechter's personality to make the performance satisfactory.

His Hamlet was 'natural'; but this was not owing, as many seem to think, to the simple fact of its being more conversational and less stilted than usual. If Shakespeare's grandest language seemed to issue naturally from Fechter's lips, and did not strike you as out of place, which it so often does when mouthed on the stage, the reason was that he formed a tolerably true conception of Hamlet's nature, and could *represent* that conception. It was his personality which enabled him to represent this conception. Many of the spectators had a conception as true, or truer, but they could not have *represented* it. This is self-evident. But what is the meaning of the natural in art? On this point great confusion prevails. By naturalism and realism, men commonly, and falsely, suppose that an imitation of *ordinary* life is meant: a reproduction of such details as may be recognized among our daily experiences. Whereas naturalism truly means the reproduction of those details which *characterise the nature of the thing represented*. Realism means *truth*, not vulgarity. Truth of the higher as of the lower forms: truth of passion, and truth of manners. The nature of a Macbeth is not the nature of an Othello; the speech of Achilles is not the speech of Thersites. The truth of the 'Madonna di San Sisto' is not the truth of Murillo's 'Beggar Girl'. But artists and critics often overlook this obvious fact. Actors are especially prone to overlook it, and, in trying to be *natural*, sink into the *familiar*; though that is as unnatural as if they were to attempt to heighten the reality of the Apollo by flinging a paletot over his naked shoulders. It is this error into which Fechter falls in Othello; he vulgarises the part in the attempt to make it natural. Instead of the heroic, grave, impassioned Moor, he represents an excitable creole of our own day.

Intellectually and physically his Hamlet so satisfies the audience, that they exclaim, 'How natural!' Hamlet is fat, according to his mother's testimony; but he is also—at least in Ophelia's eyes—very handsome—

> The courtier's, soldier's, scholar's eye, tongue, sword,
> The glass of fashion and the mould of form,
> The observed of all observers.
>
> (III, i, 154–65)

Fechter is lymphatic, delicate, handsome, and with his long flaxen curls, quivering sensitive nostrils, fine eye, and sympathetic voice, perfectly represents the graceful prince. His aspect and bearing are such that the eye rests on him with delight. Our sympathies are completely secured. And as he endeavours to *act*, not to *declaim* the part, we feel that we have Hamlet the Dane before us. All those scenes which demand the qualities of an accomplished comedian, he plays to perfection. Never before have the scenes with the players, with Polonius, with Horatio, with Rosenkranz and Guildenstern, or the quieter monologues, been better played; they are touched with so cunning a grace, and a manner so *natural*, that our delight is extreme. We not only feel in the presence of an individual, a character, but feel that the individual is strictly consonant with our previous conception of Hamlet, and with the part assigned him in the play. The passages of *emotion* also are rendered with real sensibility. His delightful and sympathetic voice, and the unforced fervour of his expression, triumph over the foreigner's accent and the foreigner's mistakes in emphasis. This is really a considerable triumph; for although Fechter pronounces English very well for a Frenchman, it is certain that his accent greatly interferes with the due effect of his speeches. [An idle attempt has been made to juggle away the objection to his foreign accent on the ground that he is not a Frenchman, having been born in London. But these biographical facts cannot weigh with an audience. His accent is a French accent; and if he is an Englishman, the accent is unpardonable.][10] But the foreign accent is as nothing compared with the perpetual error of emphasis; and *this* surely he might overcome by diligent study, if he would consent to submit to the rigorous criticism of some English friend, who would correct him every time he errs. The sense is constantly perturbed, and sometimes violated, by this fault. Yet so great is the power of true emotion, that even *this* is forgotten directly he touches the feelings of the audience; and in his great speech, 'O what a rogue and peasant slave am I!' no one hears the foreigner.

Physically then, we may say that his Hamlet is perfectly satisfactory; nor is it intellectually open to more criticism than must always arise in the case of a character which admits of so many readings. It is certainly a fine conception, consonant in general with what the text of Shakespeare indicates. It is the nearest approach I have seen to the realisation of Goethe's idea, expounded in the celebrated critique in *Wilhelm Meister*, that there is a burden laid on Hamlet too heavy for his soul to bear. The refinement, the feminine delicacy, the vacillation of Hamlet, are admirably represented; and it is only in the more tragic scenes that we feel any shortcoming. For these scenes he wants the tragedian's personality; and once for all let me say that by personality I do not simply mean the physical qualities of voice and person, but the physiological qualities which give the force of animal passion demanded by tragedy, and which cannot be *represented* except by a certain animal power.

There is one point, however, in his reading of the part which seems to me manifestly incorrect. The error, if error it be, is not peculiar to him, but has been shared by all the other Hamlets, probably because they did not know how to represent what Shakespeare has *indicated* rather than expressly set down. And as there is nothing in his physique which would prevent the proper representation of a different conception, I must assume that the error is an intellectual one. On this account I submit to his consideration the following suggestions.

10   Author's note.

Much discussion has turned on the question of Hamlet's madness, whether it be real or assumed. It is not possible to settle this question. Arguments are strong on both sides. He may be really mad, and yet, with that terrible consciousness of the fact which often visits the insane, he may 'put an antic disposition on', as a sort of relief to his feelings. Or he may merely assume madness as a means of accounting for any extravagance of demeanour into which the knowledge of his father's murder may betray him. Shakespeare has committed the serious fault of not making this point clear; a modern writer who should commit such a fault would get no pardon. Now the actor is by no means called upon to settle such points. One thing, however, he is called upon to do, and that is, not to depart widely from the text, not to misrepresent what stands plainly written. Yet this the actors do in *Hamlet*. They may believe that Shakespeare never meant Hamlet to be really mad; but they cannot deny, and should not disregard, the plain language of the text—namely, that Shakespeare meant Hamlet to be in a state of *intense cerebral excitement*, bordering on madness. His sorrowing nature has been suddenly ploughed to its depths by a horror so great as to make him recoil every moment from the belief in its reality. The shock, if it has not destroyed his sanity, has certainly *unsettled* him. Nothing can be plainer than this. Every line speaks it. We see it in the rambling incoherence of his 'wild and whirling words' to his fellow-watchers and fellow-witnesses; but as *this* may be said to be assumed by him (although the motive for such an assumption is not clear, as he might have 'put them off', and yet retained his coherence), I will appeal to the impressive fact of the irreverence with which in this scene he speaks *of* his father and *to* his father—language which Shakespeare surely never meant to be insignificant and which the actors always omit. Here is the scene after the exit of the ghost:-

[Quotes I, v, 120–66: *Marcellus*: How is't, my noble lord? . . . *Horatio*: O day and night, but this is wondrous strange!]

Now, why are these irreverent words omitted? Because the actors feel them to be irreverent, incongruous? If spoken as Shakespeare meant them to be—as Hamlet in his excited and bewildered state must have uttered them—they would be eminently significant. It is evading the difficulty to omit them; and it is a departure from Shakespeare's obvious intention.

Let but the actor enter into the excitement of the situation, and make *visible* the hurrying agitation which prompts these wild and whirling words, he will then find them expressive, and will throw the audience into corresponding emotion.

But this scene is only the beginning. From the moment of the Ghost's departure, Hamlet is a *changed* man. All the subsequent scenes should be impregnated with vague horror, and an agitation compounded of feverish desire for vengeance with the perplexities of thwarting doubt as to the reality of the story which has been heard. This alternation of wrath and of doubt as to whether he has not been the victim of an hallucination, should be represented by the feverish agitation of an unquiet mind, visible even under all the outward calmness which it may be necessary to put on; whereas the Hamlets I have seen are perfectly calm and self-possessed when they are not in a tempest of rage, or not feigning madness to deceive the King. It is part and parcel of this erroneous conception as to the state of Hamlet's mind (unless it be the mistake of substituting declamation for acting) which, as I believe, entirely misrepresents the purport of the famous soliloquy—'To be or not to be'. This is not a set speech to be declaimed to pit, boxes, and gallery, nor is it a moral thesis debated by Hamlet in intellectual freedom; yet one or the other of these two mistakes is committed by all actors. Because it is a fine speech, pregnant with thought, it has been mistaken for an oratorical display; but I think Shakespeare's genius was too eminently dramatic to have committed so great an error as to substitute an oration for an exhibition of Hamlet's state of mind. The speech is passionate, not reflective; and it should be so spoken as if the thoughts were *wrung* from the agonies of a soul hankering after suicide as an escape from evils, yet terrified at the dim sense of greater evils after death. Not only would such a reading of the speech give it tenfold dramatic force, but it would be the fitting introduction to the wildness of the scene, which immediately succeeds, with Ophelia. This scene has also been much discussed. To render its strange violence intelligible, actors are wont to indicate, by their looking towards the door, that they suspect the King, or someone else, to be watching; and the wildness then takes its place among the *assumed* extravagances of Hamlet. Fechter also conceives it thus. I cannot find any warrant in Shakespeare for such a reading; and it is adopted solely to evade a difficulty which no longer exists when we consider Hamlet's state of feverish excitement. I believe, therefore, that Hamlet is not disguising his real feelings in this scene, but is terribly in earnest. If his wildness seem unnatural, I would ask the actors what they make of the far *greater* extravagance with which he receives the confirmation of his doubts by the effect of the play upon the King? Here, it is to be observed, there is no pretext for assuming an extravagant demeanour; no one is watching now; he is alone with his dear friend and confidant, Horatio; and yet note his conduct. Seeing the King's guilt, he exclaims—

[Quotes III, ii, 249–81: 'His name's Gonzago . . . Why, then, belike, he likes it not perdy'.]

Of course the actors omit the most significant of these passages, because they are afraid of being comic; but, if given with the requisite wildness, these passages would be terrible in their grotesqueness. It is true that such wildness and grotesqueness would be out of keeping with any representation of Hamlet which made him calm, and only assuming madness at intervals. But is such a conception Shakespearian?

Fechter is not specially to be blamed for not having made Hamlet's state of excitement visible throughout; but although his personality debars him from due representation of the more tragic scenes, it would not debar him from representing Hamlet's agitation if he conceived it truly. On the whole, however, I repeat that his performance is very charming, because very natural.

(e) From: 'First Impressions of Salvini' (*On Actors and Acting*, **2nd edition**).
I cannot pretend to form an estimate of Salvini. A few years ago I saw him at Genoa in a coat-and-waistcoat comedy by Scribe (a version of *La Calomnie*), and was persuaded that he would be well worth seeing in tragedy. This summer I have seen him twice in *Othello*, once in *The Gladiator*, and twice in *Hamlet*. But this is not enough for a critical estimate; and I will therefore only set down first impressions.

His performances at Drury Lane have excited an enthusiasm that recalls the early days of Kean and Rachel; an enthusiasm which, of course, has been opposed by some fierce antagonism on the part of those who are unaffected by his passion, or who dislike his interpretation. It is always so. But for the most part there has been an acknowledgement of Salvini's great qualities as an actor, even from those who think his conception of Othello false. My object here is less to consider his insight into Shakspeare than his art as an actor. The question of his artistic skill is one which can be reduced to definite and intelligible principles. The question of insight is one which fluctuates amid the indefiniteness of personal taste and experience, complicated by traditional views, and only in rare cases capable of being fortified by reference to indisputable indications of the text. Thus whether Shakspeare paints Othello as a fiery and sensual African, superficially modified by long contact with Europeans, or as one with a native chivalry towards woman who is led to marry Desdemona less from lust, than from the gratitude of an elderly warrior towards a sympathetic maiden who naively expresses her admiration, may be left for each person to settle as he pleases; evidence may be cited in support of either view; as evidence may be cited to prove that Othello was 'not easily jealous,' or that he was very groundlessly jealous. I remarked on a previous page the great uncertainty in which Hamlet's madness is left; but whether Shakspeare meant him to be mad, or feigning madness, nothing can be less equivocal than the indications of a state of cerebral excitement in speech and conduct, and this the actor ought to represent.

These two examples point out the different attitudes which criticism must take with regard to the actor's interpretation. In the first case the critic is impertinent if he thrusts forward *his* reading of the text as that which the actor is bound to follow; the more so when a little reflection should suggest a modest hesitation as to whether on the whole the actor who has given long and continuous study to the part in all its details, and with mind alert to seize every hint, and settle every intonation, is not more likely to be right, than one who has had no such pressing motive, and whose conception of the part has been formed fitfully from occasional readings, or occasional visits to the theatre. In the second case, the critic has the plain indications of the text which he can say the actor has disregarded; that is a question which can be argued on definite and intelligible principles. No actor is to be blamed for not presenting *your* conception of Hamlet, Othello, or Macbeth; but he is justly blamed when he departs from the text such as all men understand. You may not think that Othello was a man of fierce animal passion, but you know that

Othello stabbed himself, and did *not* cut his throat. . . . [Discusses Salvini as Othello and in *The Gladiator*.]

My disappointment at his performance of *The Gladiator* abated my expectations of his Hamlet, for which part his physique so obviously ill-fitted him. Yet here—because he had again genuine dramatic material to work upon—the actor's art was once more superbly shown. It was not Shakspeare's Hamlet, one must admit; the many-sidedness of that strange character was sadly truncated—the wit, the princely gaiety which momently plays over the abiding gloom, the vacillating infirmity of purpose, the intellectual over-activity, were 'conspicuous by their absence'. The play had been cut down to suit Italian tastes. Nevertheless I think of all the Hamlets I have seen, Salvini's is the least disappointing. Of all that I have seen, it has the greatest excellences. The scenes with the Ghost erred I think psychologically in depicting physical terror rather than metaphysical awe; but this is the universal defect; and Salvini's terror was finely expressed. The soliloquies were quiet, and were real soliloquisings, except that every now and then too much was *italicised* and *painted out*: so that he seemed less one communing with himself, than one illustrating his meaning to a listener. The scene with Polonius, 'Words, words', was so admirable that it deepened regret at the mutilation of the text which reduced this aspect of Hamlet to a transient indication. The scene with Ophelia was a revelation. Instead of roaring and scolding at her like other actors, with a fierce rudeness which is all the more incomprehensible that they do not represent Hamlet as mad, Salvini is strange, enigmatical, but always tender; and his 'To a nunnery go' is the mournful advice of a broken-hearted lover, not the insult of a bully or angry pedagogue. This tenderness, dashed with insurgent reproaches, runs through the interview with his mother; and the most pathetic tones I have heard him utter were in the broken huskiness of his entreaties to her to repent. The growing intensity of emotion during the play-scene culminates in a great outburst of triumphant rage as he wildly flings into the air the leaves of the manuscript he has been biting a second before, and falls exhausted on Horatio's neck. No one who witnessed that truthful expression of powerful emotion could help regretting the excision of so many passages of 'wild and whirling words' in which Hamlet gives vent to his cerebral excitement.

Powerful and truthful also was his acting in the scene where he catches the King at prayer. But dull beyond all precedent was the talk at Ophelia's grave! The close was magnificent. No more pathetic death has been seen on the stage. Among its many fine touches there was the subtle invention of making the dying Hamlet draw down the head of Horatio to kiss him before sinking into silence: which reminds one of the 'Kiss me, Hardy', of the dying Nelson. And this affecting motive was represented by an action as novel as it was truthful—namely, the uncertain hand blindly searching for the dear head, and then faintly closing on it with a sort of final adieu.

There are two points which struck me as lessening the effect of this otherwise rare performance: the first was a tearful tendency, sometimes amounting almost to a whining feebleness; the second, nearly connected with this, was a want of perfect consistency in the presentation. There was a dissonance between the high plaintive tones, and the massive animal force, both of person and voice—it was an operatic tenor, or *un beau tenebreux*,[11] grafted on the tragic hero: an incongruous union of the pretty with the grand.

But I am only noting first impressions, and I will not by insisting on faults seem ungrateful to the great artist, who has once more proved to us what the art is capable of. Make what deductions you please—and no artist is without his comparative deficiencies—you must still admire the rare qualities of the tragedian. He has a handsome and eminently expressive face, graceful and noble bearing, singular power of expressing tragic passion, a voice of rare beauty, and an elocution such as one only hears once or twice in a lifetime: in the three great elements of musical expression, tone, timbre, and rhythm, Salvini is the greatest speaker I have heard.

---

11   *un beau tenebreux*: a fashionably dressed, melancholy man.

2. Richard Grant White

1854, 1862, (1870), 1885

Richard Grant White (1821–1885), American man of letters, friend of J.R. Lowell (q.v.) and Francis Child (editor of the English and Scottish ballads), was a learned and often acute Shakespearean scholar. His edition of *The Works of William Shakespeare* (1857–65), based on his *The Complete Works of William Shakespeare* (1857–59), reprinted as the Bankside Shakespeare in 1883, became the text for the early editions of the Riverside Shakespeare. *Shakespeare's Scholar, being Historical and Critical Studies of his Text, Characters, and Commentators, with an Examination of Mr Collier's Folio of 1632,* (1854) from which passages (a) to (d) are taken, shows White's concern with establishing a text as close to Shakespeare's own, and his meaning, as possible; and his concern with the play as performance. The editorial principles in (d) are those employed by White in his own editions of Shakespeare, and have generally been followed by scholars from the mid-nineteenth century. His notes from *Shakespeare's Scholar* also appear at the end of Vol. II of his edition of *The Works* (1857–65), from which come the introductory remarks to the play in (f). The remaining passages show the continuity of his lively interest in *Hamlet*; those from 'The Case of Hamlet the Younger' (first published in 1870) and 'On the Acting of Iago' are taken from *Studies in Shakespeare* (1885), which White was preparing for publication at the time of his death.

(a) **Comments on III, i:**
(i) *Hamlet.* **Or to take arms against a sea of troubles, / And by opposing end them. (ll. 61–2)**
Pope and others would read '*siege* of troubles', alleging that arms may be taken against a siege, but not against a sea, and that the similarity in the sound of the two words might easily have caused a substitution of one for the other. So it might: much more easily than Shakespeare could have written

> Or to take arms against a *siege* of troubles,
> And by opposing end *them*.

For, by line and plummet criticism, if it be a *siege* against which arms are to be taken, it is a *siege* which is ended; for the siege then becomes the object against which the action is to be directed, and the last line must be:

> And by opposing end *it*.

But it is the troubles against which arms are to be taken, and by opposing we end *them*. 'Sea' is but a picturesque, descriptive word in the sentence. Another writer would have said 'a throng of troubles' or something of that kind; but Shakespeare said 'sea', and by one word brings to our mind the imminent, ever succeeding woes which, innumerable, like the 'multitudinous seas', sometimes overwhelm the mind. 'Sea' makes the passage not only highly poetical and Shakesperian, but correct; *siege* makes it not only cautiously exact in following out a figure, and therefore un-Shakesperian, but incorrect to any mind which judges by other than a merely literal standard.—*A fortiori* these remarks apply to the suggestions to read *assay* or *assail* of troubles. It is mysterious to me that a doubt should ever have suggested itself, even to a child of moderate intelligence, about the passage as it stands in the original. Even in my boyish readings of Shakespeare this line was as comprehensible and as grand to me as it is now. I should have been inclined to doubt the sincerity or the sanity of any one who professed to find the passage obscure or faulty. But then I had not read Shakespeare's commentators.

(ii) *Ophelia*. Could beauty, my lord, have better/commerce than with your honesty? (ll. 111–12)
This, the reading of the folio of 1623, is rejected, and the reading of the quartos, 'with honesty', is taken. Even Mr Knight[1] departs from his rule, and rejects his favorite—and justly his favorite authority, even although he admits that the alteration from the quarto is 'clearly by design'. He does so, because 'it appears to lessen the idea we have formed of *Ophelia*

---

1 *The Pictorial Edition of the Works of Shakspeare*, ed. Charles Knight, 8 vols, London, 1839–43.

to imagine that she would put *her* beauty so directly in 'commerce' with *Hamlet's* honesty'. I am past being surprised at a miscomprehension of one of Shakespeare's characters, particularly of the character of one of his women;—yet I cannot but wonder where Mr Knight finds any thing in the delineation of *Ophelia's* character to cause him to lessen his ideas of her at finding her thus plain spoken. What does he think of the songs which she sings when derangement removes the restraint of propriety from her mind? On what do they show her thoughts to have been, in a great measure, fixed?—for it is to be borne in mind that she is not distracted or wild, but only unsettled. What does he think of her gross perversion of *Hamlet's* request in Act III. Scene 2, just before the Dumb Show begins?[2] With regard to the passage under consideration,—if a woman so far trust a man, and so far unbend herself as to speak of such matters *at all*, it seems difficult to find the peculiar and added impropriety of this expression, 'your honesty', to a lover in *Hamlet's* situation and in Shakespeare's time.

However, Mr Knight's course is but a remnant of the practice of the eighteenth century, which was, to think that the ideas which the commentator or actor had formed of a character, were more just than those of Shakespeare himself, and to take the development of character out of the hands of the poet into those of his restorers and improvers, for the stage or the closet. As for instance,—the acting *Lear, Romeo and Juliet, Richard III*, &c., &c.

(b) Comment on *Hamlet* III, iii.

This Scene, in which Hamlet finds the King on his knees alone, immediately after the Play, and yet does not avenge his father's death, is altogether omitted in the stage copy. What an outrageous liberty! how injurious to the intent of the author! Hamlet is a man of contemplation, who is ever diverted from his purposed deeds by speculation upon their probable consequences or their past causes, unless he acts too quickly and under too much excitement for any reflection to present itself,—as in the last Scene of this Act[3] and of the last Act. In the present instance

---

2 Ophelia's response to Hamlet's 'Lady, shall I lie in your lap?' (l. 107)

3 The killing of Polonius, III, iv, 23 s.d.

he finds the King alone, and in a situation that seems to tempt revenge. He instantly determines on the deed, half draws his sword, steps forward—but the idea suggests itself 'and so he goes to heaven'(III, iii, 74); and in a moment the avenger of blood is converted into the moral philosopher; he discovers that such a death would be no expiation, and gladly seizes this excuse for procrastinating the execution of his task.

By the omission of this Scene, Hamlet's character is not developed according to the author's intent; which is an offence unpardonable. There are certain Scenes and arrangements of Scenes which have naught to do with the progress of the play or the development of character, and which the improvement in stage business since Shakespeare's time renders superfluous, perhaps; and these may be omitted, though they should be eliminated with great caution and reverence; but to touch a line which portrays character, because it is thought superfluous or inconsistent by commentators or stage managers, is much as if a man who liked aquiline features should knock off the nose of the Apollo Belvedere, and say 'it's a small matter, only a nose; the face is a face without it; and besides, I would have made it Roman if I had made the statue.' Wise above what is written! will they never learn they did *not* make the Apollo, or Hamlet, or Romeo, or Lear!

(c) Comment on *Hamlet* IV, iv.

> *Ham.*   I will be with you straight. Go a little before.
>   [*Exeunt* Rosencrantz and Guildenstern]
>   How all occasions do inform against me,
>   And spur my dull revenge! . . .
>   . . .   Now, whether it be
>   Bestial oblivion, or some craven scruple
>   Of thinking too precisely on the event,
>   A thought, which, quarter'd, hath but one part wisdom,
>   And, ever, three parts coward,—I do not know
>   Why yet I live to say, *This thing's to do:*
>   Sith I have cause, and will, and strength, and means,
>   To do't.
>   (Q2, Additional passage J, ll. 22–4; 30–6)

This Scene is omitted in the folio of 1623, and also in the acting copy; but if the object of the play be the representation of Hamlet—and its action certainly has little other point—how serious an omission is this. Hamlet was one who speculated without reasoning, whose high-wrought reveries hardly ever assumed the firmness and consistency of thought, who was unyielding without firmness, determined without purpose, who contrived without plan and felt without acting. Hamlet himself, in the closing soliloquy of this Scene (Q2, Additional passage J, ll. 22–57),—to introduce which was evidently Shakespeare's only object in writing it,—gives us the key to his indecision in that self-anatomization which is the habit of such natures. They know the action of their own minds, and burrowing in the blind heaps of speculation which press upon them, they unearth only their own hidden motives. They have an intellectual perception of the excellence of action; but, fascinated by musings which hardly attain the dignity of contemplation, their noble purposes never take form; and, led on through a dreary labyrinth of speculation, they die before they reach the busy day of the actual world. Sadly enough, too, they are all the while conscious that their years glide away from them and leave naught behind; and when their last day comes, they

> close their dying eyes
> In grief that they have lived in vain.
>
> Eheu! fugaces Postume, Postume,
> Labuntur anni.[4]

(d) Note on the available texts:
It is purposely that I do not notice in detail the corruptions of the text of this play in all the editions. To point them all out would be to write a volume. The ordinary copies, printed from the *Variorum* text, are a vile compound of the texts of the quartos of 1604 and 1611 and the folio of 1623. On the other hand, Mr Knight's laudable reverence for the latter text has caused him to disregard the corruptions which evidently deform it. We need a text formed upon that of 1623 as supreme authority; but carefully corrected by the quartos.

---

4   'Alas, Postumus, Postumus, the years glide away', Horace, *Odes*, II. xiv.1

(e) From introductory remarks to *Hamlet*, in *Complete Works*, Vol. II, [1862]:

Among the numberless exquisite portraits delineated, for the delight and instruction of the world, by the hand of the great Dramatic Master, there is one which in a pre-eminent degree solicits and detains the general gaze;—'the observed of all observers' (III, i, 157). It is that of a young and amiable Prince, in whom the traits of intellect and of feeling are admirably blended; his fine and varied countenance exhibits humour and sensibility, wit and philosophy, in the justest proportions: yet over all, and through all, there is still visible that 'pale cast of thought' (III, i, 87), which might lead even the mere unacquainted spectator to infer, that the possessor had been burthened with a weight of mysterious care, which long oppressed, and finally overwhelmed him. This is that interesting and ever-eloquent friend, with whom we have held delightful converse from boyhood, even to the present hour; whose thoughts have penetrated to the innermost parts of our being; and whom, in despite of his occasional waywardness, weakness, and inconsistency, we have ever loved and respected as a dear and intimate personal friend.

—This, in a word, is HAMLET.

Of all human compositions, there is, perhaps, not one which in the same compass contains so much just, original, and profound thought, as this gigantic effort of genius; none so suggestive, so imaginative, and yet so practical; none which in an equal degree charms alike the philosopher and the simple rustic,—the poet and the man of the world. From the hour of its first appearance, it has been the especial darling of all classes; and has thus tended, more than anything else, to shew the high capabilities of the universal human mind;—to justify the high eulogium which Hamlet himself, 'the general favourite, as the general friend', pronounces so emphatically on his kindred 'quintessence of dust'. In reference to this point, it may be appropriately mentioned, that in the most remote eastern minor theatre— ... even here, the subtle wisdom and poetic beauty of the play before us, drew crowded houses, at a recent period, for upwards of sixty nights in a single season!

(f) From 'The case of Hamlet the Younger' (April 1870), republished in *Studies in Shakespeare*, 1885:
(i) Ophelia:

Ophelia, a fond, amorous, sweet, and gentle girl, but weak-souled, easily led, and easily rebuffed. Thrown into Hamlet's company, his comeliness and courtesy won her to love him after her feeble fashion; and he, first allowing himself to be loved, came at last to love her in return, and even to talk to her of marriage. Polonius, fearing that Hamlet did not wish to make Ophelia his wife, commanded her to break off her intercourse with him; which she did without much pain or remonstrance.

(ii) Did Hamlet see the ghost in the closet scene?

While Hamlet was speaking to his mother about the father whose ghost he and Horatio and Bernado and Marcellus had seen upon the platform, he thought he saw the ghost enter the chamber, and thought he heard him speak and chide him. But it was not the ghost. For the ghost was visible to every eye, and this that Hamlet saw was invisible to his mother. The ghost wore armor; but Hamlet saw his father 'in his night gown.' . . . - Hamlet, in his mother's chamber, merely fancied that he saw his father dressed as he had often seen him there in his lifetime.

(iii) Hamlet's sanity or insanity:

In the consideration of Hamlet's case nothing should be kept more clearly in mind than that from the time we hear of him until his death he was perfectly sane, and a man of very clear and quick intellectual perceptions and strong sound judgment,—one perfectly responsible for his every act and every word; that is, as responsible as a man can be who is constitutionally irresolute, purposeless, and procrastinating. They have done him wrong who have called him undecided. His penetration was like light; his decision like the Fates'; he merely left undone.

(iv) The moral lesson of *Hamlet*:

. . . that a man may have kindliness, and grace, and accomplishment, high thoughts and good impulses, and even a will that can stand firmly up against attack (as it were, leaning against opposition), and yet if he have not strong, urgent, exclusive desire, which compels him to put his impulses and will into action, and seek one single object, if indeed he be not ballasted with principle and impelled by purpose, he will be blown about by every flaw of fortune, and be sucked down into the quicksand of irresolution:—that it is better, with Fortinbras, to make mouths at an invisible event, than, with Hamlet, to be ever peering enviously into the invisible future:—that, in the words of the wicked King, which gave the key of Shakespeare's meaning,

> That we would do,
> We should do when we would; for this 'would' changes
> And hath abatements and delays as many
> As there are tongues, are hands, are accidents;
> And then this 'should' is like a spendthrift sigh,
> That hurts by easing.
>
> (Q2, Additional passage M, ll. 5–10)

They [the readers] may understand, too, how difficult it is for an actor to embody a personage who is of a high mental and moral type, and yet whose characteristic trait is a negative quality;—so difficult, that to present such personage satisfactorily demands a genius almost corresponding (I do not say equal) to his by whom it was created.

(v) Hamlet's appearance on the stage, and the text:

In the controversies over the rival Hamlets of the stage, how comes it that critics do not notice one strong and obvious argument against adopting a blonde *chevelure*[5]—the fact that Hamlet's father had black hair? The elder Hamlet's beard was, says Horatio, 'as I have seen it in his life—a sable silvered'. Now, the presumption at least is surely against a black-haired father having a yellow-haired son. On the other hand, how is it that the champions of a robust Hamlet do not make anything of the abundant proofs given in the tragedy that he was meant to be a man of fine physique and bodily strength? If anything ought to be beyond controversy in the play, this ought to be. Hamlet is always spoken of as athletic and vigorous. . . . what is the epitaph pronounced over him by Fortinbras? Does Fortinbras speak of him as a gentle scholar? He says:-

> Let four captains
> Bear Hamlet, like a soldier, to the stage;
> For he was likely, had he been put on,
> To have prov'd most royally: and, for his passage,
> The soldiers' music and the rites of war
> Speak loudly for him.
>
> (V, ii, 349–54)

5 First adopted by the French actor Charles Fechter in London in 1861.

Whatever may be said for or against other peculiarities in the personation of *Hamlet*, the evidence is irresistible in support of the presentation of the prince as a young man of splendid physique, nobly accomplished in all manly exercises. The delicate student theory has nothing whatever to sustain it except the odd notion that a man of undecided character, much given to casuistry and easy philosophizing, must necessarily be lank, lymphatic, and feeble.

(g) From: 'On the Acting of Iago', *Studies in Shakespeare***: Stage traditions: the closet scene:**
The traditions of the stage are among the most enduring of immaterial things. How enduring they are, even as to minute points, is shown by evidence which is clear and unmistakable in regard to a trifling piece of stage 'business' in *Hamlet*. In the scene of that tragedy in which the imagined appearance of the Ghost interrupts the interview between Hamlet and his mother, it was the modern custom, until very lately, for the Prince to spring from his seat with such violence as to throw down the chair on which he was sitting. Now in 1709 Nicholas Rowe published the first edited collection of Shakespeare's plays; and each play had a frontispiece illustrating one of its most conspicuous scenes. The frontispiece to *Hamlet* illustrates the scene in question, and shows us Hamlet in an enormous flowing wig, startled out of his propriety, and his chair flung down in the foreground. We thus see that even this little trick was handed down from actor to actor, and held its place upon the stage for more than a hundred and fifty years.

3. William Watkiss Lloyd

1856, 1858

William Watkiss Lloyd (1813–1893) built on his grammar school education to become a well regarded classical and Shakespearean scholar. A friend of S.W. Singer, he provided the critical essays to Singer's 1856 edition of Shakespeare 'as a labor of love' (author's preface). The following is taken from *Essays on the Life and Plays of Shakespeare, contributed to the Edition of the Poet by S.W. Singer, 1856*, London: C. Whittingham, 1858, 'a reprint, for convenience of private distribution' (author's preface). The essays were reissued in 1875 and 1888.

From 'Critical Essay on *Hamlet*'

(a) The character of Hamlet embodies the predominance of the contemplative element over the practical in a mind of the highest order, both intellectually and morally. If merely in virtue of belonging to this elevated class, the practical element is necessarily not entirely absent, it is even present in manifestations of no ordinary force; but this force is displayed fitfully, irregularly, by sudden provocation or unpremeditated impulse, and by its very effort exhausts itself and gives way to the more even reign of the tendency to plan rather than execute, and to reflect and generalize rather than to form a specific plan. And this character is placed precisely amidst circumstances that demand plan and purpose, and resolute execution, as they combine all the motives of hope and fear, of love and hatred, of personal interest and domestic sympathy and public duty, that are capable of stimulating a passion and rousing to action. The introduction of the supernatural in this play, as in *Macbeth*, is managed with such art, and has such coherence with all that is most purely natural in the play, that it does not remove the subject from ordinary nature, and we cannot therefore escape from admitting the weakness of Hamlet, by such palliation as the incongruity of his knowledge of his father's murder, with his means of bringing it home to the satisfaction of others,—a tragic motive quite conceivable, though it would require to be treated with a more romantic freedom than Shakespeare ever indulges in his more serious moods. There is therefore no enhancement of embarrassment arising from the murder being revealed to Hamlet by the ghost, a witness citable in no mortal court, of a different nature than would have accrued had his information come by ordinary circumstances, or rather by divination of his prophetic soul and damnatory disorder at witnessing the play. It is true that he proposes a doubt—'the spirit that I have seen may be the devil—abusing me to damn me' (II, ii, 599–600); but this suspicion is no leading motive, is merely a readily invented and embraced subterfuge prompted by his general disposition. The humanity of the play is in itself independent entirely of the supernatural world—if the phrase be not a contradiction, and passion and action follow on as though no ghost had ever risen. The dramatic value of the apparition is however incalculable, and it becomes the highest poetical expression of the sympathetic penetration accorded to such souls as Hamlet's, and the index of the vagaries to which wits, highly wrought by anxiety and thought, and false position and ill-assorting circumstances, are liable at the crisis of tension and distress.

When Hamlet first comes before us he stands in the black garb of filial mourning, a shadow on the splendour of the easily re-comforted court. The shameful speed of his mother's second marriage, marriage held incestuous, with her late husband's brother, and his antipathy to and mistrust of his uncle have disgusted him with life, with the world, with the sex. It is only afterwards that we learn that political disappointment of the succession to his father might have increased his depression, and that the bitterness of his mother's fault had poisoned the charm of his attachment to Ophelia. But thus minded, what does he at the court where only irritation of his misery can await him; his first act of concession in giving up his return to Wittenberg stamps the characteristic of facility in falling from a resolution, and the same scene commences the contrast in this respect that it is extended afterwards, between him and Laertes,—Laertes who carries through his own purpose of departure against his father's stubborn opposition. Thus the anger of his mind turns inward and preys upon its energies, instead of passing away by the healthier course and giving quickness and nerve to the immediate instruments of action; he already contemplates suicide, at least considers it as a refuge from his troubles which only the conscientiousness of his feelings restrains him from resorting to. Such minds so circumstanced, vexed, disappointed, objectless, depressed, declined from that harmony with bodily stimulus that gives the recruiting refreshment known as the tide of animal spirits in their sobered flow, are reckoned to be as near to derangement as to suicide, which is but the catastrophe of derangement. Whether the boundaries of sanity are really overpassed by Hamlet, whether the very warning he gives of his purposed simulation may be but one of the cunningnesses of the truly insane, are questions that belong to a class most difficult to treat whether in life or literature. I confess to be inclined to take the latter view, which by no means excludes the recognition of a main stream of sanity running through the action, and comprising very much that was really but simulation of madness. But some such extremity of excitement seems to form part of the supernaturalism of the play; such an effect was ordinarily ascribed to apparitions, and in this sense Horatio alludes to it, and it is noteworthy that Hamlet's manner is already changed, and he has already given signs of an antic disposition without obvious motive, before he has given notice that at some time thereafter he should probably think meet to affect eccentricity as a disguise. His susceptibility of irritation has received a wrench, and although he professes to his mother with every appearance of conviction to be merely mad in craft, a suspicion of something more is intimated in his thought that possibly the ghost may have been but diabolical abuse of weakness and melancholy—ever subject to such ill influence; and when he excuses his injuries to Laertes on the ground of madness, distractions, it would be, I think, unworthy of him to suppose that his apology was a mere and conscious fabrication. Some palliation moreover must be borrowed hence for his treatment of Ophelia, which otherwise more than verges on the brutal. So we must pronounce with every recognition of the irritation he was subjected to, and every allowance for the sudden irritability of a usually tranquil but highly sensitive mind. 'Frailty thy name is woman', was already impressed upon him painfully, and now his letters are repelled, his visits refused, and at last it is pretty apparent that with the quickness that is characteristic of madness, he discerns that Ophelia, seated with her book of prayers, is lending herself as a decoy to the practices of contemptible eavesdropping politicians. But while his vehemence is as genuine as when in towering passion he grapples with Laertes in her grave, it is far too severe—I may say too coarse, to be admitted as compatible with even the passionate violence of the noble spirit that Hamlet sufficiently approves himself. Ophelia herself,—the eye-witness, and subject of his rage and insult, suspects him as little of pretence as of intention, and in the beauty of her own mild nature ascribes the disorder entirely to the blasting ecstasy which she weeps and pities; and though the king, in his guilty consciousness of the drift of what he overheard, at first speaks of it as 'not like madness', though it wanted form a little,—yet he unawares makes the admission at the conclusion of the scene:-

> It shall be so:
> Madness in greatness[1] must not unwatch'd go.
>
> (III, i, 190-1)

Whatever energy in action, therefore, is manifested by Hamlet is in the form of passionate outburst, or reply to sudden provocation, or the impulse of the moment, and his liability to such accesses of excitement appears to have been increased by the excitement of the apparition—itself from another point of view a consequence of the excitability, till it carries his mind over the balance that gives fair claim to sane composure. The transitions from excessive violence to perfect repose are throughout remarkable, and the queen herself recognizes in them the recent disturbance of his mind, not its ordinary turn and character:-

> This is mere madness:
> And thus awhile the fit will work on him;
> Anon as patient as the female dove,
> When that her golden couplets are disclos'd,
> His silence will sit brooding.
>
> (V, i, 281-5[2])

So it is immediately after Ophelia laments with so much apparent cause the overthrow of his noble mind, that he enters discoursing didactically with the players, and disserts with such temperate acumen on the

---

1 *greatness*: Watkiss Lloyd's mistake for 'great ones'.
2 So Q2; in F and Q1 these lines are given to Claudius.

theory of their art, and the passionate scuffle with Laertes is as closely succeeded by the tranquil relation of his sea adventures to Horatio.

As I have said then, the elements of energy were comprised in germ or in occasional and irregular action in the character of Hamlet,—to the full extent that renders the words of Fortinbras, at his funeral, by no means suggestive of the inopportune cavil they would provoke had he been a mere sluggard or unable trifler:

> Let four captains
> Bear Hamlet like a soldier to the stage;
> For he was likely had he been put on
> To have proved most royally.
>
> (V, ii, 349–52)

Such a putting-on might have consisted in more favourable conjunction of circumstance; but, as it is, the efficiency of the character in its position is vitiated by partial overgrowth and consequent want of harmonious interplay and combination. This is a source of weakness of which Hamlet is perfectly aware theoretically, and he expresses it with admirable precision and force; but he knows it only speculatively and outwardly, not from self-knowledge, and if his self-examination leads him near the error that disables him, he dwells upon it too lightly to detect it, and straightway lapses into new misdirections. It is before his encounter with the ghost that he comments on the weakness of national character, and thus applies—with unknown aptness to his own constitution, though still apologetically:-

> So, oft it chances in particular men,
> That, for some vicious mole of nature in them,
> As, in their birth (wherein they are not guilty,
> Since nature cannot choose his origin),
> By the o'ergrowth of some complexion,
> Oft breaking down the pales and forts of reason;
> Or by some habit, that too much o'erleavens
> The form of plausive manners;—that these men,—
> Carrying, I say, the stamp of one defect,
> Being nature's livery, or fortune's star,—
> Their virtues else (be they as pure as grace,
> As infinite as man may undergo,)

> Shall in the general censure take corruption
> From that particular fault: The dram of base[3]
> Doth all the noble substance of a doubt,
> To his own scandal.
>
> (Q2, I.iv, Additional Passage B, ll. 7–22)

Hamlet fails in action not because he broods too deeply on the duty imposed upon him and the deed he has to do, entangled in the over-refinement of his foresight of difficulties, but rather from his aversion to brood upon it at all. His predilections are for the arts and elegancies of life, for the studies of Wittenberg, the companionship of chosen fellow students, for poetry and the play, the elegant accomplishments and exercises of his rank, riding and the use of weapons, and for meditation on men and manners, and the collection of recorded observations. Hence, in his great soliloquy of 'To be or not to be', he is not intent upon the purpose he has owned of punishing the murderous usurper,—he has for the time forgotten it, and is following out the remoter reflections that are more connected with his previous melancholy. He is ever reminded of the charge laid upon him by the ghost, to recognize it with a pang, to find some excuse for deferring—now mistrust of the ghost, now inaptness of opportunity, to accuse himself of dullness and tardiness, even to declare a resolution, but immediately to diverge into the generalities of a philosophical deduction, and allow himself to be carried away from any definite design entirely. He has the means, the skill, the courage, and what should be sufficient motive, but the active stimulus is unequal to the contemplative inertia that opposes it, and never thoroughly masters and possesses his nature; it gains no permanent hold on his attention; his spirit is soon wearied and oppressed by the uncongenial intrusion, and he relapses into the vein more natural to him; it is cursed spite to be called upon to bring back to order an unhinged world,—we may believe from his manner that he finds no great hardship or disgrace either, in having lost the chance of governing the kingdom, of the foreign affairs of which at least he has not cared to inform himself, and there is such entire absence of expressions of regret for his frustrate love that I am

---

3   *base*: Theobald's emendation for the mystifying 'eale', adopted by Singer, 2nd edition

not sure he does not feel some relief in getting rid of an importunate and interrupting passion. Hamlet's mind is certainly unhinged, and I would prefer to say unsettled. He is two entirely different Hamlets in different scenes, and we see him in constant alternation of hurried and lucid intervals. If we could assume for a moment that his madness is entirely feigned we should stumble over the inconsistency that it is so carried out as to answer no reasonable purpose, excites suspicion instead of diverting it, covers not, and is not fitted to cover, any secondary design, and would amount at best to a weak and childish escapade of ill humour and spleen. This is the really difficult aspect of Hamlet's character, and it is here—perhaps we may say alone in the play—that the poet has left us to our own resources, has placed the picture of nature before us, and called upon us to read and interpret it with no aid from him of marginal interpretation. It is here that the genius of a great Shakespearian actor, if ever such arise again, may be displayed, in so rendering these equivocal scenes by the inspiration that places in sympathy with the author and in its highest sense can only be allowed to actual impersonation, as to blend them harmoniously with those portions that in themselves are perfectly illuminated and defined, and bring home enlightenment and conviction at once to the understanding and the heart.

For the rest, we meet throughout the play with scholia on the leading topic of motive weakening by lapse of time, and unsustained engrossment. This is the very colour Laertes puts upon his love:-

> Think it no more,
> For nature crescent does not grow alone
> In thews and bulk; but, as this temple waxes,
> The inward service of the mind and soul
> Grows wide withal. Perhaps he loves you now,
> And now no soil nor cautel doth besmirch
> The virtue of his will,—but you must fear.
>
> (I, iii, 10–16)

So the king in the introduced play:—

> I do believe you think what now you speak,
> But what we do determine oft we break;
> Purpose is but the slave to memory

> Of violent birth, but poor validity . . . .
> What to ourselves in passion we propose,
> The passion ending doth the purpose lose.
>
> (III, ii, 177–80; 185–6)

Hamlet himself describes his own ideal of a perfect character which aptly illustrates his own,—he admires the steadfastness that is born of due commixture of thought and feeling, but still characteristically enough the error he deprecates is not his own, of sluggish answering to the requirements of exciting emergency, but the opposite fault of over sensibility to the spurs of new occasion:—

> And bless'd are those,
> Whose blood and judgement are so well co-mingled,
> That they are not a pipe for fortune's finger
> To sound what stop she please. Give me that man
> That is not passion's slave, and I will wear him
> In my heart's core, ay, in my heart of heart.
>
> (III, ii, 66–71)

In his instructions to the players it is noteworthy that, while he deprecates tameness on the one hand as well as extravagance on the other, he is mainly emphatic in denouncing turbulence and rant, the strutters and bellowers, and returns again to insist upon smoothness, temperance, the special observance not to overstep the modesty of nature. So he does not even counsel his mother to break off a course that he regards as incest with abruptness, but by gradual and temporizing estrangement.

The guilty king himself is so conscious of the tendency of time and thought to sickly o'er the native hue of resolution,—to quench passion the most violent, that he speaks thus to rouse Laertes whom he had pacified with such difficulty:—

> Laertes, was your father dear to you?
> Or are you like the painting of a sorrow
> A face without a heart?
> *Laertes.* Why ask you this?
> *King.* Not that I think you did not love your father,
> But that I know love is begun by time:
> And that I see in passages of proof

> Time qualifies the spark and fire of it.
> There lives within the very flame of love
> A kind of wick or snuff that will abate it,
> And nothing is at a like goodness still;
> For goodness growing to a pleurisy
> Dies in his own too-much. That we would do
> We should do when we would; for this 'would' changes,
> And hath abatements and delays as many
> As there are tongues, are hands, are accidents;
> And then this 'should' is like a spendthrift's sigh
> That hurts by easing.
>
> (Q2, IV, vii, 90–106)

Hamlet's own self-accusations also are so distinct that we are brought up by every aid to appreciate the difficulty that besets his weakness. In his feeling for art he has the true Attic spirit, as defined by Pericles, of passionate affection for beauty within the limits of chaste and temperate effect; but he does not reach the complement of the disciplined mind according to the idea of the great statesman,—the attachments to habits of philosophizing without relaxation of practical activity. Assuredly he is not a coward, still less oblivious, still less unimpressible by sympathies or affronts, and it is not even that his original genius utterly incapacitates him for action; it indisposes him no doubt, but this indisposition he might probably have overcome but for the disadvantage at which the occasion and the duty are presented. They might have given a direction to his interest in life, but they are powerless to revive it; the contemptibleness and grossness of the world have been brought revoltingly before him at his entrance into it, and with the same result upon a sensitive nature that occurs so often when systematic harshness and unkindness exercised towards youth deprive all future age of interest, or hope from such a pestilent congregation of noxiousness and ill-conditions. In comparison with such an injury the personal or political reverse that Hamlet has sustained is trifling and unexciting, and, this being so, the motive of revenge for his father's death is a retrospective feeling that lacks the backing and support of others more positive in nature. Originally he was destitute of that exuberant spirit of enterprise that welcomes all excitement and provides it when it does not offer, and untoward accident quenched even the warmth that excitement might have provoked into a flame.

Thus succumbing to his destiny he is rescued to our respect and sympathy by his noble qualities and accomplishments, by the very disorder of mind and passion that he gives way to, which exemplify the conflict of feelings and influences under which he suffers, and I know not, lastly, whether a main interest that we feel in him be not due to recognizing in him the martyr to a cause which more or less engages, perplexes, and persecutes all. The nature of man—of the individual, will struggle wildly and protest loudly in vindication of the rights of individuality—of the claim of his proper nature to find its proper range and exercise uncontrolled by the tyranny of accident and position: it refuses to take its cue absolutely from aught that does not establish a sympathetic title to tend it, and groans under the slavery of having to drudge perforce in a field it never had the option of declining, for ends in which it has no interest, and constraining itself to an interest in which it feels would be self-betrayal and self-corruption. Original genius enters the world with a charter of special activity; the strongest and most original minds or the minds strongest in their originality, will struggle most vehemently against the substitution of another; and when accident and necessity bear them down with all the parade of vindicating the sanctities of duty and the paramount sovereignty of society, even those who assent and take a warning will have misgivings at heart that they were not wholly wrong,—that if blame must be coupled with the cause of suffering somewhere it did not all attach to the sufferers—that, in fact, there is something more than natural in it if philosophy could find it out.

The most obvious foil to Hamlet is Laertes; the contrast between them in their first scene has already been noticed, and when Laertes is afterwards, as Hamlet himself says, much in his own position in a quarrel for the death of a father, this contrast is still further displayed in the prompt return from France, the hasty revolt, reckless approach to royalty, and demand of vengeance at all risks, temporal and eternal, concluded at last by agreement in schemes of treachery, such as it is certain Hamlet would never have been party to. The contrast therefore is at last to the advantage of Hamlet, and the composition demands still another harmonizing figure. This is provided by the seemingly episodical Fortinbras, who however is most important and indispensable for the effect of the play. We hear of his martial preparations in the first scene, hinging again upon transactions of transferred sovereignty from the death of a father,—he seeks to regain by force lands lost when his father was slain, and forfeited with all the sanctions of law and heraldry. In the course of the play we hear again of the alacrity with which he renounces this enterprize when it appears hopeless, and turns his means and levies to another where honour only is in question; he passes over the stage and is momentarily confronted with Hamlet on his way to England, and returning victorious appears in the last scene to assert the claims that are opened to him by the catastrophe, to close the scene with some generous words, and bring out at last the visible decree that sovereignty will at last, by its own propension, decline into the hands of those who have the living motives of vigorous leadership in their nature in harmony with the advantages of their position.

The players find nothing attractive in Fortinbras, and are too happy to retrench the character and extirpate all possible allusions to him; but there is a worse evil in this than the curtain falling at last on an unking'd stage, with four princely corpses, and Osric and Horatio only left alive: these foreign incidents give range to the thoughts that relieves them in this the longest of all the plays, that renders the voyage and return of Hamlet less abrupt and remote and exceptional, and the idea which they communicate of the Norwegian prince—the young and tender leader of an adventurous expedition, remains in the mind insensibly from essential congruity with the theme of the play, so that his appearance and mastery at last is satisfying as the closing in of a grand outlying circuit and fulfilment of an expectation.

It may be noticed that even in Laertes, and even in the king, a certain disposition is observable to the occasional though not predominant tone of generalization so habitual with Hamlet, as though it were in some degree proper to the climate, and this is the explanation of the 'rational and consequential' reflection on tradition and habit as the real foundation of monarchy, indulged in in the midst of his alarm by the announcer of the popular revolt. Indeed *Hamlet*, which has been the most admired of all Shakespeare's plays in Germany, must be regarded as rather Teutonic in genius than specifically Scandinavian, and so far it seems accurately expressive of the great but hitherto somewhat uncollected and vacillating nation—they will excuse us at this date above all, who, while they ascribe to England and France the domination of the sea and land, have themselves owned their special speculative realms as the region of air. But this tendency which is profound philosophy in Hamlet is exhibited in its dotage in Polonius—a tedious old fool, doubtless, as the prince splenetically calls him, and yet were it not for the ridiculousness of this character we might more easily have erred in rating too severely those weaknesses of Hamlet that are upon the verge of ridiculousness. The parroted precepts of Polonius, strung together with no leading principle, which are so much a matter of rote that he regains the thread of his discourse like an actor by a friendly cue, bring out the freshly welling originality of the diverging rather than desultory reflections that carry Hamlet from time to time away from his theme. So the backstairs, eavesdropping politics that he professes, and the gross mistakes he makes in practical judgment as to the designs of Hamlet on Ophelia, and then as to the cause and nature of his madness are such marked types of the faults and blunders that most beset the speculative when they make their sagacity a ground for interference in business that is beyond them, as to reflect back some glory on the better essays of the less experienced but far more able, as well as more intellectual, prince of Denmark. Hence the use and the effectiveness of such a scene as that between Polonius and Reynaldo, with the instructions for roundabout enquiry as to the proceedings of Laertes, in a style that it is obvious would have any other tendency than either to elicit truth or to benefit the character of the person so equivocally cared for. Compared with this, the scheme of Hamlet to entrap the conscience of the king into self-betrayal by the play, is wisdom, is simplicity itself, and we are prepared to appreciate his penetration in fathoming at once the insidious questioning of Rosencrantz and Guildenstern. These worthies, it may be observed, have their own turn for indulgence in a generalized reflection apiece which characteristically takes the form of flattery and assentation:-

> *Guild.* Most holy and religious fear it is
> To keep those many many bodies safe,
> That live and feed upon your majesty.
> *Ros.* The single and peculiar life is bound,
> With all the strength and armour of the mind,
> To keep itself from 'noyance; but much more
> That spirit, upon whose weal depend and rest
> The lives of many. The cease of majesty
> Dies not alone,
>
> (III, iii, 8–16)

—and so forth,—and so forth.

But as I have said the main difficulty in the way of our feeling that we have a perfect appreciation of the play, and of its leading character, is the conduct of Hamlet towards Ophelia; even if we exclude the scene of his excited violence towards her, and forget the dumb-show mummery that she relates, there still remains a frigidness in all his allusions to her, and in the rarity of these allusions also, that impeaches the sincerity of the passion that he once professed for her, and even the ordinary consideration and delicacy that were due to her misfortunes, though they had not originated with himself. What then is the real palliation that Shakespeare relied upon to save his hero from entire desertion by our sympathies, and which, though we may have difficulty in detecting and stating it, does have that effect. Reserving the plea of injured sanity, shall we say that the fault of Hamlet is grievous, but that pity tempers our indignation? for it is too far seen that abstract reflection is not in favour of sensibility of the sympathies, and that those who are habitually wrapt in their own thoughts will err too often in injury inflicted on the hearts of those around them, from no cruelty of temper and no conscious wantonness, but simply from inattention and disregard to hearts and feelings as incidents of life: at least if this view be wrong let philosophers defend themselves by furnishing another solution of the difficulty that suggests it.

Certainly there is a marked contrast in respect to sympathy with the sex between the musing and reflective prince and his warlike father, whose affection for his consort erred during his life rather in over fondness—as well appears from Hamlet's description of his tenderness and assiduity, and who, even when he reappears as a ghost in intervals of torment to claim revenge for murder upon her paramour, cannot bear that she should be even distressed by reproaches, much less actually punished. Both on the platform of the castle and in the chamber of the palace he qualifies his urgency of appeal for vengeance by restraints in her favour, and by injunctions to soothe and comfort her when her conscience seems to be touched with difficulty and at last.

Hamlet the Dane is apparently by his constitution, of which we have seen and said enough, of a character essentially undramatic, yet has he the leading part of unusual extent in the longest of the plays, in perhaps the most popular of all among readers, and one of the most effective even on the stage. He is the centre and the cause moreover of a series of events at the conclusion of which a larger proportion of the principal agents have met with violent deaths—the King, the Queen, Polonius, Laertes, Ophelia, and Hamlet, Rosencrantz and Guildenstern,—than in any other of the Tragedies. Whence is this? it is nothing more than an expression of the natural effect when powerful but ill-harmonized energies are led into or step into a combination they are too irregular to master and conduct. Such interference only enhances complication or checks it by fits and starts that sometimes fall at random and are speedily exhausted; the catastrophe struggles to its own extrication through manifold lapse and disaster, aggravated and prolonged, and naturally involves at last the guilty and some that are chiefly unfortunate, and the author lastly, who but for our sympathies must stand equivocally between the two.

On none of Shakespeare's plays, perhaps, has so much been written, and so excellently, as on *Hamlet*,—so much that it is hopeless either to recapitulate or to emulate, and, indeed, scarcely necessary; for much of the criticism has become inseparably associated with the play, and familiar to all students of it. Coleridge thus concludes his notes, in which, as usual, philosophical intention makes hard fight against the inertia of pedagogue and preacher:

> Shakespeare seems to mean all Hamlet's character to be brought together before his final disappearance from the scene;—his meditative excess in the grave-digging, his yielding to passion with Laertes, his love for Ophelia blazing out, his tendency to generalize on all occasions in the dialogue with Horatio, his fine gentlemanly manners with Osric, and his and Shakespeare's own fondness for presentiment: 'But thou would'st not think, how ill all's here about my heart; but it is no matter'.[4]

Excellently said, when it is qualified for the alloy; it is indeed by the closing up of the varied phases of the character in brief, with what we have been familiarized in detail, that the effect is given of such a final collision of many lines of action that in plays more dependent upon incident become the catastrophe. But for the outblazing love,—alas, I see it not in the outburst provoked by the extravagance of Laertes, though no doubt it is, as the progress of the play demanded, the most definite manifestation of the real nature and degree of his sentiment. Speculative philosophers—and possibly Coleridge himself is an instance—must permit it to be said that Love is as ungermane to their dispositions as Hatred,

4   See *CRH*, ii, 83.

and that they will find themselves not more hampered by an onerous duty sternly imposed from without to redress a political grievance or aid the execution of God's revenge for incest, tyrannous robbery, and murder, than embarrassed by a passion,—whether they are detained by confiding and admiring simplicity or limed by a flirt.

I presume, again, that Coleridge was serious when he spoke of Hamlet's fine gentlemanly manners with Osric; but he would have been nearer, though not close to the truth, had his terms been ironical, or compounded into the more equivocal word 'fine-gentlemanly'. The waterfly Osric lies under the suspicion of complicity in the treachery of the King and Laertes with the foils, though Shakespeare has not thought it worth while to render the crime definite, or to condescend to punish it; he embodies, however, at least whatever is most frivolous and contemptible in the courtier and chamberlain, and continues into the last act the motives of the departed Polonius and Rosencrantz and Guildenstern, which brought out before so admirably the contrast between the tastes, the nature of Hamlet, and the swarm,—marsh-born, miasma-nourished, that are around him. Nothing certainly can be more unroyal, or, for the position of a prince aspiring to royalty, more impolitic than his betrayal of consciousness or disdain for the falsehood and frivolity of etiquette and the unmixed selfishness lying below courtly manners. It is not thus that ceremony is handled by potentates and aspirants, who are aware that they are for the most part but ceremonies themselves, and may not long remain that, if the fact gets wind and is talked about. But it is by so much as Hamlet is recalcitrant against the habitudes of his position that he gains dignity, and interests our affections as a man. As the world goes—for that matter it goes now as it always went—the arts and habits that make up the specific manners of the gentleman have come to mean little less than cool dexterity in offensiveness in one direction, balanced by efficient self-seeking complaisance in the other, and there is probably no rarer wild bird than your gentleman of gentlemanly feelings. But Hamlet baits and perplexes and satirizes the qualities that are really base, independently of relative position, and turns with fundamental sincerity and geniality of character to familiar intercourse with friends and fellow-students, to genuine enjoyment and encouragement of struggling art in right of his own critical taste, to pregnant colloquy incognito with grave-diggers, and observation of social movement along all its intersecting tracks. Hamlet assuredly is something better than a prince and courtier-scholar; soldier as he is, he is in sympathy with that best democracy, of which Novalis said that Christianity is the base, as it is the highest fact in the rights of man.

The drama mirrors the world, we say, and Shakespeare's drama above all; but the question occurs more than once, and sometimes mistrustfully, whether the theme so common on the stage, of the mental torture of the tyrannous, is more than the rarest exception in nature; the crime doubtless brings its punishment ever, and not the less severely because not in the form most dramatically effective; though even that,—as anguish or intolerable burden—may be a more frequent inmate of palace bedchambers than we suppose.

Certainly a spirit of divination seems to have guided Shakespeare to delineate the movement of German philosophy through rationalism to a philosophical theory of the mythus both profane and sacred. I have heard, says the student of Wittenberg:—

> The cock, that is the trumpet to the morn,
> Doth, with his lofty and shrill sounding throat,
> Awake the god of day; and at his warning
> Whether in sea or fire, in earth or air,
> Th'extravagant and erring spirit hies
> To his confine; and of the truth herein
> This present object made probation.
>
> (I, i, 131–7)

This tradition, with its god of day opening wide eyes at the summons of the officious cock, is a Pagan form, and Horatio is as interested in noting the natural truth that it expresses as my friends and colleagues of the Archaeological Institute of Rome in their ingenious reductions of the mythic decoration of a Greek vase. Marcellus, of less recondite acquirements, follows up with a contemporary and living superstition:—

> It faded on the crowing of the cock.
> Some say, that ever 'gainst that season comes
> Wherein our Saviour's birth is celebrated,
> This bird of dawning singeth all night long:
> And then they say no spirit dares stir abroad;

> The nights are wholesome; then no planets strike,
> No fairy takes, nor witch hath power to charm,
> So hallowed and so gracious is that time.
>
> (I, i, 138–45)

Hamlet[5] receives the Christian illustration expressively:-

> So I have heard, and do in part believe it;

but what form his belief takes, and which part he disbelieves, he keeps to himself, with a reserve that the world has suffered less from since in Germany than elsewhere; but even there, prudence and self-interest will secure its mischievous continuance—mischievous, at least, to truth, so long as the maxim has a foundation,—*Populus vult decepi,—decipiatur.* 'The people desire to be hoodwinked,—please the people.'

Many who have seen the frequent willows drooping into the Avon about Stratford, will have had the thought that Ophelia, falling with the envious sliver, and floating awhile among her scattering flowers, is a picture of some misadventured maiden in the poet's native town; there is even something particular in the sneer at 'crowner's quest law', that may intimate an opinion of a stupid verdict in such cases that had untender consequences centuries later; however, as in so many other cases the blundering attempt of a clown to express a distinction that is a falsity,—the discrimination here between voluntary and involuntary suicide,—provides the verity with terse and strict expression.

> Give me leave. Here lies the water; good; here stands the man; good: if the man go to this water and drown himself, it is, will he, nill he, he goes, mark you that; but—(says the clown, labouring for a difference that has already evaded him, and should make him in consistency say, and again)—if the water comes to him and drown him, he drowns not himself: argal, he that is not guilty of his own death shortens not his own life.
>
> (V, i, 15–20)

But enough, enough; happy if not overmuch, though commentary may be forgiven for not knowing when to stop on a subject that is inexhaustible.

---

5 Watkiss Lloyd's error for 'Horatio'.

[Watkiss Lloyd then gives a brief account of texts, dating and sources of the play, from which the following is taken:]

(b) Comment on 'How all occasions do inform against me', IV. iv (Q2, Additional passage J, ll. 23–57)

Some of the peculiarities of the enlarged quarto are brief enough to be absent from the folio merely by accidental omission; but the soliloquy on the expedition of Fortinbras is not one of these; beautiful as it is, I am, however, disposed to think that the excision of it may have been deliberate,—as unnecessary, prolonging action, and it may be exhibiting the weakness of Hamlet too crudely, for it shows him making the most definite of his resolutions to revenge precisely as he turns his back upon the last opportunity by quitting the country. The passage, however, with some others, is too fine to be suppressed, though I am inclined to think the poet sacrificed them, and worthily and properly may take their place in brackets.

4. Henry Hope Reed

1856

Henry Hope Reed (1808–1854) was professor of rhetoric and English literature at the University of Pennsylvania. He was an enthusiastic champion of Wordsworth, producing the first American edition of his *Complete Works* (1837), notable for anticipating the poet's own later classification of his poems. As well as a later *Complete Poetical Works* of Wordsworth and an edition of Christopher Wordsworth's *Memoirs of William Wordsworth* (both published in 1851), Reed also edited the poems of Gray, and lexicographical and nineteenth century English historical works. Following his untimely death (he drowned at sea, returning to America after his only visit to Europe), Reed's lectures were edited by his brother, William Bradford Reed. The extracts below are from the English edition (1856) of *Lectures on English History and Tragic Poetry, as illustrated by Shakespeare* (1855), and demonstrate Reed's gentle and appreciative line of criticism.

From 'Four Lectures on Tragic Poetry, as illustrated in Shakespeare's Four Great Dramas', Lecture 3: '*Hamlet*':

(a) . . . in Hamlet, the philosophic habit of his intellect is the chief element in the tragedy—the ruling principle which gives to it its gentle and slow progression. Nor is this intellectual character peculiar to the chief person; for, besides the profound and feeling thoughtfulness of Hamlet, you find the insincere and declamatory reasoning of the king, the self-complacent shrewdness of the old politician in Polonius, the fraternal counsels of Laertes, and, in perfect keeping with the predominant tone of the tragedy, the logic of the captious grave-digger—a most thoughtful, reasoning company. In this respect, it seems to me that this drama, more than any other, may be regarded as eminently reflecting the constitution of Shakespeare's mind—as the production in which he incorporated, more largely than any other, the habits of his intellect. . . .

The tragedy is a story of a soul environed by all the agencies which are best fitted to reveal its functions and its aspirations; and the imagination of Shakespeare, after embodying in the character of Hamlet the elements of a susceptible spirit, has gathered around that spirit every influence which could aptly touch it. He has shown this character in the despondency of an unavailing sorrow; another while in the sunshine of a cheerful thoughtfulness; again in the distress of disturbed affections, in the perplexity of obscure and conflicting duties; and again in the solemn awe of a supernatural influence. The observation we have to take is of the starlike light of Hamlet's soul dwelling apart in the region of a lofty self-communion, and moving onward in its path like one of 'that host,' as it has been finely called, 'of white-robed pilgrims that travel along the vault of the nightly sky.' We are to observe the light of his life shining, serenely shining, from the large and placid spaces of his own gentle and noble and thoughtful nature, or else struggling with either the mists of earthly sorrow, or the lurid, supernatural reflection that reaches it from the prison-house of the suffering dead. . . .

The ghost of the murdered monarch is surely one of the most majestic phantoms that poetic imagination has ever realized. It is an apparition not so much of terror as of awe and solemnity, arrayed with all the impressive associations of the grave, of religion, and of popular superstition. Its movements are stately—the shadow, as it were, of the step of a kingly soldier; the glory of its earthly and warlike majesty is mysteriously mingled with an awful dignity brought from the regions of the dead. It is that fair and warlike form

> In which the majesty of buried Denmark
> Did sometimes march.
>
> (I, i, 46–7)

It seems to wear the very armour he had on

> When he the ambitious Norway combated.
>
> (I, i, 60)

When the soldiers vainly and rashly strike at it with their partisans, they straightway feel—

> We do it wrong, being so majestical,
> To offer it the show of violence;
> For it is, as the air, invulnerable,
> And our vain blows malicious mockery.
>
> (I, i, 124–7)

The spectre which most nearly resembles it is the imperial apparition of Caesar, which awed even the philosophic soul of Brutus before the battle of Philippi....

Hamlet's character from the time of the interview with the ghost becomes more complicated; and it is a question on which a great deal of comment has been expended, whether his insanity is feigned or real. The difficulties involving the question are of theoretical rather than of practical purport; for they do not seem to affect the poetical impression which the character is intended to make. Indeed, it may be that the interest of the character is rather increased by this very mysteriousness—the obscurity in discriminating between his affected wildness and the actual disturbance of his intellect. These difficulties are owing partly to this—that insanity is of so many degrees, and so multiform, that you can scarce define it: the English language, though not highly esteemed by all for its copiousness, furnishes, it may be, a dozen different words to express the various morbid conditions of the intellect....

The difficulty with respect to Hamlet is not so much in forming a just conception of the state of his mind, as in attaching a precise significancy to this word 'insanity.' At least there need be no such difficulty, were it not oftener caused by the logic of contracted criticism—the propensity to narrow verbal comment—which will misapprehend the whole drift of a character and destroy the spirit of a drama by dwelling upon detached passages and expressions....

Hamlet mentions to his friends a deliberate purpose of 'putting an antic disposition on,' and he is seen fulfilling his intention; and hence it is inferred that all his insanity is feigned. On the other hand, there is observed a wildness of demeanour which cannot thus be accounted for; and hence it is inferred that it is real insanity. Now, the human mind is not such a simple machine as this, and Shakespeare knew it too well ever to treat it so. The truth, as well as I can state a matter so abstruse, seems to be this: that, from combination of influences, the mind of Hamlet was in a state of undue susceptibility of both unnatural excitement and depression; and then further agitated by a supernatural visitation, by which, in his own words he felt his 'disposition horridly shaken with thoughts beyond the reaches of our souls.' This visible and audible communion with the dead has so convulsed all the spiritual elements of his nature, that he becomes conscious that the sovereignty of his reason was in jeopardy; and it is that very consciousness—the apprehension of insanity—which suggests to an intellect so active the thought of feigning madness—the device of assuming an antic disposition—which would give them an unwonted freedom, and which might always be controlled by his habitual intellectual strength. It comes, then, to this—that there was disorder in the mind—a disturbance of his intellect, something more than that which he was feigning; but, if this question of insanity involve the question whether his mind ceased to be under the mastery of his will, assuredly there was no such aberration.

In the various allusions to the condition of Hamlet's mind, you may find it variously designated. The queen tenderly speaks of the 'transformation' of her son. The king speaks of it as a 'melancholy' and a 'distemper.' Polonius calls it 'lunacy.' The grave-digger bluntly talks of 'Hamlet—he that is mad and sent to England; sent there because he was mad; he shall recover his wits there; or if he do not, it is no great matter; it will not be seen in him there; there the men are as mad as he'(V, i, 144–51).[1] But when Ophelia speaks of it, in the simplicity of her opinion, there is not only beauty but truth in the image by which she describes what seems to her the piteous overthrow of a lofty mind:

> See that noble and most sovereign reason,
> Like sweet bells, jangled, out of tune, and harsh.
>
> (III, i, 160–1)

It is an exquisite similitude of the undefinable condition of Hamlet's mind: his intellect had lost its harmony, but still there was a wild music in the changes which an untoward destiny was ringing on it.

---

1 Reed has slightly adapted the quotation.

The scene with Ophelia is one of the most difficult to interpret. There is a natural inclination to refer to real insanity Hamlet's apparent harshness; for there seems to be a rude rejecting of her, which it is hard to reconcile with the truth and gentleness of his natural disposition, and which we cannot quite believe his deep love for her would suffer him to affect. But it must be remembered, that there was a leave-taking before this, which is not dramatically presented, and which, in some respects, is more important. It is only described: it was a silent interview—that silence a better token of his deep feeling than the wild words he afterwards addresses to her. He takes her by the hand; he gazes on her face with

> Such perusal as he would draw it—
> (II, ii, 91–2–adapted)

perhaps to impress it on his imagination as something dear to his heart, and yet which an awful necessity forces him to banish. A deep and piteous sigh breaks from him; then, without a word spoken, he leaves her ... This was the real leave-taking; and if it be asked why he thus alienated himself from Ophelia, the necessity is to be explained by the fearful responsibility which filled his soul. ... What now could he have to do with such a sentiment as love? With all its purity, it could not consort with his solemn charge.

When afterwards Hamlet unexpectedly finds himself again in the presence of Ophelia, all his former affection comes back upon him:

> Soft you, now!
> The fair Ophelia!—Nymph, in thy orisons
> Be all my sins remembered.
> (III, i, 90–2)

He had over-calculated his own strength in setting aside his love for her; and of this he becomes conscious when the thought of his one paramount duty quickly returns. Hence, the revulsion of feeling in this painful scene—the desperate energy with which he recovers himself from relapse into an affection, the indulgence of which his destiny can no more admit. His apparent rudeness we must not take too literally—remember it is poetry, and not prose, we are studying now. It is not in reality indifference and heartlessness to Ophelia, but self-reproach of what he sternly condemns as his own weakness, when, with such strange impetuosity, he bids her—'To a nunnery, go'—one moment disclaiming his love, and another acknowledging it—with a wild irony accusing himself of 'pride, revenge, ambition—more offences at his beck than he has thoughts to put them in, imagination to give them shape, or time to act them in' (III, i, 126–8); then telling the innocent and artless girl of the vices and frailties, not, indeed, of herself, but of her sex, and warning her that the world is not a safe place for her to abide in:—'Get thee to a nunnery, farewell. . . . [sic] To a nunnery, go; and quickly too. Farewell. . . . [sic] To a nunnery, go'. In confirmation of the view I have taken of this scene, observe that Hamlet's asperity does not wound Ophelia as an injury. Her only feeling is pity—more for the sad calamity of his intellect than for her own dejected hopelessness.

Meditative as is the mind of Hamlet, his nature is too gentle for him to travel on in life a solitary-hearted man. The sense of loneliness is relieved by his friendship for Horatio, to whose manly judgment he could, in consultation, impart his supernatural secret and his dread, though ill-defined, purposes, which it would have been both cruel and useless to tell to one so innocent, so tender, and so artless as the 'sweet Ophelia.' . . - . Horatio is a man not only of strong, but just and well-regulated, feelings, and especially in intellectual constitution, possessed of sound, practical, common sense, strikingly contrasted with Hamlet's imaginative apprehensiveness—the deep spirit of meditation and overwrought mental activity. The character of Hamlet is overflowing with poetry and philosophy, while Horatio is matter-of-fact and prosaic. . . .

Besides this friendship, Hamlet finds relief from the sense of moral desolation, which sickens his heart, in the conscious power of his intellect.

(b) Hamlet's inaction:
The chief explanation by the best critics lies in the excessive activity of Hamlet's intellect—disproportionate mental exertion, always busy with its own suggestions and speculations, but flying from the acting point. He is conscious of this himself in some of his self-reproaches:

> What is a man,
> If his chief good, and market of his time,
> Be but to sleep and feed? a beast, no more.
> ...
> Now, whether it be
> Bestial oblivion, or some craven scruple
> Of thinking too precisely on the event—
> A thought, which quarter'd, hath but one part wisdom,
> And ever three parts coward,—I do not know
> Why yet I have to say, 'This thing's to do;'
> Sith I have cause, and will, and strength, and means,
> To do't.
>
> (Q2, Additional passage J, ll. 24–37)

But this is the exaggeration of self-accusation. Hamlet was brave, yet he was gentle too; and it seems to me that another and, perhaps, chief cause of his inaction, for which sufficient allowance has not been made, was the tenderness of his conscience—the agitation of the moral sense even more than of the intellect:

> Thus conscience does make cowards of us all;
> And thus the native hue of resolution
> Is sicklied o'er with the pale cast of thought;
> And enterprises of great pith and moment,
> With this regard, their currents turn awry
> And lose the name of action.
>
> (III, i, 85–90)

It should not be forgotten that when the ghost imposed on Hamlet the duty of vengeance, he said not how, but solemnly charged him—

> Howsoever thou pursu'st the act,
> Taint not thy mind, nor let thy soul contrive
> Against thy mother aught.
>
> (I, v, 84–7)

It was the awful duty of blood-shedding to be discharged righteously, and most natural was it that the duty was entangled in inextricable perplexity.

The tenderness of Hamlet's conscience is shown in his repenting of the chance-killing of Polonius; and afterwards when eluding the treachery of Rosencrantz and Guildenstern, he sends them to the death they had plotted for him, he makes some little excusing of himself to Horatio:

> Why, man, they did make love to their employment;
> They are not near my conscience.
>
> (V, ii, 58–9)

And then the thought of putting the king to death comes to his mind with a sense of justice—an act of dutiful vengeance:

> Is't not perfect conscience
> To quit him with this arm?
>
> (V, ii, 68–9)

It is his moral doubts which have blunted his purpose—postponing—

> The important acting of the dread command.
>
> (III, iv, 99)

These caused his misgivings that the spectre might be an evil spirit, seeking out his weakness and his melancholy to abuse him to his perdition. He sought, therefore, further assurance of his conscience by means of the play before the king . . . When Hamlet has actually drawn his sword to take the forfeit life of the usurper, he sheathes it again for an expressed reason that sounds almost like a fiendish vengeance—the thought that if the king were killed while praying, his soul, purged and seasoned for the passage, would go to heaven. But surely no one can misapprehend this for the true reason:—it is only a piece of self-deception—an excuse for delay—a palliation for his shrinking from a deed of blood. . . .

He whose mind had been so active in its purposes—whose heart had beat so quickly to all true impulses—achieves the duty, vaguely commanded by a supernatural voice, only by co-operating with the tumult of an accident, and in the heat of passion. Heretofore, always equal to the present moment, his meditations—meditations of the heart as well as of the intellect—had perpetually carried him into the distant future. Now, the certainty of the poison crowds all the future of his mortal life into a few, short, present instants. Death is in Denmark's palace. The majestic phantom of him who once tenanted the throne, is avenged by the bloody perishing of the guilty. The innocent one is implicated too deeply in the destiny of the tragedy to escape, and Horatio's words are his fitting requiem:

> Now cracks a noble heart. Good night, sweet prince;
> And flights of angels sing thee to thy rest.
>
> (V, ii, 312–13)

5. Walt Whitman

1856?

Walt Whitman (1819–1892) poet, journalist, and essayist, as a young man frequented the Bowery and Park theatres in New York, and saw many Shakespeare plays. Whitman saw Shakespeare as the great artistic genius of the feudalism of the Old World, but found un-American 'that principle of caste which we Americans have come on earth to destroy.'[1] The source of the following manuscript note (n.d.) is not known with certainty; it might have derived from Hallam's *Introduction to the Literature of Europe in the Fifteenth, Sixteenth and Seventeenth Centuries* (first published in 1839 in London) either through an intermediary source or from Whitman's quotation from memory[2].

From 'Shakespeare Born'[3]

'During the next eight or nine years—from the first year of the 17th century to about 1609 or '10—*from the poet's thirty-seventh to about his forty-sixth year*—his genius rose at once to its highest point of culmination.—It was the era of his tragic power, of *his resistless control over the emotions of terror and* of *pity*—and of his deepest and most gloomy philosophy.—This was the period when he appeared as *"the stern censurer of man,"*—when his deeper insight into the human heart led him

---

1 'Poetry To-Day—Shakespere—The Future' in *Prose Works 1892*, Vol. 2, ed. Floyd Stovall (New York: New York University Press, 1964), p. 476, *The Collected Writings of Walt Whitman*, ed. Gay Wilson Allen and Sculley Bradley.

2 See the editor's headnote to 'Shakespeare Born', *Notebooks and Unpublished Manuscripts*, Vol. 5, ed. Edward Grier (New York: New York University Press, 1984), p. 1739, *The Collected Writings of Walt Whitman*. Passage quoted from this edition.

3 The pink wove paper on which this note is written was left over from *Leaves of Grass* (1855), and according to the ed. of *Notebooks and Unpublished Manuscripts* Whitman used it for about a year (Introduction, Vol. 1, xix).

to dark and sad views of human nature—sometimes prompting the melancholy philosophy of Hamlet, sometimes bursting forth in the fiery indignation of Timon and Lear.—It was during this period that he most impressed upon his style that character which we now recognize as peculiarly Shaksperian, by *crowding into his words a weight of thought until "the language bent under it."*—His *versification becomes, like his diction, bolder, freer, careless of elegance, of regularity and even of melody,—a sterner music, fitted for sterner themes.*

6. John Charles Bucknill

1859

Sir John Charles Bucknill, (1817–1897), was a physician who became a member of the Royal College of Surgeons in 1840. Between 1844 and 1862 he was medical superintendent of Devon County Asylum and was made Lord Chancellor's medical visitor of lunatics, 1862–1876. His publications include *A Manual of Psychological Medicine*, 1858 and *The Psychology of Shakespeare*, 1859, this was republished in a second edition in 1867 under the title *The Mad Folk of Shakespeare*, from which the following extracts are taken.

(a) Hamlet

All critical study of *Hamlet* must be psychological; and as there are few subjects which have been more closely studied, and more copiously written upon, than this magnificent drama, criticism upon it might seem to be exhausted. But human nature itself is still more trite; yet, study it profoundly as we can, criticise and speculate upon it as we may, much will ever be left outside the largest grasp of those minds who undertake to elucidate so much of it as they can comprehend. Hamlet is human nature, or at least a wide range of it, and no amount of criticism can exhaust the wealth of this magnificent storehouse. It invites and evades criticism. Its mysterious profundity fascinates the attention; its infinite variety and its hidden meanings deny exhaustive analysis. Some leavings of treasure will always be discoverable to those who seek for it in an earnest and reverent spirit. Probably no two minds can ever contemplate Hamlet from exactly the same point of view, as no two men can ever regard human life under exactly the same aspect. Hence truthful criticism of this great drama is not only various as mind itself, but is apt to become reflective of the critic. The strong sense of Johnson, the subtle insight of Coleridge, the fervid eloquence of Hazlitt, the discriminating tact of

Schlegel, are nowhere more evident than in their treatment of this mighty monument of human intellect. Every man who has learned to think, and has dared to question the inward monitor, has seen some part of the character of Hamlet reflected in his own bosom.

It will form no part of the subject of this essay to criticise the dramatic construction of *Hamlet*. We may, however, confess ourselves to be among those who cannot see in its construction that perfect art which has been so abundantly shewn by Shakespeare in many other pieces. Of the petty anachronisms which sent Hamlet to school in Wittenberg, which allow Ophelia to call for a coach, and the King's palace to resound with salvos of artillery, we make small account; like spots on the sun's surface, they only impress themselves upon those who look upon the great work through some medium capable of obscuring its glories. The great length appears by no means an imperfection of this drama as a composition, whatever it may be as an acting play. The analysis of the motives of human action, which is the great object of this work, could not have been effected if the action had been rapid. Rapidity of action is inconsistent with philosophic self-analysing motives and modes of thought; while the slow and halting progress of the action in this drama not only affords to the character space and verge enough to unfold the inmost peculiarities of thought and feeling, but develops in the mind of the reader a state of receptivity scarcely less essential to its full appreciation.

Once for all, let us say, in pointing out what appear to us difficulties to a logical apprehension of this piece from that point of view which contemplates the development of character and the laws of mind, we do not urge these difficulties as objections to this great drama, which we love and prize more than any other human piece of composition. We venture to find no fault with *Hamlet*; we revere even its irregularities, as we prefer the various beauties of forest landscape to the straight walks and trim parterres of a well-kept garden. There are more irregularities and unexpected turns of action in *Hamlet* than in any other of Shakespeare's plays. Our belief is, that the poet became charmed with the creature of his own imagination as it developed itself from his fertile brain; and that as he gave loose reign to poetic fancy and philosophic reverie, he more than ever spurned the narrow limits of dramatic art. The works of Shakespeare's imagination, contrasted with those of the Greek dramatists, have been said to resemble a vast cathedral, combining in one beautiful structure various forms of architecture, various towers and pinnacles,—the whole irregular, vast, and beautiful. The drama of the Greeks, on the other hand, has been said to resemble their temples, finished in one style, perfect and regular. The *simile* is true and instructive, and in no case more so than in its application to *Hamlet*. If in our admiration of its whole effect,—if in our reverent examination of its parts, its pinnacles of beauty, its shrines of passion, its gorgeous oriels of many-coloured thought,—we venture to express the difficulties we experience in understanding how one part grew out of another, and the many parts grew to form the wondrous whole, let our criticism be accepted as that of one who examines only to learn and to enjoy.

It is known that Shakespeare devoted more time to this than to any other of his works, and that in his construction he altered and re-altered much.[1] The work bears evident traces of this elaboration, both in its lengthy and slow action, in its great diversity of incident and character, and in the perfection of its parts contrasted with some loss of uniformity as a whole. Some of his plays (as the *Merry Wives of Windsor*) Shakespeare is said to have thrown off with incredible rapidity and facility; but this certainly is not one in which he 'warbled his native wood-notes wild'. It was the laboured and elaborate result of years of toil, of metaphysical introspection and observation. It was the darling child of its great author, and ran some risk of being a little spoiled. A singular trace of this remodelling, which the commentators appear to have overlooked, is left in the different ages which are assigned to Hamlet in the earlier part and at the end of the drama. The Prince is introduced as a mere youth, whose intent,

> In going back to school in Wittenburg,
>
> (I, ii, 113)

the King opposes. His love is described as

> A violet in the youth of primy nature;
>
> (I, iii, 7)

---

1   Bucknill assumes the orthodoxy of his time: that *Hamlet* Q1 is Shakespeare's early draft of the play.

and he is so 'young' that he may walk with a large tether in such matters. He has not even attained his full stature, for

> Nature, crescent, does not grow alone
> In thews and bulk; but, as this temple waxes,
> The inward service of the mind and soul
> Grows wide withal.
>
> (I, iii, 11–14)

To his mistress he appears in the 'unmatched form and feature of *blown youth*' (III, i, 162). In fact, he is a young gentleman of eighteen or thereabouts. The inconsistency of attributing such profound powers of reflection, and such a blasé state of emotion, to a youth who could scarcely have had beard enough to be plucked, appears so forcibly to have struck Shakespeare, that he condescends to that which with him is a matter of the rarest occurrence, an explanation or contradiction of the error. With curious care he makes the Sexton lay down the age of the Prince at thirty years. He came to his office 'the very day that young Hamlet was born'; and he had been 'sexton here, man and boy, thirty years'. As if this were not enough, he confirms it with the history of Yorick's skull, which 'has been in the earth three and twenty years'; Yorick, whose qualities were well remembered by Hamlet, 'a fellow of infinite jest, of most excellent fancy; he hath borne me on his back a thousand times'; a kind of memory not likely to have stamped itself before the age of seven; and thus we have Hamlet presented to us not as an unformed youth, but a man of age competent to his power of thought, and of the age most liable to his state of feeling.

The first scene, where the Ghost appears to the sentinels on watch, is constructed with exquisite dramatic verisimilitude, and is admirably adapted to prepare the mind for that contest between the materialism of sensation and that idealism of passion, that doubting effort to discriminate between the things which are and the things which seem, which is the mark thread in the philosophy of the piece.

The Ghost appears at cold and silent midnight. ''Tis bitter cold, and I am sick at heart'. 'Not a mouse stirring', says Francisco. On this Coleridge remarks, that 'in all the best attested stories of ghosts and visions, the ghost-seers were in a state of cold or chilling damp from without, and of anxiety inwardly'[2]. As far as visions are concerned, this observation might have psychological importance, as tending to indicate the conditions of the nervous system favourable to the production of hallucination; but with regard to ghosts seen by many persons at the same time, if such things have been, it could only indicate that, escaped for a while from 'sulphurous and tormenting flames', these airy existences preferred to walk on cold nights.

We cannot consent to reduce the Ghost of *Hamlet* to physiological laws.

> We do it wrong, being so majestical,
> To offer it the shew of *science*[3]

The Ghost in *Hamlet* can in no wise be included within the category of illusions or hallucinations; it is anti-physiological, and must be simply accepted as a dramatic circumstance calculated to produce a certain state of mind in the hero of the piece. Hazlitt well says, that actors playing Macbeth have always appeared to him to have seen the weird sisters on the stage only. He never had seen a stage Macbeth look and act as if he had been face to face with the supernatural. We have experienced the same feeling in seeing the most approved representations of Hamlet; and doubtless Goethe had felt the same, since in the representation of Hamlet in *Wilhelm Meister* he produces upon the stage that which the tyro player takes for a real ghost. No person to act the part had been provided, and something marvellous had been mysteriously promised; but he had forgotten it, probably intending to dispense with the *appearance*. When it came, 'the noble figure, the low inaudible breath, the light movements in heavy armour, made such an impression on him that he stood as if transformed to stone, and could only utter in a half voice, "Angels and ministers of grace defend us". He glared at the form, drew a deep breathing once or twice, and pronounced his address to the Ghost in a manner so confused, so broken, so constrained, that the highest art could not have hit the mark so well'.[4] Besides the part it takes in the development

---

2   See *CRH*, ii, 64.

3   An adaptation of I, i, 124–5.

4   See *CRH*, ii, 41.

of the plot, the *role* of the Ghost is to account for, if not to produce, a high-wrought state of nerve in the hero: and in the acting play to produce the same effect in lesser degree on the audience. Fielding has described this, when Tom Jones takes Partridge to see Garrick in the character of Hamlet. The life-like acting of the English Roscius, combined with the superstition of the schoolmaster, produces so thorough a conviction of the actual presence of the Ghost, that the result is one of the drollest scenes ever painted by that inimitable romancist[5].

Hamlet is from the first moment represented in that mood of melancholy which vents itself in bitter sarcasm: 'A little more than kin, and less than kind'. He is 'too much i' the sun'. Sorry quips truly, but yet good enough for the hypocritical King, who wishes to rejoice and to lament at the same moment:

> With one auspicious and one dropping eye,
> With mirth in funeral and with dirge in marriage,
> In equal scale weighing delight and dole.
> (I, ii, 11–13)

To the King's unfeeling arguments that the son ought not to grieve for the death of his father, because it is a common theme and an unavailing woe, Hamlet vouchsafes no reply. But to his mother's rebuke, that the common grief 'seems' particular to him, he answers with a vehemence which shews that the clouds which hang on him are surcharged with electric fire:

> Seems, madam! nay, it is; I know not 'seems'.
> 'Tis not alone my inky cloak, etc.

He has that within that passes show; and, when left alone, he tells us what it is in that outburst of grief: [Quotes opening lines of soliloquy: 'O, that this too too solid flesh would melt', I, ii, 129–38]. It is the conflict of religious belief with suicidal desire. In his pure and sensitive mind the conduct of his mother has produced shame and keen distress. His generalising tendency leads him to extend his mother's failings to

---

5 See *CRH*, i, 159–63.

her whole sex—'Frailty, thy name is woman'; and from thence the sense of disgust shrouds as with foul mist the beauty of the world, and all its uses seem 'weary, stale, flat, and unprofitable'. To general dissatisfaction with men and the world succeeds the longing desire to quit the scene of shame and woe. In the subsequent arguments which the Prince holds with himself on suicide, he acknowledges the constraining power to be the fear of future punishment: but in this passage the higher motive of religious obedience without fear is acknowledged; a higher and a holier motive for the duty of bearing the evils which God permits, and refusing to break His law to escape from them, whatever their pressure may be. A bold man may 'jump the life to come' in the very spirit of courage; but a true servant and soldier of God will feel that there is unfaithfulness and cowardice in throwing off by voluntary death whatever burden of sorrows may freight the frail vessel of his life.

The concluding line equally marks profound sorrow, and the position of dependence and constraint in which Hamlet feels himself:

> But break, my heart, for I must hold my tongue.

And yet what rapid recovery to the quick-witted complaisance of social intercourse, when his friends break in upon these gloomy thoughts; and, again, mark the natural contiguity, in a mind equally sensitive and melancholic, of bantering sarcasm and profound emotion:

> Thrift, thrift, Horatio! the funeral baked-meats
> Did coldly furnish forth the marriage tables.
> Would I had met my dearest foe in heaven
> Or ever I had seen that day!
>
> (I, ii, 179–82)

This early passage seems to give the key-note of Hamlet's temper, namely, soul-crushing grief in close alliance with an ironical, often a broad humour, which can mock at despair. Profound life-weariness and suicidal desire indicate that from the first his emotions were morbid, and that the accusation of the King that he had

> A heart unfortified, a mind impatient,
> An understanding simple and unschooled,
>
> (I, ii, 96–7)

was as true of the heart as it was false of the intellect. Yet his rapid recovery from brooding thoughts, and his entire self-possession when circumstances call upon him for action trivial or important, prove that his mind was not permanently off its poise. Profoundly reflective, capable of calling up thoughts and ideas of sense at will, of seeing his father 'in his mind's eye', he is equally capable of dismissing them and throwing himself into the present. How thoroughly self-possessed is he in his interview with his friend and fellow-student and the soldiers, and the reception he gives to their account of the apparition, by which they were 'distilled almost to jelly by the act of fear'; how unhesitating his decision to see and speak to it, 'though hell itself should gape!' and in the seventh scene, Additional Passage B from Q2, when actually waiting for the Ghost, what cool reflection in his comments on the wassail of the country. Yet he heard not the clock strike midnight, which the less pre-occupied sense of Marcellus had caught. His address to the Ghost,

> Angels and ministers of grace defend us!
> Be thou a spirit of health or goblin damned? etc.

is marked by a bold and cool reason, at a time when the awful evidences of the future make

> us fools of nature
> So horridly to shake our disposition
> With thoughts beyond the reaches of our souls.
>   (I, iv, 20–37)

The courage of the Prince is of the noblest temper, and is made the more obvious from its contrast with the dread of his companions, who suggest that *it*, the neutral *thing*, as it has before been called, may tempt him to the summit of the cliff,

> And there assume some other horrible form,
> Which might deprive your sovereignty of reason
> And draw you into madness. Think of it:
> The very place puts toys of desperation,
> Without more motive, into every brain
> That looks so many fathoms to the sea
> And hears it roar beneath.
>   (Q2 I, iv, 53–9 Additional Passage B)

But Hamlet is beyond all touch of fear.

> My fate cries out,
> And makes each petty artery in this body
> As hardy as the Nemean lion's nerve.
>
> (I, iv, 58–60)

Horatio says, 'He waxes desperate with imagination'; but his state really appears to be that of high-wrought yet reasonable courage. After following the Ghost to some distance he'll 'go no further'; but if this is said with any touch of fear it soon becomes pity: 'Alas, poor Ghost!' And this, again, changes to revengeful resolution. He demands quickly to know the author of his father's murder, that he

> May sweep to his revenge.
>
> (I, v, 31)

But when the Ghost has told his terrible tale, and has disappeared, with the solemn farewell, 'Adieu, adieu, adieu! remember me', the reaction comes. Then it is that Hamlet feels his sinews fail their function, and invokes them to bear him stiffly up; then he recognises a feeling of distraction in the globe of his brain; then he vows forgetfulness of all things but the motive of revenge. He becomes wild at the thoughts of the 'smiling damned villain' who had wrought all this woe; and then, passing from the terrible to the trivial, he sets down in his tables a moral platitude:

> My tables! meet it is, I set it down,
> That one may smile, and smile, and be a villain;
> At least I am sure it may be so in Denmark.
>
> (I, v, 108–10)

We regard this climax of the terrible in the trivial, this transition of mighty emotion into lowliness of action, as one of the finest psychological touches anywhere to be found in the poet. There is something like it in Tennyson's noble poem, *Maud*. When the hero has shot the brother of his mistress in a duel, he passes from intense passion to trivial observation; [Quotes *Maud*, II, ii, stanza 8]. When the mind is wrought to an excessive pitch of emotion, the instinct of self-preservation indicates some lower mode of mental activity as the one thing needful. When

Lear's passions are wrought to the utmost, he says, 'I'll *do*! I'll *do*! I'll *do*!' But he does nothing. Had he been able, like Hamlet, to have taken out his note-book, it would have been good for his mental health. Mark the effect of the restraint which Hamlet is thus able to put upon the tornado of his emotion. When the friends rejoin him, he is self-possessed enough swiftly to turn their curiosity aside. Horatio, indeed, remarks on his manner of doing so, and on his expression of the intention, for his own poor part, to go pray:

> These are but wild and whirling words, my lord.

Doubtless the excitement of manner would make them appear to be more deserving of this comment than they do in reading. Yet Hamlet knows thoroughly well what he is about, and proceeds to swear his friends to secrecy on his sword. The flippant comments on the awful underground voice of the Ghost, 'the fellow in the cellarage', 'old mole', 'truepenny', are another meeting point of the sublime and the ridiculous, or rather a voluntary refuge in the trivial from the awful presence of the terrible. They are thoroughly true to the laws of our mental being. How often have men gone out of life upon the scaffold with a jest upon their lips. Even the just and cool-tempered Horatio, who takes fortune's buffets and rewards with equal thanks, is astounded and terrified at that underground voice which provokes but mocking retorts from the Prince. Horatio exclaims:

> O, day and night, but this is wondrous strange!

That Hamlet's mockery was the unreal opposite to his true feeling, like the hysteric laughter of acute grief, is evident from his last earnest adjuration:

> Rest, rest, perturbed spirit!

How it is that the resolution of Hamlet to put on the guise of madness follows so quick upon the appearance of the Ghost to him, (indeed, while the spirit is yet present, though unseen, for the resolution is expressed before the final unearthly adjuration to swear,) we are unable to explain. His resolutions are not usually taken with such quick speed; and indeed the wings of his meditation, which he refers to as swift, commonly beat the air with long and slow strokes, the very reverse of Macbeth's vehement action, framed upon the principle 'that the flighty purpose never is o'ertook, except the act goes with it'. It may, however, be said that the word *'perchance'* shews that Hamlet has not yet decided to act the madman when he swears his friends to secrecy.

> Never, so help you mercy!
> How strange or odd so'er I bear myself,
> As I *perchance* hereafter shall think meet
> To put an antic disposition on.
>
> (I, v, 170–3)

And yet the intention must have resolve in it, even at this time, or he would not swear his friends in so solemn a manner to maintain inviolate the secret of his craft. The purport of Hamlet's feigned madness is not very obvious. It does not appear to have been needful to protect him, like that of the elder Brutus. It may be that under this disguise he hopes better to obtain proof of his uncle's guilt, and to conceal his real state of suspicion and vengeful gloom. Still more probable is it that Shakespeare adopted the feigned madness as an essential part of the old story on which the drama is founded.

The old history of Hamlet relates how he counterfeited the madman to escape the tyranny of his uncle Fengon, whose expedients resemble those in the drama which were resorted to by the King to ascertain whether his madness were counterfeited or not. The feigned madness, therefore, of the Prince was so leading a feature in the original history, that Shakespeare could by no means have omitted it, even if by doing so he would not have deprived himself of a magnificent canvass on which to display his psychological knowledge. As it stands however in the drama, the counterfeit madness would seem to bring Hamlet into more danger than security. What if the King had accepted his madness from the first, and shut him up, as he might have justified himself in doing, in some strong castle. After the death of Polonius, the King says [to Gertrude]:

> His liberty is full of threats to all;
> To you yourself, to us, to every one.

> Alas! how shall this bloody deed be answer'd?
> It will be laid to us, whose providence
> Should have kept short, restrain'd, and out of haunt,
> This mad young man.
>
> (IV, i, 13–18)

And again—

> How dangerous is it that this man goes loose.
>
> (IV, iii, 2)

He puts not the strong law upon him indeed, as he says, because 'he's loved of the distracted multitude', and because 'the Queen lives but in his eyes'. These motives may explain the King's conduct, but they do not shew that, in assuming the guise of madness, Hamlet was not incurring the risk of the limitation of his own freedom.

The first demonstration of the antic disposition he actually does put on, is made before his mistress, the fair Ophelia [Quotes II, i, 75–111]. We are at a loss to explain this part of Hamlet's conduct towards his sweet mistress, unless it be accepted as the sad pantomime of separation, love's mute farewell. That his noble and sensitive mind entertained a sincere love to the beautiful and virtuous girl, there can be no doubt. Surely it must have been this love which he thus refers to in that paroxysm of feeling at the close of the Ghost scene:

> Yea, from the table of my memory
> I'll wipe away all trivial fond records.
>
> (I, v, 98–9)

Indeed, love is an autocratic passion not disposed to share the throne of the soul with other emotions of an absorbing nature. Hamlet, however, might feel his resolution, to wipe from his memory the trivial fond records of his love, strengthened into action by the conduct of Ophelia herself, who repelled his letters and denied his access, thus taking upon herself the pain and responsibility of breaking off the relationship in which she had stood to him, and in which with so keen a zest of pleasure she had sucked in the honey-music of his vows, and the reaction from which cost her so dear. In his interview with Ophelia, arranged by Polonius and the King, he speaks to her of his love as a thing of the past. That that love was ardent and sincere we learn from his passionate grief at the grave of his dead mistress, a grief which, on his own acknowledgement to his friend, we know to have been no acting, but the demonstration of which was due to the fact that he had forgot himself in the presence of Laertes, the bravery of whose grief had put him 'into a towering passion'. It is at this time, when he had forgot himself, that he exclaims with passionate vehemence,

> I loved Ophelia; forty thousand brothers
> Could not, with all their quantity of love,
> Make up my sum.
>
> (V, i, 266–8)

That Hamlet's conduct to Ophelia was unfeeling, in thus forcing upon her the painful evidence of the insanity he had assumed, can scarcely be denied. Hamlet, however, was no perfect character, and in the matter of his love there is no doubt he partook of the selfishness which is the common attribute of the passion wherever its glow is the warmest. His love was not of that delicate sentimental kind which would above all things fear to disturb the beatitude of its object, and feel its highest pleasure in acts of self-denial. It was rather of that kind which women best appreciate—an ardent passion, not a sentimental devotion; and hence its tinge of selfishness. Yet, having put on his antic disposition with the trappings and suits of madness, he might feel that the kindest act he could perform towards Ophelia would be to concur with her in breaking off their courtship. He might, indeed, have allowed others to tell her that he had gone mad, and have saved her a great fright and agitation of mind; but, under the circumstances, it cannot be considered unnatural that he should selfishly enough have rushed into her presence to take leave of her in the mad pantomime which she describes. His conduct to Ophelia is a mixture of feigned madness, of the selfishness of passion blasted by the cursed blight of fate, of harshness which he assumes to protect himself from an affection which he feels hostile to the present purpose of his life, and of that degree of real unsoundness, his unfeigned 'weakness and melancholy', which is the subsoil of his mind.

In the following scene the King explains to Rosencrantz and Guildenstern the condition of the Prince in a manner which implies that at that time he entertained no doubt of the reality of his madness:

> Something have you heard
> Of Hamlet's transformation; so I call it,
> Since not the exterior nor the inward man
> Resembles that it was. What it should be,
> More than his father's death, that thus hath put him
> So much from the understanding of himself,
> I cannot dream of.
>
> (II, ii, 4–10)

The King's anxiety to ascertain 'if aught to us unknown afflicts him thus', indicates the unrest of his conscience, and the fear that some knowledge of his own great crime may lie at the bottom of his nephew's inward and outward transformation. The same fearful anxiety shews itself immediately afterwards, when on the vain half-doting Polonius at the same time asserting that the Ambassadors from Norway are joyfully returned, and that he has found 'the very cause of Hamlet's lunacy', the King exclaims, 'Oh! speak of that, that I do long to hear'; thus bringing upon himself the retort courteous of the old man, that the news respecting Hamlet should be kept to follow the pressing business of the moment, as dessert follows a feast.

From Polonius's exposition of Hamlet's madness, which, in a manner so contrary to his own axiom 'that brevity is the soul of wit', he dilates upon with such tediousness and empty flourishes of speech as to draw upon himself the rebuke of the Queen, 'more matter with less art', one would almost think that Shakespeare might have heard some lawyer, full of his quiddets and cases, endeavouring by the sophistry of abstract definitions to damage the evidence of some medical man to whose experience the actual concrete facts of insanity were matters of familiar observation, but whose verbal expression had more of pedantry than power:

> I will be brief: your noble son is mad:
> Mad call I it; for, to define true madness,
> What is't but to be nothing else but mad?
>
> (II, ii, 93–5)

In the following lines, the old man recognises madness to be a phenomenon, for which, like every other phenomenon, some cause or other must exist; and, moreover, that madness is not in itself a distinct entity, something apart from the mind, but a *defect* in the mind.

> Mad let us grant him then: and now remains
> That we find out the cause of this effect,
> Or rather say, the cause of this defect,
> For this effect defective comes by cause.
>
> (II, ii, 101–4)

Hamlet's letter to Ophelia is a silly-enough rhapsody; of which, indeed, the writer appears conscious. It reads like an old letter antecedent to the events of the drama. The spirit it breathes is scarcely consistent with the intense life-weariness under which its author is first introduced to notice. The signature, however, is odd. 'Thine evermore, most dear lady, whilst this *machine* is to him', and agrees with the spirit of Hamlet's materialist philosophy, which is so strongly expressed in various parts of the play, and which forms so strange a contrast with the revelations from the spirit-world, of which he is made the recipient. The description which Polonius gives of the course of Hamlet's madness, after his daughter had locked herself from his resort and refused his messages and tokens, is vain and pedantic in its expression, but pregnant in meaning:

> And he, repulsed—a short tale to make—
> Fell into a sadness, then into a fast,
> Thence to a watch, thence into a weakness,
> Thence to a lightness, and, by this declension,
> Into the madness wherein now he raves.
>
> (II, ii, 146–50)

Translated into the dulness of medical prose, the psychological opinion of the old courtier may be thus expressed. Disappointed and rejected in his ardent addresses to Ophelia, Hamlet became melancholy and neglected to take food; the result of fasting was the loss of sleep; the loss of sleep and loss of food were followed by general weakness; this produced a lightness or instability of the mental functions, which passed into insanity. The suggestion made by Polonius to test the soundness of his view, that the Prince loved his daughter and had fallen from his reason thereon, was plain and practical, namely, to arrange and to watch in ambuscade interviews between him and the persons most likely to excite his emotion. Moreover, Shakespeare was in some sort bound to introduce these interviews, inasmuch as they formed an important part of the old history.

The Queen did not partake of the King's anxiety to ascertain the cause of her son's madness. When he tells her that Polonius

> Hath found
> The head and source of all your son's distemper,

she replies—

> I doubt it is no other but the main;
> His father's death, and our o'erhasty marriage.
> (II, ii, 54–7)

Hamlet now for the first time appears in his feigned character. The feint is so close to nature, and there is underlying it withal so undeniable a substratum of morbid feeling, that in spite of ourselves, in oppositon to our full knowledge that in his antic disposition Hamlet is putting on a part, we cannot from the first dispossess ourselves of the idea, that a mind fallen, if not from the sovereignty of reason, at least from the balance of its faculties, is presented to us. So much is undirection of mind blended with pregnant sense and apprehension, both however perverted from the obvious line of sane thought; so much is the universal and caustic irony tinged with melancholic self-depreciation, and that longing for death which in itself alone constitutes a form of mental disease. In the various forms of partial insanity, it is a question of intricate science to distinguish between the portions of a man's conduct which result from the sound operations of mind, and those which result from disease. Hamlet's own assertion,'I am but mad north-north-west: when the wind is southerly I know a hawk from a hand-saw', is pregnant with a psychological truth which has often engaged the most skilful and laborious investigation both of medical men and of lawyers. It has often been a question of life or death, of wealth or poverty, whether a criminal act was done, or a civil one performed, by a half-madman, when the mental wind was in the north-west of disease, or blowing from the sanatory south.

That in his actual unfeigned mental condition Hamlet is far from being in a healthy state of mind, he is himself keenly conscious, and acknowledges it to himself in his soliloquy upon the players:

> The spirit that I have seen
> May be a devil: and the devil hath power
> To assume a pleasing shape; yea, and perhaps
> *Out of my weakness and my melancholy,*
> As he is very potent with such spirits,
> Abuses me to damn me.
>
> (II, ii, 599–604)

Upon this actual weakness of mind and suicidal melancholy, combined with native humour and the biting irony into which his view of the world has sharpened it, is added the feigned form of insanity, the antic disposition wilfully put on, the dishevelled habiliments of person and wild converse. The characteristics of this feigned form are those of mania, not indeed violent, acute, and demonstrative, but mischievous, reckless, and wayward, and so mingled with flashes of native wit, and disguised by the ground colour of real melancholy, shewing through the transparency of the feigned state, that Hamlet's character becomes one of the most interesting and complicated subjects of psychological study anywhere to be met with.

He is first introduced to us in his feigning condition with a fine touch to excite pity:

> Queen. But, look, where sadly the poor wretch comes reading.
> Polonius. Do you know me, my lord?
> Hamlet. Excellent well; you are a fishmonger.
>
> (II, ii, 169, 175–6)

Coleridge and others remark upon this, that Hamlet's meaning is, You are sent to fish out this secret. But we are not aware that fishmongers are in the habit of catching their fish. May it not rather be that a fishmonger was referred to as a dealer in perishable goods, and notoriously dishonest; and thus to give point to the rejoinder—

> Then I would you were so honest a man.

The writers who insist upon a profound meaning, even in Hamlet's most hurling words, have been mightily puzzled with the lines:

For if the sun breed maggots in a dead dog, being a good kissing carrion, etc.
(II, ii, 183–4)

Coleridge refers to 'some thought in Hamlet's mind, contrasting Ophelia with the tedious old fool her father'.[6] Is it not rather a wild taunt upon the old man's jealous suspicion of his daughter, as if he had said, since the sun causes conception in such vile bodies,'let not your precious daughter walk in the sun'.

Perhaps he only intended to convey to Polonius, by a contemptuous simile, the intimation that he cared not for the daughter, and thus to throw him off the scent of his quest. The intention to offend the tedious old fool,and thus to disembarrass himself of his presence, becomes still more obvious in the description of old age which immediately follows,'Slanders, sir',etc.

The point of the satire, and the absence of unreason, strikes Polonius.

> Polonius. Though this be madness, yet there is method in't. Will you walk out of the air, my lord?
> Hamlet. Into my grave.
> Polonius. Indeed, that is out o' the air. How pregnant sometimes his replies are! a happiness that often madness hits on, which reason and sanity could not so prosperously be delivered of.
> (II, ii, 207–13)

In this, again, the old man shews that though his wits may be somewhat superannuated, yet, either from reading or observation, he has no slight knowledge of mental disease.

What depth of melancholy and life-weariness is there not apparent in the conclusion of the interview.

> Polonius. I will most humbly [sic] take my leave of you.
> Hamlet.You cannot, sir, take from me anything that I will more willingly part withal: except my life, except my life, except my life!

But when his old schoolfellows arrive, how frank and hearty his greeting; how entirely is all disguise for the moment thrown aside! The noble

---

6   *Marginalia*. See *CRH*, ii, 75.

and generous native nature is nowhere made more manifest than in the reception of these friends of his youth, men to whom he once adhered, neighbours to his youth and humour. Until his keen eye discovers that they have been 'sent for', and are mean instruments, if not spies, in the hands of the king, he throws off all dissimulation with them, greeting them with right hearty and cheerful welcome. Yet how soon his melancholy peers through the real but transient cheerfulness. The world is a prison, 'in which there are many confines, wards, and dungeons; Denmark being one of the worst'. If it is not so to his friend, yet is it so to him from thinking it so, for 'there is nothing either good or bad, but thinking makes it so: to him it is a prison'. The real prison, then, is his own mind, as, in the contrary mental state, a prison is no prison, for

> Stone walls do not a prison make,
> Nor iron bars a cage[7].

Hamlet feels that he could possess perfect independence of circumstance if the mind were free.

Rosencrantz. Why then, your ambition makes it one; 'tis too narrow for your mind.
Hamlet. O God, I could be bounded in a nutshell and count myself a king of infinite space, were it not that I have bad dreams.

(II, ii, 253–7)

The spies sound him further on the subject of ambition, thinking that disappointment at losing the succession to the crown may be the true cause of his morbid state. In this intention they decry ambition: 'it is but a shadow's shadow'. Hamlet replies logically enough, that if ambition is but a shadow, something beyond ambition must be the substance from which it is thrown. If ambition represented by a King is a shadow, the antitype of ambition represented by a beggar must be the opposite of the shadow, that is, the substance. 'Then are our beggars, bodies; and our monarchs, and outstretch'd heroes, the beggars' shadows'. He reduces the sophistry of his false friends to an absurdity, and closes the argument by declining to carry it further: 'By my fay, I cannot reason'. But Mr

7 Richard Lovelace, *Song, To Althea from Prison*, 25–6.

Coleridge declares the passage to be unintelligible, and perhaps this interpretation of it may be too simple.

So far from being able to examine and recover the wind of Hamlet, his old schoolfellows are put by him to a course of questioning as to the motives of their presence, as to whether it is a free visitation of their own inclining, or whether they have been 'sent for'. Their want of skill in dissemblance and their weaker natures submit to him the secret that they had been 'sent for', and the old 'rights of fellowship', 'the obligations of ever-preserved love', are immediately clouded by mistrust: 'Nay, then, I'll have an eye of you', he says. Yet notwithstanding he freely discloses to them the morbid state of his mind; and, be it remarked, that in this exquisite picture of life-weariness, in which no image could be altered, no word omitted or changed, without obvious damage to its grand effect, he does not describe the maniacal state, the semblance of which he has put on before Ophelia and Polonius, but that morbid state of weakness and melancholy which he really suffers, of which he is thoroughly self-conscious, and which he avows in his first speech, before he has seen the Ghost: [Quotes Hamlet's speech II, ii, 296–311, beginning 'I have of late—but wherefore I know not—lost all my mirth . . . ']. How exquisitely is here portrayed the state of the reasoning melancholiac, (melancholia without delusion,) who sees all things as they are, but feels them as they are not. All cheerfulness fled, all motive for action lost, he becomes listless and inert. He still recognises the beauty of the earth and the magnificence of the heavens, but the one is a tomb, and the other a funereal pall. His reason still shews him the place of man, a little lower than the angels, but the sources of sentiment are dried up, and, although no man-hater, he no longer derives pleasure from kindly affections. The waters of emotion are stagnant; the pleasant places of the soul are sterile and desert.

Hamlet is not slow to confess his melancholy, and indeed it is the peculiarity of this mental state, that those suffering from it seldom or never attempt to conceal it. A man will conceal his delusions, will deny and veil the excitement of mania, but the melancholiac is almost always readily confidential on the subject of his feelings. In this he resembles the hypochondriac, though not perhaps from exactly the same motive. The hypochondriac seeks for sympathy and pity; the melancholiac frequently admits others to the sight of his mental wretchedness from mere despair of relief and contempt of pity.

Although Hamlet is ready to show to his friends the mirror of his mind, he jealously hides the cause of its distortion. 'But wherefore I know not' is scarcely consistent with the truth. In his first soliloquy, which we take to be the key-note of his real mental state, he clearly enough indicates the source of his wretchedness, which the Queen also, with a mother's insight, has not been slow to perceive:

> His father's death, and our o'erhasty marriage.
>
> (II, ii, 57)

He is jealous that his friends should not refer his melancholy to love-sickness. The opinion propounded by Polonius, that he was mad for love, could not have escaped him; a theory, of his malady, which would be likely to wound his pride severely. Polonius had already made, in his presence, sundry aside observations on this point; and the significant smile of Rosencrantz at his observation, 'Man delights not me', would be likely to stimulate the sleeping suspicion that he was set down as a brain-sick, rejected lover; and some annoyance at an attempt to explain his madness as a result of his rejection by Ophelia, may combine with the suspicion that he is watched to explain his harshness towards her in his subsequent interview with her.

How are we to understand his confession to the men he already distrusts, that in the appearance of his madness the King and Queen are deceived, except by his contempt for their discrimination, and his dislike to wear his antic disposition before all company?

When Polonius returns, he immediately puts on the full disguise, playing upon the old man's infirmities with the ironical nonsense about Jephtha, king of Israel, who had a daughter, etc., and skilfully leading Polonius by the nose on the scent of his own theory, 'Still on my daughter'.

When the players enter, however, he thoroughly throws off not only the antic counterfeit, but the melancholy reality of his disposition: he shakes his faculties together, and becomes perfectly master of himself in courtesy, scholarship, and solid sense. His retort to Polonius, who objects to the speech of the player as too long, seems a valuable hint of Shakespeare's own opinion respecting the bad necessity he felt to introduce ribald scenes into his plays: 'It shall to the barber's, with your beard. Prithee, say on: he's for a jig or a tale of bawdry, or he sleeps'. A noble sentiment in homely phrase is that in which he marks the right motive of behaviour towards inferiors, and indeed towards all men. To Polonius's assurance that he will use the players according to their desert, the princely reply is—

> God's body kins, man, much better: use every man after his desert, and who should 'scape whipping? Use them after your own honour and dignity: the less they deserve, the more merit is in your bounty.
>
> (II, ii, 531–4)

Although he freely mocks the old lord chamberlain himself, he will not permit others to do so. His injunction to the player, 'Follow that lord, and look you mock him not', not only indicates that the absurdities of Polonius are glaring, but that there is less real malice in Hamlet's heart towards the old man than he assumes the appearance of.

Hamlet decides upon the use he will make of the players with a promptitude that shews that his resolve, 'sicklied o'er with the pale cast of thought', is but the inactivity of an over-reflective melancholic mind, and that there is energy enough in him to seize some forms of opportunity.

Hamlet's soliloquy, 'O, what a rogue and peasant slave am I!' resembles, with a difference, the one following his interview with the Captain: 'How all occasions do inform against me' (Q2 IV, iv, 231). The latter one, after he has obtained satisfactory proof of his uncle's guilt, is by far the least passionate and vehement, justifying in some degree the remark of Schlegel, that 'in the last scenes the main action either stands still or appears to retrograde'.[8] There is, however, an important distinction between these two soliloquies. The passionate outburst of the first has been stimulated by emotional imitation. The feigned passion of the player has touched the most sensitive chord of feeling, and given occasion to the vehemence of his angry self-rebuke. The account of the soldier's temper, 'greatly to find quarrel in a straw when honour's at the stake' (Q2, IV, iv, 46–7), sets him calmly to reflect and philosophize upon the motives of action. In these two soliloquies we have to some extent Shakespeare's

---

8   August Wilhelm Schlegel, *Lectures on Dramatic Art and Literature*, see *CRH*, ii, 50.

own exposition of Hamlet's natural character, and the motives of his conduct.

'The whole', says Schlegel, 'was intended to shew that a consideration which would exhaust all the relations and possible consequences of a deed to the very limits of human foresight, cripples the power of acting'[9]. In this tragedy of thought we have delineated a highly sensitive, reflecting, self-introspective mind, weak and melancholic, sorrow-stricken and life-weary. In a manner so awful that it might shake the soundest mind, this man is called upon to take away the life of a king and a relative for a crime of which there exists no actual proof. Surely Hamlet is justified in pausing to weigh his motives and his evidence, in concluding not to act upon the sole dictation of a shadowy appearance, who may be the devil tempting his 'weakness and his melancholy'; of resolving to 'have grounds more relative than this', before he deliberately commits himself to an act of revenge which, even had the proof of his uncle's crime been conclusive and irrefragable, would have been repulsive to his inmost nature. Hamlet's indecision to act, and his over-readiness to reflect, are placed beyond the reach of critical discovery by his own analytical motive-hunting, so eloquently expressed in the abstruse reasoning in which he indulges. Anger and hatred against his uncle, self-contempt for his own irresolution, inconsistent as he feels it with the courage of which he is conscious; disgust at his own angry excitement, and doubts of the testimony upon which he is yet dissatisfied that he has not acted, present a state of intellectual and emotional conflict perfectly consistent with the character and the circumstances. If Hamlet had had as much faith in the Ghost as Macbeth had in the Weird Sisters, he would have struck without needing further evidence. If he had been a man of action, whose firstlings of the heart are those of the hand, he would have struck in the earliest heat of his revenge. He feels while he questions, that it is not true that he is 'pigeon-liver'd, and lacks gall to make oppression bitter'; but he does lack that resolution which 'makes mouths at the invisible event'; he does make 'I would, wait upon, I will': he does hesitate and procrastinate, and examine his motives, and make sure to his own mind of his justification, and allow us to see the painful labour of a noble and sensitive

---

9   Ibid.

being struggling to gain an unquestionable conviction of the right thing to do, in circumstances most awry and difficult; he does feel balancing motives, and painfully hear the ring of the yes and no in his head.

> Che si, e no nel capo mi tenzona.[10]

Shall we think the less nobly of him because his hand is not ready to shed kindred blood; because, gifted with God-like discourse of reason, he does look before and after; because he does not take the law in his own hands upon his oppressor until he has obtained conclusive evidence of his guilt; that he seeks to make sure he is the natural justiciar of his murdered father, and not an assassin instigated by hatred and selfish revenge?

The report given to the King and Queen by the young courtiers is conceived to hide their failure in the mission of inquiry. The Prince, they say, 'does confess he feels himself distracted', while he refuses to yield to them the cause:

> But, with a crafty madness, keeps aloof,
> When we would bring him on to some confession
> Of his true state.
>
> (III, i, 8–10)

He behaves

> Most like a gentleman;
> But with much forcing of his disposition,
>
> (III, i, 12–13)

and he is falsely stated to have been 'niggard of question', but 'most free in his reply'.

They must, however, have been surprised to hear the condition in which they found their friend described by the King, as 'turbulent and dangerous lunacy', since, up to this time, this is an untrue description of Hamlet's state, whatever cause the King may subsequently have to apply it, when the death of Polonius makes him feel that Hamlet's 'liberty is

---

10   For yes and no dispute within my head.

full of threats to all'. The expression used by the King, that Hamlet 'puts on this confusion', would seem to point to a suspicion, even at this early time, that his madness is but counterfeit. The Queen, however, appears to accept its reality and, notwithstanding all the arguments of Polonius, she adheres to her first opinion of its cause. She doth *wish*, indeed, that Ophelia's 'good beauties be the happy cause of Hamlet's wildness'; since, if so, she entertains the hope that her virtues may bring the remedy. It seems here implied that the King and Queen have been made aware of Ophelia's love for Hamlet; and both in this speech of the Queen, and in the one she makes over Ophelia's grave,

> I hoped thou shouldst have been my Hamlet's wife,

it appears that the remedy by which the Queen at this time hopes to attain his recovery to 'his wonted way again', is by his marriage. This understanding, however, or arrangement, is nowhere expressed; and indeed, although the Queen may desire to think with Polonius respecting the cause and nature of her son's malady, her mother's knowledge and woman's tact lead her conviction nearer to the truth, when she avows the real cause to be 'his father's death, and our o'erhasty marriage'.

The soliloquy which follows, 'To be, or not to be', is one of the most exquisite pieces of poetic self-communing ever conceived. Imbued with a profoundly melancholy view of human life, which is relieved by no gleam of cheerfulness, illumined by no ray of hope, the mind of the unhappy Prince dwells with longing desire, not on a future and happier state of existence, but on annihilation. He wishes to end the troubles of life in a sleep without a dream, and is restrained alone from seeking it by the apprehension of

> What dreams may come
> When we have shuffled off this mortal coil;
>
> (III, i, 68–9)

by the fear, in fact, of a future state, in which the calamities of this life may be exchanged for others more enduring, in the undiscovered country of the future. This 'dread of something after death' scarcely deserves the name of conscience which he applies to it. The fear of punishment is the lowest motive for virtuous action, and is far removed in its nature from the inward principle of doing right for its own sake. The word, however, does not seem to be here applied in its higher sense, as the arbiter of right, but rather in that of reflective meditation. It is this that makes 'cowards of us all'. It is this that prevents Hamlet seeking his own rest in the annihilation he longs for. It is by this also that his hand is withheld from the act of wild justice and revenge upon which his mind sits on brood. It is thus that he accurately describes the *timbre* of his own mind, so active to think, so inert to act, so keen to appreciate the evils of life, so averse to take any active part against them:

> Thus conscience does make cowards of us all;
> And thus the native hue of resolution
> Is sicklied o'er with the pale cast of thought,
> And enterprises of great pith and moment
> With this regard their currents turn awry,
> And lose the name of action.
>
> (III, i, 85–90)

The motive against suicide here adduced is undoubtedly a mean and fallacious one. It is mean, because it is cowardly; the coward want of patience manfully to endure the evils of this mortal life being kept in check by the coward fear of future punishment. It is fallacious, because it balances the evils of this life against the apprehended ones of the future; therefore when, in the judgment of the sorely afflicted, the weight of present evils more than counterpoises those which their amount of religious faith may point to in the threatening future, the argument here advanced would justify suicide. There is nothing in which men differ more than in the various degrees with which they are endowed with the courage of fortitude and the courage of enterprise; and it is certain that of two men equally groaning and sweating under a weary life, and oppressed by the same weight of calamity, if solely actuated by the reasoning here employed by Hamlet in the contemplation of suicide, one would have the courage to endure the present, and the other would have the courage to face the perils of the future. Courage has been described as the power to select the least of two evils; the evil of pain and death, for instance, rather than that of shame. If this be so, it must yet be admitted that either one of two given evils may be the greatest to different men;

and courage may urge one man to fight and another to flee, either in the vulgar wars of Kings and Kaisars, or in the more earnest trials of the battle of life. The converse of the proposition must also be true, and cowardice may either make us stand by our arms or basely desert. The terrible question of suicide, therefore, is not to be thus solved; indeed the only motive against suicide which will stand the test is that which Hamlet in his first speech indicates, namely, obedience to the law of God; that obedience which, in the heaviest calamities, enables the Christian to 'be patient and endure'; that obedience which, in the most frantic desire to put off this mortal coil, can withhold the hand by this one consideration, that

> The Eternal hath set His canon 'gainst self-slaughter[11].

The motives made use of by Hamlet in his earlier and later contemplation of suicide, indicate his religious and his philosophic phase of character. Faith in the existence of a God, and of a future state of existence, is so ingrained in his mind that it powerfully influences his conduct, and constantly turns up to invalidate, if not to refute, that sceptical philosophy with which he is indoctrinated, and which leads him so constantly to trace the changes of matter, as in

> Imperious Caesar, dead and turn'd to clay,
> Might stop a hole to keep the wind away.
>
> (V, i, 208–9)

This, perhaps, was the philosophy which Horatio and he had learned at Wittenburg, the fallacy of which the Ghost had seemed at first to prove. Yet it is strange how entirely Hamlet appears at times to have forgotten the Ghost and its revelations. The soliloquy 'To be, or not to be' is that of a man to whom any future state of existence is a matter of sincere doubt. He reasons as one of those who would not be persuaded 'though one rose from the dead'.

---

11   Bucknill is misremembering the lines (I, ii, 131–2):
> Or that the Everlasting had not fix'd
> His canon 'gainst self-slaughter!

After the soul-harrowing recital made to him by the perturbed spirit of his father, in which the secrets of the purgatorial prison-house are not indeed unfolded, but in which they are so broadly indicated that no man who had seen so much of the 'eternal blazon' of the spirit-world could find a corner in his soul for the concealment of a sceptical doubt, after this, the soliloquy 'To be, or not to be' presumes either an entire forgetfulness of the awful revelation which had been made to him, or the existence of a state of mind so overwhelmed with suicidal melancholy as to be incapable of estimating testimony. Now it is well enough known that the most complete sensorial and intellectual proofs go for nothing when opposed to the stubborn strength of a morbid emotion; and when Hamlet reasons thus upon the future life, and hunts matter through its transmigrations with sceptical intent, it must be accepted as the result of the perverted instinct of self-preservation, which made him desire nothing so much as simple unconditional annihilation.

In his interview with the much-enduring Ophelia which follows the soliloquy, Hamlet has been accused of unworthy harshness. Two considerations will tend to modify, though not altogether to remove, this judgment. The reader is aware that Ophelia entertains the fondest love towards Hamlet; but he, ignorant of this, only knows that, after accepting the tender of his affections, she has repulsed him with every appearance of heartless cruelty. He feels her to be the cause of his 'pangs of despised love'; yet he at first addresses her in a manner indicating his own faithfulness and fond appreciation of all her goodness and virtue, as if he could best approach Heaven through her gracious intercession:

> The fair Ophelia! Nymph, in thy orisons
> Be all my sins remember'd.
>
> (III, i, 91–2)

What follows is so opposed to the tenderness of this greeting, that we are compelled to assume that he sees through the snare set for him; and that in avoiding it he works himself into one of those ebullitions of temper to which he is prone. He sees that Ophelia is under constraint of other presence, as what keen-sighted lover would not immediately distinguish whether his mistress, in whatever mood she may be, feels herself alone with him, or under the observation of others? He has before shewn his repugnance to the idea that he is love-sick mad. He knows that Polonius thus explains his conduct; and his harshness to Ophelia is addressed to Polonius, and to any others who may be in hiding, more than to Ophelia herself. Yet the harshest words, and those most unfit to be used to any woman, are the true reflex of the morbid side of his mind, which passion and suspicion have cast into the bitterest forms of expression. The true melancholy and the counterfeit madness are strangely commingled in this scene. The latter is shewn by disjointed exclamations and half-reasonings. 'Ha, ha! are you honest?' 'Are you fair?' 'I did love you once.' 'I loved you not' etc., and by the wild form in which the melancholy is here cast. 'Get thee to a nunnery: why wouldst thou be a breeder of sinners?' 'What should such fellows as I do crawling between earth and heaven!' 'Where's your father?' Ophelia tells a white lie. 'At home, my lord.' Hamlet knows better, and sends a random shaft into his ambuscade. 'Let the doors be shut upon him, that he may play the fool nowhere but in his own house.' [Quotes III, i, 123–32, 137–52.] Partly dictated by jealous fear that Ophelia may solace her pain with some other lover, it is yet an attempt to wean from himself any fondness which may remain. The burden is, Grieve not for me, but do not marry another. The latter part of the speech is directed to the Queen in ambush.

What exquisite pathos! what wail of despairing love in Ophelia's lament over the ruin of her lover's mind! What fine discrimination of the excellencies marred! What forgetfulness of self in the grief she feels for him! Not for her own loss, but for his fall, is she 'of ladies most deject and wretched', although it is the dying swan-song of her own sanity. [Quotes III, i, 153–64.] The King, in the meanwhile, whose keenness of vision has not been dimmed by the mists of affection, like that of Ophelia, nor by self-conceit, like that of Polonius, has detected the prevalence of melancholy and sorrow in the assumed wildness of the Prince:

> Love! his affections do not that way tend;
> Nor what he spake, though it lack'd form a little,
> Was not like madness. There's something in his soul,
> O'er which his melancholy sits on brood;
> And I do doubt the hatch and the disclose
> Will be some danger.
>
> (III, i, 165–70)

Polonius thinks well of the King's scheme to get Hamlet out of the way by pretext of benefitting his health by change of scene, though with senile obstinacy he still holds to his opinion that the commencement of his grief sprung from neglected love. To test this further he proposes the interview with the Queen, who is to be round with her son, and whose conference Polonius will hear. If this scheme fails, let him be sent to England without delay, or be put into confinement.

In his speech to the players, Hamlet's attention, abstracted for a moment from the view of his sorrows, leaves his mind free from the clouds of melancholy, and permits him to display his powerful and sarcastic intelligence without let or hindrance. His innate nobleness of mind is not less clearly portrayed in the conversation with Horatio which immediately follows. The character of this judicious and faithful follower, as it is manifested throughout the piece, and especially as it is here portrayed by Hamlet himself, forms a pleasing contrast to that of his princely friend. The one passionate in emotion, inert in action; the other cool in temper, prompt in conduct. The maxim *noscitur a sociis*[12] may be narrowed to the closer and truer one, 'Shew me your friend, and I'll tell your mind'; and in a true and deep friendship there will always be found much uniformity of sentiment, though it may be, and indeed often is, combined with great diversity of temperament. Deep friendship rarely exists between persons whose emotional tendencies closely resemble. A true friend is generally chosen in some contrast of disposition, as if the basis of this rare and noble affection were the longing to remedy the imperfection of one's nature by complementing ourselves with those good qualities of another in which we are deficient.

Before this time Hamlet has confided to his friend the terrible secret of the Ghost's message, the truth of which he proposes to test by the scheme of the play, and thus to sting the conscience and unkennel the occult guilt of his uncle.

When the court enter, Hamlet puts on his antics in his ironical half-reasonings with the King and Polonius, and his banter with Ophelia. The manners and playhouse licence of the time explain the broad indelicacy of the latter; but that he so publicly indulged it may be accepted as proof of his desire to mark his indifference to the woman who had, as he thought, heartlessly jilted him, and whose love he had reason to think had been 'as brief as the posy of a ring'.

---

12   One is known by one's friends.

As the play within the play draws to its climax, Hamlet becomes so excited and restless that it is a wonder he does not spoil his scheme by exposing it to the King, who, on the point of taking the alarm, exclaims,'Have you heard the argument? Is there no offence in't?' He is little likely to be reassured by Hamlet's disclaimer, 'They poison in jest; no offence i'the world'.

When the crisis has come, and the King's guilt has been unkennelled, and Hamlet is again left alone with Horatio, before whom he would not feign, his real excitement borders so closely upon the wildest antics of the madness he has put on in craft, that there is little left to distinguish between the two. He quotes senseless doggerel, will join 'a fellowship in a cry of players', will 'take the Ghost's word for a thousand pound', and is altogether in that state of flippant merriment which men sometimes assume to defend themselves from deep emotion; as they sometimes jest in the face of physical horrors or mental woe. It is like the hysterical laughter of intense emotion, though not quite. It is partly that levity of mind which succeeds intense strain of thought and feeling, as naturally as it is to yawn and stretch after one long-continued wearisome position. This mood of unfeigned flippancy continues after the re-entrance of his treacherous school friends, well expressing its tone in the doggerel,

> For if the king like not the comedy,
> Why then, belike,—he likes it not, perdy.
>
> (III, ii, 280-1)

To the courtier's request, that he will put his 'discourse into some frame', he rejoins, 'I am tame, sir: pronounce'. He affects a display of politeness, but the 'courtesy is not of the right breed'. To the entreaty to give 'a wholesome answer' to the Queen's message, he affords an indication that some at least of his wildness is also not of the right breed, since he appeals to it as a reality. 'Make you a wholesome answer; my wit's diseased'. Of a disease, however, which leaves the wit too quick for their play. He sees through them thoroughly. To the silly-enough inquiry of Rosencrantz, 'Good my lord, what is your cause of distemper? you do surely but bar the door of your own liberty, if you deny your griefs to your friend'; he gives answer, laying bare the selfish motives of the questioner, 'Sir, I lack advancement'. Suppressing irony, he becomes for a moment serious with them: 'Why do you go about to recover the wind of me, as if you would drive me into a toil?' And then that lesson of sarcastic earnestness, to prove that he knew the breed of their friendship and solicitude for him: [Quotes III, ii, 351–60].

The veil which he deigns to put on before these mean and treacherous ephemera of the court is of the thinnest counterfeit; but with Polonius the mental antics are more pronounced, for with him he rejoices in spiteful mischief, as when the tiresome old man 'fools him to the top of his bent'. 'Do you see yonder cloud?' etc. The soliloquy immediately following fully proves how thoroughly on the surface all this flippancy is. The dread purpose is gathering to action, and the mind was never more sad than all this while, under the mask of intellectual buffoonery, for 'tis even now he

> could . . . drink hot blood,
> And do such bitter business as the day
> Would quake to look on.
>
> (III, ii, 379–81)

At this juncture the King re-appears, with his mind thoroughly made up on the point that Hamlet has in him something dangerous, if his doubts are not also solved on the point of his madness. The play which has discovered the King to Hamlet, must also have discovered his knowledge of the murder to the King. Before this time Claudius thinks his nephew's madness must be watched, and although he fears that the hatch and disclose of his melancholy will be some danger, it does not appear that he yet proposes to send him to England with purpose against his life. After the play, and before the death of Polonius, the King's apprehension is excited:

> I like him not, nor stands it safe with us
> To let his madness range.
>
> (III, iii, 1–2)

> The terms of our estate may not endure
> Hazard so dangerous as doth hourly grow
> Out of his lunacies.
>
> (III, iii, 5–7)

> We will fetters put upon this fear,
> Which now goes too free-footed.
>
> (III, iii, 25–6)

Although the King speaks to the courtiers of dispatching their commission to England forthwith, and desires them to arm to this speedy voyage, it can scarcely be that at this time he is guilty of that treacherous design on Hamlet's life which he unfolds after the death of Polonius. The agony of repentance for his past crime, so vehemently expressed in the soliloquy, 'O, my offence is rank', etc., appears scarcely consistent with the project of a new murder on his mind. The King has no inconsiderable mental endowments and moral courage, though personally he is a coward and a sottish debauchee. But, notwithstanding this personal cowardice, we must accept Hamlet's abuse of him, in contrast to the manly perfection of his father, as applying rather to his appearance, and to his deficiency in those soldier-like qualities which would command respect in a nation of warriors, than to his intellect. Although the King holds fencing, that quality of Laertes which hath plucked envy from Hamlet, 'as of the unworthiest siege'; although a plotter, 'a cut-purse of the empire and the rule', and, according to the description of his son-in-law, altogether a contemptible person, intellectually he is by no means despicable. Yet that burst of eloquent remorse seems too instinct with the longing for real repentance to have been uttered by this cowardly fratricide, who even in the act of prayer is juggling with heaven itself. We feel no pity for the scheming hypocrite, in spite of the anguish which wrings from him the cry:

> O wretched state! O bosom, black as death!
> O limed soul, that, struggling to be free,
> Art more engaged!
>
> (III, iii, 67–9)

If in that fine appreciation of mercy and of Heaven's justice in which

> There is no shuffling, there the action lies
> In his true nature; and we ourselves compell'd,
> Even to the teeth and forehead of our faults,
> To give in evidence,
>
> (III, iii, 61–4)

if these thoughts appear too just to be expressed by so foul a mouth, even as the polished wisdom of the precepts given to Laertes appears inconsistent with the senile incapacity of Polonius, we must somewhat attribute it to that lavish wealth of power and beauty which we find only in Shakespeare, who sometimes in wanton extravagance sets pearls in pinchbeck, and strews diamonds on the sanded floor, who pours nectar into the wooden cup, and feeds us with ambrosia when we should have been satisfied with bread.

It will scarcely be denied by those who have escaped that blindness of bigotry, which the intense admiration Shakespeare naturally excites in those who study him closely accounts for and excuses, that he sometimes gives to one of his personages an important speech, somewhat out of harmony with the general delineation of the character; his characters being in other parts so thoroughly natural and consistent, that he is able to do this without injury to the general effect. But when he does so, what breadth of wisdom and beauty of morality does not the discursive caprice afford!

The soliloquy of the King, a homily in thirty lines, on the mercy and justice of God, and the utter folly of hypocrisy in prayer, is followed by the speech of Hamlet, 'Now might I do it pat', etc., containing sentiments which Johnson designates as atrocious.

We are inclined to think that in writing both this speech and the King's soliloquy, Shakespeare had in mind the intention of conveying instruction on the nature and office of prayer, rather than that of developing his plot. From the King's speech we learn that the mercy of the sweet Heavens is absolutely unlimited, that the force of prayer is two-fold to bring aid and pardon, that the condition of forgiveness is a true repentance which does not shame justice by retaining the offence, and the worthlessness of word prayers. We know that the prayers of the King are hollow and unavailing, but so does not Hamlet, who is made to bear testimony to the all-sufficient efficacy of prayer, since it can save so damnable a villain as his uncle. His father has been

> Cut off even in the blossom of [his] sin,
> Unhousel'd, disappointed, unanel'd.
>
> (I, v, 76–7)

> He took my father grossly, full of bread;
> With all his crimes broad blown, as flush as May
>
> (III, iii, 80–1)

so that his audit with Heaven was likely to stand heavy with him. Villain as his uncle was,

> Bloody bawdy villain!
> Remorseless, treacherous, lecherous, kindless villain!
>
> (II, ii, 581–2)

still there was that in prayer which would fit and season him for his passage to the future life, and, if taken 'in the purging of his soul', why, 'so he goes to Heaven'.

Both of these speeches seem to have been written to impress most forcibly the efficacy of sincere and prayerful repentance. It was to the religious sentiment that the revival of play-acting was due; but when Shakespeare wrote, it had already ceased to be a common subject of theatrical representation, and (*Measure for Measure* perhaps excepted) in no other of his dramas has it been very prominently brought forward. The motive for delay assigned in this speech was certainly neither Christian nor merciful. Yet the act itself was merciful, and the more horrid bent with which Hamlet excused his inaction was but speculative. A conscience yet unsatisfied that his purposed deed was a just and righteous one, rather than a cruel thirst for the full measure of revenge, appears to have been Hamlet's real motive for delay at this period. His opportunities for assassinating the King, had he so desired, were certainly not limited to this moment, yet he forbore to use them, until his uncle's murderous treachery towards himself at length resolved him to quit accounts with his own arm. Moreover, it is the Romanist theology which is represented in this play, and its doctrines must be taken into consideration in judging of the excuse which Hamlet makes for delaying to kill the King, until 'about some act which has no relish of salvation in't'. The future state of punishment is represented as a terminable purgatory; Hamlet's father is doomed 'for a certain time' to fast in fires until his crimes are burnt and purged away. Hamlet swears by the rood, and he lays the stress of a catholic upon the incest of the Queen in becoming her husband's brother's wife. At the funeral of Ophelia it is the catholic ritual which is in abeyance. Great command has overswayed *the order* of priory or abbey, where the funeral is taking place. The priest says 'her death was doubtful'; and,

> We should profane the service of the dead
> To sing a *requiem* and such rest to her
> As to peace-parted souls.
>
> (V, i, 231–3)

In this passage the Romanist idea is for the third time produced, that the soul's future depends upon the mode of leaving this life, rather than upon the manner in which this life has been spent.

In the interview with his mother, the idea of Hamlet's profound affection for her has been most skilfully conveyed in the painful effort with which he endeavours to make her conscious of her position, to set before her a glass where she may see her inmost part, to speak daggers to her, to be cruel, but not unnatural. From the speech,

> A bloody deed! almost as bad, good mother,
> As kill a king, and marry with his brother,
>
> (III, iii, 27–8)

it would appear that he entertained some suspicions of his mother's complicity in the murder of his father, and that these words were tentative to ascertain whether her conscience was sore on that side. From what follows we must suppose suspicion allayed. The readiness with which Hamlet sizes the opportunity to strike the blow which kills Polonius, under the belief that he strikes the King, is of a piece with a character too meditative to frame and follow a course of action, yet sometimes sudden and rash in action when the opportunity presents itself. The rapid action with which he utilizes the players, with which he circumvents his treacherous schoolfellows, with which he at last kills the King, resembles the quick blow which sends to his account 'the wretched, rash, intruding fool', whom he mistakes for his betters. So long as resolution can be 'sicklied o'er with the pale cast of thought', so long as time is allowed for any scruple to be listened to, he thinks too precisely on the event, and lives to say the thing's to do. But let the opportunity of action present itself, and he is quick to seize it, as he would have been dilatory in seeking it. It is the meditative, inactive man, who often seizes opportunities for action, or what he takes for such, with the greatest eagerness. Unable to form and follow a deliberate course of action, he is too ready to lend his hand to circumstances, as they arise without his intervention. Sometimes he fails miserably, as in the death of Polonius; sometimes he succeeds, as when he finds occasion to praise that rashness, which too often stands him in the place of steady purpose.

> Rashly,
> And praised be rashness for it, let us know,
> Our indiscretion sometimes serves us well,
> When our deep plots do pall; and that should teach us
> There's a divinity that shapes our ends,
> Rough-hew them how we will.
>
> (V, ii, 6–11)

The comments of Hamlet upon the death of Polonius, if they had been calmly spoken by a man holding the even tenor of his way through life, would have deserved the moralist's reprobation quite as much as his speech over the praying King. To us they tell of that groundwork of unsound emotion upon which the almost superhuman intellectual activity of the character is founded. In Hamlet's life-weary, melancholy state, with his attention fixed elsewhere, such an event as the death of Polonius would have had a very different effect to that which it would have had upon so sensitive and noble a mind, if its condition were healthy. His attention at the time is concentrated upon one train of ideas, his feelings are preoccupied, his sympathies somewhat indurated to the sufferings of others, and his comments upon them are likely, therefore, to appear unfeeling.

The Queen indeed, with affectionate invention, represents to the King the very opposite view. She says 'he weeps for what he's done'; his natural grief shewing itself pure in his very madness, like a precious ore in a base mineral. It is, however, not thus that Hamlet is represented 'to draw toward an end' with the father of his mistress, and to deposit 'the carrion'.

The ideas which almost exclude from Hamlet's thoughts the wrong he has done Polonius now become expressed with a vehemence inconsistent with sound mind. The manner in which he dallies with the idea of his mother's incest, using images of the grossest kind—the blighting comparison of that mildewed ear, his uncle, with his warrior father—the vehement denunciation of his uncle—'a murderer and a villain, a slave', 'a vice of kings, a cutpurse of the empire and the rule', 'a king of shreds and patches', 'a toad', 'a bat, a gib'—all this verifies his own sneer on himself, that while he cannot act he can curse 'like a very drab'. Although he succeeds in his purpose of turning the Queen's eyes into her very soul, and shewing black and grained spots there, it must be admitted that this excessive vehemence is not merely so much out of the belt of rule as might be justified by the circumstances, but that it indicates a morbid state of emotion; and never does Hamlet appear less sane than when he is declaring

> That I essentially am not in madness,
> But mad in craft.
>
> (III, iv, 171–2)

Hamlet's behaviour in the second Ghost scene is more excited and terrified than in the former one. The apparition comes upon him when in a less firm and prepared mood. The first interview is expected, and each petty artery is knit to hardihood. The second is wholly unexpected, and comes upon him at a time when his mind is wrought to passionate excitement; and it is far easier for the mind to pass from one state of emotional excitement to the opposite, than from a state of self-possessed tranquillity to one of excitement. It is thus with Hamlet's rapid transition from the passionate vehemence, with which he is describing his uncle's crimes and qualities, to the ecstasy of fear, which seizes him when his father's shade once more stands before him. The sting of conscience also adds force to the emotion of awe. He has neglected the dread command, the sacred behest, of the buried majesty of Denmark. With unworthy doubts and laggard procrastination, his purpose has become almost blunted. His doubts, however, have now vanished; he no longer entertains the thought that 'the spirit he has seen may be the devil'; he no longer questions whether it is 'a spirit of health, or goblin damned'; but accepts the appearance implicitly as the gracious figure of his father. Since the first appearance of the unearthly visitant he has caught the conscience of the fratricide King, and unkennelled the dark secret of his guilt; therefore it is that at this second visitation the feeling of awe is unmixed with doubt and that touch of defiance which is so perceptible on the former one. Since then, moreover, his nerves have been rudely shaken; he has lived in the torture of extreme anxiety and profound grief, and the same cause naturally produces upon him a greater effect. Even while he is vehemently railing at the criminal whom he had been called upon to punish, the Ghost appears. [Quotes III, iv, 106–15, 128–40.] It is in this agony of awe that he calls upon the heavenly guards to save and protect him, that his eyes wildly indicate alarm, that his bedded hairs stand on end, that the heat and flame of his distemper appear to lack all patience. It is in this agony of awe that he feels himself so unnerved, that he entreats his father not to look upon him, lest he should be thus rendered incapable of all action, and only live to weep. During the brief space of the Ghost's second appearance, Hamlet's extremity of fear can scarcely be overrated. Still it is the sentiment of awe, not of that horror which petrifies Macbeth in the banquet scene. Moreover, in Hamlet the reaction tends to tears, in Macbeth it is to rage.

There is something exquisitely touching in the regard which the poor Ghost shews towards the frail partner of his earthly state. The former injunction

> Taint not thy mind, nor let thy soul contrive
> Against thy mother aught
>
> (I, v, 85–6)

had scarcely been obeyed; and now the entreaty

> O, step between her and her fighting soul
>
> (III, v, 103)

is a fine touch of the warrior's heart, whose rough and simple silhouette is thrown upon the page in those two lines of unsurpassable descriptive terseness,

> So frowned he once, when in an angry parle
> He smote the sledded Polack on the ice.
>
> (I, i, 61–2)

The Ghost, indeed, is a character as never ghost was before. So far from being a neutral *it*, a *thing*, the buried majesty of Denmark is now highly personal in his simple Sclavonic majesty. Though he instigates revenge in the old viking, rather than in the Christian spirit, though he protests against the luxury and damned incest which defiles his royal bed, yet is he nobly pitiful to the wretched woman through whose frailty the transgression arises; and it is worthy of remark that after the intercession of the Ghost, Hamlet's manner to his mother entirely changes. In his former reference to the incest he makes her a full partner of the crime. In his subsequent one he represents the King as the tempter, and supposes her future conduct as that of 'a queen fair, sober, wise'; and to the end he gives her his affection and confidence.

That the apparition is not an hallucination, as the Queen thought, a bodiless creation caused by the diseased brain, is known to Hamlet and the reader of the play by its previous appearance, and by its reference to the disclosure then made. Its use of speech distinguishes it from the silent ghost of Banquo. It seems an error to put the Ghost on the stage clad in armour on this second occasion.

> My father, in his *habit* as he lived!

indicates that this time the design of the poet was to represent the dead king in the weeds of peace. The quarto edition, indeed, gives as a stage direction, 'Enter the Ghost, in his night-gown'. The appearance in this form would be suited to the place, even as the *cap-à-pie* armament to the place of warlike guard. Unlike the appearance on the battery, which is seen by all who were present, on this occasion it is only visible to Hamlet, and invisible to his mother. Ghosts were supposed to have the power to make themselves visible and invisible to whom they chose; and the dramatic effect of the Queen's surprise at Hamlet's behaviour was well worth the poetic exercise of this privilege. The Queen, indeed, must have been thoroughly convinced of her son's madness, in despite of his own disclaimer, and of the remorseless energy with which he wrings her own remorseful heart. Her exclamation, 'Alas, he's mad!' is thoroughly sincere; and though her assurance that she has 'no life to breathe' the secret that he is 'but mad in craft' seems to imply her assent to the fact, Hamlet's language and demeanour are certainly not such as are calculated to convince her of the truth of this avowal. She is therefore likely to have spoken not falsely, but according to her convictions, when she immediately afterwards says that her son is

> Mad as the sea and wind, when both contend
> Which is the mightier.
>
> (IV, i, 6–7)

The Queen in this ghost scene, and Lady Macbeth in the banquet scene, are placed in very similar circumstances. They both refer the appearances, by which the son of the one and the husband of the other are so terribly moved, to a morbid state of the brain; they both, but in very different degrees, are endeavouring to conceal remorse. But the Danish Queen is affrighted at the behaviour of her son; the Scottish Queen, incapable of fear, is mainly anxious about the effect which her husband's conduct will have upon the bystanders. The one gives free expression to her alarm,—she allows amazement to sit visible in her expression and attitude; the other, firm and self-possessed, is the ruling spirit of the hour. The one is a middle-aged voluptuary who, incestuously married to a drunkard of degraded appearance, has feelings so little refined that, until her son holds up the mirror to her soul, she is barely sensible of her own shameless position; the other, a great criminal, is as self-conscious as she is outwardly confident. The one is animated by the spirit of Belial, the other with that of Satan.

Hamlet finds that his assumed madness, which he puts on and off rather capriciously, is likely to become an impediment to a right understanding with his mother. He sees her ready to deny the reality of her own trespass, because it is mirrored to her with the demeanour and, in some sort, with the words of ecstacy. He therefore offers as tests of his sanity, that his pulse is temperate, that his attention is under command, and his memory faithful; tests which we are bound to pronounce about as fallacious as could well be offered, and which could only apply to febrile delirium and mania. The pulse in mania averages about fifteen beats above that of health; that of the insane generally, including maniacs, only averages nine beats above the healthy standard: the pulse of melancholia and monomania is not above the average. That a maniac would gambol from reproducing in the same words any statement he had made, is true enough in the acute forms of the disease; but it is not so in numberless instances of chronic mania, nor in melancholia or partial insanity. The dramatic representations which are in vogue in some asylums prove the power of attention and memory preserved by many patients; indeed, the possessor of the most brilliant memory we ever met with was a violent and mischievous maniac. He would quote page after page from the Greek, Latin, and French classics. The *Iliad*, and the best plays of Molière in particular, he seemed to have at his fingers' ends. In raving madness, however, the two symptoms referred to by Hamlet are as a rule present. The pulse is accelerated, and the attention is so distracted by thick-flowing fancies, that an account can scarcely be given of the same matter in the same words. It is, therefore, to this form alone that the test of verbal memory applies.

The death of 'the unseen good old man' Polonius, which Hamlet in his 'lawless fit' and 'brainish apprehension' had effected, adds to the alarm of the King, already excited by the 'pranks too broad to bear with' of the play. The courtiers and the Queen do not seem to have inquired how it was that the King was so marvellously distempered with choler, wherefore he became so much offended with the catastrophe of the play. Like good courtiers, they accept his humour unquestioning. Now, however, the King has a good presentable excuse for alarm. [Quotes King's speech, IV, i, 11–22.] From which it appears that the all-observing eye of the poet had noted the custom of the world to conceal the occurrence of insanity within the family circle, a custom which still prevails, and from which much evil is wrought. To keep secret the existence of this dreaded malady, the relatives of an insane person oftentimes postpone all effectual treatment until the time of its usefulness is past; and they forego measures of security until some terrible calamity results. Accepting the ignorant and wicked opinion that disease of the brain is disgraceful, they give grounds to others for holding this opinion, by the sacrifices they are willing to make that the existence of insanity in the family may be concealed. They not only sacrifice to this the safety of the public, but that of the patient himself, with his present comfort and the probable means of restoration. From motives variously compounded of selfishness and ignorance, they ignore the two great principles in the successful treatment of insanity, that it must be early, and that it must be conducted in scenes remote from those influences in which it has its origin. Under a real or assumed regard for the feelings of the unhappy patients, they retain them at homes which may once have been happy, but which have now become places of moral torture, where every look inflicts a wound, every word probes a sore. When the patient is removed to fresh scenes, and to that skilfully arranged repose of the excited mental functions, which is provided for in a judicious system of treatment, the misery inflicted by the disease abates, even as the anguish of a broken limb is allayed by simple rest and well-arranged position.

In the following scene with Rosencrantz, Guildenstern, and the King, Hamlet is again in his most antic disposition of mind. His sarcastic irony to his two old schoolfellows, whom he now trusts as he would adders fanged, is more directly insulting than before. They are sponges that soak up the King's countenance, the ape's first morsel, first mouthed, last swallowed. Still he throws a thicker cloak of counterfeit unreason over his sarcasm than he has done before. He replies,

> The body is with the king, but the king is not with the body. The king is a thing— . . . of nothing: bring me to him. Hide fox, and all after
>
> (IV, ii, 26–7, 29–30)

his answers to the King, 'Farewell, dear mother', 'My mother: father and mother is man and wife; man and wife is one flesh; and so, my mother'—are fairly on a par in unreasoning suggestiveness with his reply to Polonius, 'For if the sun breed maggots', etc. These mad absurdities are never altogether meaningless, and never altogether foreign to the natural train of his own thoughts. The description of Polonius at supper, 'not where he eats, but where he is eaten', is the foreshadowing idea of the earnest meditations on the mutability of matter in which he afterwards indulges over the churchyard skulls. 'A man may fish with a worm that hath eat of a king; and eat of the fish that hath fed of that worm'. And thus, 'A king may go a progress' etc. 'Tis the very same speculation as that so seriously expressed to his friend:

> To what base uses we may return, Horatio! Why may not imagination trace the noble dust of Alexander, till he find it stopping a bung-hole?
>
> (V, i, 198–200)

This is the philosophy he had learnt at Wittenburg, and which he toyed with to the last. He had learned, indeed, its inadequacy to explain all things by immaterial evidence, sights which make

> us fools of nature
> So horribly to shake our disposition
> With thoughts beyond the reaches of our souls.
>
> (I, iv, 35–7)

He had been compelled to acknowledge that there 'are more things in heaven and earth than are dreamt of' in this philosophy. Still this form of speculation was the habit of the mind, and whether in antic disposition of madness, or in earnest converse with his friend, it is found his frequent topic. Might not this habit of dwelling upon the material laws to which our flesh is subject, have been resorted to as a kind of antidote to those 'thoughts beyond the reaches of the soul' to which his father's apparition had given rise,—his father, 'whose bones had burst their cerements', whose sepulchre had oped its ponderous jaws to cast him up again. Was not this materialist speculation a struggle against these thoughts, and akin to the unconscious protest against the Ghost, that beyond the grave is

> The undiscover'd country, from whose bourn
> No traveller returns.
>
> (III, i, 81–2)

Alas for Hamlet! What with his materialist philosophy and his spiritual experiences, there was contention enough in that region of the intellect which abuts upon veneration, to unhinge the soundest judgment; let alone the grief, and shame, and just anger, of which his uncle's crimes and his mother's frailty were the more than sufficient cause in so sensitive a mind.

In the following scene with the captain of the army of Fortinbras, we have a comment upon the folly of useless war, and an occasion for another fine motive-weighing soliloquy; like the prayer scene, useless indeed to the progress of the piece, but exquisite in itself. Never does Shakespeare seem to have found a character so suited to give noble utterance to his own most profound meditations as in Hamlet. It is on this account that we unconsciously personify Shakespeare in this character, as we personify Byron in Childe Harold, or Sterne in Yorick, and, may we not add, Goethe in Faust.

The soliloquy 'How all things do inform against me' marks a state of inclination to act, in advance of that manifested in the soliloquy beginning 'Oh what a rogue and peasant slave am I!' but still not screwed up to the point of resolve. The gross example of soldiers, who 'for a fantasy and trick of fame' are so lavish of life and limb, places before Hamlet in the strongest light his own craven scruples, and, as he chooses to say, his apprehension of results. But on this point he does not do himself justice. His personal courage is of the most undaunted temper. In his first interview with the Ghost he does not set his 'life at a pin's fee'; and the independent evidence of Fortinbras testifies to his high promise as a soldier. It is not the lack of courage, but the inability to carry the excitements of his reason and his blood into an act so repugnant to his nature as the assassination of his uncle, that yet withholds his hand; and although he concludes,

> O, from this time forth
> My thoughts be bloody, or be nothing worth!
> (Q2 IV, iv, 56–7, Additional passage J)

he leaves his purpose unfulfilled, and allows himself to be sent out of the country—a proceeding likely to postpone his revenge indefinitely, or to defeat it altogether; and it is not until he discovers the King's villainous plot against his own life, that he determines to 'quit him with this arm'.

The colloquy with the grave-digger and Horatio in the churchyard affords abundant proof that the biting satire and quaintness of thought, which have been accepted as the antic garb of Hamlet's mind, are quite natural to him when he is playing no part. The opening observation on the influence of custom is a favourite theme with him. When he wishes to wring his mother's heart, he is apprehensive whether

> damned custom have not brass'd it so
> That it is proof and bulwark against sense.
> (III, iv, 36–67)

And when he dissuades her from her incestuous intercourse, he says,

> That monster, custom, who all sense doth eat,
> Of habits devil, is angel yet in this,

> That to the use of actions fair and good
> He likewise gives a frock or livery,
> That aptly is put on....
> For use almost can change the stamp of nature,
> And either curb the devil, or throw him out
> With wondrous potency.
> (Q2 III, iv, 152–6, 159–61, Additional passage G)

Custom, therefore, brazes the heart in vice; custom fortifies the body in habits of virtue; it also blunts the sensibilities of the mind; so that gravemaking becomes 'a property of easiness'.

> 'Tis even so: the hand of little employment hath the daintier sense.
> (V, i, 69–70)

This, however, is but half truth. The 'hand of little employment' hath not always 'the daintier sense' in use. Does custom blunt the fingers of a watchmaker, the eyes of a printer, or the auditory nerve of a musician? Did the grave-digger do his own sombre work with less skill because he had been accustomed to it for thirty years? Custom blunts our sensations to those impressions which we do not attend to, and sharpens them to those which we do. Custom in Hamlet himself had sharpened the speculative faculties which he exercised, while it had dulled the active powers which depend upon that resolution which he did not practice.

Hamlet's comments upon the skulls,—upon the politicians, who could circumvent God,—on the courtiers, who praised my lord Such-a-one's horse when he meant to beg it,—on the lawyers, whose fine of fines is to have his fine pate full of fine dirt, and whose vouchers vouch him for no more of his purchases than the length and breadth of a pair of indentures,—are the quaint prosaic expression of his melancholy, his gloomy view of the nothingness of life, combined with his peculiar speculations upon death as the mere corruption of the body. He revolts at the idea of this ignoble life, as he thinks it, ending in annihilation, and he equally recoils at the idea that it may end in bad dreams. He thinks that if death is an eternal sleep, such an end of the ills of life is a consummation devoutly to be wished, but the fear that it is an eternal dream is unendurable. His fancy is too active to permit him to rush into an eternity of unknown consciousness. Like Prince Henry, in the *Spanish Student*[13], he feels,

> Rest! rest! O give me rest and peace!
> The thought of life that ne'er shall cease
> Has something in it like despair,
> A weight I am too weak to bear.[14]

To return to his mother earth an unconscious clod seems his most earnest hope; yet when the offensive *débris* of mortality meets his eyes, such an ignoble termination of mental activity revolts both his sensibility and his reason. 'Here's a fine revolution, if one had the trick to see't'. His bones ache to think on't. When he sees the skull of his old friend the jester, from whose companionship he may have derived much of his own skill in word-fence and poignancy of wit, his imagination is absolutely disgusted. [Quotes Hamlet's speech beginning 'Alas, poor Yorick'! V, i, 180–90.] The grave-digger's jest that Hamlet's madness will not matter in England, since "twill not be seen in him: there the men are as mad as he', is legitimate enough in the mouth of a foreigner, since for ages have the continentals jested upon the mad English, who hang themselves by scores every day, and who, in November especially, immolate themselves in hecatombs to the dun goddess of spleen. By this time the jest has somewhat lost its point. At least, it may be said that if the English furnish as many madmen as their neighbours, they are somewhat better acquainted with the means of ameliorating their sad condition. Madness, however, and suicide are now known to be as prevalent in the great neighbour nation, whose writers jest upon the universal diffusion of the curse.

All men are mad, writes Boileau, the grand distinction among them being the amount of skill employed in concealing the crack: and if statistics prove anything with regard to suicides, it is that our once volatile neighbours have an unhappy advantage over us in that respect, both in numbers and variety. If it was ever a habit with us, it has now become a fashion with them.

---

13   Actually from a different work by Longfellow: *The Golden Legend*, I, 41–4.
14   From Henry Wadsworth Longfellow's *The Golden Legend*, I, 41–4.

The funeral of Ophelia, and the bravery of her brother's grief, are the occasion of conduct in Hamlet which cannot be considered either that of a reasonable man or of a counterfeit madman. He acknowledges to his friend that he forgot himself, and that he was in a towering passion. The more probable explanation is, that the shock of Ophelia's death, made known to him so suddenly, strangely, and painfully, gave rise to an outburst of passionate excitement referrable to the latent unsoundness of his mind, and that the Queen's explanation of his conduct is the true one:

> This is mere madness:
> And thus awhile the fit will work on him;
> Anon, as patient as the female dove,
> When that her golden couplets are disclosed,
> His silence will sit drooping.
>
> (V, i, 281–5)[15]

It indeed looks like madness; for why should a brother's phrase of sorrow over the grave of a sister, however exaggerated its expression, excite a sane lover to such rage,—the rage of passion, not of grief. A sane man would have been struck dumb by overwhelming grief, if he had thus accidentally met at the verge of the tomb the body of a mistress whom he devotedly loved, and whose stinted ritual betokened that with desperate hand she had foredone her own life. In Hamlet's state of mind the occurrence gives birth to rash conduct and vehement passion; passion, be it remarked, not caused by the struggle in the grave, but by the bravery of the brother's grief.

Although after this scene Hamlet converses with thorough calmness with his self-possessed friend, there are passages which strongly indicate the morbid state of his mind. Speaking of his condition on shipboard, he says:

> Sir, in my heart there was a kind of fighting,
> That would not let me sleep: methought I lay
> Worse than the mutines in the bilboes.
>
> (V, ii, 4–6)

And again, referring to his present feelings, he says: 'Thou wouldst not

---

15 Q2 assigns this speech to Gertrude, the Folio to Claudius.

think how ill all's here about my heart; but it's no matter'. 'It is but foolery; but it is such a kind of gain-giving as would, perhaps, trouble a woman' (V, ii, 158–9, 161–2).

Above all, if his conduct in the churchyard is not the result of morbidly violent emotion, uncontrolled by reason, what can we say of his own explanation: [Quotes Hamlet's apology to Laertes, V, ii, 172–90]. Except the above brief reference to the inner wretchedness, which Horatio takes for an evil augury, Hamlet shews no disposition to melancholy after the rough incidents of his sea voyage. The practice of the King upon his life appears to have fixed his resolve: He'll wait till no further evil is hatched. He that hath

> Thrown out his angle for my proper life,
> And with such cozenage; is't not perfect conscience
> To quit him with this arm? and is't not to be damn'd
> To let this canker of our nature come
> In further evil?
>
> (V, ii, 67–71)

Moreover, what there is to do he'll do quickly. The issue of the business in England, with Rosencrantz and Guildenstern, will quickly be known, but

> the interim is mine;
> And a man's life no more than to say, one.
>
> (V, ii, 74–5)

In this temper it would have been frivolous in him to have accepted the challenge of Laertes, were it not that he saw in it an opportunity to right himself with his old friend, by the image of whose cause he read the portraiture of his own. It is after a seeming reconciliation thus obtained, that he determines to accept 'this brother's wager'. Might not also the challenge be accepted as likely to offer a good opportunity to meet the King, and 'quit him with this arm', an opportunity which he now resolves to seize whenever it offers? The sentiment of coming evil lends probability to the thought.

> Not a whit, we defy augury: there's a special providence in the fall of a sparrow.
> If it be now, 'tis not to come; if it be not to come, it will be now: if it be not now,

yet it will come: the readiness is all: since no man has aught of what he leaves, what is't to leave betimes?

(V, ii, 165–70)

The final scene of indiscriminate slaughter, which, as Fortinbras says, would more become a battle-field than a palace, points the moral so obvious throughout the piece, that the end of action is not within the hands of the human agents. The blow which finally quits the King was fully deserved for his last act. His end has an accidental suddenness about it, which disappoints the expectation of judicial revenge. Like Laertes, he is a woodcock caught in his own springe. Retribution is left to the terrible future, whose mysteries have been partially unveiled; and the mind, prepared by the revelations of the Ghost, accepts the death of the King but as the beginning of his quittance.

The death of Hamlet has been objected to as cruel and needless; but would it not rather have been cruel to have left him alive in this harsh world, drawing his breath in pain? Heart-broken, and in that half-mad state which is vastly more painful than developed insanity, what could he do here, after the one act for which he was bound to live had been accomplished. Had he survived he must have sank into inert motiveless melancholy, or have struggled on in the still more painful state of contention between conscience and suicidal desire. To prevent a wounded name being left behind him, he can command his friend to 'absent him from felicity awhile'; but for himself the best is the dark mantle of oblivion, the rest with hope which his friend so gracefully expresses:

> Now cracks a noble heart. Good night, sweet prince;
> And flights of angels sing thee to thy rest!

There is no attempted poetical justice in this bloody finale to the drama. The way of the world rather is followed in the indiscriminate mischief. Sweet Ophelia and noble Hamlet meet the same fate which attends the incestuous Queen, the villainous King, the passionate Laertes, and the well-meaning Polonius. The vortex of crime draws down the innocent and the guilty, the balance of desert being left for adjustment in the dark future. The intricacy of the action and the unexpected nature of the events are copied from life as closely as that marvellous delineation of motive and feeling which brings Hamlet so intimately home to the consciousness of reflective men. Those dramas in which we accurately foresee the event in the first act are as little like the reality of human life as a geometric problem is like a landscape. Granted that there is nothing like accident in human affairs, that if a special providence in the fall of a sparrow may be doubted, the subjection of the most trivial circumstances to general laws is beyond question; still, in human affairs the multiplicity and mutual interference of these laws are such, that it is utterly beyond human foresight to trace forward the thread of events with any certainty. In Hamlet this uncertainty is peculiarly manifested. Everything is traceable to causes, which operate, however, in a manner which the most astute forecaster of events could never have anticipated; though, after their occurrence, it is easy enough to trace and name them, as Horatio promised to do.

> So shall you hear
> Of carnal, bloody, and unnatural acts,
> Of accidental judgments, casual slaughters,
> Of deaths put on by cunning and forced cause,
> And, in this upshot, purposes mistook
> Fall'n on the inventors' heads: all this can I
> Truly deliver.
>
> (V, ii, 334–40)

Although we arrive at the conviction that Hamlet is morbidly melancholic, and that the degree to which he puts on a part is not very great; that, by eliminating a few hurling words, and the description which Ophelia gives of the state of his stockings, there is little either in his speech or conduct which is truly feigned; let us guard ourselves from conveying the erroneous impression that he is a veritable lunatic. He is a reasoning melancholiac, morbidly changed from his former state of thought, feeling, and conduct. He has 'foregone all custom of exercise', and longs to commit suicide, but dares not. Yet, like the melancholiacs described by Burton, he is 'of profound judgment in some things, excellent apprehensions, judicious, wise, and witty; for melancholy advanceth men's conceits more than any humour whatever'. He is in a state which thousands pass through without becoming truly insane, but which in hundreds does pass into actual madness. It is the state of incubation of disease, 'in which his melancholy sits on brood', and which, according to the turn of events or the constitution of the brain, may hatch insanity, or terminate in restored health.

There is an apparent inconsistency between the sombre melancholy of Hamlet's solitary thoughts and the jesting levity of his conversation, even when he seeks least to put on the guise of antic behaviour; an inconsistency apparent only, for in truth this gloomy reverie, which in solitude 'runs darkling down the stream of fate', is thoroughly coherent in nature with the careless mocking spirit playing in derisive contempt with the foibles of others. The weeping and the mocking philosopher are not usually divided as of old, but are united in one, whose laugh is bestowed on the vanity of human wishes as observed in the world around, while the earnest tear is reserved for the deeply felt miseries of his own destiny. The historian of melancholy himself was a philosopher of this complexion. Deeply imbued with melancholy when his mental gaze was introverted, when employed upon others it was more mocking than serious, more minute than profound. Thence came the charming and learned gossip of the *Anatomy*; thence also the curious habit recorded of him, that for days together he would sit on a post by the river-side, listening and laughing at the oaths and jeers of the boatmen, and thus finding a strange solace for his own profound melancholy. Here is his own evidence:

> Humorous they (melancholiacs) are beyond measure; sometimes profusely laughing, extraordinary merry, and then again weeping without a cause . . . ; groaning, sighing, pensive, sad, almost distracted, . . . restless in their thoughts and actions, continually meditating.
> *Velut aegri somnia, vanae*
> *Finguntur species;*
> more like dreamers than men awake, they feign a company of antick fantastical conceits[16].

There is an intimate relationship between melancholy and humour. The fact is finely touched in the Yorick of Lawrence Sterne, and, what is more to the purpose, in the real history of many of the most celebrated humourists; and the truth even descends to those humourists of action,

---

16   Robert Burton, *The Anatomy of Melancholy*, 3 vols (London: Dent, 1932), i, 393–4. (I, iii, 1, 2)

theatrical clowns. Who has not heard the story of one of the most celebrated of these applying incognito to a physician for the relief of melancholy, and being referred for a remedy to his own laughter-moving antics? Not that humour is always attended by any tinge or tendency to melancholy, as the plenitude of this faculty exhibited by jolly Sir John fully proves. Still there is this in common to the roystering humour of Falstaff, the melancholy humour of Jacques, and the sarcastic humour of Hamlet, that they have each a perverse ingenuity in contemplating the weakness and selfishness of human motive. Wit deals with ideas and their verbal representations; humour with motives and emotions; and that melancholy cast of thought, which tends to exhibit our own motives in an unfavourable light, is apt to probe the motives of others with searching insight, and to represent them in those unexpected contrasts and those true but unusual colours which tickle the intelligence with their novelty and strangeness.

The character of Hamlet presents another contrast, which, if not more obvious than the above, has at least attracted more attention, perhaps because he himself comments upon it, and because it is a main point upon which the drama turns. It is the contrast between his vivid intellectual activity, and the inertness of his conduct. To say that this depends upon a want of the power of will to transmute thought into action, is to do no more than to change one formula of words into another. There must be some better explanation for the unquestionable fact that one man of great intellectual vigour becomes a thinker only, and another a man of vehement action. That activity of intellect is in itself adverse to decisiveness of conduct, is abundantly contradicted by biography. That activity of intellect may exist with the utmost powerlessness, or even perversity of conduct, is equally proved by the well-known biographies of many men, 'who never said a foolish thing, and never did a wise one'. The essential difference of men who are content to rest in thought, and those who transmute it into action, appears not to consist in the presence or absence of that incomprehensible function, that unknown quantity of the mind, the *will*; but in the presence or absence of clearly-defined and strongly-felt *desire*, and in that power of movement which can only be derived from the exercise of power, that is, from the habit of action. It is conceivable, as Sir James Mackintosh has well pointed out, that an intellectual being might exist examining all things, comparing all things, knowing all things, but desiring and doing nothing. It is equally conceivable that a being might exist with two strong desires, so equally poised that the result should be complete neutralization of each other, and a state of inaction as if no emotional spring to conduct whatever existed. Hence, inaction may arise from want of desire, or from equipoise of desire.

It is, moreover, conceivable that an intellectual being might exist, in whom desires were neither absent nor equipoised, but in whom the habit of putting desires into action had never been formed. We are indeed so constituted, that clearly-formed desires tend naturally to transmute themselves into action, and the idea of a being at once intellectual and emotional, in whom circumstances have entirely prevented the development of the habit of action, has more the character of metaphysical speculation than of a possible reality. Still the immense influence of habit upon the power of action is unquestionable, and the want of this habit appears to have been one chief cause of Hamlet's inert and dilatory conduct, and of the contention between that meditative cast of thought which he in vain strove to screw up to the point of action, and the desire to discharge that repulsive duty which his uncle's villainies had laid upon him. That the time was out of joint would have been for him a subject of painful reflection only, but for the accursed spite which had laid it upon him to set it right, and which was the cause of that fierce moral strife between duty and disposition which forms the innermost web of the piece. The rash execution of an unpremeditated action is entirely consistent with this sensitive motive-weighing inability to act upon mature resolve. The least resolute men are often the most rash; as quick spasm in feeble muscles is substituted for healthy, regular, and prolonged exertion. Hamlet praises rashness in the instance in which it served him, but he would scarcely have been able to have done so when it led him to slay Polonius in mistake for the King; and the incidents of the drama, no more than the incidents of real life, justify us in rough-hewing our purposes with rashness, though the Divinity may shape the ends even of our most politic arrangements.

This reasoning melancholiac, disgusted with the world, and especially disgusted with the repulsive duty which a hard fate has laid upon him, is not less different to the Hamlet of the past, to him who had been

> The expectancy and rose of the fair state,

to him who, as a soldier,

> was likely, had he been put on,
> To have proved most royally,

than he is the good feeble young gentleman whom Goethe describes, and whose 'mind is too feeble for the accomplishment' of 'the great action imposed as a duty'[17]. 'Here is an oak planted in a vase; proper only to receive the most delicate flowers. The roots strike out, the vessel flies to pieces. A pure, noble, highly moral disposition, but without that energy of soul which constitutes a hero, sinks under a load which it can neither support nor abandon altogether'. 'Observe how he shifts, hesitates, advances, and recedes!' Goethe's simile, however, beautiful though it be, appears to halt on both feet, for the great action, which is the oak, does not strike out its roots, does not increase in magnitude or responsibility; nor does the Prince deserve to be compared to a vase, senseless and inert, which cannot expand or 'shift'; and, moreover, it is not the greatness of the action which is above the energy of his soul, but the nature of it which is repulsive to its nobility. If Hamlet must be compared to a vase, let it not be to a flower-pot, but to that kingly drinking-cup, whose property it was to fly to pieces when poison was poured into it.

In addition to the above, there are other causes of turmoil in Hamlet's mind less plainly stated, but traceable enough throughout the piece. One of these is the contention between his religious sentiments and his sceptical philosophy. His mind constantly wavers between belief and unbelief; between confidence in an overruling Providence, who shapes all our ends to wise purposes, and even permits its angels and ministers of grace to attend unseen on our hours of trial; between this reverential faith and that scepticism which sees in man but so much animated dust, and looks upon death as annihilation. The pain of this same doubt has been finely expressd by him, whom future centuries will regard as the great lyric of the nation, even as Shakespeare is for aye its great dramatist:

---

17   *Wilhelm Meister*, see *CRH*, ii, 24–5.

> I trust I have not wasted breath:
> I think we are not wholly brain,
> Magnetic mockeries; not in vain,
> Like Paul with beasts, I fought with Death:
>
> Not only cunning casts in clay:
> Let Science prove we are, and then
> What matters Science unto men—
> At least, to me? I would not stay.
>
> ... And he, shall he ...
> Who loved, who suffered countless ills,
> Who battled for the true and just,
> Be blown about the desert dust,
> Or sealed within the iron hills?[18]

Indeed, the manifold points of resemblance between *Hamlet* and *In Memoriam* are remarkable. In each the great questions of eternal interest are debated by a mind to whom profound grief makes this world a sterile promontory. The unknowable future absorbs all interest. The lyric bard, however, fights his way to more light than the dramatist attains. The fear of annihilation oppresses, but does not conquer him. He rebukes Lazarus for holding his peace on that which afflicts the doubting soul, but for himself he fights his way to faith.

> He fought his doubts, and gathered strength;
> He would not make his judgment blind;
> He faced the spectres of the mind,
> And laid them ... [19]

It is not easy to estimate the amount of emotional disturbance for which Love is answerable in Hamlet's mind. Probably, if other matters had gone well with him, Ophelia's forced unkindness would easily have been seen through and overcome; but, with a mind pre-occupied with the dread mission of his father's revenge, it is likely that he would not question

---

18   Alfred Tennyson, *In Memoriam*, st. cxx, 1–8; st. lvi, 8, 17–20.
19   *In Memoriam*, xcvi, 13–16.

the earnestness of Ophelia's rejection, and that 'to the pangs of despised love' he might well attribute one of the most poignant ills that flesh is heir to. His demeanour to Ophelia, when he first puts on his antic disposition, and which she so graphically describes, not less than his own avowal at her grave, that 'twenty thousand brothers could not make up his sum of love', point to the existence, not of 'trivial fond records', but of a passion for her both deep and constant; a passion thrust rudely into the background indeed, but not extinguished or even weakened, by the more urgent emotions of revenge for his father, of shame for his mother, of scorn and hatred for his uncle. The character of Hamlet would have been incomplete if the element of love had been forgotten in its composition. Harshly as he may seem to treat his mistress, this element adds a warm sienna tint to the portraiture, without which it would have been not only cold and hard, but less true to the nature of the melancholy sensitive being delineated.

There is little trace of ambition in his character; for, although he makes the King's having stepped between the election and his hopes one in the list of his injuries, his comments upon the manner in which this was done savour of contempt for his uncle's ignoble means of success, for the manner in which he filched the crown, and was 'a cutpurse of the empire and the rule', rather than of any profound disappointment that the election had not fallen upon himself. Indeed, this character has been painted in dimensions far exceeding those of the sceptred rulers of the earth. Ambition would have dwarfed him to the type of a class; he stands forth the mighty poetical type of the race.

It is this universal humanity of the character which lies at the root of its wonderful reality and familiarity. Hamlet seems known to us like an old friend. 'This is that Hamlet the Dane', says Hazlitt,'whom we read of in our youth, and whom we seem almost to remember in our after years.' 'Hamlet is a name: his speeches and sayings but the idle coinage of the poet's brain. What, then, are they not real? They are as real as our own thoughts. Their reality is in the reader's mind. It is *we* who are Hamlet. This play has a prophetic truth which is above that of history'[20]. Are we then wrong in treating Hamlet as a reality, and in debating the

---

20 William Hazlitt, *Characters of Shakespeare's Plays*, 1817, see *CRH*, ii, 114.

state of his mind with more care than we would choose to bestow upon the insane vagaries of an Emperor Paul or a Frederick Wilhelm? Have we not more sure data upon which to exercise judgment than upon the uncertain truth of history? Buckle, in his *History of Civilization*, has elaborately argued the madness of Burke; a domestic grief, a change of temper, and above all, a change of political opinions from those which the historian thinks true to those which he thinks false, being held sufficient to establish the confirmed insanity of the great statesman. Those who read the ingenious argument will feel convinced at least of this, that history rarely or never leaves grounds relative enough to solve such a question. Nay, when we are close upon the footsteps of a man's life, when the question is not one of learned trifling, like that of the insanity of Socrates, but the practical one of whether a man just dead was competent to devise his property, when his papers and letters are ransacked, his daily life minutely examined, when scores of men who knew him intimately bear testimony to their knowledge, we often find the balance of probability so even, that it is impossible to say to which side it inclines, and the feelings of the jury as often as not fabricate the will. But when the great mind of mind speaks out as in Hamlet, it is not so. Then it is as in the justice of Heaven, then the 'action lies in its true nature', which neither ignorance can obscure nor sophistry pervert.

It is by this great faculty that Shakespeare unfolds to our view the book of the mind, and shews alike its fairest and most blotted pages, and leaves in us a thirst not for more light, but for more power to read.

If familiarity and fellow-feeling compel us at one time to regard Hamlet as a reality, reflection and curious admiration compel us at others to wonder at it as a work of man's creative power; and it has ever been to us a question of intense interest to speculate upon the manner it was worked out. There appears this great distinction between Hamlet and all other characters of Shakespeare in which real or feigned insanity is represented, that, while they are evidently all drawn from the life, it could scarcely have been drawn from observation. Ophelia, for instance, is the very type of a class of cases by no means uncommon. Every mental physician of moderately extensive experience must have seen many Ophelias. It is a copy from nature, after the fashion of the pre-Raphaelite school, in which the veins of the leaves are painted. Hamlet however is not pre-Raphaelite, but Raphaelite; like the Transfiguration, it is a glorious reflex from the mind of the author, but not a copy of aught which may be seen by other eyes. It is drawn, indeed, in accordance with the truth of nature, just as Raphael made use of anatomical knowledge in painting the Transfiguration; but there is something beyond and above that which any external observation can supply. From whence did this come? Without doubt, from within. Shakespeare has here described a broad phase of his own mind; has reflected the depth of his own great soul; has set up a glass in which the ages will read the inmost part of him; how he thought of death and suicide; how he doubted of the future, and felt the present,

> That this huge state presenteth naught but shows[21];

how he looked inwards until fair nature became dark, and spun

> A veil of thought, to hide him from the sun.

(b) Ophelia

> Che per amor venne in furore e matto.[22]

Ophelia, so simple, so beautiful, so pitiful! The exquisite creation is so perfect, yet so delicate, that we fear to approach it with the rough touch of critical remark. Child of nature in simplicity and innocence—without guile, without suspicion—and therefore without reserve, or that deceit which often simulates a modesty more dainty than the modesty of innocence. And yet, not ignorant though innocent; but with quick native intellect, which appreciated the selfishness and rebuked the fears of her brother's caution; which still more fully appreciated, and was able most eloquently to describe the noble qualities of her princely lover, 'the glass of fashion and the mould of form'; simple, yet not obtuse; but possessing quick sentiment and lively fancy to a degree which made her most impressible to all generous emotion; sensitive, but yet reticent; thrilling through every fibre of the soul to the touch of love and the anguish of despair; yet allowing no confession to be extorted, and no cry to escape,

21 Shakespeare, Sonnet 15, 3: 'state' is Malone's emendation for 'stage'.
22 Who became possessed by love and went mad. Ariosto, *Orlando Furioso*, I, ii, 3.

until she sees her lover 'quite, quite down'; when, with unselfish grief lamenting his fall, she allies her fate with his, and cries aloud in the agony of woe—'and I of ladies most deject and wretched'. It is strange how thoroughly we seem to know Ophelia, notwithstanding her taciturnity and reserve. She says nothing of herself, and yet we seem to look into the very recesses of her clear soul; thus presenting one form of contrast to the being with whose fate her own was entwined, who constantly soliloquising and self-analysing, nevertheless leaves upon us the impression that we know the vast amplitude of his thoughts and feelings but dimly and in part. The one is the translucent and limpid fountain, reflecting but one image; the other, the ever-varying river, with rapids, and smooth reaches, and profound depths, reflecting and representing the varied features of earth and heaven.

Ophelia is passive, but not impassive; her very reticence is eloquent of feeling. Her love, like that of Imogen and Desdemona, has more of sentiment than of passion in it. It does not vent itself in strong expressions, like the passions of Juliet and Cleopatra. It is imaginative, retiring, sensitive, fearful of itself, and yet without one particle of selfishness. In this, also, it is unlike the *amour passion*, which is essentially selfish. Not that Ophelia is wholly without passion; for love without passion cannot exist, except as a mere dream. But the constituents, sentiment and passion, which are in all love, though in infinitely varying degrees, appear in Ophelia to exist in the greatest possible amount of the former, and the least of the latter.

Sensitive, and imaginative, and devoted, the poor girl was endowed with all the faculties of moral suffering. That she should suffer greatly, undeservedly, irremediably, was needful, in order to make her the object of that intense pity which the character excites, and which was certainly wanted in the drama to perfect it as a tragedy. The character is not very prominent, but it so entirely seizes upon our sympathy and pity, that, in this respect, it leavens our regard for the whole play. Ulrici has called the play a 'Gedankentrauerspiel', or, tragedy of thought[23]; as if there could be any tragic emotion excited by thought alone, whose unmodified influence is to cause assent or dissent? Yet, if the character of Ophelia

23 Ulrici attributes this description to Schlegel, see *CRH*, iii, 51.

were wanting, there would be so much justice in the epithet which this critic has applied to the drama, it would appeal so much to thoughts and opinions, and so little to sentiment, that it would be too much a drama of thought and opinion to take the rank it does in the most sacred shrine of the tragic muse.

Pity, soft-eyed mother of the virtues, ever assuaging the severe aspect of their male parent, justice; pity, most unselfish of all the emotions, although in truth but one form of self-suffering; pity, that appreciation of evil which we understand and sympathize with, and therefore suffer with or compassionate when we behold others under the weight of its affliction; pity, whose Heavenly influence it is the highest aim and object of the tragic muse to invoke, is the sentiment which the character of Ophelia more powerfully elicits than that of any other of Shakespeare's female characters. For if Imogen was at one time as wretched, her misery was changed into joy; and if Desdemona was equally innocent, her agony was more brief and less intense. The sufferings of Cordelia were alleviated by active resistance against the evil power by which they were occasioned. In Lear, the king of sorrows, and in Othello, the lion poisoned by a villain's hand, are characters which excite pity as intense, though not as unmixed; for in neither is the agony felt to be quite undeserved or quite unavoidable. For it is to be remarked, that to excite the pure sentiment of pity—First, it is needful the suffering reflected from the consciousness of another upon our own sensibility should be such as we can appreciate, and bring home as it were to ourselves:

> Haud ignara mali miseris succurrere disco[24].

Secondly, that the sufferings should be great. We do not pity the petty miseries of life; and although a man's happiness may be stung to death by poisonous insects as certainly as it can be torn by the fangs of a savage monster, we are not revolted at wounds which we cannot see. Thirdly, unmixed pity can only be excited by suffering, which is undeserved and unavoidable. When a man brings upon himself only so much suffering as he deserves to endure; or when, through wilfulness or obstinacy, he endures suffering which he can avoid, justice holds up the stern

---

24 Not lacking experience of evil, I learn to undergo wretchedness.

finger and forbids pity to interfere. But avoidability of suffering and desert of suffering are so relative and varied with circumstance, that some amount of obstinacy or demerit is readily overlooked by the tender eyes of compassion. 'Treat us all according to our merits', says Hamlet, 'and who shall escape whipping?' Feel for us all according to our merits, and who shall deserve pity?

Yet justice modifies pity, nay, sometimes forbids it—even where suffering is greatest. The agonies of hell, as they are painted on the broad canvas of Milton, do not excite pity, because they are felt to be justly endured.

Ophelia is, from the first moment of her appearance, suffering the anguish of doubt and wounded love. Unlike Desdemona and Imogen, there is no bright period of the character. There is gentle but real sorrow in her first words, 'No more but so?' Must she consider herself merely the toy of her princely lover? 'The perfume and suppliance of the minute'? Has he been trifling with her love? and his own, is it nothing but youthful lust, dishonourable to himself and dangerous to her? 'No more but so?' She does not believe it; her brother sees that she does not believe it, and he gives more credit to Hamlet's earnestness. 'Perhaps he loves you now'; but he may not marry where he chooses; he may not carve for himself; therefore it behoves poor Ophelia to exercise her wisdom where wisdom is rarely exercised, and to believe Hamlet's love only so far as the probability of an honourable marriage may justify her faith. Matchmaking probabilities, which the poor girl was far enough from being able to estimate! Laertes does not advise his sister according to the truth of the saying, that 'the woman who hesitates is lost'. He advises her to believe in Hamlet's love to a certain extent, but not to give *too* credent an ear:

> Be wary then, best safety lies in *fear*;
> Youth to itself rebels, though none else near.
>
> (I, iii, 43–4)

Polonius knows that best safety lies in *flight*; he insists upon no half measures. The not very delicate warning of Ophelia's disagreeable brother, that she is likely to lose her honour to Hamlet's unmastered importunity, is evidently distasteful to the poor girl, and gives occasion to the only sparkle of displeasure which the gentle creature ever shows, in that quick witted retaliation of advice:

> But, good my brother,
> Do not, as some ungracious pastors do,
> Show me the steep and thorny way to heaven;
> Whiles, like a puff'd and reckless libertine,
> Himself the primrose path of dalliance treads,
> And recks not his own rede.
>
> (I, iii, 46–51)

Ophelia's reference to the primrose path of dalliance which her libertine brother was likely to lead, shows from the first that her purity of mind is not the result of ignorance. She seems young and ardent—her brother fears for her honour not more on account of Hamlet's importunity, than on account of her own youth, which is likely to rebel against the dictates of prudence, though unsolicited, 'though none else near'.

What the old father has to say takes a much more decisive and straightforward form than the advice of Laertes, who feels that he is treading on tender ground, and who gets repaid by counter advice. Polonius reproaches his daughter that she has been 'most free and bounteous of her audience with Hamlet'; and he tells her downright, 'you do not understand yourself so clearly, as it behoves my daughter, and your honour'. To the demand that she should give up the truth to him, the poor frightened girl at once acknowledges Hamlet's suit, but carefully conceals the state of her own heart. [Quotes I, iii, 99–115.] A green girl, indeed; a baby in the perils of court amours, having the credulity of innocence, but not that of stupidity. A sensitive unsophisticated maiden for the first time in love, wondering at the new and strange sensation, scarcely confessing it to herself, unable to distinguish the traits of the mysterious tyrant who has set up his throne in her young heart. The father and the brother fear for her chastity; and these fears may have been well founded, for she appears the very prototype of Margaret in *Faust*, who, in the spirit of unselfish devotion, could refuse her lover nothing. But they need not have feared for her modesty, or for that precious quality in women which the cold word modesty, or moral moderation, does not express, the shamefacedness of love (*pudicitia, pudeur, Keuscheit*), at once the effect and the proof of moral purity. Had Ophelia been capable of measuring and moderating her love in accordance with the advice of her worldly brother, of yielding to Hamlet so far as the probability of the voice of the nation assenting to his marriage might justify her, her chastity might have been perfectly safe; but it is certain that the true modesty of her love would have been lost. There are such beings as brazen prudes. There are also those who have fallen and are pure. Rousseau well says, 'Le vice a beau se cacher dans l'obscurité, son empreinte est sur les fronts coupables; l'audace d'une femme est le signe assuré de sa honte; c'est pour avoir trop à rougir qu'elle ne rougit plus, et si quelquefois la pudeur survit à la chastité, que doit-on penser de la chastité quand la pudeur même est éteinte?'[25]

Between this scene and the next one in which Ophelia appears, time must have elapsed during which Hamlet has pursued his suit; since Ophelia, in obedience to her father's command, has repelled his letters and denied access. These letters would scarcely have been written by Hamlet, subsequently to his interview with the ghost and his vow to erase all trivial fond records from the table of his memory. According to the progress of the love story, therefore, the last scene of the first act would appear to belong to the second act; which would leave Hamlet's mad appearance in Ophelia's closet as the first and immediate consequence of his resolve 'to put an antick disposition on'. This it is which changes the old courtier's fear that Hamlet intended to wreck his daughter's honour, into the belief in his sincerity and consequent madness; and thus arises his regret that he had not noted him with better heed and judgment.

Ophelia's plasticity and yieldingness of character, rather than her depth of filial affection, appear manifested in the readiness with which she first obeys the old man's orders to reject Hamlet's addresses, and with which she subsequently lends herself to the deceit which is practised upon her lover, to test and demonstrate his state of mind, and especially, whether, as Polonius maintained, and the Queen finely expressed, that her 'good beauties be the happy cause of Hamlet's wildness'. The arranged meeting

---

25 Vice hides in the dark in vain, its imprint is on guilty faces; a woman's audacity is the sure sign of her shame; it is for having too much to blush for that she no longer blushes; and if sometimes modesty outlives chastity, what ought one to think of chastity when modesty itself has died?

of Hamlet and Ophelia, 'as 'twere by accident', and the pretence of the maiden to read a book as a colour to her loneliness, was a species of conduct inconsistent with her ingenuousness of character, and to which she appears to have lent herself in sorrowful unquestioning obedience. The dialogue which follows is a terrible punishment for any fault she may almost unconsciously have committed. Her lover sees the snare laid for him, and recognizes the deceitful part she is taking. She has not seen him 'for this many a day', and longs to re-deliver his remembrances formerly so precious to her, now become so poor since he has proved unkind. How much she expresses in how few words. What simplicity and faith in his love—'Indeed, my lord, you made me believe so'. What patient anguish at his denial of his love—'I was the more deceived'. What unselfish forgetfulness of her own deep sorrow, to which the word forgiveness would be misapplied, since the slightest notion of resentment never seems to have entered her gentle soul. When she recognizes in his disdainful vituperation the incoherence of insanity, she cries, 'O, help him, ye sweet heavens!'—not herself, but him. Not because she is deceived and rejected, but because he is quite, quite down, is she of ladies most deject and wretched. Not for her own blighted hopes, but because his unmatched form is blasted with ecstacy, does she raise that cry of anguish—

> O, woe is me,
> To have seen what I have seen, see what I see!
>
> (III, i, 163–4)

In the whole of the play there is not a more exquisite passage than this lamentation of the desolate maid over the supposed ruin of her lover's intellect.

Ophelia appears once more as one of the audience before the players, before her own mind is 'as sweet bells jangled out of tune'; but it is to be remarked that she never makes a consecutive speech again. To Hamlet's indelicate banter she makes the curtest replies, scarcely sufficient to defend her outraged modesty. She is concealing, and, as well as may be, bearing up against the anguish gnawing at her heart. But fancy and intellect are benumbed by sorrow, only to display themselves at a later date, again active, though perverted, under the stimulus of disease.

It is left in some doubt to what extent grief at the death of Polonius concurred, with pining sorrow at the blight of her love, in giving rise to Ophelia's distraction. The King and Queen, and Laertes, evidently refer it to the former cause; yet although in her gentle ravings she constantly refers to her father's death, and never directly to her lover's unkindness, we are inclined to consider the latter as by far the most potent, though it may, perhaps, not be the sole cause of her distraction. This opinion founds itself on the form of insanity which is depicted, namely, mania with prevalent ideas of the sentiment of love, or erotomania, as it is learnedly called. 'In medicine', says Ferriar[26], 'we have fine names at least, for every species of disease', and erotomania is the fine name for that form of insanity in which the sentiment of love is prominent, as nymphomania is the fine name for an allied but sufficiently distinct variety in which the instinct is excessive.

We have somewhere read that Ophelia's snatches of song were culled from the street ballads of the day, and that Shakespeare thus obtained an easy theatrical effect. This, however, seems probable only with reference to the two longer and more indelicate effusions beginning, 'Good morrow, 'tis St.Valentine's day', and 'By Gis and by Saint Charity'. The snatches of song which precede having reference to her own circumstances, seem impromptu, strung together at the time:

> How should I your true love know
> From another one?
> By his cockle hat and staff,
> And his sandal shoon?
>
> He is dead and gone, lady,
> He is dead and gone;
> At his head a grass-green turf,
> At his heels a stone.
>
> White his shroud as the mountain snow,
> Larded all with sweet flowers;
> Which bewept to the grave did go,
> With true-love showers.
> (IV, v, 23–6; 29–32; 35, 37–9)

---

26 John Ferriar (1761–1815), physician, author of *An Essay towards a Theory of Apparitions* (1813).

They well express the confused connection in the poor head between the death of her father and the loss of her lover; the one is foremost on her lips, but it is not difficult to see that the latter is uppermost in her thoughts. The same confusion between the two sources of her sorrow is manifested in all she says. In the lines—

> They bore him barefaced on the bier; ...
> And in his grave rain'd many a tear;—
> Fare you well my dove!—
>
> (IV, v, 165, 167–8)

the two first lines seem to go for the loss of her father—the last for her lover. The same lucid confusion and imperfect concealment are still more obvious in her distribution of flowers.

> There's rosemary, that's for remembrance; pray, love, remember: and there is pansies, that's for thoughts. There's fennel for you, and columbines: there's rue for you; and here's some for me: we may call it herb-grace o'Sundays: O, you must wear your rue with a difference. There's a daisy: I would give you some violets, but they withered all when my father died: they say he made a good end.
>
> (IV, v, 179–84)

Well might her passionate brother, softened for a moment by her grief and sweetness, exclaim—

> Thought and affliction, passion, hell itself,
> She turns to favour and to prettiness.
>
> (IV, v, 186–7)

for never was sentimental mania more truly and more exquisitely depicted than in this effusion of mad song . . .

It seems impossible that Shakespeare could have done otherwise than drawn from the life in this character. He has in truth and in deed verified the introductory observation that her mood will needs be pitied, for gentleness and goodness, struggling in the deepest affliction of which human nature is capable, have never been more finely drawn; and yet not overdrawn, for in the vivid reality of the picture there is not one touch of mawkishness. Compare, in this respect, the love-lorn maiden of Sterne, poor Maria, who allowed the stranger to wipe away the tears which trickled down her cheeks with his handkerchief, which he then steeped in his own tears, and then in hers, then in his own, until it was steeped too much to be of any further use. 'And where will you dry it, Maria?' said I. 'I will dry it in my bosom', said she, 'it will do me good[27]'. One never meets with such bathos of sentiment as this in the real insane, nor in the insane characters of the great master. Ophelia's prettinesses are as natural as they are touching. The freshness of reality encircles her head like the wild flowers with which she weaves her garlands. This fantastical dress of straws and flowers is a common habit of the insane, but it seems more natural in Ophelia than in the angry and raging madness of old Lear, in whom it is also represented. The picture of her insanity is perfected by many other touches as natural and true. She

> Spurns enviously at straws; speaks things in doubt,
> That carry but half sense.
>
> (IV, v, 6–7)

She winks, and nods, and makes gestures, which have the double effect of breeding dangerous conjectures in the minds of the people, and of delineating with exactness the habits and practices of gentle but general mania. There is no consistency in her talk, or rather, there is only the consistency of incoherence, with two prominent ideas, the loss of her lover, and her father's death.

> Well, God 'ield you! they say the owl was a baker's daughter. Lord, we know what we are, but know not what we may be. God be at your table!
>
> You must sing, *Down a-Down, an you call him a-down-a.* O, how the wheel becomes it! It is the false steward, that stole his master's daughter.
>
> (IV, v, 41–3, 171–3).

Compare this perfect incoherence with the apparent incoherence of Hamlet, whose replies, as Polonius observes, are often more pregnant of indirect meaning than reason and sanity could be. There is no hidden meaning in aught that poor Ophelia says. When for a moment she wanders from her leading train of thought, the sequence of ideas is utterly lost. Even at

---

27   *A Sentimental Journey*, 'Maria: Moulines.'

the last, when she has fallen into the weeping brook, she has no appreciation of her danger.

> Her clothes spread wide;
> And, mermaid-like, awhile they bore her up:
> Which time she chanted snatches of old tunes,
> As one incapable of her own distress.
>
> (IV, vii, 147–50)

Utterly lost, except to the insane train of ideas, she is as insensible to danger as a somnambulist; and singing her life away, she passes from the melody of madness to the silence of the grave. O rose of May! too soon blighted! but whose perfume shall endure in a monument of immortal words, when the tombs of Egyptian kings shall have crumbled into the desert dust!

7. Charles Dickens

1860

Charles Dickens (1812–1870), one of Britain's greatest novelists, had a lifelong interest in the theater and greatly enjoyed taking part in amateur theatricals. The imaginary account of a performance of *Hamlet*, given here by the novel's hero, forms chapter 31 of *Great Expectations* (1860–61), 'Mr Wopsle plays Hamlet.'

On our arrival in Denmark, we found the king and queen of that country elevated in two arm-chairs on a kitchen table, holding a Court. The whole of the Danish nobility were in attendance; consisting of a noble boy in the wash-leather boots of a gigantic ancestor, a venerable Peer with a dirty face, who seemed to have risen from the people late in life, and the Danish chivalry with a comb in its hair and a pair of white silk legs, and presenting on the whole a feminine appearance. My gifted townsman stood gloomily apart, with folded arms, and I could have wished that his curls and forehead had been more probable.

Several curious little circumstances transpired as the action proceeded. The late king of the country not only appeared to have been troubled with a cough at the time of his decease, but to have taken it with him to the tomb, and to have brought it back. The royal phantom also carried a ghostly manuscript round its truncheon, to which it had the appearance of occasionally referring, and that, too, with an air of anxiety and a tendency to lose the place of reference which were suggestive of a state of mortality. It was this, I conceive, which led to the Shade's being advised by the gallery to 'turn over!'—a recommendation which it took extremely ill. It was likewise to be noted of this majestic spirit that whereas it always appeared with an air of having been out a long time, and having walked an immense distance, it perceptibly came from a closely-contiguous wall. This occasioned its terrors to be received derisively. The Queen of Denmark, a very buxom lady, though no doubt historically brazen, was considered by the public to have too much brass about her; her chin being attached to her diadem by a broad band of that metal (as if she had a gorgeous toothache), her waist being encircled by another, and each of her arms by another, so that she was openly mentioned as 'the kettledrum'. The noble boy in the ancestral boots, was inconsistent; representing himself, as it were in one breath, as an able seaman, a strolling actor, a grave-digger, a clergyman, and a person of the utmost importance at a Court fencing-match, on the authority of whose practised eye and nice discrimination the finest strokes were judged. This gradually led to a want of toleration for him, and even—on his being detected in holy orders, and declining to perform the funeral service—to the general indignation taking the form of nuts. Lastly, Ophelia was a prey to such slow musical madness, that when, in course of time, she had taken off her white muslin scarf, folded it up, and buried it, a sulky man who had been long cooling his impatient nose against an iron bar in the front row of the gallery, growled, 'Now the baby's put to bed, let's have supper!' Which, to say the least of it, was out of keeping.

Upon my unfortunate townsman all these incidents accumulated with playful effect. Whenever that undecided Prince had to ask a question, or state a doubt, the public helped him out with it. As for example; on the question whether 'twas nobler in the mind to suffer, some roared yes, and some no, and some inclining to both opinions said 'toss up for it'; and quite a Debating Society arose. When he asked what should such fellows as he do crawling between earth and heaven, he was encouraged with loud cries of 'Hear, hear!' When he appeared with his stocking disordered (its disorder expressed, according to usage, by one very neat fold in the top, which I suppose to be always got up with a flat iron), a conversation took place in the gallery respecting the paleness of his leg, and whether it was occasioned by the turn the ghost had given him. On his taking the recorders—very like a little black flute that had just been played in the orchestra and handed out at the door—he was called upon unanimously for Rule Britannia. When he recommended the player not to saw the air thus, the sulky man said, 'And don't *you* do it neither; you're a deal worse than *him*!' And I grieve to add that peals of laughter greeted Mr. Wopsle on every one of these occasions.

But his greatest trials were in the churchyard: which had the appearance of a primeval forest, with a kind of small ecclesiastical wash-house on one side, and a turnpike gate on the other. Mr. Wopsle, in a comprehensive black cloak, being descried entering at the turnpike, the gravedigger was admonished in a friendly way, 'Look out! Here's the undertaker a coming, to see how you're getting on with your work!' I believe it is well known in a constitutional country that Mr. Wopsle could not possibly have returned the skull, after moralising over it, without dusting his fingers on a white napkin taken from his breast; but even that innocent and indispensable action did not pass without the comment 'Wai-ter!'. The arrival of the body for interment (in an empty black box with the lid tumbling open), was the signal for a general joy which was much enhanced by the discovery, among the bearers, of an individual obnoxious to identification. The joy attended Mr. Wopsle through his struggle with Laertes on the brink of the orchestra and the grave, and slackened no more until he had tumbled the king off the kitchen-table, and had died by inches from the ankles upwards.

We had made some pale efforts in the beginning to applaud Mr. Wopsle; but they were too hopeless to be persisted in. There-fore we sat, feeling keenly for him, but laughing, nevertheless, from ear to ear. I laughed in spite of myself all the time, the whole thing was so droll; and yet I had a latent impression there was something decidedly fine in Mr. Wopsle's elocution—not for old association's sake, I am afraid, but because it was very slow, very dreary, very up-hill and down-hill, and very unlike any way in which any man in any natural circumstance of life or death ever expressed himself about anything. When the tragedy was over, and he had been called for and hooted, I said to Herbert, 'Let us go at once, or perhaps we shall meet him'.

We made all the haste we could down-stairs, but we were not quick enough either. Standing at the door was a Jewish man with an unnatural heavy smear of eyebrow, who caught my eyes as we advanced, and said, when we came up with him:

'Mr. Pip and friend?'

Identity of Mr. Pip and friend confessed.

'Mr. Waldengarver', said the man, 'would be glad to have the honour.

'Waldengarver?' I repeated—when Herbert murmured in my ear, 'Probably Wopsle'.

'Oh!' said I. 'Yes. Shall we follow you?'

'A few steps, please'. When we were in a side alley, he turned and asked, 'How do you think he looked?—*I* dressed him'.

I don't know what he had looked like, except a funeral; with the addition of a large Danish sun or star hanging round his neck by a blue ribbon, that had given him the appearance of being insured in some extraordinary Fire Office. But I said he had looked very nice.

'When he come to the grave', said our conductor, 'he showed his cloak beautiful. But, judging from the wing, it looked to me that when he see the ghost in the queen's apartment, he might have made more of his stockings'.

I modestly assented, and we all fell through a little dirty swing door, into a sort of hot packing-case immediately behind it. Here Mr. Wopsle was divesting himself of his Danish garments, and here there was just room for us to look at him over one another's shoulders, by keeping the packing-case door, or lid, wide open.

'Gentlemen', said Mr. Wopsle, 'I am proud to see you. I hope, Mr. Pip, you will excuse my sending round. I had the happiness to know you in former times, and the Drama has ever had a claim which has ever been acknowledged, on the noble and the affluent'.

Meanwhile, Mr. Waldengarver, in a frightful perspiration, was trying to get himself out of his princely sables.

'Skin the stockings off, Mr.Waldengarver', said the owner of that property, 'or you'll bust 'em. Bust 'em, and you'll bust five-and-thirty shillings. Shakspeare never was complimented with a finer pair. Keep quiet in your chair now, and leave 'em to me'.

With that, he went upon his knees, and began to flay his victim; who, on the first stocking coming off, would certainly have fallen over backward with his chair, but for there being no room to fall anyhow.

I had been afraid until then to say a word about the play. But then, Mr. Waldengarver looked up at us complacently, and said: 'Gentlemen, how did it seem to you, to go, in front?'

Herbert said from behind (at the same time poking me), 'capitally'. So I said 'capitally'.

'How did you like my reading of the character, gentlemen?' said Mr. Waldengarver, almost, if not quite, with patronage.

Herbert said from behind (again poking me), 'massive and concrete'. So I said boldly, as if I had originated it, and must beg to insist upon it, 'massive and concrete'.

'I am glad to have your approbation, gentlemen', said Mr. Waldengarver, with an air of dignity, in spite of his being ground against the wall at the time, and holding on by the seat of the chair.

'But I'll tell you one thing, Mr. Waldengarver', said the man who was on his knees, 'in which you're out in your reading. Now mind! I don't care who says the contrary; I tell you so. You're out in your reading of Hamlet when you get your legs in profile. The last Hamlet as I dressed, made the same mistakes in his reading at rehearsal, till I got him to put a large red wafer on each of his shins, and then at that rehearsal (which was the last) I went in front, sir, to the back of the pit, and whenever his reading brought him into profile, I called out "I don't see no wafers!" And at night his reading was lovely'.

Mr. Waldengarver smiled at me, as much as to say 'a faithful dependent—I overlook his folly'; and then said aloud, 'My view is a little classic and thoughtful for them here; but they will improve, they will improve'.

Herbert and I said together, Oh, no doubt they would improve.

'Did you observe, gentlemen', said Mr. Waldengarver, 'that there was a man in the gallery who endeavoured to cast derision on the service—I mean, the representation?'

We basely replied that we rather thought we had noticed such a man. I added, 'He was drunk, no doubt'.

'Oh dear no, sir', said Mr. Wopsle, 'not drunk. His employer would see to that, sir. His employer would not allow him to be drunk'.

'You know his employer?' said I.

Mr. Wopsle shut his eyes, and opened them again; performing both ceremonies very slowly. 'You must have observed, gentlemen', said he, 'an ignorant and a blatant ass, with a rasping throat and a countenance expressive of low malignity, who went through—I will not say sustained—the role (if I may use a French expression) of Claudius King of Denmark. That is his employer, gentlemen. Such is the profession!'

Without distinctly knowing whether I should have been more sorry for Mr. Wopsle if he had been in despair, I was so sorry for him as it was, that I took the opportunity of his turning round to have his braces put on—which jostled us out of the doorway—to ask Herbert what he thought of having him home to supper? Herbert said he thought it would be kind to do so; therefore I invited him, and he went to Barnard's with us, wrapped up to the eyes, and we did our best for him, and he sat until two o'clock in the morning, reviewing his success and developing his plans. I forget in detail what they were, but I have a general recollection that he was to begin with reviving the Drama, and to end with crushing it; inasmuch as his decease would leave it utterly bereft and without a chance or hope.

8. George Eliot

1860

George Eliot (Mary Ann Evans, 1819–1880), arguably the most widely read author of the nineteenth century, was deeply interested in the theory of tragedy from the ancients to modern times throughout her career first as editor/contributor to the *Westminster Review*, and later as novelist and poet. Her comment on *Hamlet* in *The Mill on the Floss* (1860) is the first qualification she makes of the *dictum* of Novalis; she quotes the aphorism again in *Middlemarch* (1872).

From: *The Mill on the Floss*, Book VI, Ch. 6:
For the tragedy of our lives is not created entirely from within. 'Character', says Novalis, in one of his questionable aphorisms—'character is destiny'[1]. But not the whole of our destiny. Hamlet, Prince of Denmark, was speculative and irresolute, and we have a great tragedy in consequence. But if his father had lived to a good old age, and his uncle had died an early death, we can conceive Hamlet's having married Ophelia, and got through life with a reputation of sanity, notwithstanding many soliloquies, and some moody sarcasms towards the fair daughter of Polonius, to say nothing of the frankest incivility to his father-in-law.

1   Novalis is the pseudonym of Friedrich Leopold, Freiherr von Hardenberg (1772–1801), German Romantic poet and novelist. The quotation comes from *Heinrich von Osterdinger*, Part 2: 'Ich einsehe, dass Schicksal und Gemüt Namen eines Begriffes sind.'

9. Samuel Timmins

1860

This 'Bibliographical Preface' by Samuel Timmins (1826–1902) forms the introduction to a parallel text facsimile edition of the first and second Quartos of *Hamlet* in 1860, under the general title, *The Devonshire Hamlets* (because owned by The Duke of Devonshire, to whom the volume is dedicated). The preface gives a useful summary of scholarly opinion on the relationship between the two texts as it was known at this time.

The *Tragedy of Hamlet* is not only one of the most popular of Shakespeare's plays, but, perhaps, all things considered, one of the greatest works of dramatic art yet given to the world. From the child who sees or reads it when so young that, like Dr. Johnson, he is afraid to 'read the ghost scenes alone', to the philosopher who seeks to understand its mysteries, this great drama has long received the highest meed of praise. It has taken a place in literature almost unique, and the tragic story of the melancholy Dane is as fully and as widely received from Shakespeare's version as any genuine historic fact. The literary history, however, of this wonderful tragedy is exceedingly obscure. Shakespeare, unlike Ben Jonson, took no trouble about his marvellous dramas; and it was not till seven years after his death that the collected edition of his works appeared. Heminge and Condell, the editors of this folio of 1623, caution their 'great variety of readers' against 'divers stol'n and surreptitious copies' previously published, and profess to have printed their edition from 'papers' in which they 'scarce received from him a blot'. The folio, however, is carelessly edited, and badly printed, and we are indebted to some of these 'stol'n and surreptitious copies' for some noble passages which would otherwise have been irrecoverably lost. Among these early quartos, most of which are very scarce, the first edition of *Hamlet* was till recently unique. It bore the date of 1603, and became the property of the late Duke of Devonshire in 1825, along with twelve other scarce old plays. The volume, which formerly belonged to Sir Thomas Hanmer, was bought by Payne and Foss for £180, sold to the Duke for £250, and is now estimated to be worth £400. A reprint of the *Hamlet*, very carefully and accurately made, was published in 1825, but without the last leaf, which was deficient in the original, and this leaf was not supplied till 1856, when a second copy of the play was discovered by Mr. M.W. Rooney of Dublin. This copy, which had the last leaf perfect, but wanted the title page was bought by Mr. Rooney from a student of Trinity College, Dublin, who had brought it from Nottinghamshire with his other books. After reprinting the last leaf, Mr. Rooney sold the pamphlet to Mr. Boone for £70, from whom Mr. J.O. Halliwell bought it for £120, and it is now deposited in the British Museum.

Critics, of course, differ very widely as to the real date and history of this famous quarto. Mr. Payne Collier thinks it was probably printed from short-hand notes, revised by an inferior dramatist: others consider that it is, as far as it goes, a correct copy of the first version of the famous play: while nearly all agree that the date upon the title page gives no clue to the real date when the play was first written and performed. The contemporary literature affords four passages showing that a play called *Hamlet* was known before 1598, but no trace is found of any other *Hamlet* than that which bears Shakespeare's name; it is therefore a reasonable assumption that this drama, bearing the date 1603, may have been a recognised work of Shakespeare, publicly performed several years before that date, and 'surreptitiously' printed in that year. This would allow the further inference that the subject was a favourite one with Shakespeare, and that about the beginning of the seventeenth century he revised his early drama, and 'enlarged it to almost as much againe as it was'. As the evidence is so very scanty, and the limits of this preface will not permit a discussion of probabilities, I must refer the reader to the remarks of Mr. Collier, Mr. Knight, Mr. Dyce, and Mr. Staunton, and to an article in the *Edinburgh Review* (lxxxi, 377–84), in which the question is fairly and fully discussed, and record my own conviction that both the texts now republished are most valuable, the first as a 'rough-hewn' draft of a noble drama (written probably 1587–1589, 'diverse times acted by His Highnesse servants' till 1602, when it was 'entered' for publication, and soon afterwards 'enlarged'), and 'shaped', as it appears in the second quarto, by the divine bard's maturer mind.

The 1604 quarto is also scarce, only three copies being known. One belongs to the Duke of Devonshire, another to Lord Howe, and the other to Mr. Huth, junior, of London. The history of the Devonshire copy is not publicly known, that of Lord Howe formerly belonged to Charles Jennens, Esq., and Mr. Huth's copy was discovered by Mr. Howard Staunton in the library of Mr. Plumer of Selkirk, and for which, with a folio of 1623, and 1632, Mr. Huth paid £200, leaving about £165 as the cost of the quarto *Hamlet*. All these copies are perfect and extremely valuable, not only as giving the text 'enlarged to almost as much againe as it was, according to the true and perfect coppie', but as containing many passages of extreme beauty not found in the earlier quarto. A glance at the pages of this reprint will show how large are the additions, and how singularly interesting is the collation of the two texts. Whatever theory may be adopted as to their origin or date, their rarity is remarkable and their literary value great, since (in the words of Mons. F.V. Hugo, who has recently translated both versions into French) they afford us a 'comparaison infiniment curieuse, en ce qu'elle nous permet de penetrer jusqu'au fond la pensée du poète, et de surprendre les secrets du genie en travail'.[1]

The extreme rarity and value of these two quartos has kept them almost out of the reach of the great world of Shakespeare-scholars; but the late Duke of Devonshire liberally ordered fac-similes to be made, and forty copies were issued under the superintendence of Mr. Payne Collier, and presented to various public libraries and eminent literary men. Even these, however, are too scarce to reach the great mass of readers; and the present volume (in which the pages on the *right* hand side are exact copies of the *Second Quarto*, page for page) is offered to the literary world as a careful and accurate reprint of the two scarce and valuable original editions; the *First Quarto* (occupying the *left* hand side) being so spaced out that the passages which are parallel face those of the second edition, and thus the development of the characters, and the changes of the text may be readily examined and compared.

---

1 An infinitely fascinating comparison, in that it allows us to interrogate the thought of the poet in depth and to prise out the secrets of genius at work.

10. The Times Review of Fechter's *Hamlet*

Friday, 22 March, 1861

The performance of *Hamlet* at the Princess's Theatre in London in March, 1861 with the French actor Charles Fechter playing Hamlet, caused a sensation by breaking with the long established traditions of the British stage in the interpretation of the part.

M. Fechter's performance of Hamlet should unquestionably be seen by every one who takes interest in the higher departments of histrionic art. At all events, it is a theatrical curiosity. A Parisian artist, unrivalled in his own line, which is not that of French classical tragedy, essays the most arduous of Shakspearian characters. With the conventions of our stage, with the 'points' which, to us, seem almost as needful to the play as the words of the text, he has had nothing to do. He goes straight from the book to the boards, and, though possibly he has received a few hints as to the general conduct of the business, there is every reason to believe that all his details are entirely the result of his own thought.

His very entrance makes a completely novel impression. After the fashion of the German stage, he indicates Hamlet's Scandinavian nationality by a profusion of flaxen hair, and carries to perfection an assumption of that dreamy, unpractical look which is scarcely to be associated with a dark complexion. There is no doubt that to him the meditative element in Hamlet's nature has seemed most essential. The manner in which he throws out his answers, like one unwillingly awakened from a continued abstraction, into which he presently relapses, is admirably truthful, and the pretence of madness little changes this manner, beyond the addition of a light tone of irony.

Through the predominance given to the meditative element, the soliloquies acquire a very remarkable character. He has elaborated these at a vast expense of thought, and his delivery is marked by the subtlest variations. But the novelty of his rendering consists in the peculiarity that the stronger passions intrench as little as possible upon his solitude, and that he is chiefly occupied with a play of the intellect. The birth of his thoughts is more visible than the influence of his emotions.

The gentlemanlike side of Hamlet stands also high in the consideration of M. Fechter. Throughout the whole tragedy he is the very perfection of courtesy, and this quality is especially shown in his scenes with the players. Those of our readers who have seen him in the *Corsican Brothers* will recollect the charming affability with which, as the 'Young Squire', he settled the disputes of his turbulent peasantry. He was evidently far above the others in the social scale, but his condescension was so easy that it was even more agreeable than equality. Something of the same kind may be observed in M. Fechter's representation of Hamlet's conduct towards the itinerant comedians. He is a thoroughly polite Prince, and even when he is vexed by the interruptions of Polonius there is infinite courtesy in the gestures with which he motions him to silence. Indeed, all the 'genteel comedy' which belongs to Hamlet is admirably sustained; and though we can never forget that the part is played by a Frenchman, the Frenchman seems perfectly at home in his new atmosphere, and, indeed, has been qualified for it by the polished comedy of his own stage.

In those scenes, on the other hand, in which passion cannot be resolved into meditation, but must speak out loud and strong, the fact that Hamlet is played by a foreigner is less advantageously apparent. It is not that he lacks passion or is deficient in purpose, but that physical force which we find in the words of Shakspeare when wielded by a native seems to lie beyond the reach of an alien; and while we admire his general conception it is impossible not to feel that passages to which we have been habituated to attach great importance slip away comparatively unobserved. The merits and deficiencies of M. Fechter cannot be better illustrated than by the fact that the 'play scene' and the 'closet scene' are those with which he produces the least effect, whereas in the second act he makes a most powerful impression.

We have already said that such a performance is worth seeing as a curiosity. It is also estimable from a higher point of view. The pains which M. Fechter has taken to master the diction of Shakspeare and fully to understand every line set down for him are laudable in the highest degree, and the slips which he makes are so rare that they may simply be regarded as monuments of creditable toil. The finish of his performance is not the less real because it has the nature of French polish, and because many of his gestures are unlike those to which we have been accustomed on our own stage. Probably 'Shakspeare' never has been, or will be, played so well by a foreign artist as M. Fechter has played Hamlet, and it would be wholly incorrect to measure him by an English standard.

Mr. Harris has done a great deal for the decoration of the play, and several departures from tradition seem to have been dictated by a spirit in harmony with the novel interpretation of M. Fechter. The churchyard scene is remarkably pretty and the disposition of Hamlet and Horatio during the conversation with the gravedigger is new and picturesque. Miss Elsworthy has been engaged to play Gertrude, and very efficiently sustains the part.

11. Charles Cowden Clarke

1863

Charles Cowden Clarke (1787–1877) and his wife Mary are remembered as much for their friendships with some of the major writers of the first half of the nineteenth century as for their considerable contributions to literature during their long lives. Charles was a friend and teacher of John Keats and a close friend of Leigh Hunt, Charles and Mary Lamb, Charles Dickens and Douglas Jerrold, all of whom are commemorated in the jointly written *Recollections of Writers* (1878). His essay on *Hamlet*, reproduced here, is taken from his book *Shakespeare's Characters, Chiefly Those Subordinate*, 1863.

Hamlet is the prince of *poetical* philosophers. To philosophise is the habit of his mind. To reflect and reason upon every thing and every person that comes within his sphere,—to ponder upon every event that occurs,—to consider and reconsider each circumstance that arises,—is with him a part of his nature. He can no more help philosophising than he can help breathing; it is his mental atmosphere, as the air is his vital one. He philosophises upon his mother; upon his mistress; upon his friend; upon the king; upon the old courtier, Polonius; upon the water-fly, Osric; upon 'the sponge', Rosencrantz; and upon the spy, Guildenstern. He even philosophises upon himself, and upon himself most of all. Yet, with all this, as the poet has managed it, there is nothing dictatorial or dogmatical in Hamlet; for Hamlet is a gentleman,—a more accomplished, a more courteous gentleman than he, is not to be found in all Shakespeare, (and, I was going to say,) or anywhere else. Hamlet is not either dry or prolix. He is not didactic; for his reflections are rather for his own behoof than delivered as precepts for others. He is not sententious; for his words flow on in the shape of reverie and musing rather than in that of terse, brief phrases, uttered for effect. His moral philosophy is not studied; it has no rule, no set or specific rule, but is a rich emanation of his own spiritual being—flowing from his profound heart, his noble mind, his fertile imagination, his great and lofty soul. He moralises almost unconsciously; so naturally, so spontaneously do his ideas take that form.

How artistically has Shakespeare made Hamlet fall into that habitual mode of parlance, even in the very hour of awaiting the dread apparition on the platform at midnight. On his first coming in,—when we may imagine that they have all dropped into silence, as they approach the haunted spot,—Hamlet complains of the chill night breeze:—

> The air bites shrewdly; it is very cold.

But no sooner has the cannon sounded which announces the royal carousal, and the voice of his friend Horatio is heard, asking whether this be a custom, than the Prince answers in the philosophic strain natural to him:—

[Quotes I, iv, 15–20, into which are incorporated Q2's 22 lines 'These heavy headed revels east and west . . . To his own scandal', Additional passage B.]

This is wonderfully striking; and as characteristic as it is striking. No one like Shakespeare for consistency in character, and for making that consistency a heightener of his dramatic and poetical effects, as well as of his portraiture-effects. Monsieur Guizot, in his clever book upon our great English poet,—*Shakespeare and his Times*[1],—declares 'unity of impression' to be the great law of Shakespeare's dramatic art; and the marvellous harmony and consistency in his characters forms one portion of this 'unity of impression'.

Hamlet's proneness to soliloquy bespeaks the reflective man; and it not only serves to denote his philosophic mood, but it paints the perturbed condition of his spirit under the onerous task of revenge, imposed upon him by fate. Inexpressibly affecting is that eagerness he betrays to get by himself,—to feel free and unwatched,—that he may revolve the thoughts of his burthened heart at liberty. We feel the load taken from

---

1 For François Guizot's 'A Note on Hamlet', contained in this English translation of his book, see *CRH*, iii, 279ff.

him in those words of his, '*Now I am alone*', when Polonius, the players, and the two sycophantic lords, Rosencrantz and Guildenstern, leave him. And also, afterwards, on the journey, when he bids the two latter prying personages 'Go on before', that he may indulge his reverie upon meeting with the captain of Fortibras's forces. The vast responsibility laid by the Ghost upon him constantly rises upon his tide of thought, haunting, urging him to his settled course of action. When all the company have gone on,—soldiers and courtiers,—he breaks forth:—

[Quotes soliloquy 'How all occasions do inform against me', Q2, IV, iv, 23–37, Additional passage J.]

And he concludes his twentieth vacillation with this resolve:—

> Oh! from this time forth,
> My thoughts be bloody, or be nothing worth!
>
> (Q2, IV, iv, 56–7)

Hamlet's philosophy not unfrequently takes the form of bitter jests, while foiling the eaves-dropping treachery of those two hireling courtiers. He contemptuously dallies with their curiosity, and plays with their puzzled perceptions. He even strikes off into a wild levity and startling humour at times; and this eccentricity of demeanour, it is unnecessary to observe, was prepared and adopted by him to carry out his plan of subterfuge-action in assuming the character of insanity. For instance, where he replies to the King's inquiries after the dead body of Polonius, with those scoffing answers:

King. Where is Polonius?
Hamlet. In heaven: send thither to see. If your messenger find him not there, seek him in th'other place yourself. But, indeed, if you find him not within this month, you shall nose him as you go upstairs into the lobby.
King. [*To some attendants.*] Go, seek him there.
Hamlet. [*Calling after them.*] He will stay till you come.

(IV, iii, 32–8)

This dash of the grotesque, in his occasional words, enhances the effect of the profound and settled sadness dwelling within Hamlet's soul; just as the circumstance of the skull, which the grave-digger throws up at Hamlet's feet, being that of a jester, augments the solemnity of the event.

Its being the skeleton head of that soul of whim and mad waggery, upon whose shoulder the boy Hamlet had ridden a thousand times, gives additional awe to the sympathetic shudder with which we behold him handle and moralise upon it. In the same manner, the boorish jokes of the two grave-digging clowns increase the grim melancholy of the church-yard scene.

I will say a few words upon the feigned madness of Hamlet, and, as succinctly as I am able, justify my argument by authorities from his own speech and action.

The readers of this most mysterious of all the characters in Shakespeare are divided into those who believe in his real insanity, occasioned by that awful accumulation of circumstances,—the revealing of his father's spirit; the promulgation of his murder; and the tremendous responsibility arising out of it, to avenge his violent and unnatural death:—while the other party hold the opinion that the poet intended to convey nothing more than the assumed madness of the prince, for the purpose of shrouding his course of retribution.

That this latter is the true reading of the character, the following passages appear to be confirmatory.

In the 1st Act, after the scene with the Ghost, he prepares Horatio and Marcellus for the part he is about to act:—

> As I perchance hereafter shall *think meet*
> *To put an antic disposition on.*
>
> (I, v, 172–3)

Afterwards, in the scene with his mother, (Act III, sc. iv), when he has again seen his father's ghost, she calling his behaviour upon the occasion, 'ecstacy, the coinage of his brain', he replies:—

> Ecstacy!
> My pulse, as yours, doth temperately keep time,
> And makes as healthful music: it is not madness
> That I have utter'd: bring me to the test,
> And I the matter will re-word; which madness
> Would gambol from.
>
> (III, iv, 130–5)

And at the close of the same scene, he counsels his mother not to allow the king to worm from her his secret:—

> Let him not
> Make you to ravel all this matter out,
> That I essentially am not in madness,
> But mad in craft.

But the strongest proof of all that his madness is assumed is, that in his *soliloquies* he never utters an incoherent phrase. When he is alone, he reasons clearly and consistently;—it may be inconclusively, because he seeks in sophism an excuse for deferring the task of revenge imposed upon him;—but it is always coherently. At the close of the celebrated soliloquy,—'To be, or not to be',—than which nothing more grandly reflective and heart-absorbing was ever penned by poet, he is surprised at finding that he has been overheard in his rationality by Ophelia, who is at the back of the scene; and he then immediately begins to wander, in order that he may maintain his scheme of delusion; his language to her being the naturally conceived expression of an over-heated and excited brain, and not the disjointed incoherency of the incurable maniac.

Especially fine, too, is he in that soliloquy of the 4th scene, Act iv., after meeting with the forces of Fortinbras; and which speech Schlegel justly describes as being the key to the character of the prince. Hamlet says, sedately reflecting:

> Rightly to be great,
> Is *not* to stir without great argument,
> But greatly to find quarrel in a straw,
> When honour's at the stake. How stand I then,
> That have a father kill'd, a mother stain'd,
> Excitements of my reason and my blood,
> And let all sleep? While, to my shame, I see
> The imminent death of twenty thousand men,
> That for a fantasy and trick of fame,
> Go to their graves like beds.
> (Q2, IV, iv, 44–53, Additional passage J)

This greatly reasoning scene is never represented on the stage;—and, by the way, it has not unfrequently been the practice to argue on a question in Shakespeare's plays, from what is known of them through the actors; yet the theatrical copies are so notoriously abridged, that it is impossible to judge fairly of the poet's delineation of character, who never wrote a line that did not harmonise with, and tend to define the portrait he was limning.

In the scenes, too, with his heart-friend, Horatio, Hamlet is uniformly rational:—with one exception only; and that is immediately after the play-scene, and the discovery of the king's appalled conscience, when the wild words he utters may be fairly imputed to the result of his excitement, consequent upon the confirmation of the Ghost's murder-tale.

With the players, too, and the grave-digger, where it is unnecessary to maintain the consistency of the part he had assumed, he is perfectly collected, and even utters sound criticism and profound philosophy. His apology to Laertes, wherein he decidedly imputes his former misconduct to mental aberration, is the nearest approach to a confirmation of the idea that he has been really insane: but this scene takes place in the presence of the whole court, whom he has all along intended to deceive—his revenge, moreover, being still left unaccomplished. I therefore conclude, and I think reasonably, that they have read the whole play with very little reflection who conceive that Shakespeare intended to portray real, and not feigned madness in the conduct of Hamlet.

I should suppose that there never was a more artistical piece of dramatic event achieved (at all events, my own reading cannot quote its rival) than the arrangement of the machinery in the first scene of this play, for the introduction of the Ghost. How gradual, how solemn, and withal how serene, are its approaches;—the opening eyelids of the dawn not more impressive. We first behold the soldier, Francisco, on his watch. The stillness of the scene is broken by the pass-word of his comrade, Bernardo, who comes to relieve guard, and take Francisco's post. His natural question to his predecessor,—'Have you had quiet guard?' for Bernardo knows of the spirit's appearance, and wishes to discover whether Francisco have seen it also. To him, however, 'not a mouse has been stirring'. And here I would draw attention to one of the most signal examples of the far-sightedness and comprehension of his subject on the part of the poet, which occurs in the first two sentences of this play; the purport of which is so subtle, that it must escape the casual and light reader. Francisco is the guard on duty; and Bernardo, coming in to relieve him, calls out, 'Who's there?'—which challenge the other naturally retorts, with, '*Nay, answer me*; stand, and unfold yourself'. Bernardo being full of the apparition that he and Marcellus had witnessed the night before, in his perturbation questions everything he encounters in the night gloom. And when he is about to be *left alone* on the platform,—midnight close at hand,—the awful point of time for the visitation, he anxiously commissions Francisco, 'If you do meet Horatio and Marcellus, the rivals of my watch, *bid them make haste.* Immediately upon this, the two in question enter: Horatio having come to prove the truth of what had been reported to him by the other two,—he doubting the fact. Marcellus, who had been a witness of the apparition, calls it, 'This dreaded sight twice seen of us'. Now, all this appears to me the perfection of forethought, with contrivance. Horatio, still doubtful, says: 'Tush, tush, 'twill not appear'. Then Bernardo adds circumstance to the testimony of his companion:—

> Last night of all,
> When yond' same star that's westward from the pole,
> Had made his course t'illume that part of heav'n
> Where now it burns; Marcellus and myself,
> The bell then beating one,—

'Peace! break thee off', exclaims Marcellus, 'look where it comes again'. (I, i, 34–8).

How thrillingly grand is all this! and how natural! Still, the dignity of the event is to be sustained; and Horatio being the 'scholar', also the bosom-friend of Hamlet, is urged to address the spirit:—and here again, it is noticeable, that although all three are officers and gentlemen, yet the language of Horatio is cast in a more classical mould that that of the others, and this unvaryingly so throughout. How solemn and how deprecatory is his abjuration!—

> What art thou, that usurp'st this time of night,
> Together with that fair and warlike form,
> In which the majesty of buried Denmark
> Did sometimes march?—By heaven I charge thee, speak!
> (I, i, 44–7)

The spirit stalks away, deigning no reply; the consummation of its errand is yet to be fulfilled: it is yet to speak; and to no ears but those of Hamlet. Marcellus now exclaims to his doubting comrade:—

> How now, Horatio! you tremble, and look pale.
> Is not this something more than fantasy?
> What think you on't?
> *Hor.* Before my God, I might not this believe,
> Without the sensible and true avouch
> Of mine own eyes.
>
> (I, i, 51–6)

In the midst of a conversation of conjecture and surmise that ensues upon this event, Horatio again brings forward his classical accomplishments; and, what is remarkable, Shakespeare has put into his mouth a complete anticipation of the Newtonian theory of the tides. All this byeplay is to add dignity to Horatio, the friend and companion of the hero. After speaking of the prodigies that are said to have appeared in Rome previously to the assassination of the 'mightiest Julius';—

> The graves stood tenantless, and the sheeted dead
> Did squeak and gibber in the Roman streets;—

he concludes:—

> And the moist star [the moon]
> Upon whose *influence* Neptune's empire stands,
> Was sick almost to dooms-day with eclipse.
>
> (Q2, I, i, 8–13, Additional passage A)

Then follows that sweetly solemn winding up of the scene, after the second vanishing, at the crowing of the cock, with the remembrance of that pious superstition as recorded by Marcellus;—and what an exquisitely poetical term to use!

> It *faded* at the crowing of the cock.

Let any one try to find a more apt phrase than that to describe the dissolving of a shade into the elements, and he will be lucky if he succeed. Macbeth presents an even more vivid picture to the imagination upon the vanishing of the witches:—

'What seem'd corporal', he says, 'melted as breath into the wind' (*Macbeth*, I, iii, 79–80).

Marcellus then concludes:—

> Some say, that ever 'gainst that season comes
> Wherein our Saviour's birth is celebrated,
> This bird of dawning singeth all night long:
> And then, they say, no spirit can walk abroad;
> The nights are wholesome; then no planets strike,
> No fairy takes, nor witch hath power to charm;
> So hallow'd and so gracious is the time.
>
> (I, i, 139–45)

Horatio, the scholar and the philosopher, consistently answers:-

> So have I heard, and do *in part* believe it.

It will be recollected that he was sceptical as to the appearance of the ghost. Wonderfully artistical is that discrimination between the minds of Horatio and Marcellus. And then, lastly, what poetry in the breaking up of their conference!

> But, look, the morn in russet mantle clad,
> Walks o'er the dew of yon high eastern hill.
> Break we our watch up.
>
> (I, i, 147–9)

In this introductory scene we are presented with all the chief characteristics of the sublime; and of which, not the least prevailing feature is the effect produced by the gigantic power of stillness. The quiet midnight; the cold and misty moon; the wondering under-breath discourse of those who had assembled to witness that tremendous vision. The awful and unsubstantial form itself, in silent and majestic sorrow passing among, and about them, and yet not with them; present, and yet absent; cognisable, identical, and yet intangible. This all-absorbing, this mighty abstraction, congealed, as it were, into a stern reality, in dumb eloquence and thrilling stillness announces to us the coming events of a heart-shaking tragedy. Great is the majesty of 'silence', says Thomas Carlyle; and I know of nothing comparable in grandeur with the still and silent course of the first introduction of the Ghost in *Hamlet*.

At the subsequent appearance of that awful form, which occurs in the closet scene between the Prince and his mother, Shakespeare, so far from having committed an anti-climax, (which must have happened to an ordinary dramatist,) has even more deeply rooted our interest in the sorrows of the 'perturbed spirit'; for, on his first coming, the motive for appearing to his son being to stir him to revenge, he would tardily and scantily have carried our sympathies with him; but his second appearance is blended with an emotion of tenderness towards her who had lain in his bosom in her days of innocence and happiness; in those days when—

> She would hang on him,
> As if increase of appetite had grown
> By what it fed on:
>
> (I, ii, 143–5)

and who now was stricken to the heart with blood-guiltiness and remorse.

> But look, amazement on thy mother sits:
> Oh! step between her and her fighting soul.
>
> (III, iv, 102–3)

In the first scene with his son, when charging him to revenge the 'foul and unnatural murder', he enjoins exception in behalf of his guilty queen:—

> But, howsoever thou pursu'st this act,
> Taint not thy mind, *nor let thy soul contrive*
> *Against thy mother aught; leave her to Heaven,*
> And to those thorns that in her bosom lodge,
> To prick and sting her.
>
> (I, v, 4–8)

It was just like divine humanity in our poet to foster the idea of love in that life beyond life, still hovering with angelic tenderness and pardon over his weak and repentant partner in the flesh. And how beautifully this little touch of yearning emotion on the part of the spirit harmonises with the previous character given of him by his son:-

> So loving to my mother,
> That he might not beteem the winds of heaven
> Visit her face too roughly.
>
> (I, ii, 140–2)

It is the verifying these points of harmony and consistency in the creations of this wonderful genius, that makes the study of his productions a constant source of astonishment as well as delight.

Horatio is not merely the gentleman and scholar, as has been observed, and therefore worthy to be the companion of Hamlet; but the higher attractions of his honourable nature, his bland and trusting disposition, his prudent mind, and steadfastly affectionate heart, have raised him to the highest social rank that man can attain in this world—he is his prince's confidant and bosom-friend. The character of Horatio is the only spot of sun-light in the play; and he is a cheering, though not a joyous gleam coming across the dark hemisphere of treachery, mistrust, and unkindness. The cheerfulness of the grave-digger arises from an intimacy with, and a callous indifference to his occupation, which, as Horatio says,

> Custom hath made in him a property of easiness.
>
> (V, i, 67–8)

It is the result, too, of a healthy old age; or, in some sort, it is not a sentiment, but a physical consequence; even a negation.

But in the deportment of Horatio we have the constant recognition of a placid and pensive man; making no protestations, yet constantly prepared for gentle service. Modest, and abiding his time to be appreciated, his friendship for Hamlet is a purely disinterested principle, and the Prince bears high testimony to it,—an illustrious and eloquent tribute to the qualities of his head and heart:—

[Quotes III, ii, 52–72 from 'Horatio, thou art e'en as just a man'.]

And all this is no lip-deep attestation. Horatio has it, and has earned it. As he adhered to his friend through life, so would he have followed him in death; and only consented to survive him that he might redeem his character with the world. It is worthy of notice, that Horatio's speeches, after the first scene, consist almost entirely of simple assents to the observations of Hamlet; but when the final catastrophe has ensued, he comes forward, and assumes the prerogative of his position; and, as the companion and confidant of his Prince, he takes his station by Fortinbras, and the ambassadors, and at once assumes the office of moral executor and apologist for his friend. Was there no forethought,—no contrivance in all this subtle consecution of action? To me there is an indescribable charm in this Doric order of friendship and attachment, which Shakespeare has so frequently repeated in his plays:—simple, and unornate in exterior pretension; but massive and steadfast in design and structure.

With scarcely an exception, no one character in this tragedy has, I think, been worked out with more pains and accurate consistency, than that of the Lord Chamberlain, old Polonius. In his conduct and demeanour the critical task has been achieved of blending the highest useful wisdom (the knowledge of mankind) with the garrulity of an imbecile old age. Although Polonius, however, prates away at all times, and never omits an occasion to proffer his opinion, yet he does not babble; for no one dispenses sounder advice, or speaks more practical axioms. These, it is true, from his courtly education and gold-stick employment, he frequently converts into the 'crooked wisdom' of cunning and manoeuvre; for, so carefully is his conduct laid out by the poet, that every one of his plans has in it a double-move, as it were, (like a game of chess,) before he makes his hit. Polonius is a thorough-paced diplomatist, and seems to have (like the bulk of his tribe) a positive horror of simple and sincere action: as if stratagem and circumvention were the genius and staple of political commerce. His well-known advice to his son, Laertes, upon the young man's leave-taking for France, is as fine as an essay in Bacon:—it consists of a string of axioms that would make a perfect gentleman and man of business, whether civil or commercial:—

[Quotes whole of Polonius's speech I, iii, 55–81 beginning, 'Yet here, Laertes! aboard, aboard, for shame!'.]

Here we see the instinct and native disposition of the man; but when his object is to obtain an account of the mode of life his son is leading in Paris, he descends to subterfuge and manoeuvre; even with their servant Rinaldo, who is about to join his young master; giving him licence to lie, and traduce the conduct of Laertes at home, in order that he may induce his French associates to betray any irregularities that he may have committed in their company. This scene is the first of the Second Act; and a masterpiece of writing it is;—at that point of it especially where the old man hurries himself out of breath with explanation, and suddenly forgetting the thread of his instruction, exclaims:—'Where was I? Where was I?' It is like a dialogue taken in shorthand.

Again, in the scene with his daughter, (the conclusion of the one just quoted,) when she comes running in to inform him of Hamlet's altered behaviour, how characteristic is the self-rebuke of the practised courtier, in having desired her to decline the prince's advances, and refuse his letters; and with what close and practical experience he concludes his observation upon her report:—

> *That* hath made him mad.
> I am sorry that with better heed and judgment
> I had not quoted him; I fear'd he did but trifle,
> And meant to wreck thee; but, beshrew my jealousy!
> It seems as proper to our age
> To cast beyond ourselves in our opinions,
> As it is common for the younger sort
> To lack discretion.
>
> (II, i, 111–18)

Here, we see, he regrets his over-caution; [but] for that, he would have promoted (and rationally) a safe alliance for his daughter with the heir to the throne: yet afterwards, in conversation with the king and queen, he makes a merit of having confronted her, and solely on the ground of the disparity of their conditions:—

> Lord Hamlet is a prince, out of thy star;
> This must not be: and then I precepts gave her,
> That she should lock herself from his resort,
> Admit no messengers, receive no tokens.
>
> (II, ii, 142–5)

How accurately does all this shuffling and moral imbecility square with the temporizing courtier! Yet again; his tendency to manoeuvre and insincerity are noticeable in his making Ophelia act a part in the scene he had contrived for discovering whether the madness of Hamlet were confirmed or not:—

> Ophelia, walk you here, . . .
>   read on this book;
> That show of such an exercise may colour
> Your loneliness.
>   (III, i, 45, 46–8)

And then the genuine nature of the honourable man stares out of the artificial man of society. He says to himself:—

>   We are oft to blame in this,—
> 'Tis too much prov'd,—that with devotion's visage,
> And pious action, we do sugar o'er
> The devil himself.
>   (III, i, 48–51)

So thorough, so pliant, and hard-working a courtier is he, that he even offered to act the eaves-dropper to the king, that he may report to him the result of the interview between Hamlet and his mother—an act which brings upon him so terrible a retribution; but which, at the same time, preaches a caustic moral to all disreputable, uncompromising time-servers: the moral being the more stringent in his case, because, by nature, Polonius possessed an instinct of honour and self-respect, which a course of unworthy pliancy and intrigue (perhaps almost inseparable from his office) had soiled and tainted.

In introducing the character of the ill-starred and forlorn Ophelia, I will, previously, take occasion to offer a remark or two upon that part of the celebrated dissertation on Hamlet, by Goethe, in his *Wilhelm Meister*, which bears upon one phase of her conduct.

The eminent German critic starts with the position that Ophelia possessed a temperament which would lead her to become an easy prey wherever her fancy had been attracted; and, having taken that point, he draws his conclusions from the warnings given to her by both father and brother, to be upon her guard in admitting the addresses of the Lord Hamlet; and he crowns his inferences by quoting the snatches of songs she sings during her madness, as the foregone conclusions of a mind (to use the mildest term) not tempered with the chariest discretion, or habituated to the most delicate associations.

Now, all this appears to me the question-begging of one who would merge all love into the *sensual*, at the expense of the *ideal*—a conclusion totally unwarrantable in the case of Ophelia; for the only confession we have of her love for Hamlet is wholly comprised in the absorbing adoration of his intellectual endowments—a higher order of love than Goethe seems to think her capable of even discovering. With a passionately chaste lament, she says:—

[Quotes III, i, 153–61 beginning 'Oh! what a noble mind is here o'erthrown!'.]

This is not the language of a gross or even a light-minded female, which Goethe, with all his wariness, and ingenuity of expression, would have his readers think Ophelia to be. Nor would Shakespeare have given to her a complaint of such character and tone, had she been deceived, and then deserted by Hamlet. Moreover, we may be sure that she was not—in any form—a victim to her wantonness, or his infidelity; for, after her death, in an ecstacy of genuine passion, he says:—'I loved her above forty thousand brothers!' And he would not have used that language had his intercourse with her been a merely *illicit* one.

As to that branch of the critic's argument, drawn from the warning of Ophelia's father and brother, it is unnecessary to remind any adult that such a precaution is perfectly consistent with the most spotless purity of heart, where that heart is wholly occupied and absorbed by the one sentiment and passion of love and admiration: the father and brother both recognising the irresponsible position of the prince; and this, joined with their fears and jealousy lest she bewray the family honour; while that is a natural precaution on their part, (both being men of the world, and the artificial world of a court—and such a court as that of Claudius the murderer and adulterer;) whatever the precaution (I say) on their part, it by no means involves, or even implies, a laxity on hers.

With regard to the critic's innuendo (and this is the least reputable of his insinuations) respecting her real character, drawn from the songs she sings during her insanity; Goethe, as a psychologist, ought to have known that no such conclusion can be drawn from the actions of a person under that suspension:—on the contrary, it is an argument of her native *innocence* of *character*; and Shakespeare knew this two hundred years before Goethe lived; experience constantly reminding us that insane people are wont to be, for the time, the total opposites of their real natures—your madmen plotting to kill those whom they most loved when in a state of sanity[2]; your profligates breaking forth into piety; your pious into blasphemies; and your most reserved and chaste indulging in a laxity of expression astonishing to those who knew their former course of life and principles. And, after all, these same snatches of songs, alluded to by Goethe, and which, by the way, consist of two, and not much in those, they display the constant thought and contrivance of the poet to carry on *within* as well as *without* the scene a continuity and consistency of thought, as well as of action in the character. Upon referring again to the passage for my present purpose, I can come to no other conclusion than that he intended to convey in those wanderings of Ophelia the reflected lights of *past* reflections in her sane moments, resulting from the warning and advice that had been given to her in admitting the advances and protestations of her royal lover; but that they were intended to be the foregone conclusions of an unstable virtue, could only proceed, I think, from a prurient mind, apt at catching at such a suggestion.

I regret, though I confess I am not surprised at the tone of this commentary in the eminent critic, since I have never been able entirely to shake off the idea that Goethe himself was not wholly untainted with the leaven of grossness; and therefore was the more apt at imputation. The celebrated Bettina, in one of her letters to him, makes the remark, that she wonders from what class in society he chose his heroines, they are such questionable people. I am sure that in the self-absorption of the homage toll-fee Goethe's appetite was grossness itself.

In how much finer a spirit has Doctor Bucknill, in his admirable work on the *Psychology of Shakespeare*, appreciated the character of Ophelia. Doctor Bucknill is the superintendent of a lunatic asylum, and therefore speaks with authority. He says, 'The not very delicate warning of Ophelia's disagreeable brother, that she is likely to lose her honour to Hamlet's unmastered importunity, is evidently distasteful to the poor girl, and gives

---

2 Clarke possibly has the example of Mary Lamb in mind in this example.

occasion to the only sparkle of displeasure which the gentle creature ever shows, in that quick-witted retaliation of advice:-

> But, my good brother,
> Do not, as some ungracious pastors do,
> Show me the steep and thorny way to heaven;
> Whilst, like a puff'd and reckless libertine,
> Himself the primrose path of dalliance treads,
> And recks not his own read.
>
> (I, iii, 46–51)

Ophelia's reference to the primrose path of dalliance which her libertine brother was likely to tread, *shows, from the first, that her purity of mind is not the result of ignorance.* Her belief in the honour and truth of her lover, Bucknill adds, is the *'credulity of innocence, but not of stupidity'*. Old Dan Chaucer says of the Duchess Blanche of Lancaster,

> I say not she knew no *evil*,
> Then had she known no *good*,
> So seemeth me[3]

Rosencrantz and Guildenstern are favourable samples of the thorough-paced, time-serving court knave—servants of all-work, ticketed, and to be hired for any hard or dirty job. Shakespeare has at once, and unequivocally, signified his opinion of the race, by making Rosencrantz, the time-server, the schoolfellow of Hamlet, and, under the colour of their early associations, professing a personal friendship—even an affection for him, at the very time that he had accepted the office of spy upon his actions, and traitor to his confidence. 'Good, my lord, what is your cause of distemper? You do surely but bar the door upon your own liberty, if you deny your griefs to your friend'(III, ii, 324–6). Immediately upon the heel of this protestation he accepts the king's commission to convey his 'friend' to England, where measure had been taken for his assassination. Rosencrantz and his fellow would designate themselves as thoroughly '*loyal* men'; they make no compromise of their calling; the 'broad R' is

---

3 Geoffrey Chaucer, *The Book of the Duchess*, 996–8. 'I sey nat that she ne had knowynge/What harm was; or elles she/Had koud no good, so thinketh me'.

burnt into them; they are for the king's service exclusively; and with the scavenger's calling, they would scoop all into that reservoir. The poet has sketched them in few and bold outlines; their subtleties of character stare out like the bones of a starved beast. They are time-servers by profession, and upon hire; and 'verily they have their reward'. The great Hebrew legislator has said, 'Thou shalt not muzzle the ox that treadeth out the corn'[4]; but the corn that such oxen tread out no noble beast would consider worthy of 'protective duty' at all. No one works so hard as a time-server; and, under the fairest auspices, his labour is well worthy of his pay. The machinery he constructs to accomplish his little ends, is always complicated and eccentric in movement—like the Laputan's invention for cutting a cabbage, requiring a horse-power to put it in action; or like the painstaking of Bardolph, who stole the lute-case, carried it seven leagues, and sold it for three-halfpence. The same great master-spirit—Shakespeare—has made another time-server say, 'How wretched is that poor man that hangs on princes' favours![5]' but how much more wretched is that poor prince who needs such hangers-on as Guildenstern and Rosencrantz! What a hell on earth has the man who is the suborner of meanness and villainy!—the constant sense of subjection—the instinctive sense of insincerity and sham respect—the rising of the gorge at the fawning and the mouth-honour, the self-inspection, (which will come,) the surmises, the fears, the trepidations, the heartaches: 'Verily, both parties have their reward', even here, 'on this bank and shoal of time'. I know of no bitterer satire upon the compact between state hire and state service than is put into the mouth of this Rosencrantz, addressed to such a king as Hamlet's uncle!-

[Quotes Rosencrantz's speech 'The single and peculiar life is bound . . . ' III, ii, 11–23.]

This is a specimen of time-server logic for an act of state policy: it is the argument of a hireling to sugar over the king's act to murder Hamlet, in order that the peace and safety of the suborner may be secured. Assuredly no one has been less of a flatterer, with stronger inducements to

4 Deuteronomy, xxv, 4.
5 *Henry VIII*, (*All Is True*) III, ii, 367–8.

be one, than Shakespeare. In the spirit of just retribution, these two worthies fall into the trap they had set for their old friend and schoolfellow.

On another occasion I have spoken of Shakespeare's large discourse upon the 'Philosophy of War', and its utter worthlessness. In the short scene between Hamlet and the captain of Fortinbras,—and which, as already observed, is never acted,—we have the poet again upon the same theme, but in a calm and lofty vein of satire, exposing the contemptible grounds upon which these vicegerents on earth will play their bloody gambols at the expense of the life and treasure of those uninterested in the game. Shakespeare was our first poet who saw and exposed its absurdity; and Cowper was the last, who followed it out with a dash of radicalism in the sentiment:—'But war is a game, which, were their subjects wise, kings would not play at'.

The dialogue I have alluded to is an edifying commentary upon the light causes and grave effects of strife and contention. Hamlet says to the captain:—

[Quotes dialogue between Hamlet and Captain, Q2, IV, iv, 2–20, Additional passage J.]

How searching that philosophy! and what truth and felicity in the metaphor, with its application! Hamlet, afterwards, when ruminating upon this circumstance in connexion with his own irresolute action, says, (as already quoted,)—

> To my shame, I see
> The imminent death of twenty thousand men,
> That for a fantasy and trick of fame,
> Go to their graves like beds; fight for a plot
> Whereon the numbers cannot try the cause,
> Which is not tomb enough, and continent,
> To hide the slain.
>
> (Q2, IV, iv, 50–6)

I have always been struck with the dialogue between Hamlet and Osric, the 'gilded water-fly', as he terms him, who comes to announce to the Prince the wager at fence with Laertes. Who that has ever observed the action of that peculiar insect,—skimming to and fro, and round and round upon the water's face, with no apparent purpose but mere inconsequence,—can fail to recognise the aptitude of that assimilation?—the '*gilded* water-fly' too!

The choice language and peculiar idiom of the dandy lord, with the superior bearing and regal dignity of the Prince, not carrying with it the slightest tinge of insolence or 'pride of place'—(I repeat, there is no perfecter gentleman drawn than Hamlet)—his fooling Osric to the 'top of his bent', is in the pure spirit of the highest-bred gentility:—

> Your bonnet, sir, to his right use; 'tis for the head.
>
> *Osric*. I thank your lordship; 'tis very hot.
> *Ham*. No, believe me, 'tis very cold; the wind is northerly.
> *Osric*. It is indifferent cold, my lord, indeed.
> *Ham*. But yet, methinks, it is very sultry and hot; or my complexion—
> *Osric*. Exceedingly, my lord; it is very sultry,—as 'twere,—
> I cannot tell how.
>
> (V, ii, 94–102)

With all his vapid pliancy, however, when Osric comes to speak upon the accomplishments which alone, in those days, betokened the gentleman, Shakespeare knew that he must no longer make him contemptible: in descanting, therefore, upon Laertes' pretensions, he is made to use the choicest terms, describing him as an 'absolute gentleman, full of most excellent differences, of very soft society, and great showing' (Q2 V, ii, 1–3, Additional passage N). And he dilates upon the weapons that are to be used with an accurate and professor-like technicality, and in language as polished as their blades: 'Six French rapiers and poniards, with their assigns, hangers, and so. Three of the carriages, in faith, are very dear to fancy, very responsive to the hilts, most delicate carriages, and of very liberal conceit' (V, ii, 113–17). Upon referring to this scene, it will be observed, I think, that Shakespeare, in Hamlet's mouth, intended to ridicule the dandy nomenclature of the day; for, with an amusing air of simplicity, he takes the tone of a stranger to the mysteries of the profession of arms, requiring an explanation of the terms so fluently used by Osric. It may appear affected to attach importance to a scene like this—trifling, indeed, as compared with the solemn and gigantic events that have transpired in the course of the drama; yet this simple and very natural prelude to the quenching of the noble spirit of the hero, produces, in my mind, a sense of reality and of pathos that are more easily suggested than explained, and suffers no detraction; if, indeed, it be not heightened by the gentle and modest tone in which the Prince dismisses the messenger:-

> Sir, I will walk here in the hall: if it please his majesty, it is the breathing time of day with me: let the foils be brought, the gentleman willing, and the king hold his purpose, I will win for him if I can; if not, I will gain nothing but my shame, and the odd hits.
>
> (V, ii, 134–8)

Amid the glittering firmament of beauties with which this amazing drama is studded, it is no questionable homage to turn aside and examine with interest so insignificant a character as that of Osric; and, moreover, for the mind to come to the satisfactory conclusion that even the great master-movers in the scene are not more ably conceived, or produced with greater force or truth to nature.

It is immediately after his accepting the challenge that the 'coming event' of his death, 'casting its shadow' across the mind of Hamlet, draws from him that affecting confession to his bosom friend, Horatio; and which, as associated with all the circumstances of his unhappy mission, together with the deep and solemn piety of his comment, I confess, I never even recur to without an indescribable emotion of awe and reverence. He says:-

> Thou wouldst not think how ill all's here about my heart;—but 'tis no matter.
> *Hor.* Nay, my good lord,—
> *Ham.* It is but foolery; but it is such a kind of gain-giving as would, perhaps, trouble a woman.
> *Hor.* If your mind dislike anything, obey it:—I will forestall their repair hither, and say you are not fit.
> *Ham.* Not a whit;—we defy augury: there is a special providence in the fall of a sparrow. If it be now, 'tis not to come; if it be not to come, it will be now; if it be not now, yet it will come:—*the readiness is all.*
>
> (V, ii, 158–68)

Ah! when the ignorant or the thoughtless, or, the worse than both, the hypocritical, talk of Shakespeare's immorality, refer them to this simple and beautiful little homily upon resignation and reliance.

Laertes is one of that large class in humanity of the level standard in morals,—loud, turbulent, and boisterous in profession; yet so weak in judgment, and unjust in act, (and injustice must always involve a perversion of intellect,) that, for the purposes of revenge, he will become the principal in a plot to commit treachery and murder:—at the same time, in strict accordance with such a disposition and temperament, he is remorse-stricken at the issue of his villainy. This is human nature in fac-simile. It was a touch of fine art in the poet to place the character and deportment of Laertes in contrast with that of his victim, at the immediate point of time when he was about to put his plot in action.

The apology Hamlet makes for his previous excitement towards the brother of Ophelia, at her grave, is conceived in the very highest sense of magnanimity and gentle bearing;—'gentle' in every sense;—a perfect gentleman. In concluding his speech, he says:-

> Sir, in this audience,
> Let my disclaiming from a purpos'd evil
> Free me so far in your most generous thoughts,
> That I have shot mine arrow o'er the house,
> And hurt my brother.
>
> (V, ii, 186–90)

While we are upon the subject of 'contrasts', how fruitful a theme for reflection is the whole of the grave-digging scene: how full of character; full of unexpected thought; and how free from effort and display of every kind,—in short—for the thousandth time—'*how natural!*' The thoughtless gaiety of the sexton, singing over his work; 'Custom having made it in him a property of easiness', as Horatio says; and, as Hamlet beautifully follows up the explanation, 'The hand of little employment hath the daintier sense':—a philosophical apology for those un-imaginative classes in society whose sole occupation is connected with the *last* offices of life, and the *first* of death. Indeed, our beloved Shakespeare had a considerate and gentle heart.

Again,—'in contrast',—the recognition of Yorick's skull, and the two men's characteristic associations with the same individual;—the clown remembering him for a 'pestilent mad rogue, who had poured a flagon of Rhenish on his head';—the practical jokes only of the jester remained in the sexton's memory. Hamlet recalls his social and intellectual qualities; an epitaph to his fame, and a lecture upon vanity that will be coeval with poetry itself:-

[Quotes Hamlet's speech beginning 'Alas, poor Yorick!' V, i, 180–90.]

The rise, progress, and consummation of the whole plot of the tragedy of Hamlet is a consistent theme upon the conflict between determination and irresolution, arising from over-reflection; and in nothing throughout the whole scheme of the play is the art of the poet more grandly developed than in making the vacillation of the hero to turn solely upon that over-reflectiveness of his nature; and indeed, under the circumstances, it was Shakespeare's only resource. Had Hamlet wavered from any other cause, we must have dismissed him with disrespect; as it is, we make the handsomest excuse for him; and, in short, elevate him in our esteem by the acknowledgement that he was the most unfit instrument for the mission imposed upon him, simply because he had a mind superior to the carrying of it out in detail.

And, to conclude so pygmy a comment, as the one now presented upon this giant of philosophical dramas; rise from it when we may, and as often as we may, our hearts are warmed by wiser and holier thoughts; and our sole comment upon the creative mind that was permitted to give such a work to his fellow-mortals may well be summed up in the words of his own hero:-

> How noble in reason! how infinite in faculties! in action how like an angel! in apprehension how like a God!
>
> (II, ii, 104–7)

12. Hippolyte Adolphe Taine

1863?

Hippolyte Adolphe Taine (1828–1893) was one of France's most distinguished historians. Among his works is a voluminous *History of English Literature* from which the following accounts of Shakespeare's language and of the character of Hamlet are taken. The translation is that of H. Van Laun, first published (in four volumes) in 1873–74.

(a) Shakespeare's style (ii, 67–72):
Shakspeare imagines with copiousness and excess; he scatters metaphors profusely over all he writes; every instant abstract ideas are changed into images; it is a series of paintings which is unfolded in his mind. He does not seek them, they come of themselves; they crowd within him, covering his arguments; they dim with their brightness the pure light of logic. He does not labour to explain or prove; picture on picture, image on image, he is for ever copying the strange and splendid visions which are engendered one after another, and are heaped up within him. Compare to our dull writers this passage, which I take at hazard from a tranquil dialogue:

> The single and peculiar life is bound,
> With all the strength and armour of the mind,
> To keep itself from noyance; but much more
> That spirit upon whose weal depends and rests
> The lives of many. The cease of majesty
> Dies not alone; but, like a gulf, doth draw
> What's near it with it: it is a massy wheel,
> Fix'd on the summit of the highest mount,
> To whose huge spokes ten thousand lesser things
> Are mortised and adjoin'd; which, when it falls,
> Each small annexment, petty consequence,
> Attends the boisterous ruin. Never alone
> Did the king sigh, but with a general groan.
>
> (III, iii, 11–23)

Here we have three successive images to express the same thought. It is a whole blossoming; a bough grows from the trunk, from that another, which is multiplied into numerous fresh branches. Instead of a smooth road, traced by a regular line of dry and cunningly-fixed landmarks, you enter a wood, crowded with interwoven trees and luxuriant bushes, which conceal and prevent your progress, which delight and dazzle your eyes by the magnificence of their verdure and the wealth of their bloom. You are astonished at first, modern mind that you are, business man, used to the clear dissertations of classical poetry; you become cross; you think the author is amusing himself, and that through conceit and bad taste he is misleading you and himself in his garden thickets. By no means; if he speaks thus, it is not from choice, but of necessity; metaphor is not his whim, but the form of his thought. In the height of passion, he imagines still. When Hamlet, in despair, remembers his father's noble form, he sees the mythological pictures with which the taste of the age filled the very streets:

> A station like the herald Mercury
> New lighted on a heaven-kissing hill.
>
> (III, iv, 57–8)

This charming vision, in the midst of a bloody invective proves that there lurks a painter underneath the poet. Involuntarily and out of season, he tears off the tragic mask which covered his face; and the reader discovers, behind the contracted features of this terrible mask, a graceful and inspired smile which he did not expect to see.

Such an imagination must needs be vehement. Every metaphor is a convulsion. Whosoever involuntarily and naturally transforms a dry idea into an image, has his brain on fire; true metaphors are flaming apparitions, which are like a picture in a flash of lightning. Never, I think, in any nation of Europe, or in any age of history, has so grand a passion been seen. Shakspeare's style is a compound of frenzied expressions. No man has submitted words to such a contortion. Mingled contrasts, tremendous exaggerations, apostrophes, exclamations, the whole fury of the ode, confusion of ideas, accumulation of images, the horrible and the divine, jumbled into the same line; it seems to my fancy as though he never writes a word without shouting it. 'What have I done?' the queen asks Hamlet. He answers:

> Such an act
> That blurs the grace and blush of modesty,
> Calls virtue hypocrite, takes off the rose
> From the fair forehead of an innocent love,
> And sets a blister there, makes marriage-vows
> As false as dicers' oaths: O, such a deed
> As from the body of contraction plucks
> The very soul, and sweet religion makes
> A rhapsody of words: Heaven's face doth glow;
> Yea, this solidity and compound mass,
> With tristful visage, as against the doom,
> Is thought-sick at the act.
>
> (III, iv, 39–50)

It is the style of phrensy. Yet I have not given all. The metaphors are all exaggerated, the ideas all verge on the absurd. All is transformed and disfigured by the whirlwind of passion. The contagion of the crime, which he denounces, has marred all nature. He no longer sees anything in the world but corruption and lying. To vilify the virtuous were little; he vilifies virtue herself. Inanimate things are sucked into this whirlpool of grief. The sky's red tint at sunset, the pallid darkness spread by night over the landscape, become the blush and the pallor of shame, and the wretched man who speaks and weeps sees the whole world totter with him in the dimness of despair.

Hamlet, it will be said, is half-mad; this explains the vehemence of his expressions. The truth is that Hamlet, here, is Shakspeare. Be the situation terrible or peaceful, whether he is engaged on an invective or a conversation, the style is excessive throughout. Shakspeare never sees things tranquilly. All the powers of the mind are concentrated in the present image or idea. He is buried and absorbed in it. With such a genius, we are on the brink of an abyss; the eddying water dashes in headlong, swallowing up whatever objects it meets, and only bringing them to light transformed and mutilated. We pause stupefied before these convulsive metaphors, which might have been written by a fevered hand in a night's delirium, which gather a pageful of ideas and pictures in half a sentence, which scorch the eyes they would enlighten. Words lose their meaning; constructions are put out of joint; paradoxes of style, apparently false expressions, which a man might occasionally venture upon with diffidence in the transport of his rapture, become the ordinary language. Shakspeare dazzles, repels, terrifies, disgusts, oppresses; his verses are a piercing and sublime song, pitched in too high a key, above the reach of our own organs, which offends our ears, of which our mind alone can divine the justice and beauty.

Yet this is little; for that singular force of concentration is redoubled by the suddenness of the dash which calls it into existence. In Shakspeare there is no preparation, no adaptation, no development, no care to make himself understood. Like a too fiery and powerful horse, he bounds, but cannot run. He bridges in a couple of words an enormous interval; is at the two poles in a single instant. The reader vainly looks for the intermediate track; dazed by these prodigious leaps, he wonders by what miracle the poet has entered upon a new idea the very moment when he quitted the last, seeing perhaps between the two images a long scale of transitions, which we mount with difficulty step by step, but which he has spanned in a stride. Shakspeare flies, we creep. Hence comes a style made up of conceits, bold images shattered in an instant by others still bolder, barely indicated ideas completed by others far removed, no visible connection, but a visible incoherence; at every step we halt, the track failing; and there, far above us, lo, stands the poet, and we find that we have ventured in his footsteps, through a craggy land, full of precipices, which he threads, as if it were a straightforward road, but which our greatest efforts barely carry us along.

(b) Hamlet

The history of Hamlet, like that of Macbeth, is a story of moral poisoning. Hamlet has a delicate soul, an impassioned imagination, like that of Shakspeare. He has lived hitherto, occupied in noble studies, skilful in mental and bodily exercises, with a taste for art, loved by the noblest father, enamoured of the purest and most charming girl, confiding, generous, not yet having perceived, from the height of the throne to which he was born, aught but the beauty, happiness, grandeur of nature and humanity.[1] On this soul, which character and training make more sensitive than others, misfortune suddenly falls, extreme, overwhelming, of the very kind to destroy all faith and every motive for action: with one glance he

---

1 Goethe, *Wilhem Meister* (author's note).

has seen all the vileness of humanity; and this insight is given him in his mother. His mind is yet intact; but judge from the violence of his style, the crudity of his exact details, the terrible tension of the whole nervous machine, whether he has not already one foot on the verge of madness:

> O that this too, too solid flesh would melt,
> Thaw and resolve itself into a dew!
> Or that the Everlasting had not fix'd
> His canon 'gainst self-slaughter! O God! God!
> How weary, stale, flat and unprofitable,
> Seem to me all the uses of this world!
> Fie on't! ah fie! 'tis an unweeded garden,
> That grows to seed; things rank and gross in nature
> Possess it merely. That it should come to this!
> But two months dead: nay, not so much, not two:
> So excellent a king . . . so loving to my mother
> That he might not let e'en the winds of heaven
> Visit her face too roughly. Heaven and earth!
> . . . And yet, within a month,—
> Let me not think on't—Frailty, thy name is woman!—
> A little month, or ere those shoes were old
> With which she follow'd my poor father's body . . .
> Ere yet the salt of most unrighteous tears
> Had left the flushing on her galled eyes,
> She married. O, most wicked speed, to post
> With such dexterity to incestuous sheets!
> It is not nor it cannot come to good!
> But break, my heart; for I must hold my tongue.
> (I, ii, 129–42, 145–8, 154–9)

Here already are contortions of thought, a beginning of hallucination, the symptoms of what is to come after. In the middle of conversation the image of his father rises before his mind. He thinks he sees him. How then will it be when the 'canonised bones have burst their cerements', 'the sepulchre hath oped his ponderous and marble jaws', and when the ghost comes in the night, upon a high 'platform' of land, to tell him of the tortures of his prison of fire, and of the fratricide, who has driven him thither? Hamlet grows faint, but grief strengthens him, and he has a desire for living:

> Hold, hold, my heart!
> And you my sinews, grow not instant old,
> But bear me stiffly up! Remember thee!
> Ay, thou poor ghost, while memory holds a seat
> In this distracted globe.—Remember thee?
> Yea, from the table of my memory
> I'll wipe away all trivial fond records,
> All saws of books, all forms, all pressures past, . . .
> And thy commandment all alone shall live . . .
> O villain, villain, smiling, damned villain!
> My tables,—meet it is I set it down,
> That one may smile, and smile, and be a villain;
> At least I'm sure it may be so in Denmark:
> So, uncle, there you are. [writing]
>
> (I, v, 93–100, 102, 106–11)

This convulsive outburst, this fevered writing hand, this frenzy of intentness, prelude the approach of a kind of monomania. When his friends come up, he treats them with the speeches of a child or an idiot. He is no longer master of his words; hollow phrases whirl in his brain, and fall from his mouth as in a dream. They call him; he answers by imitating the cry of a sportsman whistling to his falcon: 'Hillo, ho, ho, boy! come, bird, come'. Whilst he is in the act of swearing them to secrecy, the ghost below repeats 'Swear'. Hamlet cries, with a nervous excitement and a fitful gaiety:

> Ah ha, boy! say'st thou so? art thou there, truepenny?
> Come on—you hear this fellow in the cellarage,—
> Consent to swear . . . .
> *Ghost (beneath).* Swear.
> *Hamlet.* Hic et ubique? then we'll shift our ground.
>   Come hither, gentlemen . . . Swear by my sword.
> *Ghost (beneath).* Swear.
> *Hamlet.* Well said, old mole! canst work i'the earth so fast?
>   A worthy pioner!
>
> (I, v, 152–4, 157–9, 162–5)

Understand that as he says this his teeth chatter, 'pale as his shirt, his knees knocking each other'. Intense anguish ends with a kind of laughter, which is nothing else than a spasm. Thenceforth Hamlet speaks as though he had a continuous nervous attack. His madness is feigned, I admit; but his mind, as a door whose hinges are twisted, swings and bangs with every wind with a mad haste and with a discordant noise. He has no need to search for the strange ideas, apparent incoherencies, exaggerations, the deluge of sarcasms which he accumulates. He finds them within him; he does himself no violence, he simply gives himself up to himself. When he has the piece played which is to unmask his uncle, he raises himself, lounges on the floor, lays his head in Ophelia's lap; he addresses the actors, and comments on the piece to the spectators; his nerves are strung, his excited thought is like a surging and crackling flame, and cannot find fuel enough in the multitude of objects surrounding it, upon all of which it seizes. When the king rises unmasked and troubled, Hamlet sings, and says, 'Would not this, sir, and a forest of feathers—if the rest of my fortunes turn Turk with me—with two Provincial roses on my razed shoes, get me a fellowship in a cry of players, sir!' (III, ii, 263–6). And he laughs terribly, for he is resolved on murder. It is clear that this state is a disease, and that the man will not survive it.

In a soul so ardent of thought, and so mighty of feeling, what is left but disgust and despair? We tinge all nature with the colour of our thoughts; we shape the world according to our own ideas; when our soul is sick, we see nothing but sickness in the universe:

> This goodly frame, the earth, seems to me a sterile promontory, this most excellent canopy, the earth, look you, this brave o'erhanging firmament, this majestical roof fretted with golden fire, why, it appears no other thing to me than a foul and pestilent congregation of vapours. What a piece of work is a man! how noble in reason! how infinite in faculty! in form and moving how express and admirable! in action how like an angel! in apprehension how like a god! the beauty of the world! the paragon of animals! And yet, to me, what is this quintessence of dust? man delights not me: no, nor woman neither.
>
> (II, ii, 300–11)

Henceforth his thought sullies whatever it touches. He rails bitterly before Ophelia against marriage and love. Beauty! Innocence! Beauty is but a means of prostituting innocence: 'Get thee to a nunnery: why wouldst thou be a breeder of sinners? ... What should such fellows as I do crawling between earth and heaven? We are arrant knaves, all; believe none of us' (III, i, 122–3, 129–31).

When he has killed Polonius by accident, he hardly repents it; it is one fool less. He jeers lugubriously:

> *King.* Now Hamlet, where's Polonius?
> *Hamlet.* At supper.
> *King.* At supper! where?
> *Hamlet.* Not where he eats, but where he is eaten: a certain convocation of politic worms are e'en at him.
>
> (IV, iii, 17–21)

And he repeats in five or six fashions these gravedigger jests. His thoughts already inhabit a churchyard; to this hopeless philosophy a genuine man is a corpse. Public functions, honours, passions, pleasures, projects, science, all this is but a borrowed mask, which death removes, so that people may see what we are, an evil-smelling and grinning skull. It is this sight he goes to see by Ophelia's grave. He counts the skulls which the gravedigger turns up; this was a lawyer's, that a courtier's. What bows, intrigues, pretensions, arrogance! And here now is a clown knocking it about with his spade, and playing 'at loggats with 'em'. Caesar and Alexander have turned to clay and make the earth fat; the masters of the world have served to 'patch a wall'. 'Now get you to my lady's chamber, and tell her, let her paint an inch thick, to this favour she must come; make her laugh at that' (V, i, 188–90). When a man has come to this, there is nothing left but to die.

This heated imagination, which explains Hamlet's nervous disease and his moral poisoning, explains also his conduct. If he hesitates to kill his uncle, it is not from horror of blood or from our modern scruples. He belongs to the sixteenth century. On board ship he wrote the order to behead Rosencrantz and Guildenstern, and to do so without giving them 'shriving-time'. He killed Polonius, he caused Ophelia's death, and has no great remorse for it. If for once he spared his uncle, it was because he found him praying, and was afraid of sending him to heaven. He thought he was killing him, when he killed Polonius. What his imagination robs him of, is the coolness and strength to go quietly and with premeditation to plunge a sword into a breast. He can only do the thing on a sudden suggestion; he must have a moment of enthusiasm; he must think the king is behind the arras, or else, seeing that he himself is poisoned, he must find his victim under his foil's point. He is not master of his acts; opportunity dictates them; he cannot plan a murder, but must improvise it. A too lively imagination exhausts the will, by the strength of images which it heaps up, and by the fury of intentness which absorbs it. You recognise in him a poet's soul, made not to act, but to dream, which is lost in contemplating the phantoms of its creation, which sees the imaginary world too clearly to play a part in the real world; an artist whom evil chance has made a prince, whom worse chance has made an avenger of crime, and who, destined by nature for genius, is condemned by fortune to madness and unhappiness. Hamlet is Shakspeare, and, at the close of this gallery of portraits which have all some features of his own, Shakspeare has painted himself in the most striking of all.

13. Victor Hugo

1864

Victor-Marie Hugo (1802–1885), poet, playwright and novelist, was one of the principal figures of the French Romantic movement. His plays *Cromwell* (1827) and *Hernani* (1830) marked the beginning of the romantic revolution that was finally to break the neo-classical hold on the French stage. His novels include *Notre Dame de Paris* (1831) and *Les Misérables* (1862). His espousal of Shakespeare was part of his revolutionary program, which from 1848 was as much political as literary. He wrote his voluminous *William Shakespeare* (published in 1864) while in exile in the Channel Islands. Its English version, translated by A. Baillot and described on its title page as 'authorized', from which the following excerpts are taken, was also published in 1864.

Two marvellous Adams . . . are the man of Aeschylus, Prometheus, and the man of Shakespeare, Hamlet.

Prometheus is action. Hamlet is hesitation.

In Prometheus, the obstacle is exterior; in Hamlet it is interior.

In Prometheus, the will is securely laid down by nails of brass and cannot get loose; besides, it has by its side two watchers, Force and Power. In Hamlet the will is more tied down yet; it is bound by previous meditation, the endless chain of the undecided. Try to get out of yourself if you can! What a Gordian knot is our reverie! Slavery from within, that is slavery indeed. Scale this enclosure, 'to dream!' escape, if you can, from this prison, 'to love!' the only dungeon is that which walls conscience in. Prometheus, in order to be free, has but a bronze collar to break and a god to conquer; Hamlet must break and conquer himself. Prometheus can raise himself upright, if he only lifts a mountain; to raise himself up, Hamlet must lift his own thoughts. If Prometheus plucks the vulture from his breast, all is said; Hamlet must tear Hamlet from his breast. Prometheus and Hamlet are two naked spleens; from one runs blood, from the other doubt.

We are in the habit of comparing Aeschylus and Shakespeare by Orestes and Hamlet, these two tragedies being the same drama. Never in fact was a subject more identical. The learned mark an analogy between them; the impotent, who are also the ignorant, the envious, who are also the imbeciles, have the petty joy of thinking they establish a plagiarism. It is after all a possible field for the erudition and for serious criticism. Hamlet walks behind Orestes, parricide through filial love. This easy comparison, rather superficial than deep, strikes us less than the mysterious confronting of those two enchained beings, Prometheus and Hamlet.

Let us not forget that the human mind, half divine as it is, creates from time to time superhuman works . . . Prometheus and Hamlet are amongst those more than human works.

Hamlet, less of a giant and more of a man, is not less grand. Hamlet, appalling, unaccountable, being complete in the incomplete. All, in order to be nothing. He is prince and demagogue, sagacious and extravagant, profound and frivolous, man and neuter. He has but little faith in the sceptre, rails at the throne, has a student for his comrade, converses with any one passing by, argues with the first comer, understands the people, despises the mob, hates strength, suspects success, questions obscurity, and says 'thou' to mystery. He gives to others maladies which he has not himself: his false folly inoculates his mistress with true folly. He is familiar with spectres and with comedians. He jests with the axe of Orestes in his hand. He talks of literature, recites verses, composes a theatrical criticism, plays with bones in a cemetery, thunder strikes his mother, avenges his father, and ends the wonderful drama of life and death by a gigantic point of interrogation. He terrifies and then disconcerts. Never has anything more overwhelming been dreamt. It is the parricide saying: 'What do I know?'

Parricide? Let us pause on that word. Is Hamlet a parricide? Yes and no. He confines himself to threatening his mother; but the threat is so fierce that the mother shudders. His words are like daggers. 'What wilt thou do? Thou wilt not murder me? Help! help! ho!'—and when she dies, Hamlet, without grieving for her, strikes Claudius with this tragic cry, 'Follow my mother!' Hamlet is that sinister thing, the possible parricide.

In place of the northern ice which he has in his nature, let him have, like Orestes, southern fire in his veins, and he will kill his mother.

This drama is stern. In it truth doubts. Sincerity lies. Nothing can be more immense, more subtle. In it man is the world, and the world is Zero. Hamlet, even full of life, is not sure of his existence. In this tragedy, which is at the same time a philosophy, everything floats, hesitates, delays, staggers, becomes discomposed, scatters and is dispersed. Thought is a cloud, will is a vapour, resolution is a crepuscule; the action blows each moment in an inverse direction, man is governed by the winds. Overwhelming and vertiginous work, in which is seen the depth of everything, in which thought oscillates only between the king murdered and Yorick buried, and in which what is best realized, is royalty represented by a ghost, and mirth represented by a death's-head.

Hamlet is the *chef d'oeuvre* of the tragedy-dream.

One of the probable causes of the feigned folly of Hamlet has not been up to the present time indicated by critics. It has been said, 'Hamlet acts the madman to hide his thoughts, like Brutus'. In fact, it is easy for apparent imbecility to hatch a great project; the supposed idiot can take aim deliberately. But the case of Brutus is not that of Hamlet. Hamlet acts the madman for his safety. Brutus screens his project, Hamlet his person. The manners of those tragic courts being known, from the moment that Hamlet, through the revelation of the ghost, is acquainted with the crime of Claudius, Hamlet is in danger. The superior historian within the poet is here manifested, and one feels the deep insight of Shakespeare into the ancient darkness of royalty. In the Middle Ages and in the Lower Empire, and even at earlier periods, woe unto him who found out a murder or a poisoning committed by a king! Ovid, according to Voltaire's conjecture, was exiled from Rome for having seen something shameful in the house of Augustus. To know that the king was an assassin was a state crime. When it pleased the prince not to have had a witness, it was a matter involving one's head to ignore everything. It was bad policy to have good eyes. A man suspected of suspicion was lost. He had but one refuge, folly; to pass for 'an innocent'; he was despised, and that was all. Do you remember the advice that, in Aeschylus, the Ocean gives to

Prometheus, 'To look a fool is the secret of the wise man'. When the Chamberlain Hugolin found the iron spit with which Eldrick the vendee had impaled Edmond II, 'he hastened to put on madness', says the Saxon Chronicle of 1016, and saved himself in that way. Heraclian of Nisibe, having discovered by chance that Rhinomete was a fratricide, had himself declared mad by the doctors, and succeeded in getting himself shut up for life in a cloister. He thus lived peaceably, growing old and waiting for death with a vacant stare. Hamlet runs the same peril, and has recourse to the same means. He gets himself declared mad, like Heraclian, and puts on folly like Hugolin. This does not prevent the restless Claudius from twice making an effort to get rid of him, in the middle of the drama by the axe or the dagger in England, and towards the conclusion by poison.

The same indication is again found in *King Lear*: the Earl of Gloucester's son takes refuge also in apparent lunacy; there is in that a key to open and understand Shakespeare's thought. In the eyes of the philosophy of art, the feigned folly of Edgar throws light upon the feigned folly of Hamlet.

The Amleth of Belleforest is a magician, the Hamlet of Shakespeare is a philosopher. We just now spoke of the strange reality which characterizes poetical creations. There is no more striking example than this type, Hamlet. Hamlet has nothing belonging to an abstraction about him. He has been at the University; he has the Danish rudeness softened by Italian politeness; he is small, plump, somewhat lymphatic; he fences well with the sword, but is soon out of breath. He does not care to drink too soon during the assault of arms with Laertes, probably for fear of producing perspiration. After having thus supplied his personage with real life, the poet can launch him into full ideal. There is ballast enough.

Other works of the human mind equal *Hamlet*, none surpasses it. The whole majesty of melancholy is in Hamlet. An open sepulchre from which goes forth a drama, this is colossal. *Hamlet*, is to our mind, Shakespeare's chief work.

No figure among those that poets have created is more poignant and stirring. Doubt counselled by a ghost, that is Hamlet. Hamlet has seen his dead father and has spoken to him. Is he convinced? No, he shakes his head. What shall he do? He does not know. His hands clench, then fall by his side. Within him are conjectures, systems, monstrous apparitions, bloody recollections, veneration for the spectre, hate, tenderness, anxiety to act and not to act, his father, his mother, his duties in contradiction to each other, a deep storm. Livid hesitation is in his mind. Shakespeare, wonderful plastic poet, makes the grandiose pallor of this soul almost visible. Like the great larva of Albert Dürer, Hamlet might be named 'Melancholia'. He also has above his head the bat which flies embowelled, and at his feet science, the sphere, the compass, the hour-glass, love, and behind him in the horizon an enormous terrible sun which seems to make the sky but darker.

Nevertheless at least one half of Hamlet is anger, transport, outrage, hurricane, sarcasm to Ophelia, malediction on his mother, insult to himself. He talks with the gravediggers, nearly laughs, then clutches Laertes by the hair in the very grave of Ophelia and stamps furiously upon the coffin. Sword-thrusts at Polonius, sword-thrusts at Laertes, sword-thrusts at Claudius. From time to time his inaction is torn in twain, and from the rent comes forth thunder.

He is tormented by that possible life, intermixed with reality and chimera, the anxiety of which is shared by all of us. There is in all his actions an expanded somnambulism. One might almost consider his brain as a formation; there is a layer of suffering, a layer of thought, then a layer of dreaminess. It is through this layer of dreaminess that he feels, comprehends, learns, perceives, drinks, eats, frets, mocks, weeps, and reasons. There is between life and him a transparency; it is the wall of dreams; one sees beyond, but one cannot step over it. A kind of cloudy obstacle everywhere surrounds Hamlet. Have you ever whilst sleeping had the nightmare of pursuit or flight, and tried to hasten on, and felt anchylosis in the knees, heaviness in the arms, the horror of paralysed hands, the impossibility of movement? This nightmare Hamlet undergoes whilst waking. Hamlet is not upon the spot where his life is. He has ever the appearance of a man who talks to you from the other side of a stream. He calls to you at the same time as he questions you. He is at a distance from the catastrophe in which he takes part, from the passer-by whom he interrogates, from the thought that he carries, from the action that he performs. He seems not to touch even what he grinds. It is isolation in its highest degree. It is the loneliness of a mind, even more than the loftiness of a prince. Indecision is in fact a solitude. You have not even your will to keep you company. It is as if your own self was absent and had left you there. The burden of Hamlet is less rigid than that of Orestes, but more undulating; Orestes carries predestination, Hamlet carries fate.

And thus apart from men, Hamlet has still in him a something which represents them all. *Agnosco fratrem*.[1] At certain hours, if we felt our own pulse, we would have conscience[2] of his fever. His strange reality is our own reality after all. He is the funeral man that we all are in certain situations. Unhealthy as he is, Hamlet expresses a permanent condition of man. He represents the discomfort of the soul in a life which is not sufficiently adapted to it. He represents the shoe that pinches and stops our walking; the shoe is the body. Shakespeare frees him from it, and he is right. Hamlet—prince if you like, but king never—Hamlet is incapable of governing a people, he lives too much in a world beyond. On the other hand, he does better than to reign; he is. Take from him his family, his country, his ghost, and the whole adventure at Elsinore, and even in the form of an inactive type, he remains strangely terrible. That is the consequence of the amount of humanity and the amount of mystery that is in him. Hamlet is formidable, which does not prevent his being ironical. He has the two profiles of destiny.

Let us retract a statement made above. The chief work of Shakespeare is not *Hamlet*. The chief work of Shakespeare is all Shakespeare. That is moreover true of all minds of this order. They are mass, block, majesty, bible, and their solemnity is their *ensemble*.

Have you sometimes looked upon a cape prolonging itself under the clouds and jutting out, as far as the eye can go, into the deep water? Each of its hillocks contributes to make it up. No one of its undulations is lost in its dimension. Its strong outline is sharply marked upon the sky, and enters as far as possible into the waves, and there is not a useless rock. Thanks to this cape, you can go amidst the boundless waters, walk among the winds, see closely the eagles soar and the monsters swim, let your humanity wander midst the eternal hum, penetrate the impenetrable. The poet renders this service to your mind. A genius is a promontory into the infinite.

---

[1] I recognize a brother.

[2] I.e., consciousness

14. Thomas Kenny

1864

The Life and Genius of Shakespeare (London: Longman, Green, Longman, Roberts and Green) appears to be the only book Kenny published.

a) From 'The Men and Women of Shakespeare' (pp. 151–2)
The male figures in his drama comprise nearly all his greatest creations, and this was an inevitable result of the truthfulness of his imitation of nature. It is in man alone that all the strongest and most agitating passions are unfolded in their most unrestrained intensity. The more refined and more timid, the less selfish and less adventurous, character of woman, instinctively evades the extremity of rash reckless action. There is no female Falstaff, or Hamlet, or Othello; and even if such a being were to arise out of some unaccountable caprice of nature, we should withhold our sympathy from the monstrous combination; and the dramatist would find in it no subject on which his art could be successfully employed.

The great creations of Shakespeare's genius are never his model heroes and heroines. Like other dramatists, it is through the working of violent and irregular impulses that he affords us the deepest glance at the springs of human action. In all love stories the lovers must be made too amiable to be completely striking and original characters. The writer of impassioned fiction must not, on the one hand, give a shock to our trust in his impartiality and truthfulness, by investing his favourite figures with novel and astonishing attributes; and, on the other hand, he must not distract our interest in their persons and their fortunes, by presenting them with the drawbacks of unwelcome vices or follies. He must not help to destroy the illusion which he seeks to create. In real life the lover will forget, or altogether ignore, the existence of great defects in the object of his love; in our more impartial observation of the mimic representation of life, those defects would at once become clearly visible, and would rudely shake our sympathy with the passion which their presence cannot moderate or extinguish. Romeo, and Ferdinand, and Orlando, and Florizel, are all brave, generous, and accomplished, and are all equally destitute of any very salient or very perplexing characteristics.

Hamlet, also, is a lover; but in the great crisis of his life love is not the prevailing influence to which he yields. He is saddened and amazed; he is intensely meditative and bewildered; in him the familiar light of love pales before the lurid glare of grief and horror; and he becomes the strangest and most complex figure the genius of the great dramatist ever delineated. Lear is another of Shakespeare's largest creations. In both those characters his imagination expatiates in the wide realm of meditative passion, with a freedom which seems hardly compatible with the limited conditions of distinct individual consciousness; and the partial or complete frenzy of Hamlet and of Lear alone seems to give even an appearance of truth to the wild variety of moods through which they are passing.

b) 'Hamlet' (pp. 367–85)
Hamlet is the most universally interesting of all the dramas of Shakespeare. It is the most abrupt and the most perplexing; it unites the greatest diversity of thought and feeling in its central figure; and this figure seems to have impressed the form of its own astonishing personality on the whole vivid, agitated, rapid, and original composition.

The mere external history of this great work is involved in more or less of that petty obscurity which seems inevitably to meet us in all our attempts to follow the labours of our wonderful dramatist. But we are not, at all events, left in absolute ignorance of its probable origin. We learn from a variety of contemporary allusions that a play of *Hamlet* must have been in existence about the very earliest period to which Shakespeare's connection with the stage can with any probability be assigned. [There follows a discussion of references to *Hamlet* (Kyd's as well as Shakespeare's) and references in *Hamlet*, and of early editions of the play and their sources.]

Hamlet is the great enigma among the productions of Shakespeare's genius. For the first century and a half after its appearance no one seems to have suspected that this work occupied any exceptional position in the poet's dramas; but its strange and dark complexity has become an object of the most special fascination to the anxious, agitated, inquiring intellect of more recent generations. Goethe, in his *Wilhelm Meister*, has devoted a separate study to the elucidation of its construction, its purpose, and its ultimate meaning. Schlegel and Coleridge have also sought to penetrate its supposed mystery. We doubt, however, whether much has been added, or, perhaps, ever can be added, by the labours of the critic to the obvious impression which the work leaves on every mind of ordinary sensibility and intelligence. We are all aware that Hamlet becomes startled, amazed, saddened, and overwhelmed by the discovery of a crime which has involved all that is nearest to him in its guilt or its ruin; and that, when he is called upon to take vengeance upon its author, he dallies and procrastinates with the uncongenial mission. But we still read this stupendous tragedy with a large amount of wonder and bewilderment. We are unable perfectly to reconcile Hamlet's anomalous history with Hamlet's fine intellect and elevated character; we are lost in the 'strange labyrinth of his many moods and singularities'.

We cannot help thinking that the perplexity to which we are thus exposed is founded on conditions which, from their very nature, are more or less irremovable. It has its origin, as it seems to us, in two sources. It is owing, in the first place, to the essential character of the work itself; and, in the second place, it arises, in no small degree, from the large licence which the poet has allowed himself in dealing with his intrinsically obscure and disordered materials.

All Nature has its impenetrable secrets, and there seems to be no reason why the poet should not restore to us any of the accidental forms of this universal mysteriousness. The world of art, like the world of real life, may have its obscure recesses, its vague instincts, its undeveloped passions, its unknown motives, its half-formed judgments, its wild aberrations, its momentary caprices. The mood of Hamlet is necessarily an extraordinary and an unaccountable mood. In him exceptional influences agitate an exceptional temperament. He is wayward, fitful, excited, horror-stricken. The foundations of his being are unseated. His intellect and his will are ajar[1] and unbalanced. He has become an exception to the common forms of humanity. The poet, in his turn, struck with this strange figure, seems

1 Out of harmony, at odds.

to have resolved on bringing its special peculiarities into special prominence; and the story which he dramatised afforded him the most ample opportunity of accomplishing this design. Hamlet is not only, in reality, agitated and bewildered, but he is led to adopt the disguise of a feigned madness, and he is thus perpetually intensifying and distorting the peculiarities of an already over-excited imagination. It was, we think, inevitable that a composition which attempted to follow the workings of so unusual an individuality should itself seem abrupt and capricious; and this natural effect of the scene is still further deepened, not only by the exceptionally large genius, but by the exceptionally negligent workmanship of the poet.

Shakespeare not only used the details of his wonderful story with the most unconfined freedom, but he sometimes exaggerated its contrasts, and violated its natural proportions. He was driven, too, perhaps, in some measure, to this exaggeration, by the consciousness that he had to develop a history of thought rather than a history of action, and that it was only by the most rapid variety of moods and scenes he could give to his work the highest dramatic vitality.

There was, we think, in the original conception of the work another element of almost inevitable confusion. On the story of a semi-barbarous age the poet has engrafted a most curious psychological study; and there is naturally a certain want of probability and harmony between the refined and sensitive spirit of Hamlet and the rude scenes amidst which he is thrown, and the rude work of vengeance which he is commissioned to perform.

We believe we can discover in the history of the drama a further reason why its details were not always perfectly harmonised. It was written under two different and somewhat conflicting influences. The poet throughout many portions of its composition had, no doubt, the old story which formed its groundwork directly present to his mind; but he did not apparently always clearly distinguish between the impressions in his memory and the creations of his imagination; and the result is, that some of his incidents now seem to his readers more or less inexplicable and discordant. In the novel[2] it is distinctly stated that the woman who answers to the Ophelia of the drama was used by the King as a means of

---

2 'The History of Hamlet' in Belleforest's *Histoires Tragiques*, a source for *Hamlet*.

discovering whether Hamlet's apparent madness was only pretended, and that he was carefully warned of the danger to which he was thus exposed. This circumstance was, perhaps, remembered by the poet, and may have contributed to give much of its strange form to the language which Hamlet addresses to Ophelia; but this portion of the dialogue, as it stands in the play, looks unnecessarily extravagant and offensive, from the absence of any such preliminary explanation. Again, in the story, the officious intruder who conceals himself behind the arras is an unmistakeable enemy of Hamlet's, and we are not surprised at the fate by which he is overtaken; but in the drama Polonius cannot be supposed to occupy the same position, and the wild levity with which the death of the alleged 'foolish, prating knave' is treated by the Prince seems more or less inexplicable, as it is manifest that he does not act from any distrust of his mother, and as he addresses her with the utmost unreserve during the remainder of their interview. It is true that she afterwards says—'He weeps for what is done'; but we hardly know how to credit the statement.

The fact is, we believe, that the dramatist, using another licence, has sometimes run closely and even inextricably together the feigned madness and the real mental perturbation of Hamlet. We should have had no difficulty in accepting this representation of the character if it were only consistently maintained: it would even, under the circumstances, have been perfectly natural; but we find that, in his real mood, he retains throughout the drama, as throughout the story, the perfect possession of his faculties; his only confidant, Horatio, must evidently feel quite assured upon that point; and we are compelled, in spite of a few equivocal passages, entirely to share his conviction.

There are a few instances in which we can give but a qualified belief to the incidents which the poet himself seems to have wholly invented. We are not quite sure that Hamlet abstained from killing the King because he found him at his prayers; and this passage looks too much like a device got up for the particular occasion. We are still more perplexed by the part which he plays at the funeral of Ophelia; and here again he seems under the influence both of some real and of some pretended distraction. He afterwards expresses to Horatio his regret at having forgotten himself to Laertes, and states that he was actually moved to a 'towering passion'. But we cannot feel absolutely certain that the whole scene was perfectly free from all constraint and affectation; and we doubt, in particular, his assurance of the extremity of his love for Ophelia. That is one of the points which the poet himself seems to have left in convenient shadow. We can now only conjecture that Hamlet's attachment, though real, had but little enduringness or intensity. A man can have but one absorbing passion at a time; and love was clearly not the absorbing passion of the Danish Prince from the commencement to the close of this drama.

The mode in which the poet has treated the age of his chief personage affords another instance of his readiness to look on the minor accidents of his story with the large freedom of his imagination. In the earlier scenes Hamlet appears as a mere youth, who intends 'going back to school in Wittenberg', and who is struck with a fatal blight at the very threshold of active life, and in the most picturesque of all positions; but in a later act, with an intellect rapidly ripened, and while curiously moralising on the skull of Yorick and the dust of Alexander, he is made a mature man of thirty, although we can find no room for any large lapse of time during all the intermediate action. We have here again to make a choice for ourselves between two conflicting representations of the character; and our pervading and final impression is, that Hamlet struggled and perished in the bloom of early manhood.

Some of the minor figures in the scene bring with them their own perplexities. The King does not form one of the distinguishing creations of Shakespeare. The general moderation, and even insipidity, of character which he exhibits seems hardly compatible with the tremendous and remorseless career of crime he has pursued. The fact is, that the vigorous, and even the clear, presentment of every other agent in the scene is made subordinate to the manifestation of the wonderful personality of Hamlet himself; and hence it is, perhaps, that the Queen, too, meets us in indistinct and shadowy outline. It would, perhaps, be idle to attempt to determine whether or not she was privy to the murder of her first husband. It did not suit the immediate purpose of the poet to afford us any means of forming an absolute judgment upon that subject. Her guilt, in the early scenes, hardly admits of any extenuation; but, as we proceed, her character is naturally depicted in less repulsive colours; and we should otherwise be unable to sympathise with her attachment to her son and her resolution to save his life at all hazards. The portraiture of Polonius has also received a double treatment. The explanation of the contrasts in the character is in the main, no doubt, to be found in the circumstance that he has begun to sink into senility or dotage. But he seems to have but scanty justice dealt out to him by the dramatist; and we do not willingly witness the contempt and ridicule of which he is finally made the object. The part assigned to Laertes presents a far more reckless contrast. The impetuous, vindictive, but frank and fearless youth could not possibly have consented, on the first light offer, to become the principal agent in a scene of dark and hideous treachery, in which the presence of the King himself is barely credible.

There is one, however, of the secondary characters in *Hamlet* which must be considered decidedly Shakespearian. The poet, it is true, has still touched but lightly the passion and the sorrow of Ophelia; but it is impossible to mistake the beauty and the grace of her nature, or the immediate form of the inevitable and inexplicable destiny to which she falls a helpless victim.

There is one episode in this play which has given rise to a large amount of conjecture. The critics are divided in opinion as to the origin and purport of the lines on 'Priam's slaughter', recited by the player in Act II, Scene ii. Dryden and Pope thought they were introduced as a burlesque of the extravagant style which commonly distinguished the dramas of the age of Shakespeare. The modern commentators in general believe, on the contrary, that the poet was in earnest in the praises of them which he puts into the mouth of Hamlet; and some of them go so far as to suppose that they formed a portion of some early work which he himself had written. It seems to us that it would be a mistake to adopt either of these opinions without any reservation. We think that the passage was produced by Shakespeare himself for the occasion, and that it was written by him in that large, disengaged, mimetic mood, which was the favourite mood—which was even the natural mood—of his dramatic genius. He seems throughout the whole scene, and, indeed, throughout the whole play, to yield to the ardour of his own imaginative inspiration; but he does not, we take it for granted, appear in it in any way in his own personal character. He composed those verses in the spirit of the dramas of his time, and he praised or blamed them in imitation of the common taste of his contemporaries; but in doing so he naturally gave a certain amount of exaggeration to their distinguishing peculiarities, for the purpose of affording the requisite contrast between their artificial emphasis and the supposed directness of his own more immediate revival of the actual world.

Hamlet is, perhaps, of all the plays of Shakespeare, the one which a great actor would find it most difficult to embody in an ideally complete form. It would, we think, be a mistake to attempt to elaborate its multiform details into any distinctly harmonious unity. Its whole action is devious, violent, spasmodic. Its distempered, constant irritability is its very essence. Its only order is the manifestation of a wholly disordered energy. It is a type of the endless perplexity with which man, stripped of the hopes and illusions of this life, harassed and oppressed by the immediate sense of his own helplessness and isolation, stands face to face with the silent and immovable world of destiny. In it the agony of an individual mind grows to the dimensions of the universe; and the genius of the poet himself, regardless of the passing and somewhat incongruous incidents with which it deals, rises before our astonished vision, apparently as illimitable and as inexhaustible as the mystery which it unfolds.

It is manifest that *Hamlet* does not solve, or even attempt to solve, the riddle of life. It only serves to present the problem in its most vivid and most dramatic intensity. The poet reproduces Nature; he is in no way admitted into the secret of the mystery beyond Nature; he could not penetrate it; he only knew of the infinite longings and the infinite misgivings with which its presence fills the human heart.

Hamlet is, in some sense, Shakespeare's most typical work. In no other of his dramas does his highest personality seem to blend so closely with his highest genius. It is throughout informed with his scepticism, his melancholy, his ever-present sense of the shadowiness and the fleetingness of life. He has given us more artistically complete and harmonious creations. His absolute imagination is perhaps more distinctly displayed in the real madness of King Lear than in the feigned madness, or the fitful and disordered impulses, of the Danish Prince. But the very rapidity and extravagance of those moods help to produce their own peculiar dramatic effect. Wonder and mystery are the strongest and the most abiding elements in all human interest; and, under this universal condition of our nature, *Hamlet*, with its unexplained and inexplicable singularities, and even inconsistencies, will most probably for ever remain the most remarkable and the most enthralling of all the works of mortal hands.

15. The Hamlet Controversy

1867

This collection of seven letters, originally published in July and August 1867 in the Melbourne (Australia) *Argus* under a variety of pseudonyms, was republished in the same year as a pamphlet under the title *The Hamlet Controversy, Was Hamlet Mad?*. In it there is a marked 'ganging up' by his fellow journalists against James Smith, who was widely regarded (according to Harold Love) as 'Melbourne's leading man of letters.'[1] The debate arose from a performance of Hamlet in Melbourne by Walter Montgomery, who surprised those of the audience looking for the traditional reading, by emulating the 'romantic' and more thoughtful Hamlet made fashionable in London by Charles Fechter. The critic James Neild, who frequented the London theatres in the 1840s and whose contribution here is published under the pseudonym 'John Brown,' gives the following description of the traditional reading of the part: ' . . . a gloomy person in black velvet, who wore a long coat and had tall ostrich feathers in his hat. He walked with a measured pace, did not sit down much, spoke in a sepulchral tone and wept at intervals. His hair was black and curly and upon his breast there was a decoration of St George and the Dragon' (*The Australasian*, Sept. 29, 1877, p. 403). The other pseudonyms are explained as: 'Thomas Jones,' Charles Bright; 'Jack Robinson,' Archibald Michie, Q.C.; 'Jack Robinson, junior,' David Blair; 'R.H.H.,' R.H. Horne (q.v. *CRH*, iii, 97ff, 'Professor Grabstein').

1. James Smith.[2]

Sir—So many queries have been addressed to me, both personally and by letter, with respect to Mr. Montgomery's Hamlet[3], that I will venture, with your permission, to reply to them through the columns of the *Argus*.

1 Harold Love, *James Edward Neild, Victoran Virtuoso* (Carlton, Vic.: Melbourne University Press, 1989), p. 236.

2 James Smith, a Kentish man by birth, who was at one time editor of the *Salisbury and Winchester Journal*, became a journalist on the staff of the Melbourne *Age* in 1855.

3 Walter Montgomery, a London actor, played at Drury Lane theater in the 1860s. He played Othello at the Royal Princess's Theatre, London, in 1863 and Hotspur in the

Let me premise that every Hamlet of note I have ever seen has been largely affected by, if it has not faithfully reflected, the temperament of the actor. Mr. Montgomery's Hamlet is no exception to the rule. It is essentially lymphatic. The portrait he presents to us is that of an amiable, affectionate, self-indulgent, plaintive, and somewhat lachrymose Prince. He brings out in strong relief the vacillating, wayward, irresolute, and half-hearted traits in Hamlet's character. He shows him to be unstable as water, as variable as the clouds, as inconstant as the moon. His melancholy is not so deeply seated as to render him incapable of fugitive moods of cheerfulness. He can be diverted from his purpose by trivial incidents, and find a pretext for procrastination in dreamy reveries. His grief is the indulgence of a weak mind, and not an influential principle of action operating upon a strong one. It is content to expel itself in 'the windy suspiration of forced breath'. When it should serve as a goad or a spur, it is found to restrain him like a curb. Were his nature less gracious, his manner less urbane, and his speech less gentle, we should be provoked to despise him as a poor shiftless creature, who is always 'letting "I dare not" wait upon "I would", like the poor cat i' the adage[4].' He exhibits none of the 'stern effects' of which Hamlet speaks, and which actors of greater vigour have been accustomed to display; but on the other hand, he reveals to us—which some of them do not—the deep undercurrent of affection which he supposes the Prince to entertain for Ophelia, the mental pang which he imagines that Hamlet experiences on discovering her prevarication, and the profound reluctance which he conceives the Prince must feel in renouncing, from a sense of duty and in disregard of the dictates of his heart, the passion he has cherished for her. Mr. Montgomery's is an eminently agreeable and thoroughly artistic Hamlet. It is most effective where other representatives of the character have been least so; and it is comparatively unimpressive in those scenes—the interview with the Ghost, and the closet scene, for example—in which previous actors, and Mr. Anderson[5] especially so, have made their strongest points, and

---

Drury Lane production of the first part of *Henry IV* during the tercentenary celebrations of Shakespeare's birth in 1864. Fechter employed him briefly at the Lyceum in 1863.

4   *Macbeth*, I, vii, 44–5.

5   James Anderson, who had acted in London with Macready and was for a time manager of Drury Lane theater. He performed Hamlet in Melbourne in 1867 shortly before Montgomery's arrival.

produced their most powerful impressions. In both these instances Mr. Montgomery presents us with a striking picture of mental abstraction when, as I think, it should be one of mental absorption. His mood of mind is subjective, when it should be objective. He is occupied with his own meditations when every nerve might be supposed to be strung to the highest tension, and every faculty wholly engrossed by the awful apparition, the hour, the place, and the astounding nature of the revelation made to him by the 'dread corse'. Thus much is obvious from the text; and it derives additional sanction from the traditions of the stage, handed down to us from the time in which Shakspeare played the Ghost in his own tragedy, and is reported to have instructed Burbage in the part of Hamlet, and reproved Kemp for his 'villanous' gagging. How Garrick bore himself in presence of the spirit we know from Partridge's ingenious remark in *Tom Jones*[6]; and I think we may accept Shakspeare and Garrick as high authorities on this point, and may be justified, in this wise, for disputing the wisdom and propriety of innovations which have nothing to recommend them beyond the fact of their novelty. If the foundations of Hamlet's reason are not—as two such experts as Drs. Bucknill and Conolly assert they are[7]—overthrown by the appalling revelation which has been just made to him by the Ghost: if he does not join together—as Coleridge, as M. Villemain, and as nearly all the great critics, English, German, and French, declare he does—'the light of reason, the cunning of intentional error, and the involuntary disorder of the soul', his mind was unquestionably unsettled; while, physically, he appears to have been in a state of hysteria. Not otherwise can we account for the unfilial and scoffing language which he employs towards his father, which are so significant of Hamlet's state of mind, and which Mr. Montgomery, strange to say, altogether omits. They are these:

> Hamlet: Ha, ha, boy! say'st thou so? Art thou there Truepenny?
> Come on, you hear this fellow in the cellarage.

And again—

6 See *CRH*, i, 159–62.

7 For Bucknill see above, pp. 60–128. John Conolly's *A Study of Hamlet* appeared in 1863.

> Well said, old mole! Canst work i'the earth so fast?
> A worthy pioneer.
>
> (I, v, 152–3, 164–5)

So, too, in the play scene. Mr. Montgomery cuts out whole passages which are not less demonstrative of a disordered intellect, and not less important aids to the spectator, who is anxious to divine the true condition of the Prince's mind. The lines excised are these:—

> Hamlet: Would not this, sir, and a forest of feathers (if the rest of my fortunes turn Turk with me), with two Provençal roses on my razed shoes, get me a fellowship in a cry of players, sir?
>
> Horatio: Half a share.
> Hamlet: A whole one, ay.
> For thou dost know, O Damon dear,
> This realm dismantled was
> Of Jove himself, and now reigns here
> A very, very—peacock.
>
> (III, ii, 263–72)

This extravagance of conduct and language, it will be observed, is exhibited when none but Horatio is present, and when no necessity exists for acting the madman; while the flightiness of the couplet—

> For if the King like not the comedy,
> Why, then, belike—he likes it not, perdy—
>
> (III, ii, 280–1)

resembles that of many of Madge Wildfire's crazy speeches[8].

In the purely colloquial passages of the play Mr. Montgomery is very happy; and while, in the 'business' of the piece, he does not refuse to adopt what has been engrafted upon it by his predecessors, he gives proof of originality of conception, and endeavours, indeed, to clear up some obscurities of the text by the light which his action projects upon them. Thus, he mitigates the apparent harshness of Hamlet's language and conduct to Ophelia, in the first scene of the second act, by conveying to the

---

8 A character in Scott's novel *The Heart of Midlothian*.

audience, as explicitly as possible, the assurance of the fact that the King and his Chamberlain are eaves-dropping behind the arras; while he also renders broadly manifest the shock communicated to the Prince's moral nature when he discovers Ophelia to have paltered with the truth by declaring that her father is at home at the very moment she is aware of his being an ear-witness of all that passes in her interview with her royal lover. Mr. Montgomery represents Hamlet as actuated by conflicting emotions throughout the entire scene—grieved and exasperated by Ophelia's complicity in the espionage to which he is exposed, but still yearning towards her with a tenderness that transforms wrath into pity, and that converts the injunction, 'Get thee to a nunnery', into a loving admonition, springing either from the conviction that there she would find a haven of security and repose, or from the selfishness that would prompt him to debar others from winning that place in her affections which he had held, and had voluntarily, but reluctantly, vacated. Elegant and agreeable, however, as this is, there is nothing either in the text or the stage directions to warrant it; and harsh, violent, and cruel as Hamlet's language and demeanour are towards Ophelia, they are strictly natural, and are perfectly appropriate to his state of mind. Shakspeare well knew that in cases of mental disease or distemper, the sufferer hates and distrusts, upbraids and abuses, those whom, in mental health, he has loved and esteemed; just as—to digress for a moment—pure-minded women, if they become insane, will indulge in the lewdest conversation. And hence the dramatist, with a rare knowledge of intellectual disorder, puts snatches of coarse ballads into the mouth of the mad Ophelia. Therefore any display of tenderness towards her in the particular scene referred to, any softening down of his brutality, must be, as Dr. Conolly justly observes, 'an unauthorised departure from the delineation of his character by Shakspeare'[9]. I think that experienced physician's criticism of this part of the play is one of the best ever penned; and it derives the utmost weight from his professional experience. 'Hamlet's expressions', he writes, 'from the commencement of his directly addressing Ophelia, are all of the tissue of a madman's talk, with no clearly determined application to immediate circumstances, and addressed by a disturbed mind and heart to the empty

---

9 John Conolly, *A Study of Hamlet* (London, 1863) p. 116.

air, or to the shadows of images crowding among his troubled thoughts. They contain unconnected allusions to himself, broken reflections unconsciously wounding Ophelia, starts of general suspicion, and sudden threats which flash and disappear, but which would have been carefully refrained from if there had been only deception intended to make the path to vengeance clear. If we would unravel all these mingled expressions, we find that it is scarcely of Ophelia that Hamlet is speaking thus wildly, but of his mother, of her detested marriage, and of his own conscious imperfections; all these things are tinging his discourse, but giving it no true colour'[10].

Furthermore, Mr. Montgomery is wrong, I conceive, in his delivery—graceful and pleasing though it is—of the well-known soliloquy, 'To be, or not to be'; which is not the philosophical speculation of a Cato or a Seneca, but the passionate utterance of a soul at war with life, but dreading death, and agonised by the struggle between these two sentiments. With these abatements, and with the general objection that Mr. Montgomery does not allow Hamlet to exhibit that 'exaggerated energy under provocation' of which mild and sensitive natures like his are peculiarly capable, and in which the Prince indulges as often as his indignation gets the better of his indecision, the portraiture is graphic, consistent, and harmonious; deficient in power, but careful in finish and delicate in detail. If I were to borrow an illustration from a sister art, I should liken the picture to a clever watercolour drawing, lacking the depth and solidity of an oil-painting, but compensating for the absence of these by the presence of other qualities—by airiness of tone, simplicity of treatment, transparency of colour, lightness of touch, and a certain sobriety of effect—a pleasant twilight, equally removed from the gloom of evening and the garishness of the afternoon.

In brief, Mr. Montgomery tones down the roughness and violence of the poet's Hamlet, and presents him to us *en beau*. It is not Hamlet the moody, with a wildness that is half false, and a madness that is half real; the misanthropical, the vindictive, with a thin crust of courtly culture overlying the fundamental coarseness of his race, and broken up by fitful eruptions of fiery and ungovernable passion; but Hamlet the lover, Hamlet

---

10   Conolly, pp. 117–18.

the dawdling dreamy *fainéant*, Hamlet the *debonnaire*, Hamlet with a large infusion of Werther. I am indisposed to disparage it on that account. It is the actor's own conception of the character, and he is to be commended for thinking it out, and for embodying it in a concrete and consistent form. Let us be just to him, and let us be equally just to other actors who offer us the fruits of their genius, their study, their observation, and experience, even although we differ from them in the reading of a passage or the idea of a part.

2. 'John Brown' (James Neild).[11]

Sir-I never knew till this moment what a misfortune it is to be obscure. I am not naturally of an envious disposition, but I cannot help feeling that it is worth living for, to be able to say that a whole people is on the tiptoe of expectation to learn one's opinion. On the other hand, I trust the inhabitants of this and the neighbouring colonies are properly sensible of their obligations to Mr. James Smith, for having at last spoken, and so relieved them from the distressing uncertainty, of how they should estimate the quality of Mr. Montgomery's Hamlet. As to Mr. Montgomery himself, having now been made aware of the sad truth that he is not the great actor some of his critics and admirers have pronounced him, it can hardly help but that he will return to Europe in the 'Great Britain', and be for the rest of his life content to rate himself among the lesser lights of the theatrical firmament. Nevertheless, there be dissentients in this, as in most other matters of opinion; and, to be frank with you, I at once proclaim myself of an entirely different way of thinking from Mr. Smith. You may perhaps shudder and stand aghast at the temerity which refuses accord with the sentiments of a gentleman, who, it appears, holds the right to speak oracularly in matters of theatrical criticism; but your own experience will render it unnecessary for me to remind you that obstinate people of my complexion continually present themselves, even when so potent an authority as Mr. James Smith has to be confronted.

Freely translated, and highly condensed, Mr. Smith's letter appears to me to consist of some such declaration as this:—'Mr. Montgomery is

11 James Neild (1824–1906), erstwhile friend of James Smith, was trained in England as a physician before emigrating to Melbourne, Australia, in 1853, where he practiced medicine, but also became Melbourne's principal theatre critic.

passable, and that is about all; he walks quietly through his part, and reads fairly enough, and—*voilà tout*. If you submit this letter of mine to a similar process of transmutation, it may declare to this effect:—That Mr. Montgomery, being strongly impressed with the prevailing fault of actors in making their characters only pieces of stage mechanism, more or less skilful or clumsy, has determined on presenting them as living and breathing things, having human passions and prejudices, and so expressing these, not according to arbitrary models, but in obedience to that kind of impulse from which all the greatest works of art result.

Taking Mr. Smith's letter in detail, however, I find that he begins by informing an anxious public that 'every Hamlet of note has been largely affected by, if it has not faithfully reflected, the temperament of the actor'; and that Mr. Montgomery's temperament is 'essentially lymphatic'. I reply by denying that his temperament is 'essentially lymphatic', and I assert, on the contrary, that it is principally of the nervo-sanguineous kind. I assert, further—and in so asserting do but declare what innumerable examples have proved to be an invariable truth—that it would be simply impossible for a man whose temperament was 'essentially lymphatic' ever to attain to eminence as an actor in any line of his art, if even the desire for distinction should exist, which is not very likely. So far, therefore, from Mr. Montgomery's Hamlet 'faithfully reflecting' his temperament, it is an instance of complete subordination of temperament to the necessities of character. The endeavour, therefore, to explain his acting as consistent with a 'lymphatic temperament' needs no reply, as it is nothing else than drawing a conclusion from false data. 'But', says Mr. Smith, 'Mr. Montgomery's is an eminently agreeable Hamlet'. Logically, then, as, according to Mr. Smith, it is vastly different from all other Hamlets, I might remind him that this admission leads us to infer that all preceding Hamlets have been eminently disagreeable. But without insisting on this inference, and conceding that this is not precisely what he desires to say, I go on with the letter, and presently find myself in a fog; for one of the reasons adduced to demonstrate this quality of eminent agreeableness is that Mr. Montgomery's Hamlet is 'comparatively unimpressive in those scenes—the interview with the Ghost, and the closet scene, for example—in which previous actors, and Mr. Anderson especially so, have made their strongest points'; and then we are told 'Mr. Montgomery presents us with a striking picture of mental abstraction', which we are further informed should have been 'mental absorption', and that the state of his mind is 'subjective' instead of 'objective'. I have no doubt that many waverers in opinion about Mr. Montgomery, and Mr. Montgomery's Hamlet, wavered no longer when they got to this part of Mr. Smith's letter; because, you see, though this imposing array of terms 'abstraction', 'absorption', 'subjective', and 'objective', may convey no information whatever to a great many of Mr. Smith's readers, they are dictionary words so formidable and important that they are sure to have created a profound impression. You remember the story of some highly-impressible old ladies who always used to weep whenever they heard the Rev. Mr. Whitfield pronounce the word 'Mesopotamia'. There was no reason in the world why the old ladies should weep at the word 'Mesopotamia', any more than, let us say, at the word 'pickles'; but the fact remains that they did weep; and the fact will also remain that conviction will have followed, with an equal reason for following, the abstraction-absorption-subjective-objective appeal. Then Mr. Smith says, with a triumphant sort of flourish, 'Thus much is obvious from the text'; but I confess, with great humiliation at the consciousness of my incapacity, that I do not here see what is obvious, and that I do not know what portion of the text should make it so. But since Mr. Smith follows up the remark by telling us that, as the traditions of the stage have been handed down from the time of Shakspeare, who instructed Burbage and reproved Kemp, and that as *Tom Jones* tells us how Garrick bore himself in the part, we are justified in disputing the wisdom and propriety of certain innovations, his admirers will dispute them accordingly.

Next he brings in Drs. Bucknill and Conolly, two most learned physicians and graceful writers, it is true, but who, having been exclusively engaged many years in the treatment of lunatics, manifestly, and perhaps not unnaturally, came at last to consider madness an inevitable condition of humanity, and so found that Hamlet, despite his frequent protestation to the contrary, was really mad, the particular proof of his madness consisting in using 'unfilial and scoffing language towards his father'. I should be afraid to say how many young gentlemen in Victoria are mad, if the use of unfilial and scoffing language towards their fathers be positive proof thereof. But, without staying to inquire how far it might be desirable to make provision for the accommodation of thirty or forty thousand additional lunatics prospectively on the enforcement of this principle, let us see how it applies to Hamlet, who, Mr. Smith says, is to be deemed insane because he accosts the subterranean ghost jocularly. It is probably in the experience of every person to have felt an irrepressible desire in certain moments of great solemnity to laugh or utter a jest, or indulge in some grimace or antic, preposterously inconsistent with the time and place. It would seem as if the excessive restraint imposed by the circumstances prompted a relief in some shape; and thus it is found sometimes at funerals, that remarks are made strangely at variance with the sombre surroundings. Conformably with this propensity, Hamlet, who has just experienced a very agony of terror at the sight of his father's spirit, finds much relief in passing, even for a moment, to the extreme state of playful sportiveness. But this feeling Shakspeare very properly makes only a transient one, for, after letting Hamlet allude to the ghost as 'this fellow in the cellarage', and 'an old mole i'the ground', his reverential feelings are allowed again to predominate, and he exclaims, 'Rest, rest, perturbed spirit'. I do not doubt that Mr. Montgomery's own judgment would incline him to the restoration of these passages of jocularity; and, I dare say, it is only in unavoidable deference to the prejudices of the audience, who have so long been accustomed to a mutilated version, that for a time he consents to follow the beaten track. So again Mr. Smith informs us that the jubilant exclamation beginning with

> For thou dost know, O Damon dear,

is 'not less demonstrative of a disordered intellect', in answer to which I may reply that nothing is more common than for a person suddenly made aware of the successful termination of an experiment, or enterprise, to indulge in a mock-tragic demonstration, a bit of extemporised recitative, a snatch of some song—for Hamlet might consistently sing these lines—a quotation from Scripture, however irreverently applied, or any other interjectional mode of testifying satisfaction. For the moment, Hamlet's delight at the perfect success of his murder—test overcomes every other feeling, and being, as we know, a humourist as well as a philosopher, he bids Horatio congratulate him, and asks him if he does not think he was made for an actor? There is certainly nothing inconsistent with sanity in all this; and Mr. Montgomery, I am sure, does not omit these lines because they are inconsistent with Hamlet's reason, but because some excisions being necessary, these seem to permit of being excised without material impairment of the rest. Mr. Smith's usually careful attention, however, has been at fault for him not to have observed that Mr. Montgomery does *not* omit the couplet beginning 'For if the king', etc. Mr. Smith can only describe Mr. Montgomery's singularly original rendering of the scene with Ophelia as 'elegant and agreeable', although it throws such a light upon the meaning of the whole passage, and gives such a colour of justification for the rudeness that comes subsequently. He says:—'There is nothing either in the text or in the stage directions to warrant it'; *ergo*, I presume, it is unwarrantable. But, on the other hand, there is certainly nothing either in the text or the stage directions to forbid it; and I need hardly say how abundant are the examples in the representation of Shakspeare's plays, in which stage business has been introduced admirably auxiliary to the elucidation of the text, but without any basis of warrant in the way of stage directions in the original. If Shakspeare's own prompter's copy of his plays is ever found, we may haply light upon a good deal of information as to the manner in which they were represented: failing this, it is open to every actor, while keeping strictly within the limits of the approved text, to adopt the best mode his judgment may point out to give it emphasis and intelligibility.

Briefly to sum up my opinion of the condition of Hamlet's mind, and *malgré* Dr. Conolly, Dr. Bucknill, Coleridge, Villemain, and—Mr. James Smith, I have to remark that Hamlet's own declaration of his motive—namely, that he simulates madness the better to compass his purpose—is by far the most reasonable estimate to entertain of his mental condition. He is eccentric, fitful, vacillating, or, as Mr. Smith would put it, given to the 'subjective' rather than the 'objective'; but what then? If these qualities be attributes of madness, then is the world a lunatic asylum, and certificates of insanity are but insolent assumptions of power by the majority as against the minority of lunatics.

Thus of the psychology of Hamlet. Mr. Smith, in addition to the other objections, likes not Mr. Montgomery's delivery of the soliloquy. He admits it is 'graceful and pleasing'; but to his thinking it wants 'agony'. It is not piled up enough; to use an Americanism, it wants more 'fireworks'. He says in effect if not in words that it ought to be delivered according to Bottom's notion as 'a part to tear a cat in, to make all split'[12].

12   *A Midsummer Night's Dream*, I, ii, 25–6.

And then, passing from the soliloquy to the character generally, he says, 'It is like a clever water-colour drawing, lacking the depth and solidity of an oil-painting'; or, it is 'a pleasant twilight, neither morning nor afternoon'. With Mr. Smith's understood acquaintances with pictorial art, it is something remarkable that he should have selected so unfortunate an illustration to prove Mr. Montgomery's inferiority, for he should know that the watercolours of this day have all the force and more than the finish of oil-paintings. Let him take comfort, however. If he will go a little higher up the street, he will get his oil-painting with the colours plastered on 'thick and slab'; and as to the other comparison, he will there also find the sun so hot and blazing that ordinary people do not soon recover from its effects. Finally, I am Pagan enough to thank the gods they have sent us an actor who—in obedience to the promptings which urged on John Millais and Holman Hunt to tread a new road in painting, and Ruskin, with Scott to second him, to demolish the bastard abortions of eighteenth century architectural art—has charged himself with the great and noble mission of interpreting Shakspeare unclogged by tradition, and guided only by the light of nature and a fine intelligence.

3 'Thomas Jones' (Charles Bright),[13] Melbourne, July 31 (1867).

Sir—As I have reason to anticipate that a large number of persons are about to inquire of me my opinion of Mr. Montgomery's Hamlet, I will venture, with your permission, to reply to them through the columns of the *Argus*.

After the elaborate letter from Mr. James Smith which appeared in your issue of yesterday, it is scarcely necessary for me to premise that, were not my convictions materially opposed to those of that practised critic, I should not now address you. However, it so happens that I differ from him almost *in toto*, and cannot conceal my gratification at finding, by to-day's *Argus*, that so excellent an authority as Mr. John Brown has arrived at a conclusion very similar to my own. I dissent from Mr. Smith's *dicta* relative to Mr. Montgomery; I protest against his assumptions regarding the character of Hamlet. Mr. Brown has replied to Mr. Smith

---

13   Charles Bright, a friend of Neild, was also a Melbourne journalist and for a time editor of the Melbourne *Examiner* and the *Weekly Review*.

convincingly on most of the topics contained in his letter; and I now modestly desire to unfold myself upon one or two points which Mr. Brown has thought proper to treat with indifference.

Mr. Smith's principal cause of complaint against Mr. Montgomery is, that he does not represent Hamlet as really mad—that, in short, he takes Hamlet's word in preference to that of many of his critics, and believes that he

> —essentially is not in madness,
> But mad in craft[14].

This, which to Mr. Smith is so serious a ground of offence, is to me Mr. Montgomery's surpassing merit. Nothing can be easier than to represent Hamlet as an occasional madman. The actor—incapable of comprehending the full scope of Hamlet's varied and complex character, disinclined to piece out and supplement the meagre stage directions which accompany the text—falls back upon the ready plea of madness, and in a moment finds an excuse for his wildest extravagances, his densest stupidities. Any meaning, or no meaning, can with ease be covered by it. Does the Prince seem to be gratuitously harsh and cruel to Ophelia—it is madness. Is he apparently merry where good Monsieur Critic thinks he should be doleful, and sad where he should be playful—it is his madness. For resourceless actor and soulless critic, this is alike a city of refuge. But it is a Zoar[15] which cannot much longer be tolerated, and, spite of the illustrious names gilding the imposture, it will come to be regarded as a remnant of the system of false criticism of which Nahum Tate is the arch-apostle[16], which seeks to twist the mighty utterances of Shakspere into harmony with foregone conclusions, rather than reverently to investigate, by the best light the age can furnish, the true meaning of his grand creations. And in setting about this task, we must not forget that Shakspeare's plays are eminently acting plays; that if we have but capable

---

14 An adaptation of III, iv, 171–2.

15 '... his fugitives shall flee unto Zoar,' Isaiah, xv, 5.

16 Nahum Tate (1652–1715), a Restoration poet most notorious for re-writing *King Lear* to provide it with a happy ending.

actors, the enjoyment derivable from the presentation of these dramas on the stage must far surpass that to be obtained from closet study. But, though conceived with an immediate eye to theatrical exhibition, and fitted for the stage as are no other dramatic compositions, they are singularly barren of stage direction. When Hamlet requests young Osric to 'put his bonnet to its right use', we are informed for the first time that the latter has entered bare-headed; and so when Macduff is besought not to hide his face with his hat, but to give sorrow vent[17], the earliest intimation is conveyed of the natural action which marked his reception of the news of his irreparable loss. In these cases the 'business' of the scene is unmistakeable; but there are others of equal importance where it is more obscure. Among these I rank such scenes as that between Hamlet and Ophelia in the third act; and in these it is not only justifiable, but it is the bounden duty of every actor of mark to study to discover in what way the 'business' may be made best conducive to the elucidation of the text. When Shakspeare was by to explain his own ideal, it mattered not that the stage directions were few and meagre; but now, when instead of Shakspeare we have stage tradition, burdened with the fancies of two and a half centuries, the omission of these finger-posts becomes an important feature, and every original actor must seek by study of the text, and perhaps the text alone, to reconstruct them. It is this which Mr. Montgomery seems to me to have done, and in this way he has produced a Hamlet perfectly sane and consistent with human nature, though not, perhaps, the model, orthodox, methodical character which, if he is not to be mad, some critics would have him be.

The more closely I look into this character of Hamlet the more revolting does the assumption of semi-madness appear. Was there ever mind more thoroughly sane? It is so sane that it cannot take a leap in the dark, though prompted to it by almost ungovernable impulse, but must have

<pre>   —grounds
          More relative than this.</pre>

It is so sane that, when firmly resolved on a course which it clearly sees to be right, it adheres to it in spite of the most terrible obstacles, as

17   *Macbeth*, IV, iii, 209–10.

witness the scene in the Queen's chamber, where, though Hamlet has by an unhappy chance killed the father of her he loves, he yet, with most ruthless decision, continues the interview with his mother, and strives to make her

> Repent what's past, avoid what is to come.

If this be madness, it is of a strange nature, which can be prearranged by himself, and put on or off as his purpose serves. The passages Mr. Smith quotes in token of Hamlet's craziness might well be incorporated in the current acting copy, without in the slightest degree impairing the conception of the character which Mr. Montgomery presents to us. Besides, Mr. Smith proves too much. If Hamlet be mad when he asks if the success of his 'mouse-trap' scheme might not get him 'a fellowship in a cry of players', Horatio cannot be sane to reply, 'Half a share'. And while on this subject, I may remark how strange it is that, if Hamlet be really touched, he should be deemed mad by all saving the two who may be supposed best acquainted with his 'heart of hearts'—his father's ghost, and his dear friend Horatio. Ordinarily it is those most closely attached to a man who first discern his flightiness.

Another grave fault which Mr. Smith discovers in the Hamlet of Mr. Montgomery is that it lacks force, that it has a large infusion of Werther. Strange how minds differ! It is this very absence of mere brute force, this admixture of German dreaminess, which forms in my estimation one of the charms of this conception. Hamlet is the realization, the embodiment—if I may use the word in this sense—of mental not physical greatness. He is no savage hodman, who having found out his wronger goes and punishes him, but a man of genius of 'large discourse', a free thinker, who dares to condemn the customs of his country when he conceives them to be at odds with reason. He is irresolute through excess of mental clear-seeing, and his is too highly strung a nervous organization to be forcible.

On this theme one might write by the yard, and still have much to say, but as I cannot hope to induce you to publish a Hamlet supplement, I will conclude. Mr. Smith has had his say, happily for mankind; Mr. Brown has had his; and now, by your leave, I have had mine. The world may not be much the wiser by our utterances; for, after all, what can we poor criticlings do in front of such a play as *Hamlet*, and such a representative of the noble Prince? Mainly, to my thinking, be very thankful. As to comparing this Hamlet with any of those we have seen before in this colony, it is idle. This is flesh and blood, which they were not; and I should as soon think of comparing the genial Artemus Ward, who died at Southampton, with the figure in Mr. Sohier's window[18]. So far as our stage history extends, I may say of Mr. Montgomery in this character, to quote a somewhat hackneyed phrase of Macaulay's, 'He has distanced all his competitors so decidedly, that it is not worth while to place them. Eclipse is first, and the rest nowhere'.

4 'Jack Robinson' (Archibald Michie, Q.C.), August 1 (1867).
Sir—I think it is only what the public expect of the editor of the *Argus*, that he should keep his columns open for me. I do not write these words in any light spirit, for during the growing interest generated of the criticism of Smith, Brown, and Jones, my neighbours have been, one and all, at me with such expressions as this—'Well, Robinson, what are *you* going to say to all this?' or, 'Robinson, are you a Smithian or a Brownist', etc. Apprehending, therefore, as I do, that the vital statistics of the colony may be most unfavourably affected from mere anxiety of mind unless I complete the quartette, I at once, without apology, conquer my constitutional indolence, and throw my critical cap into the ring.

And surely, at starting, my excellent friend Jones is on the right track for truth when he calls attention to the great fact that Shakspeare's plays are, and were intended by their author to be, acting plays. As affording a boundless field for subsequent criticism, it was an advantage that Shakspeare was an actor as well as an author. In every line he wrote he had evidently, and almost instinctively, an eye to the *mise en scène*: and thus his men and women always talk and act as do men and women in real life. Action and passion, impulse and reason, storm and calm, interrupt and cross each other, just as they do wherever our nature is wrought upon by the actual business of the world. What has traditional acting to do with such scenes as these? What is it, or what should it be, to Mr. Montgomery how Garrick played Hamlet, or what Partridge thought of

18 Sohier was the proprietor of a waxworks museum in Melbourne.

it? If Mr. Montgomery can see a ghost as well as Garrick, and feel the presence of a ghost as well as Garrick, he will (physical qualities being equal) play Hamlet as well as Garrick. Those who cultivate the superstitions of the stage will, of course, laugh at bringing Garrick's and Montgomery's names in juxtaposition. So has tradition derided the mention of Garrick's name by the side of Betterton's; and yet, different as they were from each other, both were excellent, because both were natural and original. The same remark may be made on the exceedingly diverse styles—if Hazlitt and all the critics of that day are to believed—of John Kemble and Edmund Kean.

Why, therefore, should Mr. Smith subject Mr. Montgomery to a standard—the traditional one—which every original actor has a right to disregard wherever that standard conflicts with his own convictions? Mr. Smith relies (in his second letter of yesterday) on 'nearly all the commentators of Shakspeare' as authority for requiring us to believe that the Hamlet of Shakspeare is really mad. But if an actor by close study of the part, lighted up by his observation of human creatures, shall come to a different conclusion, what is the choice before him? He must give us a mechanical, lifeless, unreal copy of the rendering authorised by the commentators, or he must trust to nature and his convictions, and give us his own conception. Mr. Montgomery has, I think, wisely acted on the latter alternative. I have not seen (it is my loss) his Hamlet, but crediting Jones, Brown, and the apparent responsive public, Mr. Montgomery has done wisely. Relying, therefore, on nature and observation—as I think every great actor has always done, and to be really great must always do [Edmund Kean once, as Richard III, thrilled the house by a last abortive attempt to strike Richmond, an attempt acknowledged to have been borrowed from an exhausted and fainting prize-fighter in the ring], he becomes a true and honest interpreter at any rate, and stands just as good a chance of being a faithful interpreter as if he were to become the copy of a copy. Rachel, the little orange girl of Paris, was wise enough to know this. Fechter[19] has achieved his fame by knowing this, and acting on it. *Melius est petere fontes, quam sectari rivulos*[20], is

19   Charles Fechter, the French actor, had caused a sensation in London with his new interpretation of the part of Hamlet at the Princess's Theatre in March 1861.

20   'It is better to seek out the springs, than follow the streams'.

a sound old maxim, which, freely rendered, assures us that it is better to seek the fountain-head, human nature, than slavishly to follow the commentators.

For doing this, it appears, from the testimony of Brown and Jones, that Mr. Montgomery may be left to his own resources. That he is not wrong in giving us a sane Hamlet will, I think, appear by portions of the text not yet referred to by Brown or Jones. Following the 'Well said, old mole', which, in its apparently shocking irreverence towards his father's ghost, is only, as Mr. Smith thinks, to be explained by insanity, we have the not very insane words—

> There are more things in heaven and earth, Horatio,
> Than are dreamt of in your philosophy. But come:—
> Here, as before, never, so help you mercy
> How strange or odd soe'er I bear myself—
> As I, perchance, hereafter shall think meet
> To put an antic disposition on;
> That you, at such times, etc.
>
> (I, v, 168–74)

Have we not here a distinct intimation that Hamlet purposes to assume madness—'to put an antic disposition on'—a passage frequently altogether disregarded by the 'commentators'. And as to the 'Well said, old mole', which so staggers Mr. Smith's sense of filial duty, the expression is consistent with perfect, although highly-excited sanity. It is akin to the light jests sometimes heard under the scaffold at a public execution. There is a condition of the mind—especially in nervous and highly-organised natures, such as Hamlet's—not unlike hysteria; your correspondent Brown refers to it, and it is common in Italy and other southern climes. Whilst a man is in this state, you cannot always tell what is in the heart merely from what comes out of the mouth. Shakspeare understood this fact in our nature so well that he frequently employs it with marvellous effect. After the awful scene between Hamlet and his father's ghost, the former utters the magnificently sane soliloquy, commencing—

> O, all you host of heaven! O earth!

interrupted by Horatio and Marcellus—

> Horatio (within)—Hillo, ho, ho, my lord.
> Hamlet—Hillo, ho, ho, boy: come, bird, come.
>
> (I, v, 118–19)

Does Mr. Smith think that Hamlet is at this point suddenly struck mad, or that he says, 'Come, bird, come', as a sportsman might say it? In *Lear* and other plays are many other indications of the feeling to which I refer—indications as true to human nature as they are apparently incongruous.

I venture to think that the charge against Hamlet of being irresolute is not much better founded than the suggestion of his madness. Where, and when, and how is he irresolute? Hamlet was a scholar, a gentleman, a man of thought: not a headstrong fool to kill his uncle, when that killing might be a murder. An ignorant rustic might have been resolute enough to act on the Ghost's evidence alone; not so Hamlet—

> —Give me that man
> That is not passion's slave, and I will wear him
> In my heart's core.
>
> (III, ii, 69–71)

Hamlet, distrusting the Ghost, gets up the play to see how the king's demeanour will answer to and confirm the Ghost's revelations. He says to Horatio—

> There is a play tonight before the king;
> One scene of it comes near the circumstance
> Which I have told thee of my father's death.
> I prythee when thou see'st that act a-foot,
> Even with the very comment of thy soul
> Observe mine uncle: if his occulted guilt
> Do not itself unkennel in one speech,
> It is a damned ghost that we have seen,
> And my imaginations are as foul
> As Vulcan's stithy.
>
> (III, ii, 73–82)

It is not, indeed, until the scene where Hamlet enters and finds his uncle in the very act of confession and prayer that he shows any symptom of vacillation—

[Quotes Hamlet's speech: 'Now might I do it pat' III, iii, 73–92.]

This, the first good opportunity Hamlet has—after reasonable conviction of his uncle's guilt—for revenge, is about the only good opportunity he loses. He would have been overpowered by guards and attendants in the interview with his uncle, after the disastrous killing of old Polonius. Hamlet does his work promptly enough in the fencing scene. He has fulfilled his destiny—

> The time was out of joint; oh, cursed spite,
> That ever he was born to set it right[21].

Yet, in the last grand scene, we learn how sane, and thoughtful, and unselfish Hamlet's soul was; how it could forget its own personal sorrows in the high thoughts which became a great prince. We there see the real greatness which, having shown itself in public affairs (not before us in the play), had made him 'loved of the distracted multitude'. With his last breath he thinks only of the charge which might have been his—

> I cannot live to hear the news from England:
> But I do prophecy the election lights
> On Fortinbras: he has my dying voice;
> So tell him, with the occurrents, more and less,
> Which have solicited. The rest is silence. (Dies)

(V, ii, 306–10)

I have altogether outrun my own purpose, and committed an unwitting trespass on your columns, by the length of this letter. The offence, however, is committed, and it may be that other members of our numerous family are erring in like fashion. If so, you have the editorial remedy in your own hands, by choosing from amongst us, and for yourself, your own Jack Robinson.

21 An adaptation of I, v, 189–90.

5. 'Jack Robinson (Jun.)' (David Blair)[22], Ballarat, August 1, (1867).
Sir—*Et ego in Arcadia*[23]. Pray, of your goodness, allow this particular member of the distinguished family of Robinson to have his brief say touching the topic which his celebrated form-fellows, Smith, Brown, and Jones, are so hotly debating in your generously open columns.

I start with claiming to be a far more competent critic of Mr. Montgomery's Hamlet than either of my three friends aforesaid, and for the simple reason that I have never seen it. A disadvantage, you call it? Well, there you are wrong. Was it not Sydney Smith's fixed canon of criticism never to read a book before reviewing it, because 'it prejudices one so'? And did not Mr. James Mill, father of the illustrious member for Westminster, preface his very able *History of India* with an elaborate dissertation, proving that the best man to write the history of any country is a man who has never seen it? Here is warrant more than sufficient for the modest claim I prefer. Unprejudiced and unbiassed, I am also enthusiastic, ' 'Tis distance lends', etc.[24]

With the unhesitating frankness of perfect impartiality, then, I at once take side with Mr. Montgomery, and with my friends, Brown and Jones, and against Mr. Smith, albeit he is backed up by those two noted experts, Drs. Bucknill and Conolly. I declare war to the knife with the specious but baseless and untenable theory of a mad Hamlet. Mad! indeed. No doubt had the noble Prince of Denmark lived in these our days, those three noted experts, Drs. Smith, Bucknill, and Conolly, would have had out a writ *de lunatico* at once, clapped him into Hanwell[25] without any circumlocution, and then set zealously to work to exercise their joint professional skill on him. How the three would have revelled in psychological analysis! What an infinite deal of professional prattle there would

---

22   David Blair, in addition to being ordained as a Presbyterian clergyman, was a professional journalist and editor of the *Age* and subsequently the *Weekly Review*. He was a long-standing friend of James Neild.

23   'And I am in Arcadia'—referring to the fact that the letter is sent to Melbourne from the gold mining town of Ballarat.

24   ' 'Tis distance lends enchantment to the view,' Thomas Campbell, *The Pleasures of Hope*, i, 7.

25   The lunatic asylum of which Conolly was superintendent.

have been about the poor patient's 'subjective' and 'objective' moods! how positive in its terms the certificate of insanity, clear and undoubted, which these practised adepts in all forms of mania would have sent to the old King at Elsinore.

But Hanwell and its psychological doctors apart, the question still remains open for discussion—Did Shakspeare design to depict a mere phase of madness in his character of Hamlet? Mr. Smith says 'Yes', and claims to have all the critics with him. Now I, on the other side, concede to Mr. Smith the two mad doctors from Hanwell. The critics, I maintain, are with me. Every one of them worth the name goes dead against the madness theory. In proof I name Hazlitt, Schlegel, Goethe, Tieck, Franz Horn, and in fact all the later German critics, with G.H. Lewes, W.S. Walker, and generally all the English critics since Hazlitt's time. Even Coleridge's view (of Hamlet's undoubted madness) is qualified with so many limitations, that one may justly say that Coleridge himself was to the last in doubt upon the point. And Hartley Coleridge, the finely-gifted son, ably vindicates the view of Hamlet's perfect sanity in one of the most delightful Shakspearian essays ever written[26]. It is entitled *On the Feigned Madness of Hamlet*, and was published first in *Blackwood*, and afterwards in Hartley's collected writings (*Marginalia*). I think I may venture to assert that the old theory of Hamlet's insanity has now become as obsolete as the text of Malone and Steevens, or the notes of Warburton. Mr. Montgomery's conception of the character is, therefore, in entire accord with the latest results of Shakspearian criticism; and, I may add, with the soundest principles of psychology. Mr. Smith seems to have got no further in his philosophy than the old Kantian principle of the categorical imperative. He stops at the 'subjective' and 'objective'. Did he never hear of Schelling, with his doctrine of the absolute correlation of the subjective and the objective? or of Hegel, with his magnificent theory of the subjectivity of the objective, and the objectivity of the subjective? This is the famous theory which solves all mundane problems with infallible certainty, while one may say Jack Robinson (Jun).

6. James Smith, Melbourne, August 3, 1867.

Sir—With your permission, I will reply to your correspondents on the only material point in controversy between us—the sanity or insanity of

---

26   See *CRH*, ii, 190–203.

my Lord Hamlet. The theory I hold is this:—That he originally feigned madness; his motive for doing so being left in doubt by the dramatist. It is not improbable that Hamlet's introspective habit of mind had apprised him of the alarming fact that the germs of insanity were latent in his nature, and were liable to be quickened into pernicious activity by severely depressing or greatly exciting circumstances. From the moment the Ghost communicated to him the particulars of the murder, and urged him to revenge, Hamlet's reason was unsettled. But the malady was intermittent. He had lucid intervals, in which he conversed and acted rationally; and it was this very inconsistency of conduct that puzzled the courtiers and has perplexed the critics. Polonius who, with all his garrulity and pomposity, was an eminently shrewd observer, and who, knowing nothing of Hamlet's supernatural shock, imputed his derangement to love, has described, with perfect accuracy, the stages of physical disorder through which Hamlet passed before reaching a condition of *dementia*. He

> Fell into a sadness; then into a fast;
> Thence to a watch; and thence into a weakness;
> Thence to a lightness; and, by this declension,
> Into the madness wherein now he raves,
> And we all wail for.
>
> (II, ii, 148–52)

Now this, as Dr. Conolly points out, 'might have been copied from the clinical notes of a student of mental disorders. We recognise all the phenomena of an attack of mental disorder consequent on a sudden and sorrowful shock; first, the loss of all habitual interest in surrounding things; then, the indifference to food, incapacity for customary and natural sleep; and then a weaker stage of fitful tears and levity, the mirth so strangely mixed with 'extremest grief'; and then subsidence into a chronic state in which the faculties are generally deranged'[27]. Hamlet, it is true, protests more than once or twice that he is not mad; but such asseverations are constantly made by the insane. He challenges inquisition; but so do madmen, and frequently baffle for hours and days together the inquiries

---

27 John Conolly, *A Study of Hamlet*, p. 77.

of the ablest barristers and the most experienced physicians. His language is coherent, his reflections are philosophical, and his replies are 'pregnant'; but as Polonius sagaciously observes, this is 'a happiness that often madness hits on, which reason and sanity could not so prosperously be delivered of' (II, ii, 211–13). But in the last act Shakspeare makes Hamlet himself resolve all doubts in the minds of his family and friends as to the reality of his madness by acknowledging to Laertes that he (Hamlet) had destroyed Polonius and driven Ophelia to distraction, despair, and death under the influence of lunacy:—

> You must needs have heard how I am punish'd
> With a sore distraction. What I have done,
> That might your nature, honour, and exception
> Roughly awake, I here proclaim was madness.
> Was't Hamlet wronged Laertes? Never, Hamlet.
> If Hamlet from himself be ta'en away,
> And when he's not himself does wrong Laertes,
> Then Hamlet does it not: Hamlet denies it.
> Who does it then? His madness. If't be so,
> Hamlet is of the faction that is wrong'd;
> His madness is poor Hamlet's enemy.
>
> (V, ii, 175–85)

Here, then, Hamlet is impaled on the horns of a dilemma. He had been either mad or sane. If sane, such an attempt to evade the moral responsibility of his actions by pretending to Laertes that he had been out of his mind, and excusing his conduct on that plea, would stamp him as guilty of the basest falsehood, chicanery, and cowardice. It is impossible to believe him capable of either. He was brave, honourable, and truthful, though vacillating and irresolute. His brutality to Ophelia and his murder of her father were the acts of a madman; and in this lucid interval, when his mind had been solemnised and tranquillised by the presentiment of his own death, he freely confesses and deplores his madness, and speaks of himself with a self-pity which is very natural and infinitely touching. The shadow of impending death was settling down upon his mind. 'Thou would'st not think', he pathetically exclaims to Horatio,'how ill all's here about my heart'. His friend interposes with a gentle 'Nay, good my lord', but the Prince, interrupting him, observes, 'It is but foolery; but it is such a kind of gain-giving (i.e. misgiving) as would, perhaps, trouble a woman'. Horatio offers to employ his mediation with a view to postpone the duel, but Hamlet rejoins, 'We defy augury', and proceeds to reason like a fatalist—'If it be now, 'tis not to come', etc. The next moment his opponent appears upon the scene, and it is at this solemn juncture that Hamlet 'proclaims' the reality of his madness, and adjures Laertes to believe him while making this public 'disclaimer of a purposed evil'. Is it conceivable that if Hamlet had been feigning insanity throughout, he would, at such a time, in such a presence, and with such a presentiment of death at his heart, dare to confront the dread 'something after death' with a cowardly lie upon his lips? Would Horatio—of whom Hamlet had said that he was 'e'en as just a man as e'er his conversation coped withal'—with a full knowledge of (and who could have known so well?) the falsehood of the plea, have talked of 'flights of angels singing' the soul of a slain perjurer 'to its rest'? As I have already intimated, many of the doubts which have been entertained with respect to Hamlet's derangement have arisen from the surprising brilliancy and profundity of his mental speculations. But what says one of the greatest French authorities (M. Esquirol) on this very point? 'Presque tous les alienés confiés à mes soins ... avoient eut une grande activité de faculté intellectuelle et morale qui avoient redoublés d'energie quelque tems avant l'accès'[28], Again, after every such access of frenzy, Hamlet appears to have had a lucid interval; a circumstance which Shakspeare, with his amazing knowledge of mental derangement or disease, has not omitted to acquaint us with; for when the Prince and Laertes, after wrestling on Ophelia's coffin, leap out of the grave, and Hamlet 'mouths' and 'rants', the Queen exclaims:—

> This is mere madness;
> And thus a while the fit will work on him,
> Anon as patient as the female dove,
> When that her golden couplets are disclosed,
> His silence will sit drooping[29].
>
> (V, i, 281–5)

---

28 'Nearly all the mad confided to my care ... have had a considerable intellectual and moral vigor whose energy has been redoubled some time before an attack.'

29 So Q2; in Q1, F these lines are spoken by Claudius.

If any one will be at the trouble to turn up the *Anatomy of Melancholy*, of Shakspeare's contemporary, Burton, he will find all the symptoms of Hamlet's disorder—the '*melancholia attonita* of nosologists'—described with the minutest accuracy in a chapter from which I cannot forbear making the following quotation:—'They (i.e., the persons so afflicted) are of profound judgments in some things, excellent apprehensions, judicious, wise, and witty; for melancholy advanceth men's conceits more than any humour whatever. Fearful, suspicious of all, yet again many of them desperate hairbrains; rash, careless, fit to be assassinates, as being void of all ruth and sorrow. *Tedium vitae* [boredom with life] is a common symptom; they are soon tired with all things—*sequitur nunc vivendi nunc moriendi cupido* [the desire to live is quickly followed by the wish to die]; often tempted to make away with themselves—*vivere nolunt, mori nesciunt*[30]: they cannot die, they will not live; they complain, lament, weep, and think they lead a most melancholy life'[31]. To those who lay great stress on Polonius's remark, 'Though this be madness, yet there's method in it', as implying that the chamberlain suspected the reality of Hamlet's frenzy, I would reply in the words of Horace—*Insanire paret certo ratione modoque*. (Horace, Satires, II, iii, 271: 'he aimed at going mad by fixed rule and method') Horatio's absolute silence on the subject has little or no significance either way; yet it is interesting to observe that, after the first act, everything he says to Hamlet is soothing and acquiescent. He never thwarts him, never argues with him, never contradicts him—he humours and indulges him. He assents to all he says with an invariable 'Ay, my good lord', and conducts himself towards the distempered Prince with a delicate and sympathetic consideration, with a lenitive gentleness, in which compassion for his malady is blended with a tender friendship for his old friend and fellow-student. It is unnecessary to occupy your columns with quotations from the tragedy—since everybody can consult it—to show that Hamlet was believed to be mad by his mother, his uncle (whose opinions, however, wavered on the subject), Polonius, Ophelia, and the people of Denmark; but it would help us to

---

30 Seneca, *Morales*.

31 Robert Burton, *Anatomy of Melancholy*, I, iii, memb. 1, ii 'Symptoms or Signs in the Mind.'

a settlement of the matter in controversy if we could ascertain how the character of Hamlet was played in Shakspeare's theatre, under his instruction, or with his sanction. This can only be arrived at inferentially. The lines in Burbage's *Funeral Elegy*—

> No more, young Hamlet, though but scant of breath,
> Shall cry 'Revenge' for his dear father's death—

will not assist us much: but in the writings of contemporary poets and dramatists—of men who had seen Hamlet played at the Globe or at the Blackfriars Theatre, and had spent convivial evenings with 'Gentle Will' at the Mermaid—we find allusions to the hero of the tragedy, which denote, I think, that his insanity was a commonly-accepted fact. Thus in *Eastward Ho*, the joint production of George Chapman, Ben Jonson, and John Marston, published in 1605, a footman named Hamlet enters, and is accosted by a tankard-bearer in these words:— ' 'Sfoote, Hamlet, are you mad?' So, too, in Decker's *Belman's Nightwalkes*, published in 1612, we read the following:—'But if any *mad Hamlet*, hearing this, smell villanie, and rush in to see what the tawny devils are doing', etc. And again, in Antony Skoloker's poem entitled *Daiphantus*, published in 1604, occurs this couplet:—

> Puts off his clothes; his shirt he only weares,
> Much like mad Hamlet; thus as passion teares[32].

It only remains to quote the opinion of some of the greatest of Shakspearian critics and commentators on this much-vexed question. Goethe's well-known dictum is that 'Shakspeare meant, in the present case, to represent the effects of a great action laid upon a soul unfit for the performance of it. In this view the whole piece seems to me to be composed. There is an oak-tree planted in a costly jar, which should have borne only pleasant flowers in its bosom—the roots expand, the jar is shivered'[33].

32 See *CRH*, i, 2.
33 See *CRH*, ii, 24–5.

Professor Gervinus, the latest and not the least eminent of Shakspeare's expositors in Germany, quotes and adopts Goethe's view of Hamlet's distemper, which he analyses and unfolds:—'The cause of this extremity of dejection lies in the events which befall him—events which suddenly impoverish him, which rob him, as Goethe says, of the true conception he had formed of his parents, which unhinge his mind, and roll upon him a tide of affliction, sorrow, uneasiness, and dire forebodings, which, in the course of their fulfilment, produce unrestrained derangement.'[34]

Coleridge declares that 'Hamlet's wildness is but half false'[35]. Guizot asserts that he was 'mad from calculation, and perhaps slightly mad from nature'. Thomas Campbell, while disbelieving that Hamlet's mind was absolutely diseased, observes:—'Most certain it is that his whole perfect being had received a shock that had unsettled his faculties'[36]. Dr. Maginn says: 'Hamlet is doubtless insane; but the species of intellectual disturbance, the peculiar form of mental malady under which he suffers, is of the subtlest character'. Dr. Ferriar, the learned author of an *Essay on Apparitions*, published in 1813, terms Hamlet's mental distemper 'latent lunacy', and remarks—'He feigns madness for political purposes, while the poet means to represent his understanding as really (and unconsciously to himself) unhinged by the cruel circumstances in which he is placed'. Mr. R.G. White, the highest Shakspearian authority in the United States, contrasts 'the fierce madness' of Lear with the 'weak intellectual disorder of Hamlet'. M. Philarète Chasles traces the derangement of the melancholy prince to the ghostly revelation he had received:—'Sa communication récente avec le monde des esprits jette dans son intelligence les premiers germes de la folie.[37]' And Professor Villemain has thus felicitously indicated the mixture of simulated and real insanity in Hamlet's conduct:—'Par une combinaison singulière, Shakspeare a representé la folie feinte aussi souvent que la elle-même; enfin il a imaginé de les

---

34 See *CRH*, iii, 258

35 See *CRH*, ii, 74.

36 Not Thomas Campbell, but 'T.C.' pseudonymic initials of 'Christopher North' (John Wilson). See *CRH*, ii, 136.

37 '... it is his recent communication with the world of phantoms that sows the first seeds of madness in his mind.' *CRH*, ii, 205.

mêler toutes deux dans le personnage bizarre d'Hamlet, et de joindre ensemble les éclairs de la raison, les ruses d'un égarement calculé, et le désordre involontaire de l'âme[38].'

Cardinal Wiseman considered that the question of Hamlet's insanity had been finally disposed of by Dr. Conolly, who had conclusively shown that the Prince was 'labouring under real madness, yet was able to put on a fictitious and artificial derangement for the purposes which he kept in view'.

I am aware that a contrary opinion was held by Sir Henry Halford: but his excellent essay on this subject was effectually dealt with by a Quarterly Reviewer, in 1833, whose article may be consulted with advantage by Shakspearian students and psychologists.

Postscript.—
While these sheets are passing through the press a friend informs me that 'Amleth' is an old Danish word signifying intellectual disturbance or 'crankiness': and allied, I presume, to Gaelic words 'Ahmluadh' and 'Ahmluaidh', which have the meaning *animi perturbatio*'.

7 'R.H.H.' (R.H. Horne[39])

Sir—In one of the earlier numbers of Forbes Winslow's *Journal of Psychological Medicine*, an article will be found entitled 'Madness, as treated by Shakspeare'. It was written by me at the request of Dr. Winslow, and certainly the more the subject was studied the more deeply interesting it became, and the more wonderful appeared Shakspeare's intuitive perception, not only of the varieties and peculiarities of the forms of demonstration, but of the fine gradations, as in King Lear, or the abrupt transitions and fitfulness of the lucid intervals, as in Hamlet—supposing him to be, so far, in a state of aberration of intellect. But in any case, among the whole tribe—nation, one might almost say—of Shakspeare's characters,

---

38   In a unique combination, Shakespeare has represented feigned folly as often as the real thing; and then he thought of mixing them both together in the bizarre character of Hamlet, and to combine the perspicacity of reason, the cunning of a calculated deviousness and involuntary mental disorder.

39   Richard Henry Horne (1803–1884) had a colorful career as scholar, administrator and military man. He had been appointed as commissioner for the Australian gold mines. For further notes on his career see *CRH*, iii, xiiiff and 97.

the great psychological puzzle has always been, and perhaps always will be, the character of Hamlet—the fine analyses of Goethe, Schlegel, Hazlitt, and others notwithstanding.

Another great German author and critic (Ludwig Boerne) puts the question of Hamlet's character in a new light. I have not the work at hand, but having translated the whole essay, I am quite clear as to the main points. If Hamlet was not mad, he must have been a very bad fellow. If he had not that excuse for what he says and does in several instances, more shame for him. Boerne thinks he was not mad, and that 'the glass of fashion and the mould of form' was a prince of villains. One may feel shocked and indignant when reading such arguments and opinions; but Ludwig Boerne is entitled, like my accomplished literary friends of the firm of Smith, B., J., and R., to his independent judgment.

In the first place, then, according to this German critic, it seems clear that Hamlet had seduced Ophelia. Certain things she utters during her madness greatly help to prove this. According to Boerne's view, Hamlet's desertion of her might or might not be heartless, but his cruel personal conduct towards her was quite inexcusable, or at least unnecessary; it drove her mad, and caused her to commit suicide. Perhaps the critic is wrong as to his first proposition; but the rest may be regarded as unquestionable. When he finds he has killed the father of the lady thus deeply wronged (in any view), so far from displaying the slightest shock of dismay or touch of grief at the moment, he calls the dead body 'names' and says, 'I took thee for thy better'. His method of hiding the corpse under the staircase is very like the half-cunningness, half-carelessness, of madness; and when, after equivocating with horrible jests about Polonius being 'at supper' (with the worms), he is obliged to confess where he has hidden the corpse, he tells the interrogator he 'may *nose* him, as he goes up the stairs'. Let us hope all this was said during at least a temporary fit of madness. What else could excuse it? Not even the excellent and nicely-discriminating phrase of 'hysteria' employed by one of the learned critical firm of Smith, B., J., and R.

What would be thought, felt, and said of such conduct in real life if recorded as facts of history? If brought home to modern times, how intolerable! Suppose some young duke or prince—say, of Denmark—came out here, and, after winning the affections of the elegant and accomplished only daughter of one of our most eminent official magnates, treated her in so outrageous a manner as to drive her into madness and suicide! It is scarcely possible that we could regard such a prince as being in his proper mind. Then look at the Lord chamberlain, Polonius—not as he is too commonly misrepresented on the stage, but as an amiable gentleman and scholar; an aged, but faithful official; a man of varied attainments, or the intellect of Claudius would not have held him in such esteem and confidence; one also of great knowledge of men and manners, as specially evidenced by his description of the gradations from love and melancholy into madness, and by his parting advice to his son: and when we thus consider the courtly old Lord Chamberlain, must we not feel that the treatment of him, when alive, by the Prince of Denmark was rude and offensive in the extreme—like the behaviour of one who had lost all command over himself; while the treatment of him when dead was to the last degree revolting? What, then, should we think of the mental condition of any young duke or prince of modern Denmark who treated the father of a deserted young lady—say, one of our learned judges or the Honourable the Minister of Justice—in so insulting a style when living; who then killed him like a rat, virtually said it served him perfectly right for 'intruding', and then dragging his dead body under the stairs, left him there to rot? It does not bear thinking about. Old times or new times are not the question; it would have been shocking in the time of Nebuchadnezzar or Nero. Let us hope that Hamlet had fits not merely of hysteria, but also of madness, and that he was not the wicked villain of Ludwig Boerne.

I had written thus far, when the last letter of Mr. James Smith appeared in this morning's *Argus* (5th August), and I think he has very well summed up the arguments, and is right in the main. He takes the view of Professor Villemain and Dr. Conolly, and with good grounds. My own opinion has also been that Hamlet presents an extraordinary instance of sudden alternations of madness and sanity. That he could not be mad while uttering the consecutive thoughts of philosophy and meditative speculation for which he is so remarkable, I feel convinced; but it is equally evident that his brain was at the mercy of the next moment of excitement. Madmen reason at times, like the best of us, but they 'gambol' from the theme, as Hamlet himself remarks. Madmen are often self-conscious of their state. I think Hamlet sometimes pretended to be more mad than he really was, in order to disguise the fact of that degree of which he was conscious. He also did some things that may be regarded as the intermediate stages—such as the hiding the body of Polonius under the stairs, where it was sure to be found; and his stealing the dispatches on shipboard, in the night, and forging fresh documents, with signature and seal, in order to get the heads of Rosencrantz and Guildenstern cut off instead of his own. It is, however, the sudden alternations of an intellect of the first order, with an intellect and with actions which denote a diseased volition, that have rendered his character a psychological problem in years gone by, if not a puzzle, as it certainly has proved a battlefield, at the present day.

So much has been said in the way of criticism of the acting of this tragedy at the Theatre Royal that I must not intrude upon the department of the dramatic critic. Permit me, however, to touch upon a few points. Thoughtful actors do what they intend, but they often do more than they know. Mr. Montgomery may not intend to show Hamlet as mad, but his performance throughout is so profoundly sad and pathetic, that the author of the *Anatomy of Melancholy* would have had no doubt as to the illustration. But apart from this question, the acting of Mr. Montgomery in several scenes is of the highest class, both in pathos and in artistic finish. The fine expressions of his face are among the rarest things ever seen on the stage, and often remind one of the pictures of Titian and Guido. His scene with Ophelia when he discovers she is telling him an untruth; his scene with his mother when the ghost of his father appears; and the scene at the grave of Ophelia, are events to the mind that can never be forgotten. It is not only an elegant performance throughout, but more touching and tearful than any Hamlet I have seen. His death is perfectly true to nature, and at the same time the finest example of the histrionic art. It is the most beautifully pathetic picture I ever saw on stage. Whoever has watched with breathless emotion a beautiful dying face, or a beautiful expression in dying, cannot fail to recognise this as something deep beyond tears, whatever tears may flow.

The lateness of the hour prevents me from saying what I would wish about Claudius, and Mr. Vincent's clear and excellent version of this finely-drawn character. Claudius is the practical mover of the tragedy; the Ghost strives to be so, but fails, for at the last moment Hamlet kills the king, not on account of any of the Ghost's exhortations, but from a mad, or half mad, rage and indignation at finding the treachery that has been practised upon him with the poisoned foils. It is a compliment to a Melbourne audience, not always deserved, to say that the house was crowded in every part. So may it be every time Mr. Montgomery plays Hamlet. It is a fine lesson for a public far too much given to burlesque and vulgarity, to the love of laughing at serious emotions, and at fine subjects made ridiculous.

16. James Russell Lowell

1868

James Russell Lowell was born in 1819 at Cambridge, Massachusetts and was educated at Harvard University, where, in 1855, he succeeded Longfellow as professor of Belles-Lettres. He became the United States ambassador to Spain in 1877 and to Britain in 1880. He was in turn editor of the *Atlantic Monthly Magazine* (from 1857) and then of the *North American Review* (from 1863). The excerpt on *Hamlet* reproduced here is from the essay 'Shakespeare Once More' first published in 1868; it is here published from the volume of six essays entitled *Among My Books*, 1870 (pp. 196–217).

[Goethe] says . . . 'there is a destructive criticism and a productive. The former is very easy ; for one has only to set up in his mind any standard, any model, however narrow' (let us say the Greeks), 'and then boldly assert that the work under review does not match with it, and therefore is good for nothing,—the matter is settled and one must at once deny its claim. Productive criticism is a great deal more difficult; it asks, What did the author propose to himself? Is what he proposes reasonable and comprehensible? and how far has he succeeded in carrying it out?' It is in applying this kind of criticism to Shakespeare that the Germans have set us an example worthy of all commendation. If they have been sometimes over-subtle, they at least had the merit of first looking at his works as wholes, as something that very likely contained an idea, perhaps contained a moral, if we could get at it. The illumination lent us by most of the English commentators reminds us of the candles which guides hold up to show us a picture in a dark place, the smoke of which gradually makes the work of the artist invisible under its repeated layers. Lessing, as might have been expected, opened the first glimpse in the new direction; Goethe followed with his famous exposition of *Hamlet*; A.W. Schlegel took a more comprehensive view in his Lectures, which Coleridge worked over into English, adding many fine criticisms of his own on single passages; and finally, Gervinus has devoted four volumes to a comment on the plays, full of excellent matter, though pushing the moral exegesis beyond all reasonable bounds[1]. With the help of all these, and especially of the last, I shall apply this theory of criticism to *Hamlet*, not in the hope of saying anything new, but of bringing something to the support of the thesis, that, if Shakespeare was skilful as a playwright, he was even greater as a dramatist,—that, if his immediate business was to fill the theatre, his higher object was to create something which, by fulfilling the conditions and answering the requirements of modern life, should as truly deserve to be called a work of art as others had deserved it by doing the same thing in former times and other circumstances. Supposing him to have accepted—consciously or not is of little importance—the new terms of the problem which makes character the pivot of dramatic action, and consequently the key of dramatic unity, how far did he succeed?

Before attempting my analysis, I must clear away a little rubbish. Are such anachronisms as those of which Voltaire accuses Shakespeare in *Hamlet*, such as the introduction of cannon before the invention of gunpowder, and making Christians of the Danes three centuries too soon, of the least bearing aesthetically? I think not; but as they are a piece with many other criticisms upon the great poet, it is worth while to dwell upon them a moment.

The first demand we make upon whatever claims to be a work of art (and we have a right to make it) is that it shall be *in keeping*. Now this propriety is of two kinds, either extrinsic, or intrinsic. In the first I should class whatever relates rather to the body than the soul of the work, such as fidelity to the facts of history (wherever that is important), congruity of costume, and the like,—in short, whatever might come under the head of *picturesque* truth, a departure from which would shock too rudely our preconceived associations. I have seen an Indian chief in French boots, and he seemed to me almost tragic; but, put upon the stage in tragedy, he would have been ludicrous. Lichtenberg, writing from London in 1775, tells us that Garrick played Hamlet in a suit of the French fashion, then commonly worn, and that he was blamed for it by some of the critics;

1   I do not mention Ulrici's book, for it seems to me unwieldy and dull,—zeal without knowledge (author's footnote).

but, he says, one hears no such criticism during the play, nor on the way home, nor at supper afterwards, nor indeed till the emotion roused by the great actor has had time to subside. He justifies Garrick, though we should not be able to endure it now. Yet nothing would be gained by trying to make Hamlet's costume true to the assumed period of the play, for the scene of it is laid in a Denmark that has no dates.

In the second and more important category I should put, first, co-ordination of character, that is, a certain variety in harmony of the personages of a drama, as in the attitudes and colouring of the figures in a pictorial composition, so that, while mutually relieving and setting off each other, they shall combine in the total impression; second, that subordinate truth to Nature which makes each character coherent in itself; and, third, such propriety of costume and the like as shall satisfy the superhistoric sense, to which, and to which alone, the higher drama appeals. All these come within the scope of *imaginative* truth. To illustrate my third head by an example. Tieck criticises John Kemble's dressing for Macbeth in a modern Highland costume, as being ungraceful without any countervailing merit of historical exactness. I think a deeper reason for his dissatisfaction might be found in the fact, that this garb, with its purely modern and British army associations, is out of place on Forres Heath, and drags the Weird Sisters down with it from their proper imaginative remoteness in the gloom of the past to the disenchanting glare of the foot-lights. It is not the antiquarian, but the poetic conscience, that is wounded. To this, exactness, so far as concerns ideal representation, may not only not be truth, but may even be opposed to it. Anachronisms and the like are of themselves of no account, and become important only when they make a gap too wide for our illusion to cross unconsciously, that is, when they are anacoluthons to the imagination. The aim of the artist is psychologic, not historic truth. It is comparatively easy for any author to *get up* any period with tolerable minuteness in externals, but readers and audiences find more difficulty in getting them down, though oblivion swallows scores of them at a gulp. The saving truth in such matters is a truth to essential and permanent characteristics. The Ulysses of Shakespeare, like the Ulysses of Dante and Tennyson, more or less harmonizes with our ideal conception of the wary, long-considering, though adventurous son of Laertes; yet Simon Lord Lovat is doubtless nearer the original type. In *Hamlet*, though there is no Denmark of the ninth century, Shakespeare has suggested the prevailing rudeness of manners quite enough for his purpose. We see it in the single combat of Hamlet's father with the elder Fortinbras, in the vulgar wassail of the King, in the English monarch being expected to hang Rosencrantz and Guildenstern out of hand merely to oblige his cousin of Denmark, in Laertes, sent to Paris to be made a gentleman of, becoming instantly capable of any the most barbarous treachery to glut his vengeance. We cannot fancy Ragnar Lodbrog or Eric the Red matriculating at Wittenberg, but it was essential that Hamlet should be a scholar, and Shakespeare sends him thither without more ado. All through the play we get the notion of a state of society in which a savage nature has disguised itself in the externals of civilization, like a Maori deacon, who has only to strip and he becomes once more a tattooed pagan with his mouth watering for a spare-rib of his pastor. Historically, at the date of *Hamlet*, the Danes were in the habit of burning their enemies alive in their houses, with as much of their family about them as might be to make it comfortable. Shakespeare seems purposely to have dissociated his play from history by changing nearly every name in the original legend. The motive of the play—revenge as a religious duty—belongs only to a social state in which the traditions of barbarism are still operative, but, with infallible artistic judgment, Shakespeare has chosen, not untamed Nature, as he found it in history, but the period of transition, a period in which the times are always out of joint, and thus the irresolution which has its root in Hamlet's own character is stimulated by the very incompatibility of that legacy of vengeance he has inherited from the past with the new culture and refinement of which he is the representative. One of the few books which Shakespeare is known to have possessed was Florio's Montaigne, and he might well have transferred the Frenchman's motto, *Que sçais-je?* to the front of his tragedy; nor can I help fancying something more than accident in the fact that Hamlet has been a student at Wittenberg, whence those new ideas went forth, of whose results in unsettling men's faith, and consequently disqualifying them for promptness in action, Shakespeare had been not only an eye-witness, but which he must actually have experienced in himself.

One other objection let me touch upon here, especially as it has been urged against *Hamlet*, and that is the introduction of low characters and comic scenes in tragedy. Even Garrick, who had just assisted at the

Stratford Jubilee, where Shakespeare had been pronounced divine, was induced by this absurd outcry for the proprieties of the tragic stage to omit the grave-diggers' scene from *Hamlet*. Leaving apart the fact that Shakespeare would not have been the representative poet he is, if he had not given expression to this striking tendency of the Northern races, which shows itself constantly, not only in their literature, but even in their mythology and their architecture, the grave-diggers' scene always impresses me as one of the most pathetic in the whole tragedy. That Shakespeare introduced such scenes and characters with deliberate intention, and with a view to artistic relief and contrast, there can hardly be a doubt. We must take it for granted that a man whose works show everywhere the results of judgment sometimes acted with forethought. I find the springs of the profoundest sorrow and pity in this hardened indifference of the grave-diggers, in their careless discussion as to whether Ophelia's death was by suicide or no, in their singing and jesting at their dreary work.

> A pickaxe and a spade, a spade,
> For—and a shrouding-sheet:
> O, a pit of clay for to be made
> For such a guest is meet!

We know who is to be the guest of this earthen hospitality,—how much beauty, love, and heartbreak are to be covered in that pit of clay. All we remember of Ophelia reacts upon us with tenfold force, and we recoil from our amusement at the ghastly drollery of the two delvers with a shock of horror. That the unconscious Hamlet should stumble on *this* grave of all others, that it should be *here* that he should pause to muse humorously on death and decay,—all this prepares us for the revulsion of passion in the next scene, and for the frantic confession,-

> I loved Ophelia; forty thousand brothers
> Could not with all *their* quantity of love
> Make up my sum!
>
> (V, i, 266-8)

And it is only here that such an asseveration would be true even to the feeling of the moment; for it is plain from all we know of Hamlet that he could not so have loved Ophelia, that he was incapable of the self-abandonment of a true passion, that he would have analyzed this emotion as he does all others, would have peeped and botanized upon it till it became to him a mere matter of scientific interest. All this force of contrast, and this horror of surprise, were necessary so to intensify his remorseful regret that he should believe himself for once in earnest. The speech of the King, 'O, he is mad, Laertes', recalls him to himself, and he at once begins to rave:-

> Zounds! show me what thou'll do!
> Woul't weep? woul't fight? woul't fast? woul't tear thyself?
> Woul't drink up eysil? eat a crocodile?
>
> (V, i, 271–3)

It is easy to see that the whole plot hinges upon the character of Hamlet, that Shakespeare's conception of this was the ovum out of which the whole organism was hatched. And here let me remark, that there is a kind of genealogical necessity in the character,—a thing not altogether strange to the attentive reader of Shakespeare. Hamlet seems the natural result of the mixture of father and mother in his temperament, the resolution and persistence of the one, like sound timber wormholed and made shaky, as it were, by the other's infirmity of will and discontinuity of purpose. In natures so imperfectly mixed it is not uncommon to find vehemence of intention the prelude and counterpoise of weak performance, the conscious nature striving to keep up its self-respect by a triumph of words all the more resolute that it feels assured beforehand of inevitable defeat in action. As in such slipshod housekeeping men are their own largest creditors they find it easy to stave off utter bankruptcy of conscience by taking up one unpaid promise with another larger, and a heavier interest, till such self-swindling becomes habitual and by degrees almost painless. How did Coleridge discount his own notes of this kind with less and less specie as the figures lessened on the paper! As with Hamlet, so it is with Ophelia and Laertes. The father's feebleness comes up again in the wasting heartbreak and gentle lunacy of the daughter, while the son shows it in a rashness of impulse and act, a kind of crankiness, of whose essential feebleness we are all the more sensible as contrasted with a nature so steady on its keel, and drawing so much water, as that of Horatio,-the foil at once, in different ways, to both him and Hamlet. It was natural, also, that the daughter of self-conceited old Polonius should have her softness stiffened with a fibre of obstinacy; for there are two kinds of weakness, that which breaks, and that which bends. Ophelia's is of the former kind; Hero is her counterpart,[2] giving way before calamity, and rising again so soon as the pressure is removed.

I find two passages in Dante that contain the exactest possible definition of that habit or quality of Hamlet's mind which justifies the tragic turn of the play, and renders it natural and unavoidable from the beginning. The first is from the second canto of the *Inferno*:-

> E quale è quei che disvuol ciò' che' volle,
> E per nuovi pensier cangia proposta,
> Si che del cominciar tutto si tolle;
> Tal mi fec'io in quella oscura costa:
> Perche pensando consumai l'impresa
> Che fu nel cominciar cotanto tosta.

> And like the man who unwills what he willed,
> And for new thoughts doth change his first intent,
> So that he cannot anywhere begin,
> Such became I upon that slope obscure,
> Because with thinking I consumed resolve,
> That was so ready at the setting out.

Again, in the fifth of the *Purgatorio*:-

> Chè sempre l'uomo in cui pensir rampoglia
> Sovra pensier, da sè dilunga il segno,
> Perchè la foga l'un dell'altro insolla.

> For always he in whom one thought buds forth
> Out of another farther puts the goal,
> For each has only force to mar the other.

Dante was a profound metaphysician, and as in the first passage he describes and defines a certain quality of mind, so in the other he tells us

---

2 The romantic heroine of *Much Ado About Nothing*.

its result in the character and life, namely, indecision and failure,—the goal *farther* off at the end than at the beginning. It is remarkable how close a resemblance of thought, and even of expression, there is between the former of these quotations and a part of Hamlet's famous soliloquy:-

Thus conscience [i.e. consciousness] doth make cowards of us all:

> And thus the native hue of resolution
> Is sicklied o'er with the pale cast of thought,
> And enterprises of great pitch and moment
> With this regard their currents turn awry,
> And lose the name of action!
>
> (III, i, 85–90)

It is an inherent peculiarity of a mind like Hamlet's that it should be conscious of its own defect. Men of his type are for ever analysing their own emotions and motives. They cannot do anything, because they always see two ways of doing it. They cannot determine on any course of action, because they are always, as it were, standing at the cross-roads, and see too well the disadvantages of every one of them. It is not that they are incapable of resolve, but somehow the band between the motive power and the operative faculties is relaxed and loose. The engine works, but the machinery it should drive stands still. The imagination is so much in overplus, that thinking a thing becomes better than doing it, and thought with its easy perfection, capable of everything because it can accomplish everything with ideal means, is vastly more attractive and satisfactory than deed, which must be wrought at best with imperfect instruments, and always falls short of the conception that went before it. 'If to do', says Portia in the *Merchant of Venice*,—'if to do were as easy as to know what 'twere good to do, chapels had been churches, and poor men's cottages prince's palaces' (I, ii, 12–14). Hamlet knows only too well what 'twere good to do, but he palters with everything in a double sense: he sees the grain of good there is in evil, and the grain of evil there is in good, as they exist in the world, and, finding that he can make those feather-weighted accidents balance each other, infers that there is little to choose between the essences themselves. He is of Montaigne's mind, and says expressly that 'there is nothing good or ill, but thinking makes it so'. He dwells so exclusively in the world of ideas that the world of facts seems trifling, nothing is worth the while; and he has been so long objectless and purposeless, so far as actual life is concerned, that, when at last an object and an aim are forced upon him, he cannot deal with them, and gropes vainly for a motive outside of himself that shall marshal his thoughts for him and guide his faculties into the path of action. He is the victim not so much of feebleness of will as of intellectual indifference that hinders the will from working long in any one direction. He wishes to will, but never wills. His continual iteration of resolve shows that he has no resolution. He is capable of passionate energy where the occasion presents itself suddenly from without, because nothing is so irritable as conscious irresolution with a duty to perform. But of deliberate energy he is not capable; for there the impulse must come from within, and the blade of his analysis is so subtle that it can divide the finest hair of motive 'twixt north and northwest side, leaving him desperate to choose between them. The very consciousness of his defect is an insuperable bar to his repairing it; for the unity of purpose, which infuses every fibre of the character which will avail whenever wanted, is impossible where the mind can never rest till it has resolved that unity into its component elements, and satisfied itself which on the whole is of greater value. A critical instinct so insatiable that it must turn upon itself, for lack of something else to hew and hack, becomes incapable at last of originating anything except indecision. It becomes infallible in what *not* to do. How easily he might have accomplished his task is shown by the conduct of Laertes. When *he* has a death to avenge, he raises a mob, breaks into the palace, bullies the king, and proves how weak the usurper really was.

The world is the victim of splendid parts, and is slow to accept a rounded whole, because that is something which is long in completing, still longer in demonstrating its completion. We like to be surprised into admiration, and not logically convinced that we ought to admire. We are willing to be delighted with success, though we are somewhat indifferent to the homely qualities which insure it. Our thought is so filled with the rocket's burst of momentary splendour so far above us, that we forget the poor stick, useful and unseen, that made its climbing possible. One of these homely qualities is continuity of character, and it escapes present applause because it tells chiefly, in the long run, in results. With his usual tact, Shakespeare has brought in such a character as a contrast and foil to Hamlet. Horatio is the only complete *man* in the play,—solid, well-knit, and true; a noble, quiet nature, with that highest of all qualities, judgment, always sane and prompt; who never drags his anchor for any wind of opinion or fortune, but grips all the closer to the reality of things. He seems one of those calm, undemonstrative men whom we love and admire without asking to know why, crediting him with the capacity of great things, without any test of actual achievement, because we feel that their manhood is a constant quality, and no mere accident of circumstance and opportunity. Such men are always sure of the presence of their highest self on demand. Hamlet is continually drawing bills on the future, secured by his promise of himself to himself, which he can never redeem. His own somewhat feminine nature recognises its complement in Horatio, and clings to it instinctively, as naturally as Horatio is attracted by that fatal gift of imagination, the absence of which makes the strength of his own character, as its overplus does the weakness of Hamlet's. It is a happy marriage of two minds drawn together by the charm of unlikeness. Hamlet feels in Horatio the solid steadiness which he misses in himself; Horatio in Hamlet that need of service and sustainment to render which gives him a consciousness of his own value. Hamlet fills the place of a woman to Horatio, revealing him to himself not only in what he says, but by a constant claim upon his strength of nature; and there is great psychological truth in making suicide the first impulse of this quiet, undemonstrative man, after Hamlet's death, as if the very reason for his being were taken away with his friend's need of him. In his grief, he for the first and only time speaks of himself, is first made conscious of himself by his loss. If this manly reserve of Horatio be true to his Nature, not less so are the communicativeness of Hamlet, and his tendency to soliloquize. If self-consciousness be alien to the one, it is just as truly the happiness of the other. Like a musician distrustful of himself, he is for ever tuning his instrument, first overstraining this cord a little, and then that, but unable to bring them into unison, or to profit by it if he could.

We do not believe that Horatio ever thought he 'was not a pipe for Fortune's finger to play what stop she please', till Hamlet told him so. That was Fortune's affair, not his; let her try it, if she liked. He is unconscious of his own peculiar qualities, as men of decision commonly are, or they would not be men of decision. When there is a thing to be done, they go straight at it, and for a time there is nothing for them in the whole universe but themselves and their object. Hamlet, on the other hand, is always studying himself. This world and the other, too, are always present in his mind, and there in the corner is the little black kobold of a doubt making mouths at him. He breaks down the bridges before him, not behind him, as a man of action would do; but there is something more than this. He is an ingrained sceptic; though his is the scepticism, not of reason, but of feeling, whose root is want of faith in himself. In him it is passive, a malady rather than a function of the mind. We might call him insincere: not that he was in any sense a hypocrite, but only that he never was and never could be in earnest. Never could be, because no man without intense faith in something ever can. Even if he only believed in himself, that were better than nothing; for it will carry a man a great way in the outward successes of life, nay, will sometimes give him the Archimedean fulcrum for moving the world. But Hamlet doubts everything. He doubts the immortality of the soul, just after seeing his father's spirit, and hearing from its mouth the secrets of the other world. He doubts Horatio even, and swears him to secrecy on the cross of his sword, though probably he himself has no assured belief in the sacredness of the symbol. He doubts Ophelia, and asks her, 'Are you honest?' He doubts the ghost, after he has had a little time to think about it, and so gets up the play to test the guilt of the king. And how coherent the whole character is! With what perfect tact and judgment Shakespeare, in the advice to the players, makes him an exquisite critic! For just here that part of his character which would be weak in dealing with affairs is strong. A wise scepticism is the first attribute of a good critic. He must not believe that the fire-insurance offices will raise their rates of premium on Charles River, because the new volume of poems is printing at Riverside or the University Press. He must not believe so profoundly in the ancients as to think it wholly out of the question that the world has still vigour enough in its loins to beget some one who will one of these days be as good an ancient as any of them.

    Another striking quality in Hamlet's nature is his perpetual inclination to irony. I think this has been generally passed over too lightly, as if it were something external and accidental, rather assumed as a mask than part of the real nature of the man. It seems to me to go deeper, to be something innate, and not merely factitious. It is nothing like the grave irony of Socrates, which was the weapon of a man thoroughly in earnest,—the boomerang of argument, which one throws in the opposite direction of what he means to hit, and which seems to be flying away from the adversary, who will presently find himself knocked down by it. It is not like the irony of Timon, which is but the wilful refraction of a clear mind twisting awry whatever enters it,—or of Iago, which is the slime that a nature essentially evil loves to trail over all beauty and goodness to taint them with distrust: it is the half-jest, half-earnest of an inactive temperament that has not quite made up its mind whether life is a reality or no, whether men were not made in jest, and which amuses itself equally with finding a deep meaning in trivial things and a trifling one in the profoundest mysteries of being, because the want of earnestness in its own essence infects everything else with its own indifference. If there be now and then an unmannerly rudeness and bitterness in it, as in the scenes with Polonius and Osrick, we must remember that Hamlet was just in the condition which spurs men to sallies of this kind: dissatisfied, at one neither with the world nor with himself, and accordingly casting about for something out of himself to vent his spleen upon. But even in these passages there is no hint of earnestness, of any purpose beyond the moment; they are mere cat's-paws of vexation, and not the deep-raking ground-swell of passion, as we see it in the sarcasm of Lear.

    The question of Hamlet's madness has been much discussed and variously decided. High medical authority has pronounced, as usual, on both sides of the question. But the induction has been drawn from too narrow premises, being based on a mere diagnosis of the *case*, and not on an appreciation of the character in its completeness. We have a case of pretended madness in the Edgar of *King Lear*; and it is certainly true that that is a charcoal sketch, coarsely outlined, compared with the delicate drawing, the lights, shades, and half-tints of the portraiture in Hamlet. But does this tend to prove that the madness of the latter, because truer to the recorded observation of experts, is real, and meant to be real, as the other to be fictitious? Not in the least, as it appears to me. Hamlet, among all the characters of Shakespeare, is the most eminently a metaphysician and psychologist. He is a close observer, continually analysing his own nature and that of others, letting fall his little drops of acid irony on all who come near him, to make them show what they are made of.

Even Ophelia is not too sacred, Osrick not too contemptible, for experiment. If a man assumed madness, he would play his part perfectly. If Shakespeare himself, without going mad, could so observe and remember all the abnormal symptoms as to be able to reproduce them in Hamlet, why should it be beyond the power of Hamlet to reproduce them in himself? If you deprive Hamlet of reason, there is no truly tragic motive left. He would be a fit subject for Bedlam, but not for the stage. We might have pathology enough, but no pathos. Ajax first becomes tragic when he recovers his wits. If Hamlet is irresponsible, the whole play is a chaos. That he is not so might be proved by evidence enough, were it not labour thrown away.

This feigned madness of Hamlet's is one of the few points in which Shakespeare has kept close to the old story on which he founded his play; and as he never decided without deliberation, so he never acted without unerring judgment. Hamlet *drifts* through the whole tragedy. He never keeps on one tack long enough to get steerage-way, even if, in a nature like his, with those electric streamers of whim and fancy for ever wavering across the vault of his brain, the needle of judgment would point in one direction long enough to strike a course by. The scheme of simulated insanity is precisely the one he would have been likely to hit upon, because it enabled him to follow his own bent, and to drift with an apparent purpose, postponing decisive action by the very means he adopts to arrive at its accomplishment, and satisfying himself with the show of doing something that he may escape so much the longer the dreaded necessity of really doing anything at all. It enables him to *play* with life and duty, instead of taking them by the rougher side, where alone any firm grip is possible,—to feel that he is on the way toward accomplishing somewhat, when he is really paltering with his own irresolution. Nothing, I think, could be more finely imagined than this. Voltaire complains that he goes mad without any sufficient object or result. Perfectly true, and precisely what was most natural for him to do, and, accordingly, precisely what Shakespeare meant that he should do. It was delightful to him to indulge his imagination and humour, to prove his capacity for something by playing a part; the one thing he could not do was to bring himself to *act*, unless when surprised by a sudden impulse of suspicion,—as where he kills Polonius, and there he could not see his victim. He discourses admirably of suicide, but does not kill himself; he talks daggers, but uses none. He puts by the chance to kill the king with the excuse that he will not do it while he is praying, lest his soul be saved thereby, though it is more than doubtful whether he believed it himself. He allows himself to be packed off to England, without any motive except that it would for the time take him farther from a present duty: the more disagreeable to a nature like his because it *was* present, and not a mere matter for speculative consideration. When Goethe made his famous comparison of the acorn planted in a vase which it bursts with its growth, and says that in like manner Hamlet is a nature which breaks down under the weight of a duty too great for it to bear, he seems to have considered the character too much from one side. Had Hamlet actually killed himself to escape his too onerous commission, Goethe's conception of him would have been satisfactory enough. But Hamlet was hardly a sentimentalist, like Werther; on the contrary, he saw things only too clearly in the dry north-light of the intellect. It is chance that at last brings him to his end. It would appear rather that Shakespeare intended to show us an imaginative temperament brought face to face with actualities, into any clear relation of sympathy with which it cannot bring itself. The very means that Shakespeare makes use of to lay upon him the obligation of acting—the ghost—really seems to make it all the harder for him to act; for the spectre but gives an additional excitement to his imagination and a fresh topic for his scepticism.

I shall not attempt to evolve any high moral significance from the play, even if I thought it possible; for that would be aside from the present purpose. The scope of the higher drama is to represent life, not every-day life, it is true, but life lifted above the plane of bread-and-butter associations, by nobler reaches of language, by the influence at once inspiring and modulating of verse, by an intenser play of passion condensing that misty mixture of feeling and reflection which makes the ordinary atmosphere of existence into flashes of thought and phrase whose brief, but terrible, illumination prints the outworn landscape of every-day upon our brains, with its little motives and mean results, in lines of tell-tale fire. The moral office of tragedy is to show us our own weaknesses idealized in grander figures and more awful results,—to teach us what we pardon in ourselves as venial faults, if they seem to have but slight influence on our immediate fortunes, have arms as long as those of kings, and reach forward to the catastrophe of our lives, that they are dry-rotting the very fibre of will and conscience, so that, if we should be brought to the test of a great temptation or a stringent emergency, we must be involved in a ruin as sudden and complete as that we shudder at in the unreal scene of the theatre. But the primary *object* of a tragedy is not to inculcate a formal moral. Representing life, it teaches, like life, by indirection, by those nods and winks that are thrown away on us blind horses in such profusion. We may learn, to be sure, plenty of lessons from Shakespeare. We are not likely to have kingdoms to divide, crowns foretold us by weird sisters, a father's death to avenge, or to kill our wives from jealousy; but Lear may teach us to draw the line more clearly between a wise generosity and a loose-handed weakness of giving; Macbeth, how one sin involves another, and for ever another, by a fatal parthenogenesis, and that the key which unlocks forbidden doors to our will or passion leaves a stain on the hand, that may not be so dark as blood, but that will not out; Hamlet, that all the noblest gifts of person, temperament, and mind slip like sand through the grasp of an infirm purpose; Othello, that the perpetual silt of some weakness, the eddies of a suspicious temper depositing their one impalpable layer after another, may build up a shoal on which an heroic life and an otherwise magnanimous nature may bilge and go to pieces. All this we may learn, and much more, and Shakespeare was no doubt well aware of all this and more; but I do not believe that he wrote his plays with any such didactic purpose. He knew human nature too well not to know that one thorn of experience is worth a whole wilderness of warning,—that, where one shapes his life by precept and example, there are a thousand that have it shaped for them by impulse and by circumstances. He did not mean his great tragedies for scare-crows, as if the nailing of one hawk to the barn-door would prevent the next from coming down souse into the hen-yard. No, it is not the poor bleaching victim hung up to moult its draggled feathers in the rain that he wishes to show us. He loves the hawk-nature as well as the hen-nature: and if he is unequalled in anything, it is in that sunny breadth of view, that impregnability of reason, that looks down all ranks and conditions of men, all fortune and misfortune, with the equal eye of the pure artist.

Whether I have fancied anything into Hamlet which the author never dreamed of putting there I do not greatly concern myself to inquire. Poets are always entitled to a royalty on whatever we find in their works; for these fine creations as truly build themselves up in the brain as they are built up with deliberate forethought. Praise art as we will, that which the artist did not mean to put into his work, but which found itself there by some generous process of Nature of which he was as unaware as the blue river is of its rhyme with the blue sky, has somewhat in it that snatches us into sympathy with higher things than those which come by plot and observation. Goethe wrote his *Faust* in its earliest form without a thought of the deeper meaning which the exposition of an age of criticism was to find in it: without foremeaning it, he had impersonated in Mephistopheles the genius of his century. Shall this subtract from the debt we owe him? Not at all. If originality were conscious of itself, it would have lost its right to be original. I believe that Shakespeare intended to impersonate in Hamlet not a mere metaphysical entity, but a man of flesh and blood: yet it is certainly curious how prophetically typical the character is of that introversion of mind which is so constant a phenomenon of these latter days, of that over-consciousness which wastes itself in analysing the motives of action instead of acting.

The old painters had a rule, that all compositions should be pyramidal in form,—a central figure, from which the others slope gradually away on the two sides. Shakespeare probably had never heard of this rule, and, if he had, would not have been likely to respect it more than he has the so-called classical unities of time and place. But he understood perfectly the artistic advantages of gradation, contrast, and relief. Taking Hamlet as the key-note, we find in him weakness of character, which, on the one hand, is contrasted with the feebleness that springs from overweening conceit in Polonius and with frailty of temperament in Ophelia, while, on the other hand, it is brought into fuller relief by the steady force of Horatio and the impulsive violence of Laertes, who is resolute from thoughtlessness, just as Hamlet is irresolute from overplus of thought.

If we must draw a moral from Hamlet, it would seem to be, that Will is Fate, and that, Will once abdicating, the inevitable successor in the regency is Chance. Had Hamlet acted, instead of musing how good it would be to act, the king might have been the only victim. As it is, all the main actors in the story are the fortuitous sacrifice of his irresolution. We see how a single great vice of character at last draws to itself as allies and confederates all other weaknesses of the man, as in civil wars the timid and the selfish wait to throw themselves upon the stronger side.

> In Life's small things be resolute and great
> To keep thy muscles trained: know'st thou when Fate
> Thy measure takes? or when she'll say to thee,
> 'I find thee worthy, do this thing for me'?

I have said that it was doubtful if Shakespeare had any conscious moral intention in his writings. I meant only that he was purely and primarily a poet. And while he was an English poet in a sense that is true of no other, his method was thoroughly Greek, yet with this remarkable difference,—that, while the Greeks took purely national themes and gave them a universal interest by their mode of treatment, he took what may be called cosmopolitan traditions, legends of human nature, and nationalized them by the infusion of his perfectly Anglican breadth of character and solidity of understanding. Wonderful as his imagination and fancy are, his perspicacity and artistic discretion are more so. This country tradesman's son, coming up to London, could set high-bred wits, like Beaumont, uncopyable lessons in drawing gentlemen such as are seen nowhere else but on the canvas of Titian; he could take Ulysses away from Homer and expand the shrewd and crafty islander into a statesman whose words are the pith of history. But what makes him yet more exceptional was his utterly unimpeachable judgment, and that poise of character which enabled him to be at once the greatest of poets and so unnoticeable a good citizen as to leave no incidents for biography. His material was never far-sought; (it is still disputed whether the fullest head of which we have record were cultivated beyond the range of grammar-school precedent!) but he used it with a poetic instinct which we cannot parallel, identified himself with it, yet remained always its born and questionless master. He finds the Clown and Fool upon the stage,—he makes them the tools of his pleasantry, his satire, and even his pathos; he finds a fading rustic superstition, and shapes out of it ideal Pucks, Titanias, and Ariels, in whose existence statesmen and scholars believe for ever. Always poet, he subjects all to the ends of his art, and gives in *Hamlet* the churchyard ghost, but with the cothurnus on,—the messenger of God's revenge against murder; always philosopher, he traces in *Macbeth* the metaphysics of apparitions, painting the shadowy Banquo only on the o'erwrought brain of the murderer, and staining the hand of his wife-accomplice (because she was the more refined and higher nature) with the disgustful blood-spot that is not there. We say he had no moral intention, for the reason, that, as artist, it was not his to deal with the realities, but only with the shows of things; yet, with a temperament so just, an insight so inevitable as his, it was impossible that the moral reality, which underlies the *mirage* of the poet's vision, should not always be suggested. His humour and satire are never of the destructive kind; what he does in that way is suggestive only,—not breaking bubbles with Thor's hammer, but puffing them away with the breath of a Clown, or shivering them with the light laugh of a genial cynic. Men go about to prove the existence of a God! Was it a bit of phosphorus, that brain whose creations are so real, that, mixing with them, we feel as if we ourselves were but fleeting magic-lantern shadows?

17. George Henry Miles

1870

George Henry Miles (1824–1871), novelist, poet, and playwright, became professor of English Literature at the University of Mount St. Mary's, Maryland. His book, *A Review of Hamlet*, published in Boston in 1870, was begun as a lecture intended to be given by the Shakespearean actor Edwin Forrest, but was expanded for use as a textbook for his undergraduate students. It was well received and its view of the play was made the basis of Edwin Booth's interpretation of Hamlet. A second edition (from which these excerpts are taken) was published in 1907, after Miles's death.

The difference between a strong man and a weak one, though indefinable, is infinite. The prevalent view of Hamlet is, that he is weak. We hear him spoken of as the gentle prince, the doomed prince, the meditative prince, but never as the strong prince, the great prince, the terrible prince. He is commonly regarded as more of a dreamer than a doer; something of a railer at destiny; a blighted, morbid existence, unequal either to forgiveness or revenge; delaying action till action is of no use, and dying the victim of mere circumstance and accident. The exquisite metaphor of Goethe's about the oak tree and the vase predestined for a rose, crystallizes and perpetuates both the critical and the popular estimate of Hamlet. The Wilhelm Meister view is, practically, the only view; a hero without a plan, pushed on by events alone, endowed more properly with sentiments than with a character,—in a word, *weak*. But the Hamlet of the critics and the Hamlet of Shakespeare are two different persons. A close review of the play will show that Hamlet is strong, not weak,—that the basis of his character is *strength*, illimitable strength. There is not an act or an utterance of his, from first to last, which is not a manifestation of power. Slow, cautious, capricious, he may sometimes be, or seem to be; but always strong, always large-souled, always resistless.

The care, the awe, with which Shakespeare approached his work, are visible in the opening scene. You cannot advance three lines without feeling that the poet is before you in all his majesty, armed for some vast achievement, winged for the empyrean. In all that solemn guard relief, there is not a word too much or too little. How calm and sad it is! sadness prefiguring the the unearthly theme,—grand syncopated minor chords,—the Adagio of the overture to *Don Giovanni*! the super-human is instantly foreshadowed, and hardly foreshadowed before revealed. The dreaded twice-seen sight is scarcely mentioned. Bernardo has just begun his story,—

> Last night of all
> When yon same star that's westward from the pole
> Had made his course to illume that part of Heaven
> Where now it burns, Marcellus and myself,
> The bell then beating one,—
>
> (I, i, 33–7)

when, without further prelude, the sepulchral key-note of the plot is struck, and enter Ghost, dumb, majestic, terrible, defiant, and, above all, *rapid*. An honest ghost, a punctual ghost; no lagging Rawhead and Bloody-bones, expected indefinitely from curfew to cock-crow. Mark the pains with which this magnificent apparition is gradually got up; observe how crisply and minutely the actor is instructed to *dress* the part. First the broad outlines:

> —that fair and warlike form
> In which the majesty of buried Denmark
> Did sometimes march,—
> —the very armor he had on
> When he the ambitious Norway combated;
> So frown'd he once, when in an angry parle
> He smote the sledded Polacks on the ice.
>
> (I, i, 45–7, 59–62)

The second touches are more precise and vivid.

> Ham. Arm'd, say you?
> Mar., Bern. Arm'd, my lord.

> Ham. From top to toe?
> Mar., Bern. My lord from head to foot.
> Ham. Then saw you not his face?
> Hor. O yes, my lord, he wore his beaver up.
> Ham. What, looked he frowningly?
> Hor. A countenance more in sorrow than in anger.
> Ham. Pale or red?
> Hor. Nay, very pale.
> Ham. And fixed his eyes upon you?
> Hor. Most constantly . . .
> Ham. Stayed it long?
> Hor. While one with moderate haste might tell a hundred.
> Mar., Bern. Longer, longer.
> Hor. Not when I saw it.
> Ham. His beard was grizzled? no!
> Her. It was as I have seen it in his life,
> A sable silver'd.
>
> (I, ii, 226–41)

No misconception now, my heavy friend who plays the ghost; no room for speculation in the wardroom now. You cannot go wrong if you would. 'Armed from top to toe', 'his beaver up', 'frowning', but the eyebrows not *too* bushy, for the frown is more in sorrow than in anger. Not a particle of rouge, but pale, very pale; nor any rolling of the eyes, sir, either, but a fixed gaze. The very pace at which you are to move is measured: count a hundred as you make your martial stalk and vanish. The delineation is Pre-Raphaelite, even to that last consummate touch, the sable silvered beard. It seems easy, this slow portraiture of a Phantom, just as all perfectly executed feats seem easy; but it is painting the rainbow. And lest this honest Ghost should become *too* human, with one wave of the wand it is rendered not only unearthly, but impalpable.

> Hor. Stop it, Marcellus!
> Mar. Shall I strike it with my partisan?
> Hor. Do if it will not stand.
> Bern. 'Tis here!
> Hor. 'Tis here!
> Mar. 'Tis gone. (Exit Ghost)
> We do it wrong, being so majestical,
> To offer it the show of violence;

> For it is, as the air, invulnerable,
> And our vain blows malicious mockery.
>
> (I, i, 120–7)

Manlike, magnificent, but ghastly too,—for our blood is made to curdle by that start at cock-crow.

> Bern. It was about to speak when the cock crew.
> Hor. And then it started like a guilty thing
> Upon a fearful summons.

What a dark, weird whisper! How it goes home to the popular heart,—all that awful majesty crouching at cock-crow!

And when the picture is thus marvellously finished, observe how lovingly it is framed in gold:

> Some say, that ever 'gainst that season comes
> Wherein our Saviour's birth is celebrated,
> The bird of dawning singeth all night long:
> And then, they say, no spirit dares stir abroad;
> The nights are wholesome; then no planets strike,
> No fairy takes, nor witch hath power to charm:
> So hallowed and so gracious is that time.
>
> (I, i, 139–45)

Where, save by the pencil of the Paraclete, has such divine use been made of the music of the bird 'that is the trumpet to the morn'!

There is a loving care, a sedulous finish, about the whole portraiture, assuring us that Shakespeare wrote the part for himself. We know that he acted it, and that it was 'the top of his performance'[1]. What a treat to have seen him! Better even than listening to Homer chanting his fiery epics. Perhaps the poet dared not trust his Ghost to other hands; for the fate of the whole tragedy hinges upon the masterly rendering of this perilous part. Although Burbage, and other players of the Blackfriars were more popular general actors, yet the elaborate impersonation of a departed soul differs, almost as much as its conception, from the coarser

---

1   See Nicholas Rowe's *Life of Shakespeare*, *Eighteenth Century Essays on Shakespeare*, ed. D. Nichol Smith (Glasgow, 1903), p. 4.

eloquence and action by which mortal passions and emotions are counterfeited. That awful monotone, that statuesque repose with which the Ghost still walks the stage, are probably a reminiscence of him who gave such immortal advice to the Players, and who first acted 'the Ghost in his own *Hamlet*'.[2] But more than this. Aubrey had heard that Shakespeare was 'a handsome, well-shaped man';[3] the Stratford Bust and the engraving by Martin Droeshout confirm the tradition. Connecting this tradition with our positive knowledge, that, not withstanding his invincible modesty and propriety, he ventured to undertake a part which, although predestined for himself, he scrupled not, in obedience to the compulsion of the plot, to consecrate for all time as the supreme type and model of manly beauty, may we not be permitted to associate his likeness, in some measure at least, with that of the majesty of buried Denmark?

> See what a grace was seated on his brow;
> Hyperion's curls; the front of Jove himself;
> An eye like Mars to threaten and command;
> A station like the herald Mercury
> New-lighted on a heaven-kissing hill;
> A combination and a form, indeed,
> Where every god did seem to set his seal,
> To give the world assurance of a man.
>
> (III, iv, 54–61)

But prompt as the apparition is to come, it is slow to speak. That it means to speak, we know; that it means to make some fearful unfolding, we feel; but it remains deaf and dumb to all Horatio's pleading,—more terrible, more significant, more obstinately mute than the Prophetess in the *Agamemnon*. This superb visitant, so carefully, so cunningly constructed, is not to be fathomed or unriddled at sight. It does not pay its first visit to Hamlet and blurt out all at once, as a vulgar, unauthenticated phantom would have done. We are allowed first to hear of it; then to steal a glimpse of it; then to watch it 'while one with moderate haste may tell a hundred'. But just when expectation is kindled to the highest pitch, the scene shifts, and we are consigned by Horatio

2 Ibid.

3 See Aubrey's *Brief Lives*, ed. O. Lawson Dick, Harmondsworth, 1962, p. 334.

> Unto young Hamlet; for, upon my life,
> This spirit, dumb to us, will speak to him.
>
> (I, i, 151–2)

Not only is the interest heightened by this wise suspense, but it is artistically essential to the perfect intelligibility and effect of the Ghost's long revelation that we should have some antecedent acquaintance with the guilty King and his infatuated Queen. And not less important that we should behold this same young Hamlet and his attitude at Court before the advent of the superhuman—a Hamlet uninfluenced by anything more terrible than his father's sudden death and mother's sudden marriage, yet most profoundly influenced by that double woe. How briefly, yet how completely, this is done.

> King. But now my cousin Hamlet and my son,—
> Ham. A little more than kin and less than kind. (*Aside*)
> King. How is it that the clouds still hang on you?
> Ham. Not so, my lord; I am too much i'the sun.
>
> (I, ii, 64–7)

Notice the first keen flashes of this noble and most sovereign reason sparkling in its own gloom like polished jet. Disarmed at the first pass that uncle-father. Nor does the Queen fare better.

> Queen. Good Hamlet, cast thy nighted colour off,
>   And let thine eye look like a friend on Denmark.
>   Do not forever with thy vailed lids
>   Seek for thy noble father in the dust:
>   Thou know'st 'tis common—all that live must die,
>   Passing through nature to eternity.
> Ham. Ay, madam; it is common.
>
> (I, ii, 68–73)

Her maternal platitudes are shivered by the easy scorn of his reply. But this resolute woman, then undergoing perhaps her first experience in being silenced, answers very much to the purpose:

> If it be,
> Why seems it so particular with thee?
> Ham. Seems, madam!—
>
> (I, ii, 73–5)

It is like 'the flash and motion' of Geraint.[4] No more questionings, but *'we pray you'*, *'we beseech you'*, *''tis sweet and commendable in your nature'*, 'let not thy mother lose her prayers', 'be as ourself in Denmark'. And *he?*—he is hardly listening: he will, in all his best, obey them: he will stay at home and *not go back to school at Wittenberg*. For let it not be forgotten, that this superb intelligence, whose career has charmed and perplexed mankind for three centuries, was not too old to go 'back to school in Wittenberg'. This immaturity should be carefully remembered in the estimate of his character. A Collegian, even of thirty, summoned by the visible ghost of a murdered sire from love and life and the fair orchards of ripening manhood, to revenge and ruin, may exhibit much hesitancy and vacillation, without being tainted with inherent infirmity of purpose.

That wondrous first soliloquy is the simultaneous presentation of a plot and of a character,—of all the tragic antecedents of the Play, and of Hamlet struggling through the gloom, the incarnation of eloquent despair.

> O, that this too—too solid flesh would melt,
> Thaw, and resolve itself into a dew!
> Or that the Everlasting had not fix'd
> His canon 'gainst self-slaughter! O God! O God!
> How weary, stale, flat and unprofitable
> Seem to me all the uses of this world! etc.

Is this a sample of the imputed 'wavering melancholy and soft lamenting'? Since the Psalms of David, and the still deeper pathos of the Passion, where has mental agony found such awful utterance? Nor is the final line,—

> But break, my heart,—for I must hold my tongue!

any evidence of weakness. For what *could* the man say? The throne was not hereditary; his mother was mistress of her own hand; he had no proof, not even a fixed suspicion, of foul play. His tongue was sealed until the coming of the Ghost.

4 The French painter of heroic scenes.

It is manifest from the King's speech at the opening of the second scene, that the royal pair are then giving their *first* audience of state. Cornelius and Voltimond are dispatched to Norway; the suit of Laertes is heard and granted; and Hamlet, *who was not to be trusted abroad*, forbidden to return to Wittenberg. Most assuredly, it is Hamlet's first public reappearance. Since his father's funeral, he has lived in the strictest seclusion, or he could not else be ignorant of Horatio's presence in Elsinore. It may be as well to remember this; for the play is so elliptical, that one is apt to marvel why the two friends have not sooner met. Some hint of Hamlet's having been summoned to Court to be publicly warned from re-entering the University, must have leaked out, or we should scarcely have Marcellus saying—

> And I this morning know
> Where we shall find him most conveniently.
>
> (I, i, 155–6)

Horatio respected the Prince's privacy until forced by love and duty to invade it. But he could scarcely have been prepared for the sad change in his schoolmate. He, as well as Ophelia, had only known him as

> The courtier's, soldier's, scholar's, eye, tongue, sword;
> The expectancy and Rose of the fair state,
> The glass of fashion and the mould of form,
> The observ'd of all observers.
>
> (III, i, 154–7)

With too much reason, Hamlet had lost all trust in his mother; and when we cease to trust our mothers, we cease to trust humanity. Hamlet belonged to that middle circle of the Sons of Light, who become cynics, instead of villains, in adversity. Characters of perfect sincerity, of exhaustless tenderness, of ready trust, when once deceived by the few that were dearest, become irrevocably mistrustful of all. Your commonplace neighbor who knows himself a sham, accepts, perhaps prefers, a society of shams; has no idea of being very true to anybody, or of anybody's being very true to him; leads a sham life and dies a sham death,—as near as the latter achievement is possible,—leaving a set of sham mourners behind him. But the heart whose perfect insight is blinded only by its perfect love, once fooled in its tenderest faith, must be either saint or cynic; must belong either to God or to doubt forevermore. A blighted gentleness is as savage in the expression of its scorn as your born misanthropist or your natural villain; save that the hatred of the one is for vice, and cant, and cunning, of the other for credulity and virtue; save that the last is cruel in word and deed, the first in word alone.

Yet Hamlet is less a cynic than a satirist, and less a satirist than a Nemesis. Though merciless in plucking the mask from a knave, a villain, or a fool, yet the dormant tenderness which underlies his character, flashes fitfully out through his interviews with his mother, Laertes and Polonius, as well as being steadily manifest in his unquestioning trust in Horatio after their *reunion*. For such a thorough political change has overshadowed Denmark, that their meeting is rather a spiritual reunion than an interview. By the inexorable logic of events, Hamlet is ranged *against* the throne, the conspicuous head and front of a moral opposition, an inevitable, though passive, rebel. If Horatio is *loyal*, no matter what their previous friendship, they are thenceforth foes. One must have lived through civil war to appreciate the dexterous nicety with which Hamlet feels his former friend. And yet this early association of excessive mistrust with excessive morbidity, inclines us to suspect that the subsequent shock of the Ghost was rather an arrest of the slow degeneration of fixed melancholy into madness, than an aggravation of antecedent lunacy.

>(*Enter* Horatio, Marcellus, and Bernardo.)
>Hor. Hail to your lordship.
>Ham. I am glad to see you:
>Horatio,—or I do forget myself.
>Hor. The same, my lord, and your poor servant ever.
>Ham. Sir, my good friend,—I'll change that name with you:
>*And what make you from Wittenberg, Horatio?—*
>Marcellus?
>Mar. My good lord—
>Ham. I am very glad to see you.—Good even, Sir.-
>*But what, in faith, make you from Wittenberg?*
>Hor. A truant disposition good my lord.
>Ham. I would not hear your enemy say so,
>Nor shall you do mine ear that violence,
>To make it truster of your own report
>Against yourself. I know you are no truant.
>*But what is your affair in Elsinore?*
>
>(I, ii, 160–73)

For the third time. And see the dark hinting in the next line at the royal 'rouse' and 'wassail'; at the orgies of the scandalous wedding—as if Horatio might possible have come to share *them*.

> We'll teach you to drink deep ere you depart.

Horatio instantly detects and answers the innuendo.

> My lord, I came to see your father's funeral.
> Ham. I pray thee, do not mock me, fellow-student;
> I think it was to see my mother's wedding.
> Hor. *Indeed, my lord, it follow'd hard upon.*

Even this little, from a man like Horatio, is enough; they are on the same side, rebels both. Quick as lightning the glance is given and returned; he can trust Marcellus and Bernardo too, and bears his heart to them with a fierce sigh of relief. [Miles quotes I, ii, 179–187: from 'Thrift, thrift, Horatio' to 'I shall not look upon his like again'.] This brief introduction to the main theme is inimitable. How exquisitely the ear is made to long for Horatio's blunt transition:

> My lord, I think I saw him yesternight.
> Ham. Saw! who?
> Hor. My lord, the King, your father.
> Ham. The King, my father!
> Hor. Season your admiration for awhile
> With an attent ear, till I may deliver,
> Upon the witness of these gentlemen,
> This marvel to you.

instead of being unnerved by the story, the Prince is calm, collected, determined; cautious, reticent, and longing for night. He dismisses them with the stately courtesy which distinguishes him throughout the play; enjoining silence and promising to share their watch betwixt eleven and twelve.

Once more on the Platform before the Castle, the poet's verse resumes the awful minor in which his tragic preludes are so often conceived. [Miles quotes I, iv, 1–18 and follows this with a discussion of the significance of the omission in the Folio of Hamlet's lines against drunkenness in Q2, I, iv, 19f., preferring the Folio version. Hamlet's encounter with the Ghost is discussed.]

Amidst all the emotions with which Hamlet is simultaneously overwhelmed by the interview, the first to assert itself definitely is pity. One brief appeal to heaven, earth, and hell,—one call on heart and sinews to bear him stiffly up,—then pity, pure and profound. And, at such a moment, the capacity to pity reveals an almost infinite strength.

> Remember thee!
> Ay, *thou poor ghost*, while memory holds a seat
> In this distracted globe—Remember thee!
> Yea, from the table of my memory
> I'll wipe away all trivial fond records
> That youth and observation copied there;
> And thy commandment all alone shall live
> Within the book and volume of my brain,
> Unmixed with baser matter; yes, by heaven.
> (I, v, 95–104)

Up to this point nothing can be saner. But just here, for a single second, his 'distracted' brain gives way, as the vision of the 'smiling, damned villain' replaces that of the vanished ghost.

> O most pernicious woman!
> O villain, villain, smiling, damned villain.
> My tables,—meet it is I set it down,
> That one may smile, and smile, and be a villain;
> At least I'm sure it may be so in Denmark: (*Writing*)
> So, uncle, there you are. Now to my word;
> It is, 'Adieu, adieu! remember me':
> I have sworn't.
> (I, v, 105–13)

Whatever may be thought of the words, the *action*—that doomed figure, crouching over its tables in the dim midnight,—is a flash of positive madness, brief as lightning, but as terrible too. In this moment of supreme trial, his mind gives way: the remainder of the act is a struggle to restore the lost equilibrium. And in all the annals of tragedy, there is nothing half so frightful as this tremendous conflict of a godlike reason battling for its throne against Titanic terror and despair. Lear is comparatively an easy victim. The transition from senility to dotage, from dotage to frenzy, owing to its milder contrasts cannot be as appalling as the sharp conflict between mind in its morning splendor, and the hurricane eclipse of sudden lunacy. The first soliloquy revealed a predisposition to madness; but here the man actually goes mad before our eyes—just as Lear goes mad before our eyes, save that instead of lapsing into fixed insanity like the old King, Hamlet emerges from the storm, radiant, calm, convalescent, victorious, but with a scar which he carries to his dying day.

But will you call him *weak* because his reason sinks awhile beneath the double pressure of natural anguish and supernatural terror? Was Macbeth weak? Yet, in his own lighted halls, how quite unmanned in folly one glimpse of the blood-boltered Banquo makes him. Not till the horrible shadow is gone, is Macbeth a man again; not till the questionable shape that makes night hideous departs, does the braver soul of Hamlet betray its exhaustion; and then only after a long sigh of pity! Was Richard weak? Yet in the milder midnight of his tent, how 'the cold, fearful drops stand on his trembling flesh', [adapted from *Richard III*, V, vi, 135] before those phantoms of a dream.

> By the apostle Paul, shadows tonight
> Have struck more terror to the soul of Richard,
> Than can the substance of ten thousand soldiers
> Armed in proof, and led by shallow Richmond.
>
> (*Richard III*, V, vi, 170–3)

Yet the shapes that awed those men of steel were but coinage of the brain; unreal mockeries, all; while Hamlet confronts, and confronts unappalled, a well-authenticated ghost—a ghost as visible as Horatio, Marcellus, and Bernardo, as to himself. Nor should his comparative sinlessness affect our estimate of their relative courage. The walking ghost of a murdered king, fresh from the glare of penal fires, swearing an only son to vengeance, must be quite as trying to the soul of innocence, as the chimeras of remorse to the nerves of guilt. If Hamlet's reason is momentarily dethroned, it is only to reassert its supremacy—only to pass triumphantly through the ordeal of delirious reaction. For that moment of madness has its sure sequel of delirium,—a delirium that could only have flowed from an antecedent moment of madness. The exhibition of this delirium is the crowning achievement of the Act, of the Play,—of all dramatic art. See how he staggers back with 'wild and whirling words' from the perilous edges of madness; see how dexterously, yet grotesquely, he baffles the pardonable curiosity of his companions; see how he jests and laughs over the sepulchral '*Swear!*' of the fellow in the cellarage, lest sheer horror should compel his friends to divulge their ghastly secret. [Quotes I, v, 114–82.]

There is a purpose in all this minute precaution. One unwary syllable, one indiscreet hint of the apparition, and instead of becoming an avenger, the chances are that he will become a victim. As for *now* sweeping to revenge on wings as swift as meditation, or the thoughts of love, it is simply absurd. His mission is too vast and complicated to be solved in one fiery second; his life is no longer merely consecrated to woe, but summoned to a perilous and unwelcome *duty*. That grim, ocular demonstration of the existence of penal fires, has clogged the impulse of human revenge with a salutary appreciation of eternal justice. The future is vague and hopeless, but, come what may, he means to be master of the situation. His manner must necessarily change, but he will mask the change with madness—an easy mask for one whose whole life is spent in holding real madness at bay,—whose reason would be lost in dark abysses of despair, but for the quenchless truth and splendor of an imagination which encircles and upholds him like an outstretched angel's wing. As if that one instant of aberration were providentially suggestive, 'he plays', as Coleridge observes, 'that subtle trick of pretending to act the lunatic only when he is very near being what he pretends to act'[5]. It is not the past, but a clear vision of the future, that extorts that prophetic sigh.

> The time is out of joint; O cursed spite
> That ever I was born to set it right.
>
> (I, v, 189–90)

The inspiration of that sigh is Ophelia; for, as we shall see, the gloom of that first soliloquy is not without its solitary ray of light.

---

5   See *CRH*, ii, 74.

Now mark with what consummate art it happens, that on the very eve of that fearful midnight,—precisely as Hamlet is about to undergo the most appalling ordeal that ever man sustained, the tragic muse foreshadows another crowning sorrow for the doomed scion of Denmark. The fair Ophelia is made to flit before us, graceful, reticent, tender,—saying the very word that's wanted and nothing more; witty, high-bred, resolute—just such a lady as such a prince might love,

> —whose worth . . .
> Stood challenger on mount of all the age
> For her perfections:
>
> (Q2 IV, vii, 28–9)

a 'Rose of May' that turned

> to favour and to prettiness
> Thought and affliction, passion, hell itself.
>
> (IV, v, 187, 186)

What a *lady* she is! How archly she turns the tables on her light-headed, loud-mouthed brother, in words as memorable as any in the play:

> But good my brother,
> Do not as some ungracious pastors do,
> Show *me* the steep and thorny way to heaven;
> Whilst, like a puff'd and reckless libertine,
> Himself the primrose path of dalliance treads,
> And recks not his own read.
> Laer. O fear me not,
> I stay too long.
>
> (I, iii, 46–52)

Too long, decidedly; that home-thrust was sharper than the sword of Saladin. But observe how differently she encounters her father; though infinitely more insulted and nettled by the broad sarcasms of the Premier, she never permits herself to be stirred an inch from maidenly dignity, or to violate the completest filial respect and obedience. [Quotes I, iii, 88–93, 98–136.] Observe that it is of *late* he [Hamlet] hath given private time to her; of *late* he hath made many tenders of his affection; so that in spite of the first soliloquy, in spite of his wish to return to Wittenberg, it may fairly be inferred that elastic youth was striving to repair its first great sorrow, with its first great love,—that the '*O cursed spite!*' is not the lament of a laggard, but of a lover. And, as he proudly rallies from the agonies of that eventful midnight, asserting a quiet mastery, not only over his two friends, but over the impatient Ghost, our hearts bleed for him, as we think of the blow that Polonius is stealthily preparing.

So much has been said about the vacillation and procrastination of this much misrepresented Prince, that one would suppose the action of the Play consumed a year or two. Let us endeavor to fix the extent of his loitering.

The First Act occupies exactly twenty-four hours. The interval between the First and Second Acts is less easily determined. Hamlet himself is scarcely an authority as to time; his indignant rhetoric openly disclaims fidelity to arithmetic. First, his father has been '*two* months dead' when his mother re-married, then '*not two*', then '*within* a month', 'a little month—' and finally less than 'two hours'. But the reiteration of the same numeral is something; and Ophelia lets us know, in the Third Act, that it is then just 'Twice *two months*' since the regicide. So, allowing a *two* months' widowhood to the Queen, and counting some weeks or days between the second marriage and the first appearance of the spectre, we have less than two months, as the interval between the Acts and the measure of Hamlet's delay—the only delay with which he can be rationally reproached, since after the killing of Polonius he was a State prisoner.

The First and Second Acts, however, are so inseparably linked in horror by Ophelia's terrible picture of her interview with her discarded lover, that it is difficult to escape the impression that Hamlet stalked straight from the haunted platform into her chamber. [Quotes II, i, 75–101.] We are not permitted to see Hamlet in this 'ecstacy of love'. But what a picture! What vivid detail! What awful light and shade! How he must have loved her, that love should bring him to such a pass? his knees knocking each other?—knees that had firmly followed a beckoning ghost, now scarce able to bear him to his Mistress' chamber! There is more than the love of forty thousand brothers in that hard grasp of the wrist—in that long gaze at arms' length—in the force that *might*, but *will* not, draw her nearer! And never a word from this king of words!

His *first* great silence—the *second* is death! They may meet again—meet a thousand times—meet tomorrow, or next day, or the day after; but with the open grave of their dead love between them forevermore!

The cause of this despair is palpable:

> Pol. What! have you given him any hard words of late?
> Oph. No, my good lord; but, as you did command,
> I *did repel* his *letters* and *denied*
> His *access to me.*
>
> (II, i, 108–11)

So that in the interval between those acts, he has sought her *more* than once; she has repelled his *letters*—plural. Yet he could only have sought her to whisper some sad parting, for he knew that he was doomed! Perhaps he may have dreamed of finding counsel in her eyes—of resting that tormented forehead for the last time on her knees! Instead of this, the doors are closed against him! Dismissed, forsaken, just as the glance of a fond woman's eye, the touch of a true woman's hand, was most needed! Was it not enough to madden him? Was it not enough to turn him mercilessly against the sly old trimmer whose finger he detected in the transaction—whom he must always have detested as his uncle's Premier, had he not been Ophelia's father? Would he have been mortal, would he have been a lover, had he not hated Polonius? And yet when they next meet, we are startled by the savage flash of scorn, for which we are unprepared only because the grand Master has not deigned to restate the provocation.

This is one of the most amusing of Hamlet's engagements. How confidently the veteran sails into action!—

[Quotes II, ii, 163–220, including the whole of Hamlet's encounter with Polonius.]

This is pitiless. But there is nothing so insufferable to a lofty and morbidly acute intelligence in its prime, as the devices of a wily, aggressive old age—the 'slyness blinking through the watery eye of superannuation'. Yet, with all his drivel, the ancient diplomat is no despicable antagonist: he is still an overmatch for most men. Though on a false trail now, there is no telling when he may strike the true one. He is 'too *busy*', and that alone is 'some danger'. Still, we could hardly forgive the grim delight with which Hamlet lashes the bewildered and discomfited politician, were it not for that triple wail, 'except my life, except my life, except my life!' This arrests our sympathy just as it is about to side with Polonius, by reminding us of the insignificance of the pain the prince inflicts when weighed against the torture he endures. The Premier's advance of Rosencrantz and Guildenstern to cover his own retreat, is exceedingly humorous.

Enter Rosencrantz and Guildenstern.
Pol. You go to seek the lord Hamlet; *there* he is:—(accented just as if he had said, You go to seek the devil; *there he is!*)—
(*Exit* Polonius.)

Through Rosencrantz and Guildenstern Hamlet is presented to us under his subtlest intellectual aspects. These two young gentlemen have been summoned to Court, and delicately commissioned to 'draw out' Hamlet, and gather the secret cause of his affliction; in consideration whereof they are to receive such thanks *as fits a King's remembrance*. They had been brought up with him, 'neighbour'd to his youth and humour', old schoolmates and friends; yet, at the first intimation of their royal master, they cheerfully sink into paid spies. In their very first interview at Court, they display a talent for self-abasement.

> Thanks, Rosencrantz and gentle Guildenstern.
> Thanks, Guildenstern and gentle Rosencrantz.
> (II, ii, 33–4)

They are bought up, body and soul, and the Queen says amen to the bargain.

Hamlet, though entirely ignorant of the transaction, is instinctively on his guard, and divines their mission at sight.

The best and most characteristic portion of the scene, one of the finest in the Play, is omitted in the Quarto—another indication, we think, that the Quarto was from an earlier version, and that we must regard the Folio as the standard. For, in this omitted passage, two *essential* points are introduced; namely, Hamlet's total lack of ambition, and the circumstance of his having servants of his own; which latter fact would facilitate his fitting out or engaging a privateer, or negotiating with Fortinbras to intercept his voyage to England—a point to be considered presently.

> Guild. Mine honour'd lord.
> Ros. My most dear lord.
> Ham. My excellent good friends! How dost thou,
> Guildenstern? Ah, Rosencrantz! Good lads, how do ye both?
>
> (II, ii, 223–7)

Very genial in expression; *but instead of giving them his hand*, he institutes a cross-examination.

[Quotes II, ii, 237–70, pointing out that the passage is omitted in Q2 from line 241: 'Let me question more in particular.']

How vainly, yet how persistently, they endeavor to convict him of ambition! How superbly he disclaims! He is King already! King wherever reason may clamber, wherever imagination may soar! Monarch of all the realms of earth, and air, and ocean! Emperor of infinite space! What cares *he* for the crown of Denmark? He never once alludes to its loss, save in that final summing up against his uncle; and then only as an item on the side of 'perfect conscience':

> He that hath . . .
> Popped in between the election and my hopes. (V, ii, 65, 66)

His insecure, uninfluential, beggared position at Court, is only glanced at in excuse for not being better able to serve his friends: once at the end of the First Act,

> And what so poor a man as Hamlet is
> May do to express his love and friending to you
> God willing, shall not lack:—
>
> (I, v, 185–7)

and twice in the scene we are now examining [II, ii].

[Miles briefly discusses the rest of the dialogue between Hamlet and Rosencrantz and Guildenstern and the entry of Polonius and then the introduction of the Players and their recitation of the lines from the Trojan play, quoting II, ii, 271–411, with the omission of the "little eyases" passage of the Folio (338–62).]

But all this while Hamlet has been silently planning his Mousetrap.

> Ham. Can you play the murder of Gonzago?
> First Player. Ay, my lord.
> Ham. We'll ha't *tomorrow night.* You could, for a need, study a speech of some dozen or sixteen lines, which I would set down and insert in't, could you not?
> First player. Ay, my lord. (*Exit First Player.*)
> (*Exeunt Ros. and Guild.*)
> Ham. Now I am alone!
>
> (II, ii, 538–50)

With what fierce delight he hails the moment! His fingers are itching for his sword hilt! His rage must have vent, or it will kill him. Maddened by the forced delay, he turns on himself like a scorpion walled with fire.

[Quotes Hamlet's soliloquy 'O, what a rogue and peasant slave am I!' (II, ii, 551–87, 588–9.]

It is true, that Hamlet is constitutionally averse to violence; that he is not 'splenitive and rash'; that he 'lacks gall to make oppression bitter'; that his weakness and his melancholy 'have increased his apathy to all things, even to revenge'; that he habitually exhibits that chronic antipathy to action which accompanies extreme nervous depression. But as for cowardice?—from such cowards defend us heaven! Once roused, he never sets his life at a pin's fee: the 'something dangerous' becomes something terrible. There is not a hero in Shakespeare—Macbeth, with harness on his back,—Lear, with his good, biting falchion,—Othello, with that little arm uplifted,—ay, even Richard, when a thousand hearts are great within his bosom—who would not quail before the Berserker wrath of this Viking's son!—while, in the blaze of his dazzling irony, Falstaff himself would shrivel up into Slender?

But it is time to explain the true causes of Hamlet's delay. He is not merely the heir of a swift revenge but the princely representative of a 'cause and a name', which must be *reported aright to the unsatisfied*. How could he *then* kill the King without passing for a common cutthroat? Shall the annals of Denmark be allowed to perpetuate his uncle as a martyr and himself as an assassin? He more than half believed the Ghost's story, and hence his vehement self-accusal; but to proceed to extremities, without corroborate testimony, would have been both a crime and a blunder. *We* want no farther proof: we are initiated spectators, and have full faith in the word of the majestic apparition. But were we called upon to *act* as Hamlet was, we should think twice before we astonished our friends in particular and mankind in general by exterminating a royal uncle at the special private request of the ghost of a defunct Paterfamilias. Whatever may have been Hamlet's shortcomings, he was distinctly not a fool. And it is impossible to conceive any better, swifter or surer way of accomplishing his complicated mission than by that very assumption of lunacy on the one hand, and the expedient of the Interlude on the other. The first would mitigate the verdict of posterity if sudden fury should goad him into premature assault, as happened once and nearly twice; the second, by startling the King into some word or gesture of self-betrayal, would serve to justify or palliate a more deliberate revenge. Public verification—human testimony to the truth—of that ghostly charge was not to be obtained in a day or an hour. Hamlet seized the very first opportunity that offered: and it required both consummate ingenuity and consummate daring to devise and carry out the expedient. Away with idle *words* and cursing like a scullion!

[Quotes II, ii, 589–606: Hamlet decides to use the Play of Gonzago to catch the King's conscience.]

But there is a spiritual necessity for retarded instead of precipitate action. That smiling damned villain is a fascination: it would be a mistake to *slay* him out of hand: the joy of one sharp second is nothing to the delight of watching him, day by day, unconsciously moving nearer to his doom. Had the King a thousand lives, to take them one by one were less enjoyment than the revelry of deepening hatred, the luxury of listening to the far music of the forging bolt. Who has not recognized, in some degree, the charm of the suspended claw, or comprehended the stern joy of the lion in his lair? The crimes of this sceptered fratricide are stale: the murdered man is dust: his widow old in incest: there is no fresh, living horror to clamor for instant retribution. Indeed there is no adequate retribution possible, except such as the soul of the Avenger can find in saturating itself with the spectacle of its victim. The naked fact of killing the King would be poor revenge save as the climax of antecedent torture,—not physical, but mental and spiritual torture. For when mind and heart are outraged, they seek to be avenged in kind. To haunt that guilty court like a spectre; to hang destruction by a hair above the throne; to wean his mother from her low cleaving; to vex the state with turbulent and dangerous lunacy; to make that sleek usurper quail and cower in every conflict; to lash him with unsparing scorn; to foil him at every turn; to sting him to a new crime; to drag him from his throne, a self-convicted felon, and, ultimately, with one crowning sword-thrust to make all even,—this is the nearest approach to *atonement* of which the case is susceptible.

But the impulse of conscience, as well as of nature, was against a precipitate, headlong assault. Hamlet is represented not only as a prince and a man, but as a Christian; and as a Christian he may be pardoned, *even at this day*, for being *partially* influenced by his faith. The manifest Christian duty under the circumstance was forgiveness: there is no such word as revenge in the lexicon of Calvary. Tried by the Christian standard, the very poorest revenge he could take would be to send his own soul helplessly after his sire's just for the sake of shortening the life and accelerating the perdition of one who was pretty sure in due season to damn himself.

The classics have so profoundly paganized our taste, that our secret wish is, not that he should shut both ears to the vindictive whispers of a *questionable* shape, but that he should finish up the matter like a man and play the executioner with less mouthing. But Hamlet is not '*the passion puppet of fate, but the representative of an august will*' (De Quincey). Free will and conscience both rebel at this dictation of the grave, this super-position of destiny. The soul immortal as *itself* consents to follow the phantom so far, but no farther; and although sorely tempted to aggression, remains virtually defensive to the end, expectant of the mediation of Providence, but disdaining the compulsion of destiny.

> There's a divinity that shapes our ends,
> Rough-hew them how we may.
>
> (V, ii, 10–11)

The power referred to is God, not fate. Even before that glance beyond the grave, that verification of penal fire, he respects the 'canon 'gainst self-slaughter'. On meeting the ghost, his first ejaculation is a prayer,

> Angels and ministers of grace defend us,
>
> (I, iv, 20)

just as afterward in the interview with the Queen,

> Save me and hover o'er me with your wings,
> You heavenly guards!
>
> (III, iv, 94–5)

The surmise that the spirit he has seen may be the devil, and that the devil hath power to assume a pleasing shape, so far from being an overnice after-scruple, is his first misgiving.

> Be thou a spirit of health or goblin damn'd,
> Bring with the airs from *heaven* or blasts from *hell*;
> Be thy intents wicked or charitable,
> Thou com'st in such a questionable shape
> That I will speak to thee.
>
> (I, iv, 21–5)

Questionable from the first. And even after his love and pity are fully enlisted, he cannot ban that grim suspicion of diablerie,

> O all you host of heaven! O earth! What else?
> And shall I couple hell?
>
> (I, v, 92–3)

'So art thou to revenge when thou shalt hear', is hardly the language of a soul in Purgatory, the sphere to which the spirit professes to belong. He cannot divest himself of the darker supposal:

> He took my father grossly, full of bread;
> With all his crimes broad blown, as flush as May;
> And how his audit stands, who knows [save] heav'n?
> But, in our circumstance and course of thought
> 'Tis heavy with him.
>
> (III, iii, 80–4)

So that although the fear of *the worst* deepens and intensifies his wrath, he cannot, without more or less misgiving, wholly abandon himself to a revenge prompted, as he says, by *hell* as well as heaven.

It is precisely this influence of faith, and this consequent confusion of purpose, that lends such a deep, uncertain, unfathomable interest to the Play. The human, at its best, is beautiful, as well as the divine; and most especially attractive when enriched with just so much of the divine as enters into the composition of your average Christian. A Christian rarely presents the same harmonious front to fate which the antique not only permitted, but exacted. When the grave is the consummation, the absolute finale of existence, except as a dim shade, it is comparatively easy to round the heroic evenly and symmetrically up to that margin. But when death is the door to vaster spheres and wider experiences, when this little life is but the prelude to unending futurities of infinite bliss or infinite despair, the deeper faith should find its echo in deeper art. In *Hamlet*, as in *Faust*, more grandly, though less avowedly, the immortal weal or woe of a *human soul* is at stake; and we catch ourselves listening for the spirit voices at the end,

> 'He is judged!'—'He is saved!'

It is precisely here that he explains himself in that marvellous monologue which fills the heart of this troubled symphony with an Adagio of calm, infinite, unearthly beauty. From the first, Hamlet neither cared for nor expected to survive his revenge. *'To be or not to be'*, is not a question of suicide, but of *sacrifice*. He must perish with his victim; there is no escape. He is ready! For his body he recks not; better thaw and resolve itself into a dew. But his mind? Life had still one delight for this 'fellow of Wittenberg'—the inexhaustible splendor of his own *mind*, the glory and majesty of thought, the ecstacy of perfect expression. It was his vocation, his genius, his supreme happiness, to think, to speak, to imagine. He enjoys the play of his sovereign reason, as the horse of the desert enjoys the play of its arching neck and flying mane,—as the eagle enjoys its pinions while fanning the sun,—as all things divinely beautiful enjoy their own manifestations. Love itself, though his nature is exceptionally tender, is but a secondary transport to the rapture of eloquence. What wonder that he clings to the lighted torch of such an intelligence! What wonder that he strives to bear it unextinguished through the whirlwinds that sweep the dark passes between time and eternity! And yet he would gladly surrender this beautiful mind to the quietus of final and complete extinction: it is only the *distortion* of the dreams that haunt the sleep of death that gives him pause.

[Quotes opening of the soliloquy III, i, 58–70.]

Still less will he force a lawless passage into that

> ... undiscovered country from whose bourn
> No traveller returns ...

even for an enterprise of great pith and moment. 'The dread of something after death'

> puzzles the will,
> And makes us rather bear those ills we have
> Than fly to others that we know not of,
> Thus *conscience* does make cowards of us all;
> And thus the native hue of resolution
> Is sicklied o'er with the pale cast of thought.

But apart from all these motives and reasons for delay, Hamlet *could afford to wait*. In the first place, he was personally safe in waiting:

> He's lov'd of the distracted multitude,

(IV, iii, 4)

to such an extent that the King dare not 'put the strong law on him':

> —The queen, his mother,
> Lives almost by his looks:-
> —the great love the general gender bear him.
>
> (IV, vii, 11–12, 18)

is such that the royal arrows,

> Too lightly timber'd for so loud a mind
> Would have reverted to the bow again
> And not where they were aimed.
>
> (IV, vii, 22–4)

There is a vulgar impression, owing perhaps to the usual insignificance of stage royalty, that the King was constantly at Hamlet's mercy: whereas, but for Hamlet's personal prowess and popularity, the case must have been exactly the reverse. As it is, he haunts that guilty palace, pacing the lobby *four* hours together: as it *is*, ever since Laertes went into France, he has been in *continual practice with his rapier*[6]. If suddenly assailed, he is sure of a chance to use it—*once* at least. Always on guard, always vigilant, always armed; reckless and irresistible in his wrath; masked by lunacy and shielded by popular and maternal affection, he felt more than a match for the utmost cunning of the King. Young, unadvised, inexperienced; the representative of the better genius of Denmark; with national interests to regard as well as individual wrongs to redress; watched by an intriguing statesman; worried by a brace of friends turned spies; discarded by the lady of his love; bent on the reformation of his mother as well as on the chastisement of her wretched spouse; passive because uncertain whether his mission is from demon or divinity, yet equal to all odds and any emergency; there is no grander figure in fable or history than Hamlet, Prince of Denmark.

The Second Act was a lull, after the storm of the First: the Third Act, beginning only one day later, is an uninterrupted process of events, moving swiftly and sternly on to their terrible consummation. Polonius is setting another snare, and baiting it with Ophelia. Hamlet has been '*sent for*' to 'afront her', as't were 'by accident'; Ophelia is 'loosed', book in

---

6   See V, ii, 157.

hand, to receive him; the King and his minister so bestowed that, 'seeing unseen', they may frankly judge and gather,

> If 't *be* the affliction of his love or no
> That thus he suffers for.
>
> (III, i, 38–9)

That Ophelia is *not* aware of the lawful espials is distinctly intimated by Polonius himself after the interview:—

> How now Ophelia!
> You need not tell us what Lord Hamlet said;
> We heard it all.
>
> (III, i, 181–3)

The King's speech to the Queen, 'Sweet Gertrude, leave us too', etc., as well as the Premier's

> Gracious, so please you,
> We will bestow ourselves,
>
> (III, i, 45–6)

must therefore be delivered apart, or aside, from Ophelia, who accepts the proposed encounter, simply as an opportunity of reconciliation. But her woman's wit and maiden love suggest a much better apology for the interview, than the old statesman's rather weak invention,

> Read on this book;
> That show of such an exercise may colour
> Your loneliness.
>
> (III, i, 46–8)

Infinitely better her own honest, proud, instinctive action:—

> My lord, I have remembrances of yours
> That I have longed to re-deliver;
> I pray you now receive them.
>
> (III, i, 95–7)

She ignores their last dumb meeting:

>How does your honour for *this many a day*?

And yet, womanlike, although she had repelled his letters and declined his visits without receiving a single provocation or vouchsafing a single explanation, she now immediately assumes the attitude of injured innocence:

>Take these again; for to the noble mind
>Rich gifts wax poor when givers prove unkind.
>*There*, my lord.
>
>(III, i, 102–4)

Alas, she knew not with whom she was dealing. The delicious feminine insincerity, which makes a sound man smile in fancied superiority, was gall and wormwood to this morbid lover of truth. The wound she had dealt his soul was mortal; she had silenced the last hope of his heart; and yet she undertakes to invent unkindness on his part to excuse severity on her own! The whole plot flashes on him at once. He sees the two spies behind the scenes, as plainly as if they stood before him. He sees in *her* only a puppet or a decoy. The tenderness which deepened his voice into richer music when he first perceived her—

>Soft, you now!
>The fair Ophelia. Nymph, in thy orisons
>Be all my sins remembered—
>
>(III, i, 90–2)

all this is gone; and instead of it, harsh bewildering laughter:—'Ha, ha! are you honest? Are you fair?—Get thee to a nunnery!' How significant that fierce, sudden question,

'Where's your father?'
Oph. At home my lord.
Ham. Let the doors be shut upon him, that he may play the fool nowhere but in's own house.

(III, i, 134–5)

Sure that Polonius is a listener, *and with her connivance*, he cannot help believing her answer, a direct falsehood,—a falsehood that brings down upon her the cruel levity occurring just before the interlude, and that now embitters and corrodes his passionate but well-considered and well-meant warning.

[Quotes III, i, 136–52 (Hamlet's exit), and reiterates his justification of Hamlet's behaviour in this scene.]

... 'Get thee to a nunnery' was the best and only advice he could give her. A nunnery was her best and only refuge from the impending storm. Destruction for himself and all else around him; but, for her the cloisters' timely shelter . . .

The King has gained nothing by playing the spy; he detects too much method in his nephew's madness; that wicked parting threat is ringing in his ears, '*All but one* shall live!' His soul is on the rack; restless, apprehensive, overawed. The weaker mind already quails before the stronger; the executioner of the father begins to tremble before the son.—

> There's something in his soul,
> O'er which his melancholy sits on brood;
> And I do doubt the hatch and the disclose
> Will be some danger; which for to prevent
> I have in quick determination
> Thus set it down; he shall with speed to England.
>
> (III, i, 167–72)

But the pliant monster, overruled as usual by his minister, concludes to postpone the threatened banishment until the Queen mother has a chance to be 'round with him', *after the play*. Meanwhile the play within the play is preparing; and those wooden strollers, who in other hands would have proved clumsy or unmanageable, are here the occasion of a quiet eloquence, more effective than most dramatic action. 'Speak the speech, I pray you', is a lesson for all time to all humanity.

The facility with which Hamlet counterfeits madness, is strikingly instanced in the sudden transition from his pre-eminently sane discourse with Horatio, to his outrageous behavior before the royal pair and their attendants. How calm, how measured, those solemn words to his friend, as if designed to anticipate any misconstruction in that quarter. For it sometimes happens we play the madman so very perfectly, that our best friends are precisely those who are the first to pronounce our sanity counterfeit, and our lunacy natural. But what a superb compliment he pays Horatio; how dearly he loves to praise where praise is due,—that rarest human grace . . . [Quotes Hamlet's lines in praise of Horatio, III, ii, 52–3, 60–3, 69–72.] This is the friend whom he now commissions to watch the one scene that comes near the circumstance, 'Which I have told thee, of my father's death' . . . [Quotes III, ii, 75–85.] Then, as the first notes of the Danish March announce the coming of the King and court, he plunges instantaneously and without effort, into the reckless, impenetrable, frightful levity, that carries him through the scene. King, Queen, Polonius, Ophelia, are one by one impaled on his savage irony.

[Quotes dialogue from the King's entry to *'Exeunt all but Hamlet and Horatio* III, ii, 89–258, omitting much of Hamlet's bawdy and most of the text of the play of Gonzago.]

Any other poet would have been content to fix the climax of the scene, in the disordered flight of the palsied murderer; but in Shakespeare, it is only a stepping stone to loftier achievements. The rest of the act is a *tour de force*, a torrent of eloquence, passion and power; a stream of intellectual glory. The dramatic workmanship is inimitable. After the signal triumph of this scheme, after this conclusive confirmation of the ghostly tale, Hamlet abandons himself to the capricious impulse of the moment, as a strong swimmer abandons himself to a current, only to breast it with recovered strength. Whatever is uppermost in his mind, is the first to find expression. Half remembered fragments of verse, whether applicable or not; tumultuous raillery, in which Horatio is swept along, like a leaf in a whirlwind; swift serious questions; sharp yearnings for music; are all blended together, with unparalleled power and truth.

[Quotes dialogue between Hamlet and Horatio, III, ii, 259–82, then (with occasional comments) the interview between Hamlet and Rosencrantz and Guildenstern III, ii, 283–321, 339–60.]

The breach between them [Hamlet and Rosencrantz and Guildenstern] is widening; a dead friendship is rapidly developing into an active hatred. Throughout the interview, Hamlet preserves a frozen calm which they can neither penetrate nor disturb, though all the while his blood is boiling. With masterly self-control, he bids Polonius, 'God bless you, sir!' little knowing what immediate need there was for such a blessing. There is even a pale evanescent tenderness glimmering through that too palpably counterfeit lunacy, as if the Premier's superannuated slyness were a relief, after the baseness of the two adolescent spies.

[Quotes dialogue between Hamlet and Polonius summoning Hamlet to the Queen, III, ii, 362–76.] He has hardly time to hurry them from his presence, before the dark thought underlying all this mirth betrays itself: he is trembling on the verge of matricide. [Quotes Hamlet's soliloquy ''Tis now the very witching time of night', III, ii, 377–88.] In this mood he seeks the Queen's closet, and in this mood encounters the King at prayer. He must have overheard, on his way there, the interview between the King and Rosencrantz and Guildenstern; he *must* have witnessed or overheard them 'making love' to their pitiful employment. For scarcely in any other way could he have foreknown the royal determination, which he immediately after refers to.

> Ham. I must to England: you know that?
> Queen.   —Alack,
> I had forgot: 'tis so concluded on.
>
>   (III, iv, 183–4)

That ominous interlude has not improved the King's repose. [Quotes King's words to Rosencrantz and Guildenstern III, iii, 1–7.] Remorse, instilled by bodily fear, has driven the drunkard murderer to attempt repentance. [Quotes end of King's prayer and Hamlet 'Now might I do it pat', III, iii, 69–95.] Hazlitt calls this ghastly, livid wrath, 'a refinement in malice, to excuse his own want of resolution'[7]. A shallow plausibility, demolished by that resolute pass through the arras, aimed an instant later, at this same King of shreds and patches! And besides, there is the drama to consider. To kill the King *then*, would have been an anticlimax and the play have been cut short, as it would also had the King, and not Polonius, been behind the arras! In both these instances the plot required

---

7   See *CRH*, ii, 116.

that the King should live, but Hamlet showed himself perfectly willing to kill him out of hand if caught eavesdropping.

The main sorrow of the Ghost is the manner of his taking off:

> Cut off in the blossom of my sin,
> —sent to my account
> With all my imperfections on my head.
>
> (I, v, 76, 78–9)

Hamlet's main sorrow is less his father's sudden death, than eternal doom. Once fully abandoned to the terrible temptation which besets him, once mad enough to 'dare damnation', he is not going to sell his soul for a song; not going to kill the King *at his prayers*: he will give measure for measure, eternal doom, for eternal doom. The depths of faith are revealing darker possibilities of revenge; but the whole frightful passage is a fiendish suggestion, vividly presented, rather than deliberately embraced. It is the first wild, natural imprecation of a son *for the first time* sure that his uncle is the assassin of his father. This bitter *certainty* transforms him for the moment almost into a demon; and though his conscience re-asserts its sway, this is clearly the mood in which he afterwards meets his mother. Had the Prince known that the King, far from being truly repentant, was sending him *to his death* in England, he would assuredly have slain the wretch upon the spot and the play would have had a totally different ending. Shakespeare's art avoided the anticlimax in both these situations.

Polonius is playing the eavesdropper once too often: how dexterous, sly, and busy he is:—

> Pol.—Look you, lay home to him:
> Tell him his pranks have been too broad to bear with.
> And that your grace hath screen'd and stood between
> Much heat and him. I'll sconce me even here.
> Pray you be round with him.
>
> (III, iv, 1–5)

She *means* to be round with him, to 'lay home to him'. 'I'll warrant you', she says; 'Fear not *me*'. She is very bold and confident and self-contained. She is used to conquest. Her dominion over both her royal husbands was supreme: the first is true and tender to her, even in that sulphurous prison-house to which her fickle beauty helped to doom him: the second quotes her, though she must then be near fifty, as the central sun round which he circles.

> She's so conjunctive to my life and soul,
> That, as the star moves not but in its sphere,
> I could not but by her.
>
> (IV, vii, 14–16)

She is morally weak, but otherwise strong: fascinated by a brute, but not cognizant of his crime: the slave of one sin, yet the mistress of more than one virtue. The character is not an uncommon one. Her prostitution cannot be sufficiently detested; but there is not the shadow of a ground to suppose her conscious of the fratricide. As often happens with these magnetic unfortunates, her tender-heartedness survives her personal degradation. She has a kind word for everybody, and it flows unaffectedly from her heart: but, once roused, she displays the spirit of an Amazon. When the mutineers overbear the officers and break the doors, she strides between the armed rabble and the craven King, with a flash of the same fierce wrath which her son inherits.

> How cheerfully on the false trail they cry!
> O this is counter, you false Danish dogs.—
>
> (IV, v, 107–8)

Not easily crushed, this fair, false, haughty matron:—not easily shaken off, with one wave of the lion's mane, like Polonius and Guildenstern. The encounter is stern from the start.

[Quotes III, iv, 8–24, entry of Hamlet to killing of Polonius.]

Observe three things: the instantaneous assumption of lunacy, the sharp, unhesitating lunge,—the perfect nerve and composure *after* the deed is done. Weak? why, action is even easier than words to this terrible son of the sea-kings.

But the Queen-mother, unsubdued even by this frightful proof of Hamlet's determination to carry his point, is still every inch a Queen.

> Queen. O me, what hast thou done?
> Ham.—Nay, I know not.
>   Is it the king?
> Queen. O what a rash and bloody deed is this!
> Ham. A bloody deed!—almost as bad, good mother,
>   As kill a King, *and marry with his brother.*
> Queen. As kill a King!
> Ham. Ay, lady, 'twas my word.
>
> (III, iv, 24–9)

Had she flinched beneath that sudden test, had she faltered beneath the long and searching gaze with which these decisive words were accompanied, he might have slain her in his fury on the spot. There was no escaping that infallible ordeal: guilt or innocence was written unmistakably in her face; and it needs not the weak assurance of the Quarto of 1603 to convince us of her innocence.

> Queen. But as I have a soul, I swear by heaven,
>   I never knew of this most horrid murder.
>
> (Q1 sig. G3r)

The stronger assurance is in her face, in her whole behavior. That question and that gaze have satisfied him: his denunciations are henceforth restricted to her infidelity.

[Quotes III, iv, 33–52, to 'Look here upon this picture'.]

It requires all the tremendous sequel of the speech, to humble her thoroughly: but beneath the blast of that resistless invective, she melts away at his feet. 'O Hamlet, speak no more!' But his brain and heart are on fire; his words flow like lava, fiercer, faster, hotter, till stayed in mid career by the fancied or real reappearance of the Ghost. Its *speech* to Hamlet implies its reality; its invisibility to the Queen, its unreality. To the audience, it should be as visible as when it swept the platform before the Castle. Its invisibility to the Queen may be accounted for by supposing a merciful forbearance in the royal spectre and thus ascribing another grace to the proud, tender shade of the buried majesty of Denmark. Indeed, the brief visitation is more like an errand of love than of revenge.

After a rapid, causeless admonition, the phantom's sole anxiety centres on the Queen, about whose ultimate fate he is a thousandfold more solicitous than about his victim son's. Here, as well as earlier in the Play, Hamlet may have felt this ghostly *neglect*—felt the little more of earth than Heaven in this jealous eagerness to cleanse 'the royal bed of Denmark', of 'luxury and damned incest';—felt, amidst all his vast pity, that his own spirituality, his own welfare, were slighted by this *negotio in nocte perambulante*.[8] Nothing short of the jealous impatience of indestructible love could have imputed to Hamlet 'an almost *blunted* purpose', while Polonius, slain for the King, was still lying in his blood; unless, indeed, the Ghost were singularly ignorant of that unhappy transaction. It was a signally *sharp* purpose that slew the Premier. Hotspur himself, in Hamlet's place, could not well have gone through this terrible scene with more dash, decision, and reckless scorn of consequences, while all that lurid eloquence, all those frozen tears, would be missing! Measureless conjugal love makes the apparition real, and explains its being both invisible and inaudible to the Queen. Hamlet's heated imagination and filial piety, dormant as to her, could never have invented a speech of such heroic doting. At all events, the reappearance of the Ghost, so far as the audience and the part itself are concerned, is a dramatic necessity. But do not let us allow the impatient reproaches made by a questionable shape to blind us to the fatal vigor of that pass behind the arras.

Hamlet's attitude towards his mother is that of an inspired prophet. He moulds her like wax to his better will by the miraculous energy of his expressions. He labors giant-like to save her 'fighting' soul; reaching down a redeeming hand through the darkness of deep abysses; dragging her half willing, half reluctant, bruised, trembling, bleeding, into the full daylight of God's holy summits.

> Ham. Mother, for love of grace,
> Lay not that flattering unction to your soul,
> That not your trespass, but my madness speaks;
> ... —Confess yourself to heaven;
> Repent what's past; avoid what is to come;
> ... —Forgive me this my virtue:

---

8 'perambulating thing of the night'

> For in the fatness of these pursy times
> Virtue itself of vice must pardon beg.
>
> (III, iv, 135–7, 140–1, 143–5)

Precisely what he himself must do to most of his readers, for not being more bloodthirsty and vindictive. His irony assumes a momentary plaintiveness:

> Once more, good night:
> And when you are desirous to be blest,
> I'll blessing beg of you.
>
> (III, iv, 154–6)

He can afford to be tender: his barbed invective has apparently exterminated the sin at which it is aimed: shaft has followed shaft, until the air is darkened. But one temptation still survives; and the quiver of this young Apollo is inexhaustible. By a fine climax of sarcasm, intermixed with a grotesque but significant menace, he contrives to diminish the novel danger to which her infatuation exposes her; namely the allurements occasioned by the vivid recital of the details of her guilt: [Quotes III, iv, 172–80].

It is terrible to hear a son thus threatening a mother, face to face: but, taken all in all, his bearing is not entirely unwarranted. And this brings us to what is, perhaps, the very deepest problem in the play.

A mission, inaugurated by what may be called a miracle, can hardly fail to furnish its own opportunities. Chance, in Hamlet's case, will be unseen direction. Since his life is manacled to one issue by preternatural interposition, let the same dread agency also indicate the manner of arriving at that issue. In the frenzy inspired by the conviction that the Ghost's word is 'true for a thousand pound', he would have slain the King, had he been sure of thus dealing out eternal as well as temporal ruin. But ever after and before that horrible impulse, he is steadily *on the defensive*. Even that swift pass through the arras is defensive; he does not strike until his own safety has been compromised by his mother's cry for help. From the moment that he has satisfied himself of the Ghost's veracity, he is eager to obey its behests. There is but an hour or two, at most, between the self-betrayal of the King at the interlude, and the killing of

Polonius,—a mistake which he regrets rather as a misfortune than as a crime;

> For this same lord
> I do repent; but heaven hath pleased it so
> To punish me with this, and this with me,
> That I must be their scourge and minister.
>
> (III, iv, 156–9)

With men of Hamlet's mould, intellectual scorn is as unchangeable as truth itself. And it may be added that his exquisitely truthful nature constantly exhibits a stern unforgivingness of calculated, persistent insincerity and fraud; an unforgivingness which, but for vast, wondrous, inexplicable miracles of mercy, must belong to supreme Truth itself. A deed, a sight, that might well dismay the warrior of a hundred fields, makes no perceptible impression upon the nerves of this premature veteran in woe.

> Indeed, this Counsellor
> Is now most still, most secret, and most grave,
> Who was in life a foolish, prating knave.
> Come, sir, to draw toward an end with you—
> Good night, mother.
>
> (III, iv, 187–91)

Yet beneath this desperate apathy lurks the silent grace of tears. If the Queen may be believed, he is weeping while he speaks.

We do not know by what or whose authority the Act is made to end here; certainly not by Shakespeare's. The text of the Quarto runs straight on from beginning to end, without numbering a single Act or Scene. The Folio numbers them only so far as the Second Scene of the Second Act. Instead of '*Exeunt* severally', as the stage direction now stands, it is '*Exit*' in the Quarto, and '*Exit Hamlet, lugging in Polonius*', in the Folio. In *both*, the Queen remains on the stage; the King enters, and the action proceeds uninterruptedly. The present arrangement not only ruins the Fourth Act, but confuses and enfeebles the whole play. For reasons presently given, we shall review the Third Act to its legitimate conclusion.

True to her vow, the Queen represents Hamlet to the King as

> Mad as the sea and wind when both contend
> Which is the mightier.
>
> (IV, i, 6–7)

And observe how admirably that rapid assumption of lunacy now serves his turn:

> He whips his rapier out and cries, 'A rat, a rat!'
> And in this brainish apprehension, kills
> The unseen good old man.
>
> (IV, i, 9–11)

The King is in a most unroyal panic. [Quotes IV, i, 11–14, 28–9, 31, 35, 37, 39–40.]

The next scene is the arrest. Hamlet's unmitigated, open contempt of the inevitable pair, so different from his former constrained courtesy, reassures us that he overheard their pitiful willingness to superintend his exile. Guildenstern was peacefully silenced; but the more inquisitive and less manly Rosencrantz is spurned and abolished, as Geraint's sword would have abolished the angry dwarf. [Quotes IV, ii, 4–30.] That the arrest is a literal military arrest, see a few lines later.

> King.   But where is he?
> Ros. Without, my lord, *guarded*, to know your pleasure.
> King. Bring him before us.
> Ros. Ho, Guildenstern! bring in my lord.
>
> (IV, iii, 13–16)

The haughty questioning of the King is pitilessly demolished by the sublime ferocity of an attack, rapid and resistless as lightning. The spear of Lancelot o'erthrew whate'er it smote: Hamlet's electrical scorn withers and annihilates. [Quotes IV, iii, 17–50, Hamlet is sent to England.] Does not this point, in its beautiful way—like a star at sea—toward the pirate of very warlike appointment? But of this hereafter. The King is all aghast: [Quotes IV, iii, 56–70].

All the might of Denmark, and her dependencies arrayed against the exiled Prince! But just then, the martial figure of Fortinbras emerges from the distance and flits by in the foreground. '*Enter Fortinbras with his army over the stage: Enter Fortinbras, Drumme and Soldiers*'; as the old copies have it. And in this pomp and circumstance of a rival power, we recognize the hope on which Hamlet is silently but securely building. With this significant array of benignant strength, with this flash of a better fortune for Denmark athwart the deepening drama, the act should end. Ending here, the interval consumed by the voyage to England, the return of Laertes from Paris, and the expedition of Fortinbras to Poland and back, is thrown *between* the Acts,—its natural place. Greek tragedy, restricted by its organic law to the culmination of events, was necessarily an unbroken march from its first chorus to its catastrophe. Modern tragedy aiming rather at the development of character, through a *series* of events, has wisely divided these events into groups separated from each other by the interposition of a curtain. By this brief but total eclipse of the fictitious world, the mind is prepared for intervals of time or space. A year elapsed, or an ocean crossed, during the fall of that mysterious screen, does less violence to the imagination than the supposition of a month between consecutive scenes. In fact, the fancy is almost as free, save to consequences, at the second rise of the curtain as at the first. We accept Claude Melnotte[9] as a recruit in one act, and a Colonel in the next: but when looking dead into the open heart of a spectacle, we are asked to believe that the Prince who embarked for England under our eyes, is back again in five minutes, after a sea fight, and a week's cruise, the imagination rebels. The proposed extension of the Third Act, would make this greatest of tragedies the most symmetrical too; while the Fourth Act, relieved of a confusion which is now mistaken for an anticlimax, would be devoted with a single purpose to its two superb contrasts—the revenge of Laertes with the revenge of Hamlet, and the utter madness of Ophelia with the semi-counterfeit lunacy of her lover. A gain almost as great for the closet, as for the stage.

And what a tremendous Act that Third one is! unrivalled in wealth of imagery, in exhaustless variety and steadily culminating power, by anything in creative art, unless it be the almost equally marvellous festival Act of *Don Giovanni*. Mozart, like Shakespeare, had the faculty of perfect articulation; and hence the intense self-delight they constantly exhibit.

---

9   The hero of Bulwer-Lytton's romantic comedy, *The Lady of Lyons* (1838).

They alone, and Raphael, have the faculty of projecting the *whole* shy and ever reluctant idea from the dim chambers of conception, into full, unclouded sunlight. Like all perfect embodiments, the works of Mozart, Raphael and Shakespeare cast their own shadows: the works of others—Beethoven, Goethe, Angelo—are shadows of the master's selves. It is a common vice to prefer the second *chiar-oscuro* to the first.

The present Fourth Scene of the Fourth Act, except the nine opening lines, is omitted in the Folio ... With the Quarto before them and every temptation to expand, the long pendant to the entry of Fortinbras, must have been advisedly rejected by the editors of the Folio. Heminge and Condell were at least as familiar with this scene as we are. Minor errors in abundance may have crept into the First Folio; minor omissions and additions may disfigure its text: it may be, as Horne Tooke says, 'the only edition worth regarding'; and, as Mr. Knight says, 'the most correctly printed book on record'; or it may have been, as Mr. Dyce believes, 'dismissed from the press with less care and attention than any book of any extent and reputation in the whole annals of English typography'. But the certainty still remains that Heminge and Condell, 'sober, earnest critics', would never have dared to repudiate a long soliloquy that had a place in the *standard* acting copy—the standard ultimately fixed by Shakespeare himself, or with his distinct approval. A jest or two in Richard, an indecisive scene in *Lear*, might escape them; but not, of all things on earth, a *soliloquy* of Hamlet's—the *final* soliloquy too!

Unquestionably, all that stately dialogue with the Captain is Shakespeare's: possibly he wrote the whole soliloquy, every line of it, just as it stands. Even in that age of giants 'sturdy but unclean', there may have been no second touch to equal the felicity of

> Now whether it be
> Bestial oblivion or some craven scruple
> Of thinking too precisely on the event,—
> A thought, which, quartered, hath but one part wisdom,
> And ever three parts coward.—
> (Q2 IV, iv, 30–3, Additional passage J)

It may have been written to *strengthen* the Acts, or to please Burbage or whoever played the part: written, *tried*, and abandoned. For though a leading tragedian might cling to so tempting a bit of declamation, the house, the company, and the author, would be sure to reject it in the end. It is most awkwardly introduced—lugged in by the head and heels like a dead afterthought. It is the one speech too many that palsies both actor and audience; that fails alike on the stage or in the closet; that superficially countenances the imputation of weakness and needlessly complicates the character. We can imagine the more than half-created Hamlet, statue-like uplifting his hand in sublime protest against the threatened malformation. After the other noble monologues, it is weak as water. But the supreme reason for its rejection is that it is *false*.—

> —I do not know
> Why yet I live to say, 'This thing's to do;
> Sith *I have cause and will and strength and means*
> *To do it.*
>
> (ibid., ll. 34–7)

He had not *strength* and *means* to do it, and could not have, until rescued from captivity and impending death by that well-appointed pirate. So, apart from its comparative feebleness, apart from its superfluity, apart from its being most lamely and discordantly introduced, 'I'll be with you straight—go a little before', there is a *positive necessity* for its rejection: it is **false**! False and unnatural! For however happily his counterplot may terminate, it is surely not as a prisoner on the brink of exile, environed by the royal guards, that such a motive for self-reproach would occur. Though no one could *now* have the temerity to reject the scene, were it not rejected by the Folio; yet consciously and deliberately repudiated there, we may well feel at liberty to prefer the professional and disinterested verdict of Heminge and Condell, who certainly give no intimation in their preface that the original papers 'received from him' with scarce a blot, were destroyed as Mr. Dyce supposes, when the Globe Theatre was burned down in 1613. This ill-timed monologue though weak itself does not *really* make *Hamlet* essentially weaker; but there is no reason why the discarded superfluities of genius should be perpetuated only to obscure the pure gold of it priceless bequests. One thing however is clear: unless Hamlet planned the subsequent piratical capture, the Soliloquy is not only superfluous and contradictory, but absurd. Unhappy as it is in all other respects, it serves to demonstrate conclusively that in Shakespeare's own mind, the piratical capture was a premeditated certainty.

With its present Fifth Scene, the Fourth Act properly begins. One victim has already fallen—Polonius: Ophelia is the next. The shock of her father's death by the hand of her lover, has crazed her. It would have suited most artists to exhibit the first crash of the tragical fact; but Shakespeare mercifully spares us the sight of the blow descending on that vestal forehead. Her mind is murdered *off* the stage. The grand master will not over-charge his canvas with details which a lesser soul would grasp at. The spiritual transformation is complete before she reappears. Instead of horror heaped on horror, the very mad-ness of this Rose of May is turned 'to favor and to prettiness'. She softens the gloom and terror of the play into overpowering pathos. Though her character has been only sketched, as if by the finger of a god, in snow, what a vast dramatic purpose it serves! Her madness is the pivot of one Act, her burial of another; her maiden beauty the inspiration of both; while, over the whole tragic expanse, her image flits like the dove that followed the raven! What can be sadder than her story! But a little while ago she was bewailing the overthrow of 'that noble and most sovereign reason', and now the sweet bells of her own mind are not only jangled out of tune, but ruined, broken! One tithe of the woe that Hamlet carries, suffices to crush her. As if in rebuke of that impatient Ghost, the first attempt at revenge involves the sacrifice of this unblemished innocent. But Hamlet escapes the spectacle. By an inspired fitness of events, his banishment just precedes her madness. His self-contained lunacy could never have endured the test of her hopeless, absolute madness. The side by side contrast of real with simulated insanity, though sustained to advantage in *Lear*, between a young noble and an old king, would be a ghastly impossibility between lovers.

Ophelia is stark mad. The only gleam of a purpose left is in the brief threat that Laertes will avenge her father: 'My brother shall know of it': her only memories are dim, distracted impressions of the events that crazed her; songs of Polonius—

[Quotes snatches of Ophelia's songs, IV, v, 30–2, 35, 37–9, 188–97.] Songs of Hamlet too: 'To-morrow is St.Valentine's day'. The whole ditty is but the reflex of her discarded lover's passionate jesting, the dark shadow of masculine yearning projected athwart the snows of virgin purity, deeper and distincter in this intellectual eclipse; the wild echo of his own fierce raillery resounding from the living sepulchre wherein her maiden mind lies buried.

And sometimes too, the twin ideas to which her bewildered brain is feebly clinging, her love and her grief, run incoherently together:

> They bore him barefaced on the bier;
> Hey non nonny nonny, hey nonny;
> And on his grave rain'd many a tear,—
> Fare you well, my dove!

And again:

> There's a daisy:—I would give you some violets, but they withered all
> When my father died: they say he made a good end.—
> For bonny sweet Robin is all my joy.—
>
> (IV, v, 165–8, 182–5)

Ah, how true, how mournful, but above all, how marvellous this inspired imagination in whose imperishable mirror humanity seems more tangible, more intelligible, than even in its own bodily substance! Seeing nature with Shakespeare's eyes, is like reading the heavens with a glass of infinite range and power; wonder on wonder rolls into view; systems, dependencies, mysteries, relations, never before divined; tokens of other atmospheres, gleams of erratic luminaries that seem to spurn all law yet move obedient to one complex impulse; glimpses of fresh courier light cleaving the vast immensity on its way to our yet unvisited world, and all the while, the soul, uplifted by the vision, is flooded with the very music of the spheres.

If aught were wanting to render this play the supreme masterpiece of human genius, it is found in the contrast between Hamlet and Laertes, each with a father murdered, and each impatient for revenge. Laertes is a hero after the popular heart; gallant, passionate, resolute; moving as level to his aim 'as cannon to his blank'. He hardly hears of his father's death, before he is in Denmark; hardly in Denmark, before he storms the Palace. Unscrupulous, unconscientious, irreligious, he drives madly on where Hamlet is compelled to halt.

> To hell allegiance! vows to the blackest devil!
> *Conscience and grace* to the profoundest pit!

> *I dare damnation*: to this point I stand,
> That *both* the worlds I give to negligence,
> Let come what comes; only I'll be revenged
> Most thoroughly for my father.
>
> (IV, v, 129–34)

With inimitable skill the mighty dramatist details precisely the forfeiture of soul from which Hamlet, except in one wild tumult of delirious wrath, steadily recoils.

Hamlet's hands are tied by conscience and faith: Laertes has, practically, neither; has a talent for blasphemy; delights in daring the gods to do their worst; would be glad to cut a throat in the Church. Yet how pitifully dwarfed is the son of Polonius, beside the son of the Sea-King! How he quails before the royal pair that in Hamlet's grasp were powerless as sparrows in the clutches of an eagle! It seems as if Shakespeare had anticipated the demand for more dash in his hero, and presented this type of a fast young soldier only to exalt the grandeur of the much misconstrued prince. Those who point to Laertes' prompt action to revenge his father's death, in contrast to Hamlet's delay, forget that Hamlet's father was thought to have died a natural death. Hamlet had *no proof* to verify his suspicions;—his only witness was the Ghost! Beside the measured, principled retribution of Hamlet, the revenge of Laertes is vulgar, cowardly and criminal; his anathemas but the coarse mouthing of a schoolboy. Imagine for a moment that 'Cutpurse of the Empire' venturing to say to Hamlet,—

> Why now you speak
> Like a good child, and a true gentleman.
>
> (IV, v, 147–8)

Or conceive, in Hamlet's mouth, that rant about 'the life-rendering pelican'.

Midway between these two extremes,—the unreflecting braggart and the self-accuser 'thinking too precisely on the event',—lie the classical hero and the Christian saint. Either would have disposed of the case in a more summary way; the saint by unhesitating and complete forgiveness; the hero proper by a revenge less dilatory than Hamlet's and less treacherous than Laertes'. That the patience of a saint may be rendered as sublimely dramatic as the vindictiveness of a sinner, is proved by Calderon in his *Principe Constante*. But Shakespeare has not chosen to represent a saint, but to show how even a fair infusion of Christian faith must modify the ancient heroic model. The hero in whom religion dominates, would be a higher ideal; the hero in whom unhesitating and unsullied valor dominates, a greater personal favorite: but neither perhaps would have such a hold on the wide heart of humanity, or prove such a permanent joy and wonder, as this prolonged uncertain struggle of matchless intellect and bewildered conscience with madness and despair.

Hamlet is exalted over the mere man of animal courage and passion, not only intellectually and physically, but morally too. The reckless 'darer of damnation' is unfortunately ready to dare dishonor too. The King might have spared himself the pains of feeling his way so nicely how far in villainy he could venture without shocking his man. They are both of a mind, although the master villain is the King: [Quotes IV, vii, 109–13, 131–4].

Thus thickens the plot: in the foreground, the two conspirators, vindictive, eager, aggressive; in the distance, with Horatio, the great defensive avenger, moving ghostlike to his doom and theirs!

The King has been driven to these desperate measures by the news of Hamlet's escape and return:—

> Mess. Letters, my lord, from Hamlet.— . . .
> King. From Hamlet! (*reads*) 'High and mighty,—you shall
> know I am set naked on your kingdom. Tomorrow shall I beg leave to see your kingly eyes'.—
>
> (IV, vii, 36, 38, 42–4)

'*High and mighty!*' What grim sardonic scorn! How it smites him between the brows, as if with an axe! '*High and mighty!*' How the outmanoeuvred assassin starts and staggers beneath the blow.

> What should this mean? Are all the rest come back?
> Or is it some abuse, and no such thing?
> . . . *Can you advise me?*
>
> (IV, vii, 48–9, 52)

He is stretched on a prolusory rack, to which instant death were mercy.

The letter to Horatio is longer:

Ere we were two days old at sea, a pirate of very warlike appointment gave us chase: Finding ourselves too slow of sail, we put on a compelled valour, etc.
(IV, vi, 14–17)

Before discussing the rest of the letter, let us examine this perpetually misunderstood piratical capture. We have already noticed Hamlet's first glance at it, '*I see a cherub that sees them*' (IV, iii, 50). But there is a previous most positive and most specific allusion to it, at the close of the interview with his mother:

O 'tis most sweet
Where in one line two *crafts* directly meet.
(Q2 III, iv, 193–4)

If the word *crafts* had its present maritime significance in Shakespeare's time,[10] the double meaning is suggestive of a prearranged capture. *How* arranged, is neither here nor there; but opportunities of chartering a free cruiser could not have been wanting to a prince of Denmark; and what is more significant, *the fleet of Fortinbras was then in port at Elsinore*. There is an understanding, just ever so vaguely glanced at, between the two young princes. But the following lines admit of but one interpretation; especially in connection with his *perfect willingness* to go:

There's letters sealed: and my two school-fellows,-
Whom I will trust as I will adders fang'd,—
They bear the mandate: *they* must sweep my way,
And marshall me to knavery. *Let it work;*
For 'tis the sport to have the enginer
Hoist with his own petard; and 't shall go hard
But I will delve one yard below their mines
And blow them to the moon!
(Q2 III, iv,186–93, Additional passage H)

One would think it required a miraculous allowance of critical obtuseness

---

10   It probably did. The OED gives 1671 as the first recorded instance of such a meaning ('Craft V9') but appends a note: 'These uses were probably colloquial with watermen, fishers and seamen some time before they appeared in print, so that the history is not evidenced.' Coles's *English Dictionary* (1676) includes under 'Craft': 'small vessels as ketches etc.'

to ignore a counterplot so strikingly pre-announced. Yet, opening Coleridge, you find 'Hamlet's capture by the pirates: how judiciously in keeping with the character of the over-meditative Hamlet, ever at last *determined by accident* or by a fit of passion!' And opening Ulrici you find, 'He cheerfully obeys the command to visit England, evidently with the view, and in the hope, of there obtaining the means and opportunity (perhaps the support of England, and a supply of money and men, for an open quarrel with his uncle) to set about the work in a manner worthy both of himself and its own importance'.[11] God save the mark! '*Accident* frustrates his plans. Captured by pirates, he is set on shore in Denmark against his will', etc. And opening *Wilhelm Meister* you find Hamlet's 'capture by pirates, and the death of the two courtiers by the letter which they carried', regarded as 'injuring exceedingly the unity of the piece, *particularly as the hero has no plan*'.[12] After such obvious, amazing misconception, one may be pardoned for believing he sees

> —Two points in Hamlet's soul
> Unseized by the Germans yet.[13]

To make assurance doubly sure, comes the letter to Horatio, 'In the grapple, *I boarded them;* on *the instant* they got clear of *our ship:* so I *alone* became their prisoner. They have dealt with me like *thieves of mercy;* **but they knew what they did**' (IV, vi, 17–20). Can circumstantial proof go farther? Could any twelve men of sense, on such a record, acquit Hamlet of being an accessory before, as well as after, the fact?

The act ends with the Queen's narration of Ophelia's death, swanlike, singing her soul away under the willow aslant the brook. But before passing to the Fifth Act, notice how the Grand Master has summed up and defined in one word the exact amount of disease in Hamlet's mind:

> That I *essentially* am not in madness,
> But mad in craft.
>
> (III, iv, 171–2)

With this flashing line of light, the great poet marks the precise limits of

---

11 Coleridge, *Marginalia*, Note on IV, vi. See *CRH*, ii, 82. For Ulrici see *CRH*, iii, 51.

12 See *CRH*, ii, 31.

13 Browning, 'Bishop Blougram's Apology', 11. 946–7.

Hamlet's melancholy so sharply, that any attempt at a clearer statement is but to gild refined gold, or paint the lily. If the text is abstruse, any comment must be more so.

Up to the end of the Third Act, the material was so superabundant that the story of Hamlet may be said to have thus far written itself. But the most consummate art was required to furnish incident enough for the two remaining Acts, and invent a catastrophe that should prove an adequate solution of all this tangled skein of action, thought and agony.

We have seen how perfectly the Fourth Act manages to connect the past and future of the drama by a present which, although replete with a tragic interest of its own, is also in an eminent degree both retrospective and prophetic. But the development of the Fifth Act was inconceivably more difficult: it is the creation of a world, not out of mental chaos, but out of nothing. In this wonderful Act, paltry accessories, small side-bits of detail, are so exalted, transfigured and divinely illuminated, that they assume the dignity of events. Here, in marked perfection we see—

> 'The grace and versatility of the man.'
> 'His power and consciousness and self-delight.'

We accept as matters of course,—we make no marvel now over those wonderful clowns, and Yorick's skull; the funeral procession, the grapple in the grave, and Osric: but viewed solely as dramatic contrivances, they are miracles of construction. The deep funereal gloom, the weird sepulchral torch-light, which was thrown around the first three acts by means of the Ghost, is extended over the last two by means of Ophelia.

Hamlet's tilt with the sexton is not the least enjoyable of his encounters, or the easiest of his victories. In a trial of wit between prince and clown, as in a battle between a lion and a fly, insignificance is apt to have the better of it. But even at this disadvantage, Hamlet's patient courtesy is eventually an overmatch for the sexton's shrewd and superhumanly aggravating incivility. The caustic old curmudgeon absolutely grows genial beneath the calm unruffled smile of him that was mad and sent to England. [Quotes V, i, 168–80.]

> Ham. But soft! but soft! aside; here comes the King,
> The Queen, the courtiers: who is it that they follow
> And with such maimed rites?
>
> (V, i, 212–14)

Horatio is silent: apprehensive of mischief should Hamlet and Laertes meet: unable to tell his friend that Ophelia is dead. [Quotes V, i, 217–42 ending with the Queen's lament for Ophelia.] How different this high-bred, graceful lament from the low wailing of Laertes. This choleric stripling, whose heart was in Paris; who cowers before a 'King of shreds and patches', yet bullies an irresponsible and discretionless priest; who had even more than the full fraternal indifference to his sister until she lost her reason and her life; this small Hector must now make a scene over her dead body. And such a scene! His plunge into the open grave is unworthy of the mountebank from whom he bought the mortal unction; his invocation enough to madden any honest onlooker. All that palpable rant, all that sham despair, all that base mortal thunder, in the holy grave of the unpolluted girl! [Quotes V, i, 242–50.]

Hamlet's instant advance is like the swoop of an eagle, the charge of a squadron, the levelled curse of a prophet. [Quotes V, i, 250–81, Hamlet's fight with Laertes in the grave of Ophelia.] What can be juster, what can be grander! Mortal love and manly scorn were never strung before or since to such sublime intensity. The foot of true love lies on the prostrate sham love, like the foot of Michael on Lucifer; though here the angelic brow is flushed and ruffled with the rage of combat. The 'living monument' promised by the King is already in position: over the dead maiden stands the doomed lover, proclaiming his full faith before assembled Denmark in tones, whose echoes ringing down the aisles of death, must have conveyed to her ransomed soul and reillumined mind the dearest tribute of mortality to perfect the chalice of spiritual bliss. That sweet face on the threshold of another sphere, must have turned earthward awhile to catch those noble, jealous words. Yet this superb and well-merited rebuke has been criticised as a mere 'yielding to passion', as a 'sudden fall, from the calm height of philosophical reflection on the frailty of human life, into the degrading depths of youthful passion and inconsiderateness'; while the whole scene has been charged with 'meditative excess', and with impeding the proper march of the action, forgetting that it is pardonable, and natural, under the terrible shock of this first sudden knowledge of Ophelia's death while standing by her open grave! Heaven help us, how we grumble over God's best manna in the desert! Time, place, and circumstance considered, that annihilation of Laertes is one of the sublimest assertions of moral and intellectual supremacy in all Shakespeare.

Minds of surpassing reach, hearts of love, souls of truth, enjoy the lordly right to acquit others and blame themselves. And when, as in Hamlet's case, this magnanimity is accompanied by refined idealism and morbid delicacy, the smallest approach to violence, however pardonable, is apt to furnish a ground for self-reproach. Even before leaving the grave-yard he attempts a reconciliation,—

> Hear you, Sir;
> What is the reason that you use me thus?
> I loved you ever.
>
> (V, i, 285–7)

His subsequent regret is but another grace of his 'most generous' nature.

> But I am very sorry, good Horatio,
> That to Laertes I forgot myself;
> For, by the image of my cause, I see
> The portraiture of his: I'll court his favours.
>
> (V, ii, 76–9)

He has *then* had time for reflection: time for conversation with his invaluable friend; time to realize the heart-rending fact that Ophelia must have believed him the *wilful* murderer of her father, and that Laertes and all the world, except his mother, were justified in so regarding him. It was under the spell of conscious innocence and ignorant or forgetful of this constructive guilt that he leaped into the grave. He now comprehends and pardons the indignation of Laertes; but his own conduct was far less influenced by the violence of the son, than by the exaggerated ranting of the brother. For he cannot help adding, with a glow of reanimated disdain:

> But, sure, the *bravery* of his grief did put me
> Into a towering passion.
>
> (V, ii, 80–1)

Just as Hamlet's exact mental condition was determined by the line of light,

> That I *essentially* am not in madness
> But mad in craft:—

so in this scene, the essence of his character is revealed by another flash of discriminating genius:

> For though I am not splenetive and rash,
> Yet have I in me something *dangerous*.
>
> (V, i, 258–9)

Yet the King, relying on the double death prepared by himself and Laertes, is singularly tranquil.

> Good Gertrude, set some watch over your son . . .
> *An hour of quiet* shortly shall we see;
> Till then, in patience, our proceeding be.
>
> (V, i, 293, 295–6)

That hour of quiet never arrives. In the conversation with Horatio, that opens the last scene, there is more about the voyage to England. Hamlet knew well enough that his conductors were marshalling him to knavery; but the unsealing of their grand commission, and the device of a new one, was a sudden inspiration.

> There's a divinity that shapes our ends
> Rough-hew them how we will.—

Much follows from this unpremeditated and most legitimate theft: it is as fertile of results as the dropping of the handkerchief in *Othello*. In the first place, besides ascertaining the full extent of the royal knavery, he obtains full proof, under the royal seal, of the King's villainy. In the second place, this royal commission, which, in the presentiment or rather in the assurance of speedy death, he entrusts to Horatio, will be a justification before the world of the blow which must soon be delivered; will shield the princely name, about which he is so solicitous, from posthumous obloquy, and assist in consigning the seeming-virtuous wearer of the precious diadem to everlasting infamy. In the third place, Rosencrantz and Guildenstern, those supple traitors to all the rights of fellowship, to all the consonancy of youth, to all the obligations of ever preserved love, are finally though most cruelly disposed of by this *de jure* King of Denmark, who carries his father's signet in his purse. *They* are not even *near* his conscience;

>   —their defeat
> Does from their own insinuation grow:
> 'Tis dangerous when the baser nature comes
> Between the pass and fell incensed points
> Of mighty opposites.
>
> (V, ii, 59–63)

What perfect nerve, what ready wit, what jubilant power, in sitting calmly down and writing *fairly* out that earnest conjuration from the King. Nor is that earnest conjuration dictated by malice against his former friends, but purely in self-defense. It is the only *second* hope on which he can count; for if the chances of the sea prevent the contemplated rescue, he is infallibly lost without that earnest conjuration.

The whole 'rash' undertaking is a supplemented plot; a reserved escape; an 'indiscretion' only meant to serve in case his pirate plot should fail. For, two days at sea without sign of the friendly pirate, it was not unnatural that his fears should forget his manners. Besides, there was more than a chance, in the event of his escape, that Rosencrantz and Guildenstern returning to Denmark, *as they should have done* when they lost Hamlet, instead of keeping on to England. What determined them to 'hold their course', could only have been either the fear of facing their royal master after Hamlet's escape, or an absurd supposal that Hamlet would follow them, if released, rather than risk a return to Elsinore. Be that as it may, Hamlet's measures are strictly defensive and strictly justifiable; their doom is exclusively the result of their own obtrusiveness and folly. Still, we cannot acquit the Prince of the same cold cruelty that he showed at the death of Polonius. He might have made prison their doom instead of death, though it is true that in Shakespeare's time cruelty and torture were terribly prevalent and men were callous. Horatio's ignorance of the capture is no argument against its being premeditated. It would have been very unlike Hamlet, either to compromise his friend, who remained at court in service of the King, or to extend his secret needlessly.

Indeed it is only after hearing all the details of the royal knavery, that Horatio, true liegeman to the Dane, although belonging to the party of the future, exclaims, '*Why, what a king is this?*'—And it is only then that Hamlet ventures far enough to this noble, single-minded soldier, whom he never could or would have tempted into treason, whose good opinion is the only human verdict he cares for,—it is only then he ventures on that fearful summing up:

> Does it not, think'st thee, stand me now upon?
> He that hath kill'd my king,—
> Popp'd in between the election and my hopes,
> Thrown out his angle for my proper life,
> And with such cozenage; is't not *perfect conscience*,
> To quit him with this arm? and is't not to be damn'd,
> To let this canker of our nature come
> In further evil?
>
> (V, ii, 64–71)

The honorable officer and gentleman is silent; but the fast friend and wary man of action answers:

> It must be shortly known to him from England
> What is the issue of the business there.
>
> (V, ii, 72–5)

Hamlet's reply includes all that need be said between them; two such men soon understand each other:

> *It will be short: the interim is mine;*
> And a man's life no more than to say—one?

After that the conversation instantly changes.

It must have been observed that *Hamlet* is the most elliptical, as well as the profoundest, of the tragedies. Here, especially, Shakespeare unrolls his grand, mysterious panorama, without vouchsafing a word of explanation; here, especially, he imitates the great Creator, in permitting us the inexhaustible delight of penetrating the veiled secrets of his mighty works; here, especially, he arrays his tragic events as they occur in real life, leaving great gaps to be filled by inference or conjecture; here, especially, although far from aiming at the significant obscurity which Goethe constantly affected, he seems to disdain wearing his secret on his sleeve: and instead of tying his reader down to a single view, allows him a standpoint and speculations of his own. We are left to *infer* the interval, and objects of delay; to *infer* the reasons of all that singular behaviour to Ophelia; to *infer* the piratical capture; to *infer* a thousand subtle things everywhere beneath the surface. The farther the play progresses, the more elliptical it becomes. The last scene is the most elliptical of all: it *begins* with an ellipsis. You never suspect the errand Hamlet is on, until you happen to hear that little word '*The interim is mine!*' It means more mischief than all the monologues! No threats, no imprecations; no more mention of smiling, damned villain; no more self-accusal; but solely and briefly—

It will be short: the interim is mine!

Then, for the first time, we recognize the extent of the change that has been wrought in Hamlet; then, for the first time, we perfectly comprehend his quiet jesting with the clown, his tranquil musings with Horatio, his humorous recital of the events of the night aboard the vessel, when the fighting in his heart would not let him sleep. The man is transformed by a great resolve: *his mind is made up!* He has now placed in the safe possession of Horatio the Royal Commission containing the full proof of the king's villainy. The return of the vessel from England will be the signal for his own execution and therefore the moral problem is solved: the only chance of saving his life from a lawless murderer, is to slay him; it has become an act of self-defense: he can do it with *perfect conscience*. He has calculated the return voyage; he has allowed the longest duration to his own existence and the King's; he has waited to the very last moment for the intervention of a special providence. 'Now or never must the blow be struck!'

All this and more is revealed by that one word, '*The interim is mine!*' At the very moment he encounters the clown in the churchyard, he is on his death march to the Palace at 'Elsinore'. The only interruption of the calm resolve by which he is now possessed, is the affair with Laertes, to which he turns the conversation in princely care of Horatio's spotless honor. Is not all this indirectly but unerringly conveyed? And yet how curiously our standard criticism ignores it.

Horatio starts at the coming footstep, as if he had been listening to treason: 'Peace! who comes here?' As the vexed stream of Hamlet's life approaches the abyss, the foam and anguish of the rapids subside; and just over the level brink of calm and light that edges the fall, hovers the 'water-fly', Osric. Hamlet is patient with him—almost as patient as with the sexton—although constitutionally merciless to a fool; whether a fool circuitous like Polonius, a fool rampant like Laertes, or a fool positive like Osric. It is the last of his intellectual engagements, this singular duel between a dunce on the threshold of existence, and the stately gentleman but three steps from the grave. All forms and degrees of intellect have been dwarfed beside this most sovereign reason: the final contrast is between godlike apprehension and sheer fatuity. The King's 'Give them the foils, young Osric', inclines us to think that Osric was even more knave than fool. The creature appointed to *shuffle* those unequal foils could hardly have failed to detect the *one* unbated point. But he is too slight for dissection.

With the extinction of this water-fly, the great catastrophe approaches. Only once, and for a moment, the shadow of the coming death depresses him [Quotes V, ii, 155–70]. After this last inevitable sigh, there is no more repining. His smile is that of the *morituri te salutant!*[14] He longs to be at peace with all mankind but one; most of all with *Ophelia's brother*. The Quarto ruins his whole exquisite apology, by making it a suggestion of the Queen's; the Folio, by another masterly omission, leaves it his own free, spontaneous offering. His superabundant penitence completes itself in this acme of courtesy. Alas Laertes!—

> I do receive your offered love like love,
> And will not wrong it:

his fingers itching, as he speaks, for that unbated and envenomed foil. What a refined tenderness in the remote suggestion of Ophelia that lurks in Hamlet's answer:

14   Those who are about to die salute you.

> Ham. I embrace it freely,
> And will this *brother's* wager frankly play,
> Give us the foils.—Come on.
>
> (V, ii, 197–200)

The ocular pathos of the scene is terrible; yonder skipping water-fly; the King less patient with the chalice for the nonce, than Laertes with his anointed steel; trumpets and cannon without; Lords and attendants within: and, circled by this pageant of death, supported only by Horatio and the sympathy of his unsuspecting mother, the chosen victim of the holiday, passionless, fearless, and seemingly powerless; without a fixed 'plan for the execution of his just revenge', to quote the words of Mr. Strachey, 'but what is much better, the faith that an *opportunity* will present itself, and the resolution to seize it instantly'. Let the Embassy from England enter! He is face to face with his foe, sure of his man, even were the smiling villain twice a king!

Hamlet justifies the sinister calculation on his innate nobility of soul.

> —he, being remiss,
> Most generous and free from all contriving,
> Will not peruse the foils.
>
> (IV, vii, 107–9)

He asks but one matter of course question:

> Ham. These foils have all a length? . . .
> Osric. Ay, my good lord. (*They prepare to play*)
> King. Come, begin;
>   And you the judges bear a wary eye.—
> Ham. Come on, Sir.
> Laer. Come, my lord. (*They play*)
> Ham. One.-
> Laer. No.
> Ham. Judgement.
> Osric. A hit, a very palpable hit.—
> Laer. Well; again.
>
> (V, ii, 212, 225–33)

Footnote: See *CRH,* iii, 202.

The King cannot kill him fast enough. The first bout is hardly over before he orders up the supplemental bowl. But memories of the 'juice of cursed Hebanon' may have crossed Hamlet's mind; he will not touch the leprous distilment:

> King. Give him the cup.—
> Ham. I'll play the bout first; set it by awhile.—
> Come another hit, what say you? (*They play*)
> Laer. A touch, a touch, I do confess.
> King. Our son shall win.
> Queen. He's fat and scant of breath.—
> Here, Hamlet, take my napkin, rub thy brows:
> The Queen carouses to thy fortune, Hamlet.
> Ham. Good, madam!
> King. Gertrude, do not drink.
> Queen. I *will*, my lord; I pray you pardon me.
> King. It is the poison'd cup; it is too late, (*Aside.*)
> Ham. I dare not drink yet, madam; by and by.
> Queen. Come let me wipe thy face.
>
> (V, ii, 235–47)

How characteristic of the Queen! doting on her son, dictating to her husband to the last! Woe and confinement have left their mark on the outward as well as the inward Hamlet: the 'mould of form' has lost its earlier grace, his breath is short, the sweat stands on his brow; but at the first visitation of that Berserker wrath, he is terrible, as resistless as ever. [Quotes V, ii, 248–55.]

Laertes wounds Hamlet: then in scuffling, they change rapiers, and Hamlet wounds Laertes. No accidental exchange, for Laertes would only have surrendered his unbated foil to the sternest compulsion of superior force; nor could Hamlet well have been unaware of that venomed stuck and the warm blood that followed it. [Quotes V, ii, 255–60.] What a fearful triumph is Hamlet's '*Nay, come again!*' His wound is older,—the poison longer in his veins, than in his murderer's; yet, statue-like he stands at bay, erect, alert, defiant, comprehending all at a glance, absolute master of the situation! The mutes and audience to the act are less awed by the terror of the spectacle, than spell-bound, by the majestic attitude of the avenger [Quotes V, ii, 261–74] . . . Without pause, or with such pause as the panther makes when crouching for the leap, the final blow is delivered at last:

> Then venom do thy work!—(*Stabs the King.*)
> All. Treason! treason!
>
> (V, ii, 274–5)

They find their voices at last, these lords, attendants, guards and soldiers. But to what purpose? They *dare* not cross the path of that solitary champion of the grave,—not though invoked by the piteous appeal of their bleeding King!—

> O, yet defend me, friends; I am but hurt.

An instant more, and the hand of Hamlet is on his throat. If the archangel of judgment stood amongst them, they could not crouch more helplessly paralyzed beneath the lifted sword of fire, than before this awful incarnation of doom!

> Here, thou incestuous, murderous, damned Dane,
> Drink of this poison:—*is thy union here?*
> Follow my mother!—

O the awful irony of that fell interrogative! deadlier, bitterer than steel or bowl! The last lightning of that departing intelligence! With one outstretched arm he plucks their monarch from their midst, drags him to the ground, pinions him between his feet; with the other, forces the 'potent poison' down the reluctant throat,—overwhelming, in one tremendous second, the prostrate villain with a thousand deaths.

The King is ground to dust in that lurid hurricane of passion! mind, soul, and body shrivel up in that furnace of wrath! And so it might have been, at almost any moment, since that night on the platform. The Prince was conscious of this latent, immeasurable force; it never yet failed him at need; at the right moment, it was ever sure to come at his call. An avenger so justly confident of his strength may safely await the hour when retribution is so righteous and complete that it resembles less a human intervention than a divine dispensation.

The last prayer, even more than the last confession, of Laertes, extorts our compassion: [Quotes V, ii, 281–4]. There is nothing so pathetic, nothing so heroic in literature, as the last moments of this superb young Prince,—pierced with an envenomed wound, bleeding, reeling, dying, yet making that unbated and thrice ensanguined foil, the unquestioned sceptre of the moment for friend and foe; wrestling with Horatio for the bowl, as fiercely as with Laertes in Ophelia's grave; triumphant up to the very gates of death. He has more the flash and motion of a Homeric god than of a man. [Quotes V, ii, 285–310.]

In this supreme hour, his mission accomplished; 'winning, not losing, the cause for which he dies'; sure, through Horatio, of the verdict of posterity, and calmly fronting the dread tribunals of eternity with a radically inviolate conscience; he says, half reproachfully, to death, as though it were his sole regret at leaving life, *'The rest is silence!'* Alas, for us as well as for him, the rest is silence! Silence for the lips whose music has had no equal since the birth of time; silence for the voice whose least recorded utterance remains an inspiration for all the ages! The solution is complete. The wide repose of a perfect catastrophe extends to the remotest fibres of the plot. In the masterly lines assigned to Osric, the simultaneous arrival of Fortinbras and England is announced in one breath. Rosencrantz and Guildenstern have fallen: once more the princely Norwegian, who represents the future, marches broadly into view, irradiating all that scene of havoc with the promise of a better day for Denmark. Nothing remains but for Horatio to tell

> —the yet unknowing world
> How these things came about:

to sustain Fortinbras in claiming his vantage,

> And from *his* mouth *whose voice will draw no more!*

How beautiful that passing tribute to the eloquence of his dead friend!

In the sad, soldierly orders and martial praise of Fortinbras the play finds its perfect consummation. [Quotes V, ii, 349 to end.]

This is the only play of Shakespeare's in which our interest in the central figure is compelled to extend itself beyond the grave. When Lear,

Macbeth, or Othello die, our connection with them is dissolved: their mortality is the only thing that concerns us. Whereas, in Hamlet, we find ourselves gazing after him into that undiscovered country from whose bourne no traveller returns, uniting in Horatio's exquisite adieu,

> Good night, sweet prince:
> And flights of angels sing thee to thy rest!

Hamlet is not directly on trial for his soul, but the question of eternal loss or gain is constantly suggested. It is the management of this deep shadow of the world to come; this complicated war between conscience and passion; this sharp contrast between providence and fate; this final appeal from time to eternity, that gives the drama such universal, indestructible interest. Its felicities of diction, miracles of invention, exhaustless variety of character; its splendor of imagery, constructive symmetry, and pre-eminent glory of thought, would abundantly account for the critical admiration it inspires; but the critical *awe* and popular love it never fails to awaken can only be attributed to that rare but sovereign charm with which the highest human genius can sometimes invest a religious mystery. There is a poetic compulsion that after the fatal defeat of so blameless a youth, after a career of such unexampled, unprovoked agony, there should be in distinct perspective the ineffable amends of the hereafter. In Hamlet, Shakespeare has created not only a character but a soul. The deep spirituality of the part not only fills the play itself, but, acting as a centre of light, diffuses an ethereal lustre over all his works, and supplies the most imperishable element of his immortality. Strike any other single play from the list, and though the loss would be irreparable, yet the main characteristics of the entire fabric would remain radically the same. Strike out Hamlet, and the aspect of the whole structure is hopelessly altered.

18. Alfred Lord Tennyson

1855, 1873, 1874, 1875, 1892

Alfred Lord Tennyson (1809–1892), the greatest of the Victorian poets, became poet laureate in 1850, the year of the publication of *In Memoriam*. *Maud* (1855) was his first substantial work after this event. Tennyson wrote several poetic dramas in the mid-eighteen seventies and eighteen eighties: Henry Irving and Ellen Terry acted successfully in *The Cup* (1881) and *Becket* (1883). As the extracts show, Tennyson was deeply interested in the theater, Shakespeare (he was a member of the New Shakspere Society founded in 1874), and had a special admiration for and artistic interest in *Hamlet*.

The following passages come from Hallam Tennyson's *Alfred Lord Tennyson: a Memoir, by his Son*, 2 vols. (1897); the chronological and anecdotal nature of the material and presentation in that labor of love and filial piety justify the entry under his father and the ascribed dates. Hallam, like his mother Emily before him, protected his sensitive father from adverse criticism in his life, and recreated his voice and presence after his death.

---

a) *Maud* **as a nineteenth-century** *Hamlet*:
As he said himself, 'This poem is a little *Hamlet*', the history of a morbid poetic soul, under the blighting influence of a recklessly speculative age. He is the heir of madness, an egotist with the makings of a cynic, raised to sanity by a pure and holy love which elevates his whole nature, passing from the height of triumph to the lowest depth of misery, driven into madness by the loss of her whom he has loved, and, when he has at length passed through the fiery furnace, and has recovered his reason, giving himself up to work for the good of mankind through the unselfishness born of his great passion.

b) From Tennyson's letter to Dr Mann[1]:
Without the prestige of Shakespeare, *Hamlet* (if it came out now) would be treated in just the same way, so that one ought not to care for their cackling, not that I am comparing poor little 'Maud' to the Prince, except as, what's the old quotation out of Virgil, *sic parvis componere*, etc.[2] Would it not be better that all literary criticisms should be signed with the name or at least the initials of the writer? To sign political articles would perhaps be unadvisable and inconvenient, but my opinion is that we shall never have a good school of criticism in England while the writer is anonymous and irresponsible.

c) Memoranda of two theater visits, 1873, 1874[3]: Tennyson among the players:
Nov. 8th. A[lfred] and the boys went with Annie Thackeray[4] to Irving's *Richelieu*.

He did not care for *Richelieu*[5] ...

He described to Irving his conception of the manner in which *Hamlet* ought to be acted.

Mrs Thackeray Ritchie wrote of a similar evening in 1874 after *Hamlet*:

> The play was over, and we ourselves seemed a part of it still; here were the players, and our own prince poet, in that familiar simple voice we all know, explaining the art, going straight up to the point in his own downright fashion, criticising with delicate appreciation, by the irresistible force of truth and true instinct carrying all before him. 'You are a good actor lost', one of them, the real actors, said to him, laughing as he spoke.

1. Robert James Mann, M.D. (1817–86), whose books and articles helped to popularize science. His '*Maud* Vindicated', 1856, was an answer to hostile criticism of the poem.
2. Tennyson's meaning is rather the inverse of Virgil's 'sic parvis componere magne solebam,' *Eclogues*, I. 23: 'thus I measured great things by small.'
3. The date of Irving's celebrated first production of *Hamlet*.
4. Anne Isabella Thackeray, Lady Ritchie, eldest daughter of W. M. Thackeray; novelist and author of reminiscences of the literary figures she knew in her youth. The quotation comes from her *Records of Tennyson, Ruskin and Robert and Elizabeth Browning*, 1892.
5. By Bulwer-Lytton.

The parts of Irving's *Hamlet* which my father thought best were the dreamy and poetical asides, and when he showed the 'method in his madness as well as the madness in his method'. To Irving he said, '*Hamlet* is a many-faceted gem, and you have given more facets than anyone I have seen'.

d) Tennyson on Irving's Hamlet:
In March 1875 I find a note after he had seen Irving in *Hamlet*:

'It is not a perfect Hamlet: the pathetic side of him well done, and the acting original. I liked it much better than Macready's'.

e) From 'Criticisms on Poets and Poetry': Tennyson on *Hamlet*, 1892:
'*Hamlet* is the greatest creation in literature that I know of: though there may be elsewhere finer scenes and passages of poetry. Ugolino and Paolo and Francesca in Dante[6] equal anything anywhere. It is said that Shakespeare was such a poor actor that he never got beyond his ghost in this play, but then the ghost is the most real ghost that ever was. The Queen did not think that Ophelia committed suicide, neither do I.'

---

6   In cantos 33 and 5 respectively of the *Inferno*.

19. 'Mr. Irving's Hamlet'

1874

This anonymous article prompted by Irving's first production of *Hamlet* in October 1874 is reproduced from the December issue of Dickens's periodical *All the Year Round*.

'Do not imagine for a moment that in what are commonly called the "palmy" days of drama, people knew nearly so much about Shakespeare as they know now'.

This remark was addressed by the elder to the younger of two gentlemen who, having formed part of the vast throng assembled within the walls of the Lyceum Theatre to witness Mr. Henry Irving's performance of Hamlet, were now seated at a table in their club room to discuss the evening's experience, and to con over the reminiscences which it might have awakened.

'Well, I have been told,' observed the junior, 'that in bygone days nothing delighted fellows of my age more than the announcement that Edmund Kean, say, or Macready, would appear in one of his noted Shakespearian parts; that, in order to see the play, they would run the risk of being crushed almost to death in the pit entrance; and that the word "slow", as applied to one of our standard tragedies,would have been altogether unintelligible. Now I have known the theatrical world of London for some few years, and I can safely affirm that I never in my life saw any-thing approaching the excitement which everywhere prevailed, as the time approached for the appearance of Mr. Irving as Hamlet'.

'You have been correctly informed, and what you say is perfectly true', said the senior; 'but you have inadvertently thrown together two names that represent distinctly separate orders of things. Mr. Edmund Kean took the Shakespearian plays as he found them adapted for the stage by some one of his predecessors, and illustrated them by his brilliant acting;

whereas Mr. Macready, a gentleman of decided literary taste, was a dramatic reformer, who did much to dispel that ignorance of Shakespeare to which I have just referred. With him began the practice of reverting to original texts, instead of accepting without question the modifications of a Garrick or a Kemble'.

'Pardon me', interposed a listener, looking up from his arm-chair,'but if I recollect right, the credit is due to Edmund Kean of restoring *King Lear* to something like the shape which it wore before it was spoiled by Nahum Tate'.

'The fact had escaped my memory', replied the senior, 'and I stand properly corrected. But the restoration to which you refer did not go a great way. As far as the virtuous personages were concerned, Nahum Tate made the story end happily. The old king recovered his reason, and Edgar was rewarded with the hand of Cordelia, who did not die, and had never been married to any king of France. Mr. Edmund Kean, reviving the play after its representation on the stage had been prohibited for many years, on account of the malady of George III., restored Shakespeare's tragical termination. Lear and Cordelia both died, but the love passages between the latter and Edgar, of which Shakespeare, as you know, is perfectly innocent, were retained, and the Fool remained in the abyss of nonentity into which he had been flung by Tate. The circumstance that *Lear*, on the rare occasions when it is now performed, accords with the Shakespearian text, has its origin in Mr. Macready's management of Covent Garden. This takes me back to the assertion I made just now, that people know much more about Shakespeare now than they did in the olden time. That nothing like a return to Tate's *Lear* would now be tolerated I am certain'.

'Are you not illustrating the old adage which teaches that over familiarity is not accompanied by increase of respect?' asked the junior. 'The people who accepted a sham Shakespeare for the genuine article, at any rate showed veneration for the name. They might not consult the text at home, but they went to the theatre, happy to obtain what they could get; they cheered histrionic excellence with enthusiasm, and they went away perfectly satisfied that they had seen a work of the immortal bard, the fact of modification being to them utterly unknown. We seem now to have lost in enthusiasm what we have gained in learning.

'How can you say that enthusiasm for the name of Shakespeare has lessened, after what we have witnessed this evening? Do not estimate merely the numerical force of the audience—though that is great indeed—but observe the mood in which the entire performance of *Hamlet* is watched. People admire intensely, but they will not allow their expression of admiration to mar their intellectual enjoyment. They will applaud to the echo when applause does not cause interruption, but while Mr. Irving is speaking they want to hear him'.

'Just here comes my puzzle', interposed the junior. 'I have seen *Hamlet* tolerably often—indeed, much too often for my personal comfort—but I don't recollect, on former occasions, either the enthusiasm which shows itself in numbers or that which is manifested by self-control. The impression had gradually been made upon me that Shakespeare, except for the studious, is an institution of the past, not fitted to the play-goers of the present day. I don't suppose that we are more frivolous than the fellows were forty years or fifty years ago, but we are hard-worked, very hard-worked indeed, and in our hours of recreation we want to be amused'.

'And is the hard work of which you complain so highly intellectual, that the need of change renders it impossible for your recreation to be intellectual likewise? As far as your own individual feelings are concerned, the impression of which you speak must have been entirely effaced; for, as far as I can judge from appearances, no one could have been more thoroughly gratified by this evening's performance than yourself'.

'Nay, I was pleased, certainly', said the junior. 'To tell you the honest truth, I had never thought much of Hamlet before. My general notion was that he was a man who indulged in the habit of making long speeches to himself, and of doing everything that he told the players to avoid'.

'You never thought that he was a human being like yourself?' asked the senior.

'Oh dear, no', was the response. 'I never thought that he belonged to humanity at all. The poet sang—

> Oh, cuckoo, shall I call thee bird,
> Or but a wandering voice?[1]

In like manner I have regarded Hamlet as a stationary speech'.

1 William Wordsworth, 'To the Cuckoo,' ll. 3–4.

'But to this view, if I may venture to surmise, Mr. Irving put an end?' said the senior.

'Most decidedly', answered the junior. 'And I was much annoyed at the observation of some old-fashioned folks in my immediate vicinity, who evidently thought that the entire importance of the character depended on the number of points which the actor had an opportunity of making'.

'That worship of points, as they are called, was one of the prevalent vices of my early days', observed the senior. 'One would ask how Hamlet looked when he first saw the ghost, and quoted the recorded miracle of Betterton, who is said to have turned as white as his own neckcloth. Another object of curiosity was the manner in which, after killing Polonius, Hamlet enquired whether the victim was the king. Many persons seemed, indeed, to think that the sole purpose of the actor's art was to produce a number of startling effects, and that he who could make seven points was a better man than he who made only five'.

'Now I begin to understand', remarked the junior, 'why Shakespeare becomes such a bore. The points had all been learned by heart, and consequently ceased to produce the wonted result, and the intervals between them were all filled up with stilted declamations that awakened no sympathy. Now when I reflect on the performance of this evening, the very last things that occur to me are those isolated points about which so much fuss has, it seems, been made. I look upon Mr. Irving's Hamlet as a personage in whose joys and sorrows I can readily participate; nay, if he came back from the grave, like his father, I should be very happy to make his acquaintance'.

'What sort of personage, then, did you consider him to be?' asked the senior; 'I mean as regarded in the new light'.

'Well, I look upon him', replied the junior, 'as a man with a large heart, placed amid circumstances under which a keen sensibility could be only a source of mental agony. As Mr. Carlyle said of Dante, he was the sorrowfullest looking person I ever saw[2]. And it is to Mr. Irving's

---

2   Thomas Carlyle, *On Heroes, Hero Worship*, 'The Hero as Poet.' Carlyle is discussing the Giotto portrait of Dante: 'I think it is the mournfulest face that ever was painted from reality.'

power of exhibiting this sustained sorrow that I ascribe the greatness of the performance'.

'Your expressed opinion seems to point towards rather a dismal sort of entertainment, and to be somewhat one-sided. Surely there is nothing sorrowful in the advice to the players', objected the senior.

'Certainly not', answered the junior; 'but the cheerful familiarity with which it was given is perfectly in keeping with the rest of the part. I have heard some people talk of Hamlet as of one melancholy by nature, but I am sure the portraiture of such a man is not contemplated by Mr. Irving. A melancholy man can stand many hard buffets and bear many heavy fardels; but he who is of a cheerful, genial disposition, is just the one who suffers most, when his yearnings for reciprocal affection meet no response. Under pleasant circumstances I can imagine Mr. Irving's Hamlet being even lively above the average; but as it is, the man's spirit is crushed, and he can only be merry by fits and starts. He lives in a court where he knows that he is regarded by the reigning monarch with suspicion and dislike, where he is disgusted by the indecorous marriage of his mother, and where he feels that everyone, with the single exception of Horatio, is a spy. The youthful innocence of Ophelia seems alone to defy mistrust, but even his confidence in her is at last shaken, and the conviction is forced upon him that she is but one of a bad lot.

'Of course', asked the senior, 'you approve of the unusual arrangement by which, in the third act, the listeners are made visible to the audience?'

'Entirely', was the reply. 'And I am not ashamed to confess that I now comprehend for the first time why Hamlet so suddenly loses his temper'.

'Ay', observed the senior, 'even the most inveterate point-seeker may find ample matter for admiration in the scene with Ophelia, and in the subsequent scene with the two courtiers. How wild is the storm of rage!'

'And how very transient!' added the junior. 'How the whole deportment illustrates the nervous irritability and irresolution of the character! You remember Horatio's description of the ghost as having "a countenance more in sorrow than in anger"?'

'Certainly', answered the senior.

'Well', continued the junior. 'And yet this was the ghost of a murdered man, who had no doubt of the crime committed against him. Does not the description, especially when taken into consideration with the tenderness with which the ghost always regards the Queen, justify us in assuming that the 'pigeon-livered' disposition of which Hamlet accuses himself in the soliloquy which becomes such a splendid psychological essay in the hands of Mr. Irving—that his 'lack of gall' is in a great measure hereditary, and that the absolute incapacity for a thorough-going hatred, of the sort that Dr. Johnson would have commended, is to be regarded as a family failing'.

'From which', interposed the senior, 'the uncle is assuredly exempt'.

'No doubt', was the reply; 'and observe that in the very speech to which I have just referred, Hamlet, after bestowing upon his uncle such a variety of opprobrious epithets, adds the word 'kindless' as the climax of them all'.

'Then I suppose', said the senior, 'that you object to the restoration of Hamlet's soliloquy in the third act, uttered while the king is at prayer?'

'Not at all', replied the junior. 'In the first place, it is useful for the purpose of the fable; in the second, I agree with those who regard the horrible sentiments uttered by Hamlet as really alien from his nature, and intrinsically no more than a pretext for deferring the deed of vengeance. But what do you think of that more startling innovation, the omission of visible pictures in the closet-scene?'

'That question is not to be hastily answered', said the senior, gravely. 'In the text there is no direction by which the stage-manager can be guided, and so far the interpretation seems left to the discretion of the actor. On the other hand, the words 'counterfeit presentment of two brothers' apparently indicate something more material than mere creations of the fancy'.

'But again', objected the junior, 'Hamlet's description of the picture seems more properly applicable to a vision of the mind than to an actual painting. At all events, Mr. Irving's representation of the workings of a vivid imagination is so accurate and effective, that one is inclined to give him the benefit of the doubt'.

'Agreed!' ejaculated the senior. 'And let us rejoice that we once more have a tragic actor who, unfettered by convention, is able from his own mind to work out such a consistent whole as Mr. Irving's Hamlet. The time, I trust, has come when the serious study of Shakespeare, which is a characteristic of the present day, being utterly distinct from the ignorant worship of the past, will find its expression in the encouragement of that poetical drama which is among the glories of our country. The Americans have always stood high as Shakespearian scholars; and if that desired reform takes place, it will be in a great measure due to the American gentleman who now rules the Lyceum Theatre[3], and has given Mr. Irving the opportunity of which he makes so noble a use'.

3 H. L. Bateman.

20. Henry Irving's first night as Hamlet

1874

Percy Fitzgerald's *Henry Irving, a Record of Twenty Years at the Lyceum* (1893) here gives us two eye-witness accounts of Irving's first attempt in the role of Hamlet at the Lyceum, 31 October, 1874. Henry Irving (baptised John Henry Brodribb), was born in 1838 and became the most famous Shakespearean actor of his generation. He died in 1905.

But now was to be made a serious experiment, on which much was to depend. Hitherto Irving had not travelled out of the regions of conventional drama, or of what might be called romantic melodrama; but he was now to lay hands on the ark, and attempt the most difficult and arduous of Shakespearian characters, Hamlet. Every actor has some dream of performing the character, and fills up his disengaged moments with speculations as to the interpretation. Again and again he thinks complacently of the effects he can produce in familiar passages. The vitality of this wonderful play is such that it nearly always is a novelty for the audience; because the character is fitfully changeful, and offers innumerable modes of interpretation. A living character, strongly marked and original, presents the same variety to those who are in contact with it; and even in private life, friends will find an inexhaustible interest and equal uncertainty in judging the acts and intentions of many whom they know and esteem. But in the case of notable public characters this appreciation is ever fluctuating, and there are always new judgments and revisions of judgments.

The momentous trial was made on October 31, 1874. It had long and studiously been prepared for: and the actor, in his solitary walks during the days of his provincial servitude, had often pondered over the great drama, and worked out a regular, formal conception of the character. He was prepared with a consistent view. There was much curiosity and expectation; and it was noted that so early as three o'clock in the afternoon a dense crowd had assembled in the long tunnel that leads from the Strand to the pit door. I was present in the audience, and can testify to the entrancing excitement. Nothing I have ever seen on the stage, except perhaps the burst that greeted Sarah Bernhardt's speech in *Phèdre* on the first night of the French Comedy in London, has approached the tumult of the moment when the actor, after the play scene, flung himself into the King's chair. The different judgments of the performance testify to the interest that was excited; the performance, indeed, brought out quite a body of intelligent criticism, and in this way was of benefit in cultivating public taste.

I will here give the views of an intelligent, careful, thoughtful critic, Mr. Frederic Wedmore—

> Most of us have cause to know that heretofore, with all his merits, Mr. Irving has broken now and then into rant. It was the remark of a Frenchwoman, after Saturday's performance, that this was the first Hamlet who never ranted at all.
> As to the mere delivery of Shakespeare's words—apart from action and facial expression—Mr. Irving's mannerism is far less noticeable than before. In praise of this delivery, we may single out one passage, given with special profundity of meaning. He is anticipating death, and it is impossible to give a greater pregnancy and depth to any words than Mr. Irving gives to these: 'If it be now, 'tis not to come; if it be not to come, it will be now; if it be not now, yet it will come: *the readiness is all*'. With Mr. Irving, the sense at first of his self-questioning and all-questioning temperament, and then of the particular and accidental problems which this always problem-haunted nature is born to solve, is never lost. His abstraction is always with him, though not always upon the surface of him. He jests lightly with the players—he can talk of the weather with Osric—he talks of it as naturally as any dull Cockney of to-day. But below his lightness is always this abstraction, and it is most visible when he is most at home. That is a delicate touch of the actor's which makes him, when Horatio is offended with his 'wild and whirling words', say, with an indifference too obvious to be permitted save in the presence only of his most chosen intimate, 'I'm sorry they offend you'. It must be quite clear to Horatio that he doesn't care a straw about it.
> In the main, the absence of all exaggerated emphasis is to be commended in this latest Hamlet. The traditional exits are disregarded: of the final couplets no actor's 'point' is made. Speech ceases as in common talk—dies out like embers of a fire.
> Of course there are frequent flashes of passion, and one more brilliant than the rest. That one carries away the audience, leaving the actor still fully in possession

of his means. It occurs in the play-scene (Act the third), when Hamlet sits as usual at the feet of Ophelia, within good view of the King, and watches him narrowly, while in the background the players play their tragedy. Mr. Irving lolls upon a wild-beast skin, and toys with it, and yawns a little while the players are mouthing what is not much to his purpose. His attention is more fixed as the application draws near, and excitement grows on him as the thing proceeds: 'Gonzago is the Duke's name; his wife Baptista, you shall see anon: 'tis a knavish piece of work'—he is watching almost too eagerly to be closely keen—'but what o' that? Your Majesty and we that have free souls, it touches us not'—*does* it, though? he is asking by his eyes—'so let the galled jade wince: our withers are unwrung'. And he waits again for a moment. Then, and now no longer explaining and no longer with civil though eager reassurance, the actor, crawling unawares in his excitement away from Ophelia and towards the throne, points at the King, and hisses out like an accusation, 'He poisons him in the garden for's estate . . . You shall see anon how the murderer gets the love of Gonzago's wife'. Whereat the King rises, and it is not so much by his rising, nor by Ophelia's word of surprise, as by the actor's seething excitement, that you perceive the enterprise has succeeded. The gradual growth of this excitement, now subtly checked, now varied by a word of reassurance or commentary—'the story is extant, and writ in choice Italian'—and now overmastering his will, so that he leaps in momentary wildness, when the King has gone—all this told so plainly upon the audience that it forgot to cheer. It hardly knew its own mind for a minute, as to any expression of approval. But when somebody began to applaud, the contagion spread. Clapping of hands got louder and louder, but the audience was not content. It rose to its feet and fairly satisfied itself at last with a great roar in recognition of this power.

Our actor judiciously took account of all criticisms, and with later performances subdued or toned down what was extravagant. The whole gained in thoughtfulness and in general meditative tone, and it is admitted that the meaning of the intricate soliloquies could not be made more distinctly, or intelligibly conveyed to an audience. He played a good deal with his face, as it is called: with smilings of intelligence, as if interested or amused. But, as a whole, his conception of the character may be said to remain the same as it was on that night.

The play was mounted with the favourite economy of the manager,[1] and contrasted with the unsparing lavishness of decoration which characterized its later revival. But the actors were good . . . Actor and manager expected much success for *Hamlet*, and counted on a run of eighty nights,

---

1   The American H. L. Bateman.

but it was performed for two hundred! To the present hour it has always continued—though sparingly revived—the most interesting of the actor's performances, looked for with an intellectual curiosity.

21. The Times Review of Irving's Hamlet

Monday, November 2 1874

The great event which has been expected with eagerness by the whole theatrical world for many months came off on Saturday evening.

Mr. H. Irving appeared as Hamlet at the Lyceum Theatre.

The amount of expectation by which the event had been preceded was in itself so remarkable that many persons will find it difficult to account for. Mr. Irving has 'done' his Shakespeare in the provinces, and Hamlet has been among his parts; but no particular account has come to us as to the manner in which he filled it before he had become a London celebrity. The principal parts he has sustained in the capital have all, with the exception of Richelieu, been more or less of a melo-dramatic kind. Why, then, all this anxiety about an actor who had no Shakespearian reputation? Under ordinary circumstances, if there can be one occurrence in the course of the theatrical year less significant than another, it is the *début* of an actor as Hamlet. Everybody who has played anything in the tragic line has represented the Royal Dane, and it is among the traditions of the stage that nobody has failed. The aspiring artist may afterwards have broken down under the weight of Othello or Macbeth, but on the first night of his Hamlet, if he had never been seen before, he was sure to play a safe card which would, at any rate, win for him a *succès d'estime*. The worst of it was that the success was generally worth nothing. A part which could be carried through by mere declamation had been respectably declaimed, and there was no palpable fault to reprehend. Where no mischance could be anticipated there could be no anxiety as a result of the venture. Among all the implements of gambling none is less productive of excitement than the old-fashioned lucky-bag, containing prizes without blanks, for one result of this comfortable arrangement is that the prizes are exceedingly small. For years past the announcement of a new Hamlet has been regarded as little else than a prediction that the weight of 'boredom' by which the world is encumbered is to be increased, and the knowing ones of young England pass hurriedly before the door at which the terrible proclamation is affixed, and hasten to regale themselves with an *opéra bouffe*. Why, then, should there be such unbounded curiosity about the new Hamlet of Saturday evening? Some sceptics were of opinion within the last 48 hours that the curiosity was itself a fiction cunningly invented. At an early hour, even in the afternoon, their doubts were scattered to the winds. The crowds which besieged the pit entrance of the Lyceum long before the doors opened, the numbers who, after the doors were opened, were turned back when they showed themselves in Wellington-street and could not produce a ticket to justify this intrusion showed that the London public had been stimulated to a degree to which it would be difficult to find a precedent. The question returns. Why all this excitement about a new Hamlet?

It can only be answered by those who appreciate the deep impression made by Mr. Irving upon the London public within the last three years. In the *Bells*, in *Charles I*, in *Eugene Aram*, in *Richelieu*, in *Philip* he gave evidence of independent thought to which it is not easy to find a parallel. His gesture might sometimes be imaginary, faults might be found with the upper register of his voice, he might be charged with monotony, but the zeal of an artist thoroughly in earnest, working for his art's sake, could not be overlooked. Nor did this zeal express itself in flashing manifestations. It did not take the form of point-making. Happy moments, telling lines, were not the goal to which it was directed; it had led the actor to a course of serious reflection, of complete study, to a determination to grasp a character as a whole, not to take advantage of the salient points which it may present. It could be readily foreseen that his Hamlet, whether good or bad (and the latter alternative was scarcely possible), would come forth as a result of profound meditation on the text with which convention had nothing to do. Of late *Hamlet* had become a sort of Westminster Play, performed according to prescribed rules, in which the Pamphilus of the past might see himself accurately reflected by the Pamphilus of the present[1]. On Saturday, at all events, there was to be something new.

Nor were expectations disappointed. Mr. Irving's Hamlet is original throughout. It is more than probable that he has never seen any predecessor of extraordinary eminence enact the part. At all events, it is certain

1 Pamphilus was a Macedonian painter of the time of Philip, who may be the same as the philosopher and art historian of that name who taught Aristotle.

that the Hamlet in the play-book has been realized by Mr. Irving upon the stage without passing through any medium but that of his own thoughts. Those who hold that the cut-and-dried Hamlet is the genuine article, and who guide their judgment by the manner in which certain well-known points are made, will be grievously disappointed. Play-goers of the old school will be sorely perplexed when we tell them that the famous question, 'Is it the King?' uttered by Hamlet when he kills Polonius, was one of the least effective of the whole performance, and be inclined to think that we are indicating a failure, whereas we are recording one of the most extraordinary theatrical triumphs that was ever achieved. The learned will turn over their books to discover what was done by Betterton, what by Kemble, what by Charles Young; but their studies will avail them nothing towards an estimate of Mr. Irving, who stands aloof from the pedigree beginning with Betterton and ending with Charles Kean. We have no doubt that many intelligent persons are at this moment grievously offended by Mr. Irving's upset of received, respectable notions. They expected to see something new, something a little different here and there from what had gone before. But this Hamlet is so very new. Why could not Mr. Irving be original in old-world fashion?

Before attempting to describe the details of the performance, we will venture to surmise what, in Mr. Irving's mind, is the fountain-head whence flows that singular stream of thoughts and words to which is given the name Hamlet. That the Prince of Denmark is an irresolute man called upon to do a work, for which the firmest resolution was required is generally admitted. Most literary men are aware that Goethe compared him to a vase in which is set a plant too large for its size and strength, and much more recently a German critic, whose name we forget, regarded him, on account of his lack of purpose, as an exceedingly contemptible person, and looked upon his uncle as a far better man. He therefore likened him, as did Freiligrath in a poem, to Germany, the country prone to theorize but slow to act. (Critique and poem, be it remarked, were both written long before the year 1870.)

The irresolution of Hamlet could easily be accounted for by the assumption that he is of a timid nature. But the timidity of one to whom Ophelia emphatically ascribes

> The courtier's, soldier's, scholar's eye, tongue, sword,

we have no right to assume. Why, then, is Hamlet so irresolute? Why is he so slow to obey the promptings of the ghost?

If we rightly interpret Mr. Irving's performance, his reply to this question is to the effect that the nature of Hamlet is essentially tender, loving, and merciful. He is not a weak man called upon to do something beyond his powers, but he is a kindly man urged to do a deed, which, according to the *lex talionis*, may be righteous, but which is yet cruel. In Mr. Henry Taylor's *Philip von Arteveldt* one of the personages asks Philip, in order to ascertain his fitness to become a ruler in very stormy times, 'Can you be cruel?' thereby implying that without something like an element of cruelty in his nature his appointed work cannot be effectually done. According to Mr. Irving—as we suppose—it is to the utter lack of cruelty in his nature that Hamlet's shortcomings are to be attributed. He is a judge to whom the black cap is so abhorrent that he can never persuade himself to put it on. Mercy will always usurp the seat of Justice when her usurpation is least desirable. He is capable of any amount of sorrow—sorrow for his dead father, sorrow for Ophelia. An undercurrent of tearfulness runs through all his discourse, but of unmitigated hate he is unsusceptible, if we answer in the negative Shylock's question, 'Hates any man the thing he would not kill?'—more unsusceptible than he himself suspects. The hideous crime revealed by the ghost may cause him to 'fall a-cursing like a very drab', and bestow upon his uncle a large number of ugly adjectives; but for all that he does not like to kill him.

This view of the character is first made known in the soliloquy at the end of the second act, beginning,

> O, what a rogue and peasant slave am I,

in which the descent from frantic determination to no determination at all is most delicately traced. Sorrow for the loss of his father, awakened by the players' apparent sympathy with Hecuba, is at first the only feeling in the mind of the speaker, and it asserts its supremacy to the end. Then comes Hamlet's rage against himself for lacking gall, and he would if he could arouse himself to a most terrible state of vindictiveness. But the effort does not succeed; he is glad to accept the hypothesis that the ghost may, after all, be mendacious, and to desire 'grounds more relative' to his purpose, and the great feature of the interpretation is that the gradual change may be traced to a natural want of gall.

Whenever an opportunity offers Mr. Irving drops into a thoroughly colloquial manner of speaking, and this is no where more conspicuous than in his address to the players, to whom he talks as a familiar friend. Here he may be charged with compromising the dignity proper to the princely station, and the charge will not be unfounded. For his Hamlet is not to be compared with other Hamlets; it is right to show that he is consistent with himself. Dignity in his Hamlet is not a predominating quality. His heart is too large and too kindly to attach much importance to a social distinction which has brought him nothing but misery, and placed in a world where he has one only friend, he is glad to talk freely to persons with whom guile is impossible. Be it composed of strolling players or gravediggers, any company is better than that of the courtly spies who are at the beck of his uncle-father and his aunt-mother. We hear many persons talk fluently of a metaphysical Hamlet, without understanding in the slightest degree the meaning of the adjective thus applied, unless, indeed, a person who has arrived at a conclusion that people may be deterred from committing suicide by a belief in future punishments is to be deemed a metaphysician on that account—in which case metaphysicians would be formidably numerous. We are inclined to suspect, however, that the word 'metaphysical' is applied to Hamlet as a showy substitute for meditative. If so, it is utterly inapplicable to the Hamlet of Mr. Irving, a fine genial creature, who would willingly have clasped all the world to his bosom had not untoward events rendered its 'uses' so stale and unprofitable. If he soliloquizes much it is because he can find no one else wherewith he can freely talk; but it is his nature to be sociable.

There is a theory to the effect that Hamlet, while assuming madness, is really somewhat insane. From this theory we entirely dissent, at the same time admitting that his sensitive nature subjects him to the highest degree of nervous excitement. This could not be more clearly expressed than by Mr. Irving. His frequent changes from sitting to standing, his fitful walks up and down the stage, the frequent visits of his hand to his forehead, represent to perfection the acme of what in common parlance is called 'fidget'. Most powerful is the nervous condition exhibited in the scene with Ophelia. The pretended madness, the unquenchable love, and the desire to utter stern truths seemed to hustle against each other. The words seemed to be flung about at random, and the facial movements corresponded to the recklessness of the words. The storm of applause which followed this display of genius denoted not only admiration, but wonder.

For the present we content ourselves by stating what, in our opinion, is Mr. Irving's conception of the greatest of Shakespearian characters. Of particular points, some of which are novel and ingenious, we may speak hereafter; but we again warn the reader that the impersonation is not to be judged by points, but as a consistent whole. That opinions will vary as to the correctness of the conception itself there can be no doubt; but this much is certain, that Mr. Irving out of his own mind has evolved a Hamlet whom every Shakespearian student is bound to see.

He was admirably supported. The truly pathetic representation of Ophelia by Miss I. Bateman was rewarded by a general call and a shower of bouquets before the fall of the drop-scene . . . Though the play lasted till midnight, very few persons left the house before the final descent of the curtain, and the calls for the principal actors were followed by another for Mr. H.L. Bateman, who thanked the audience for their kindly feeling, and requested that, on account of the lateness of the hour, they would dispense with the performance of a farce, with which the evening's entertainment was to have terminated. The favour was readily granted, and the enterprising manager retired amid reiterated cheers.

22. Edward Dowden

1875, 1899

Edward Dowden (1843–1913) was educated at the University College of Cork, in Ireland and became professor of English literature at Trinity College, Dublin in 1867. He is best known for his critical survey of Shakespeare's plays, *Shakspere: A Critical Study of his Mind and Art* from the first edition of which the opening extracts (a) are taken. The work had achieved its eleventh edition by 1897. Section (b) is taken from the introduction to Dowden's edition of *Hamlet*, Methuen, 1899.

(a) *Shakspere: His Mind and Art*
From the *Preface*, pp. [v]-vi:
The reader must not fall into the error of supposing that I endeavour to identify Shakspere with any one of his dramatic personages. The complex nature of the poet contained a love-idealist like Romeo—(students of the Sonnets will not find it difficult to admit the possibility of this); it contained a speculative intellect like that of Hamlet. But the complete Shakspere was unlike Romeo, and unlike Hamlet. Still it is evident, not from one play, but from many, that the struggle between 'blood' and 'judgment' was a great affair of Shakspere's life; and in all his later works we observe the effort to control a wistful curiosity about the mysteries of human existence. And therefore, I say, a potential Romeo and a potential Hamlet, taking these names as representative of certain spiritual tendencies or habits, existed in Shakspere.

***Preface to the Third Edition*, pp. [v]-vi (and subsequent editions):**
I wish to insist upon the statement made on p. 278 that *Julius Caesar* lies in point of time beside *Hamlet*. Both are tragedies of thought rather than of passion; both present in their chief characters, the spectacle of noble natures which fail through some weakness or deficiency rather than

crime; upon Brutus as upon Hamlet a burden is laid which he is not able to bear; neither Brutus nor Hamlet is fitted for action, yet both are called to act in dangerous and difficult affairs. *Julius Caesar* was probably complete before *Hamlet* assumed its latest form, perhaps before *Hamlet* was written. Still,—giving the reader a caution as I did in the case of the *Tempest*—I am not unwilling to speak of *Hamlet* as the second of Shakspere's tragedies. *Hamlet* seems to have its roots so deep in Shakspere's nature, it was so much a subject of special predilection, it is so closely connected with older dramatic work. We acquire the same feeling with reference to *Hamlet* which we have for Goethe's *Faust*—that it has to do with almost the whole of the deeper part of the poet's life up to the date of its creation.

[From Chapter III: 'The First, and the Second Tragedy; *Romeo and Juliet; Hamlet*', pp. 125–61.]

When *Hamlet* was written Shakspere had passed through his years of apprenticeship, and become a master-dramatist. In point of style the play stands midway between his early and his latest works. The studious superintendence of the poet over the development of his thought and imaginings, very apparent in Shakspere's early writings, now conceals itself; but the action of imagination and thought has not yet become embarrassing in its swiftness and multiplicity of direction. Rapid dialogue in verse, admirable for its combination of verisimilitude with artistic metrical effects occurs in the scene in which Hamlet questions his friends respecting the appearance of the ghost (act i. scene ii); the soliloquies of Hamlet are excellent examples of the slow, dwelling verse which Shakspere appropriates to the utterance of thought in solitude; and nowhere did Shakspere write a nobler piece of prose than the speech in which Hamlet describes to Rosencrantz and Guildenstern his melancholy. But such particulars as these do not constitute the chief evidence that proves that the poet had now attained maturity. The mystery, the baffling, vital obscurity of the play, and in particular of the character of its chief person, make it evident that Shakspere had left far behind him that early stage of development when an artist obtrudes his intentions, or distrusting his own ability to keep sight of one uniform design, deliberately and with effort holds that design persistently before him. When Shakspere completed Hamlet [sic] he must have trusted himself and trusted his audience;

he trusts himself to enter into relation with his subject, highly complex as that subject was, in a pure, emotional manner. Hamlet might so easily have been manufactured into an enigma, or a puzzle; and then the puzzle, if sufficient pains were bestowed, could be completely taken to pieces and explained. But Shakspere created it a mystery, and therefore it is for ever suggestive; for ever suggestive, and never wholly explicable. It must not be supposed, then, that any *idea*, any magic phrase will solve the difficulties, presented by the play, or suddenly illuminate everything in it which is obscure. The obscurity itself is a vital part of the work of art which deals not with a problem, but with a life; and in that life, the history of a soul which moved through the shadowy borderlands between the night and day, there is much (as in many a life that is real) to elude and baffle enquiry. It is a remarkable circumstance that while the length of the play in the second quarto considerably exceeds its length in the earlier form of 1603, and thus materials for the interpretation of Shakspere's purpose in the play are offered in greater abundance, the obscurity does not diminish, but, on the contrary, deepens, and if some questions appear solved, other questions in greater number spring into existence.

We may at once set aside as misdirected a certain class of *Hamlet* interpretations, those which would transform this tragedy of an individual life into a dramatic study of some general social phenomenon, or of some period in the history of civilization. A writer, who has applied an admirable genius for criticism, comprehensive and penetrative, to the study of this play,[1] describes it as Shakspere's artistic presentation of a phenomenon recurrent in the world with the regularity of a law of nature, the phenomenon of revolutions. Hamlet cannot escape from the world which surrounds him. In the wreck of a society, which is rotten to the core, he goes down; with the accession of Fortinbras a new and sounder era opens. We must not allow any theory, however ingenious, to divert our attention from fixing it self on this fact, that Hamlet is the central point of the play of *Hamlet*. It is not the general cataclysm in which a decayed order of things is swept away to give place to new rough material; it is not the downfall of the Danish monarchy, and of a corrupt society, together with the accession of a new dynasty and of a hardier civilization

---

1   H. A. Werner, 'Ueber das Dunkel in der *Hamlet*-Tragödie,' *Jahrbuch der Deutschen Shakespeare-Gesellschaft*, v, 37–81 (author's note).

that chiefly interested Shakspere. The vital heart of the tragedy of Hamlet cannot be an idea; neither can it be a fragment of political philosophy. Out of Shakspere's profound sympathy with an individual soul and a personal life, the wonderful creation came into being.

It is true, however, as the critic referred to maintains, that the weakness of Hamlet is not to be wholly set down to his own account. The world is against him. There is no such thing as naked manhood. Shakspere, who felt so truly the significance of external nature as the environing medium of human passion, understood also that no man is independent of the social and moral conditions under which he lives and acts. Goethe in the celebrated criticism upon this play contained in his *Wilhelm Meister* has only offered a half interpretation of its difficulties; and subsequent criticism, under the influence of Goethe, has exhibited a tendency too exclusively subjective. 'To me', wrote Goethe, 'it is clear that Shakspere meant . . . to represent the effects of a great action laid upon a soul unfit for the performance of it. In this view the whole piece seems to me composed. There is an oak tree planted in a costly jar, which should have borne pleasant flowers in its bosom: the roots expand, the jar is shivered.'[2]

This is one half of the truth; but only one half. In several of the tragedies of Shakspere the tragic disturbance of character and life is caused by the subjection of the chief person of the drama to some dominant passion, essentially antipathetic to his nature, though proceeding form some inherent weakness or imperfection,—a passion from which the victim cannot deliver himself, and which finally works out his destruction. . . . We may reasonably conjecture that the Hamlet of the old play,—a play at least as old as that group of bloody tragedies inspired by the earlier works of Marlowe,—was actually what Shakspere's Hamlet, with a bitter pleasure in misrepresenting his own nature, describes himself as being, 'very proud, revengeful, ambitious'. This revengeful Hamlet of the old play exhibited, we may suppose, a close kinship to the Hamlet of the French novelist, Belleforest, and of the English 'Historie',—the Hamlet who in the banquet-hall burns to death his uncle's courtiers, whom he had previously stupefied with strong drink. But Shakspere, in accordance with his dramatic method, and his interest as artist in

---

[2] *Wilhelm Meister*, book 4, chapter 13. See *CRH*, ii, 24–5.

complex rather than simple phenomena of human passion and experience, when re-creating the character of the Danish Prince, fashions him as a man to whom persistent action, and in an especial degree the duty of revenge is peculiarly antipathetic. Under the pitiless burden imposed upon him Hamlet trembles, totters, falls. Thus far Goethe is right.

But the tragic *nodus* in Shakspere's first tragedy—*Romeo and Juliet*—was not wholly of a subjective character. The two lovers are in harmony with one another, and with the purest and highest impulses of their own hearts. The discord comes from the outer world: they are a pair of 'star-crossed lovers'. Their love is enveloped in the hatred of the houses. Their life had grown upon a larger life, a tradition and inheritance of hostility and crime; against this they rebelled, and the larger life subdued them. The world fought against Romeo and Juliet, and they fell in the unequal strife. Now Goethe failed to observe, or did not observe sufficiently, that this is also the case with Hamlet:

> The time is out of joint: O cursed spite,
> That ever I was born to set it right.
>
> (I, v, 189–90)

Hamlet is called upon to assert moral order in a world of moral confusion and obscurity. He has not an open plain or a hillside on which to fight his battle; but a place dangerous and misleading, with dim and winding ways. He is made for honesty, and he is compelled to use the weapons of his adversaries, compelled to practise a shifting and subtle stratagem; thus he comes to waste himself in ingenuity, and crafty devices. All the strength which he possesses would have become organised and available had his world been one of honesty, of happiness, of human love. But a world of deceit, of espionage, of selfishness surrounds him; his idealism, at thirty years of age, almost takes the form of pessimism; his life and his heart become sterile; he loses the energy which sound and joyous feeling supplies; and in the wide-spreading waste of corruption which lies around him, he is tempted to understand and detest things, rather than accomplish some limited practical service. In the unweeded garden of the world, why should he task his life to uproot a single weed?

If Goethe's study of the play, admirable as it was, misled criticism in one way by directing attention too exclusively upon the inner nature of

Hamlet, the studies by Schlegel and by Coleridge tended to mislead criticism in another, by attaching an exaggerated importance to one element of Hamlet's character. 'The whole,' wrote Schlegel, 'is intended to show that a calculating consideration, which exhausts all the relations and possible consequences of a deed, must cripple the power of acting.'[3] It is true that Hamlet's power of acting was crippled by his habit of 'thinking too precisely on the event;' and it is true, as Coleridge said, that in Hamlet we see 'a great, an almost enormous intellectual activity, and a proportionate aversion to real action consequent upon it.'[4] But Hamlet is not merely or chiefly intellectual; the emotional side of his character is quite as important as the intellectual; his malady is as deep-seated in his sensibilities and in his heart as it is in the brain. If all his feelings translate themselves into thoughts, it is no less true that all his thoughts are impregnated with feeling. To represent Hamlet as a man of preponderating power of reflection, and to disregard his craving, sensitive heart is to make the whole play incoherent and unintelligible.[5]

It is Hamlet's intellect, however, together with his deep and abiding sense of the moral qualities of things, which distinguishes him, upon the glance of a moment, from the hero of Shakspere's first tragedy, Romeo. If Romeo fails to retain a sense of fact and of the real world because the fact, as it were, melts away and disappears in a solvent of delicious emotion, Hamlet equally loses a sense of fact because with him each object and event transforms and expands itself into an idea. When the play opens he has reached the age of thirty years,—the age, it has been said, when the ideality of youth ought to become one with and inform the practical tendencies of manhood,—and he has received culture of every kind except the culture of active life. During the reign of the strong-willed elder Hamlet there was no call to action for his meditative son. He has slipped on into years of full manhood still a haunter of the university, a student of philosophies, an amateur in art, a ponderer on the things of life and death, who has never formed a resolution or executed a deed.

---

3 *Lectures on Dramatic Art and Literature*, see *CRH*, ii, 50.

4 *Notes on Hamlet*, see *CRH*, ii, 62.

5 See W. Oehlmann's article 'Die Gemüthsseite des Hamlet—Characters' in *Jahrbuch der Deutschen Shakespeare-Gesellschaft*, iii, 208 (author's note).

This long course of thinking, apart from action, has destroyed Hamlet's very capacity for belief; since in belief there exists a certain element contributed by the will. Hamlet cannot adjust the infinite part of him to the finite; the one invades the other and infects it; or rather the finite dislimns and dissolves, and leaves him only in presence of the idea. He cannot make real to himself the actual world, even while he supposes himself a materialist; he cannot steadily keep alive within himself a sense of the importance of any positive, limited thing,—a deed, for example. Things in their actual, phenomenal aspect flit before him as transitory, accidental and unreal. And the absolute truth of things is so hard to attain and only, if at all, is to be attained in the *mind*. Accordingly Hamlet can lay hold of nothing with calm, resolved energy; he cannot even retain a thought in indefeasible possession. Thus all through the play he wavers between materialism and spiritualism, between belief in immortality and disbelief, between reliance upon providence and a bowing under fate.[6] In presence of the ghost a sense of his own spiritual existence, and the immortal life of the soul grows strong within him. In presence of spirit he is himself a spirit:-

> I do not set my life at a pin's fee;
> And for my soul, what can it do to that,
> Being a thing immortal as itself?

(I, iv, 46–8)

When left to his private thoughts, he wavers uncertainly to and fro; death is a sleep, a sleep, it may be, troubled with dreams. In the graveyard, in the presence of human dust, the base affinities of our bodily nature prove irresistibly attractive to the curiosity of Hamlet's imagination; and he cannot choose but pursue the history of human dust through all its series of hideous metamorphoses. Thus, as Romeo's emotions, while he lived in abandonment to the life of feeling for feeling's sake, are not genuine

---

6   Giordano Bruno lived in London from the year 1583 to 1586, where he seems to have received the patronage of Sir P. Sidney, Lord Buckhurst, and the Earl of Leicester. He became professor at Wittenberg. In *Shakspere-Forschungen I. Hamlet*, by Benno Tschischwitz (Halle, 1868), the author endeavours to prove that Shakspere was acquainted with the philosophy of Bruno, and embodied portions of it in the play of Hamlet.

emotions, so Hamlet's thoughts, while he is given over to the life of brooding meditation, are hardly even so much as real thoughts; but are rather phantom ideas which dissolve, reform, and dissolve again, changing forever with every wind of circumstance. He is incapable of certitude.

When Hamlet first stands before us, his father has been two months dead; his mother has been for a month the wife of Claudius. He is solitary in the midst of the court. A mass of sorrow, and of wounded feeling, of shame and of disgust has been thrown back upon him; and this secretion of feeling which obtains no vent is busy in producing a wide-spreading, morbid humour. The misery of self-suppression leaves him in a state of weak and intense irritability. Every word uttered pricks him, and he is longing to be alone. A little bitterness escapes in his brief acrid answers to the king, and when his mother, in her insensibility to true feeling, chances upon the word 'seems' his irritation breaks forth, and after his fashion (that of one who relieves himself by speech rather than by deeds) he unpacks his heart in words. The queen who is soft and sensual, a lover of ease, withal a little sentimental, and therefore incapable of genuine passion, does not resent the outbreak of her strange son; and Hamlet, somewhat ashamed of his demonstration, which has the look of a display of superior feeling, endures in silence his uncle's tedious moralizing on the duties of mourners. Then with grave courtesy he yields to his mother's request that he should renounce his intention of returning to Wittenberg,

> I shall in all my best obey you, madam.

What matters it whether he go or stay! Life is all so flat, stale, and unprofitable, that the difference between Wittenberg and Elsinore cannot be worth contending for. [Observe the contrast between Hamlet and Laertes. The latter wrings by laboursome petition leave from his father to return to Paris. Laertes had come from Paris to the coronation; Horatio, from Wittenberg to the late king's funeral.[7]] But when at length he is alone, Hamlet feels himself enfranchised,—free to shed abroad his sorrow, to gaze intensely and mournfully upon his own aridity of spirit, and to compensate in the idea for the expenditure of kindness in act made on

---

7 Author's footnote.

his mother's behalf. A frail mother, an incestuous mother, a mother endowed with less discourse of reason than the beasts! He has satisfied the queen with an act; and action, this way or that, is profoundly insignificant to Hamlet. But in his mind she shall get no advantage of him. He will see her as she is, and if he is gracious to her in his deeds, he will, in his thoughts, be stern and inexorable.

In this scene we make acquaintance with two important persons in Hamlet's world. 'Something is rotten in the state of Denmark,' exclaimed Marcellus. Rather all is rotten—the whole head is sick and the whole heart faint. On the throne, the heart of the living organism of a state, reigns the appearance of a king; but under this kingly appearance is hidden a wretched, corrupt, and cowardly soul, a poisoner of the true king and of true kingship, incestuous, gross and wanton, a fierce drinker, a palterer with his conscience, and as Hamlet vehemently describes him 'a vice of kings,' 'a villain and a cutpurse,' 'a paddock, a bat, a gib.' Such is kingship in Denmark.

And the queen, Hamlet's mother, one of the two women from whom Hamlet must infer what womanhood is, what is she? For thirty years she had given the appearance. The *similacrum* of true love to her husband, one on whom

> Every god did seem to set his seal
> To give the world assurance of a man,
>
> (III, iv, 60–1)

one who even in the place of penance still retains his solicitude for her; and this show of thirty years' love had proved to be without reality or root in her being; it had been no more than a sinking down upon the accidental things of life, its comforts and pleasures; her husband had passed out of her existence like any other casual object; during all those years of blameless wifehood she had never once conceived the possibility of a love which is founded upon the essential, not the accidental elements of life; she had never once known what is the bond of life to life, and of soul to soul. The timid, self-indulgent, sensuous, sentimental queen is as remote from true woman's virtue as Claudius is from the virtues of royal manhood.

The third scene of the first act introduces another group of personages, distinguished figures of the Danish Court. Laertes is the cultured young gentleman of the period.[8] He is accomplished, chivalric gallant; but the accomplishments are superficial, the chivalry theatrical, the gallantry of a showy kind. He is master of events up to a certain point, because he sees their coarse, gaudy, superficial significance. It is his part to do fine things and make fine speeches; to enter the king's presence gallantly demanding atonement for his father's murder; to leap into his sister's grave and utter a theatrical rant of sorrow. Hamlet sees in his own cause an image of that of Laertes. Each has lost a father by foul means, and Laertes delays not to seek revenge. But Shakspere does not make the contrast between Hamlet and Laertes favourable to the latter. No over-weight of thought, no susceptibility of conscience retard the action of the young gallant. He readily falls in with the king's scheme of assassination, and adds his private contribution of villainy—the venom on his rapier's point. Laertes has been no student of philosophic Wittenberg.[9] The French capital, 'so dear to the average, sensual man,' is Laertes' school of education. What lessons he learnt there we may conjecture from the conversation of Polonius with his servant Reynaldo.

Laertes' little sister, Ophelia, is loved by the Lord Hamlet. What is Ophelia? Can she contribute to the deliverance of Hamlet from his sad life of brooding thought, from his weakness and his melancholy? Juliet had delivered Romeo from his dream of self-conscious egoistic feeling into the reality of anguish and joy. What can Ophelia do? Nothing. She is a tender little fragile soul, who might have grown to her slight perfection in some neat garden-plat of life. Hamlet falls into the too frequent error of supposing that a man gains rest and composure through the presence of a nature weak, gentle, and clinging; and that the very incapacity of such a nature to share the troubles of heart and brain which beset

8   Gervinus has described Hamlet as a man of a civilized period standing in the centre of a heroic age of rough manners and physical daring.—*Shakespeare Commentaries*, vol. ii, p. 161. No piece of criticism could fall more wide of the mark. The age of Claudius, Polonius, Laertes, Osric, and of the students of philosophy at Wittenberg is an age complex and refined, and in all things the reverse of heroic. see Kreyssig, *Vorlesungen über Shakespeare*, vol. ii, p. 222 (ed. 1862) (author's note).

9   Shakspere remembered Luther, thinks Gervinus. He had Giordano Bruno in his mind, says Tschischwitz. The University was famous; Giordano Bruno names it the Athens of Germany (author's note).

one must be a source of refreshment and repose. And so it is, for moments, when the pathos of slender joy, unaware of the great interests and sorrows of the world, touches us. But a strong nature was what Hamlet really needed. All the comfort he ever got in life came from one who was 'more an antique Roman than a Dane,' (V, ii, 293). If he had found one who to Horatio's fortitude, his passive strength, had added ardour and enthusiasm, Hamlet's melancholy must have vanished away; he would have been lifted up into the light and strength of the good facts of the world, and then he could not have faltered upon his way.

As things were Hamlet quickly learned, and the knowledge embittered him, that Ophelia could neither receive great gifts of soul, nor in return render equivalent gifts. There is an exchange of little tokens between the lovers, but of the large exchange of soul there is none, and Hamlet in his bitter mood can truthfully exclaim, 'I never gave you aught'. Hamlet was conscious of no constraining power to prevent him, when he thought of his mother's frailty, from extending his words to her whole sex, 'Frailty, thy name is woman'. Had a noble nature stood in Ophelia's place to utter such words would have been treason against his inmost consciousness. Let the reader contrast Juliet's commanding energy of feeling, of imagination, of will with Ophelia's timidity and self-distrust, the incapable sweetness and gentleness of her heart, her docility to all lawful guardians and governors. Juliet throws off father, mother, and nurse, and stands in solitary strength of love; she always uses the directest word, always counsels the bravest action. In his later plays Shakspere can still be seen to rejoice and expand in presence of the courage of true love. Desdemona,

> A maiden never bold;
> Of spirit so still and quiet that her motion
> Blush'd at herself,
>
> (*Othello*, I, iii, 94–6)

standing by Othello's side can confront her indignant father, with the Duke and magnificence. Imogen, for Posthumus' sake, can shoot against the king her shafts of indignant scorn, so keen and exquisite, yet heavily timbered enough to wing forward through the wind of Cymbeline's anger.

But Ophelia is decorous and timid, with no initiative in her own heart; unimaginative; choosing her phrases with a sense of maidenly propriety:-

> He hath, my lord, of late made many tenders
> Of his affection to me.
>
> (I, iii, 99–100)

And Polonius inquires, 'Do you believe his tenders, as you call them?' 'I do not know, my lord, what I should think.' It may be that her brother and her father are right; that the 'holy vows' of Hamlet on which she, poor little soul, had relied, are but 'springes to catch woodcocks'. In her madness, the impression made upon her by the words of Polonius and Laertes, which she had until then concealed, finds utterance: 'She says she hears there's tricks i' the world' (IV, v, 4–5). Juliet resolved her doubts, not by consulting old Capulet or her nurse, but by pressing forward to perfect knowledge of the heart of Romeo, and by occupying that heart with a purity of passion only less than her own. Ophelia, when her father directs her to distrust the man she loves, to deny him her presence, to repel his letters, has only her meek, little submission to utter, 'I shall obey, my lord.'

The comic element in this scene is present, but is not obtruded. Shakspere, 'der feine Shakspere, der Schalk',[10] smiles, visibly, but restrains himself from downright laughter. Laertes has read his moral lecture to Ophelia, and she in turn ventures upon a gentle, little piece of sisterly advice. Laertes suddenly discovers that he ought to be aboard his ship: 'I stay too long'. Ophelia 'is giving the conversation a needless and inconvenient turn; . . . for sisters to lecture brothers is an inversion of the natural order of things'.[11] But at this moment the venerable chamberlain appears. Laertes, who was supposed to have gone, is caught. There is only one mode of escape from the imminent scolding—to kneel and ask a second blessing. What matter that it has all been said once before? Start the old man on his hobby of uttering wisdom, and off he will go:

---

10 'The great Shakespeare, the joker.' F. Th. Vischer, in *Jahrbuch der Deutschen Shakespeare-Gesellschaft*, vol. ii. p. 149.

11 C. E. Moberly. Rugby edition of *Hamlet*, p. 21 (author's note).

> A double blessing is a double grace;
> Occasion smiles upon a second leave.
>
> (I, iii, 53–4)

The advice of Polonius is a cento of quotations from Lyly's *Euphues*.[12] Its significance must be looked for less in the matter than in the sententious manner. Polonius has been wise with the little wisdom of worldly prudence. He has been a master of indirect means of getting at the truth, 'windlaces and assays of bias'. In the shallow lore of life he has been learned. Of true wisdom he has never had a gleam. And what Shakspere wishes to signify in this speech is that wisdom of Polonius' kind consists of a set of maxims; all such wisdom might be set down for the headlines of copy-books. That is to say, his wisdom is not the outflow of a rich or deep nature, but the little, accumulated hoard of a long and superficial experience. This is what the sententious manner signifies. And very rightly Shakspere has put into Polonius' mouth the noble lines,

> To thine own self be true,
> And it must follow as the night the day
> Thou canst not then be false to any man.

Yes; Polonius has got one great truth among his copy-book maxims, but it comes in as a little bit of hard, unvital wisdom like the rest. '*Dress well, don't lend or borrow money; to thine own self be true.*'[13]

But to appreciate and enjoy fully the Chamberlain's morality, we must observe him in the first scene of the second act. Reynaldo is despatched

---

12   Mr W.L. Rushton, in his *Shakespeare's Euphuism*, pp. 44–7 (London, 1871), places side by side the precepts of Polonius and of Euphues. *Pol.* Give thy thoughts no tongue. *Euph.* Be not lavish of thy tongue. *Pol.* Do not dull thy palm, etc. *Euph.* Every one that shaketh thee by the hand is not joined to thee in heart. *Pol.* Beware of entrance to a quarrel, etc. *Euph.* Be not quarrelous for every light occasion. *Pol.* Give every man thine ear, but few thy voice. *Euph.* It shall be better to hear what they say, than to speak what thou thinkest. Both Polonius and Euphues speak of the advice given as 'these few precepts' (author's note).

13   Compare and contrast with the advice of Polonius the parting words of the Countess to Bertram—(*All's Well That Ends Well*, Act i, Sc. i.). Observe how the speech of the Countess opens and ends with motherly passion of fear and pride, in which lies enclosed her little effort at moral precept (author's note).

as a spy upon the conduct of the son on whom the paternal blessing had been so tenderly bestowed. Polonius does not expect morality of an ideal kind from the boy. As is natural, Laertes in Paris will sow his wild oats. If he come back the accomplished cavalier, skilful in manage of his horse, a master of fencing, able to finger a lute, Polonius will treasure up in his heart, not discontented, the knowledge of his son's 'wild slips and sallies.' [14]

Meanwhile Hamlet, in the midst of his sterile world-weariness, has received a shock, but not the shock of joy. With Horatio and Marcellus, Hamlet on the platform at night is awaiting the appearance of the ghost. The sounds of Claudius' revelry reach their ears. Hamlet is started upon a series of reflections suggested by the Danish drinking customs; his surroundings disappear; he has ceased to remember the purpose with which he has come hither; he is lost in his own thoughts. The Ghost is present before Hamlet is aware; it is Horatio who interrupts his meditation, and rouses him to behold the apparition. No sooner has Hamlet heard the word 'Murder' upon his father's lips than he is addrest to 'sweep to his revenge',—in the idea,-

> With wings as swift
> As meditation or the thoughts of love.
>
> (I, v, 29–30)

He will change his entire mental stock and store; he will forget his arts and his philosophies; he will retain no thought save of his murdered father. And when the ghost departs he draws—'not his sword, but his notebook'.[15] There at least he can get it down in black and white that the

---

14   The last words of Polonius to Reynaldo are—'And let him [Laertes] ply his music'. On these words Vischer observes—'Die paar Wörtchen erst enthalten den ganzen Sclüssel; der Sohn darf spielen, trinken, raufen, fluchen, zanken, in saubre Häuser, '*videlicet* Bordelle' gehen, wenn er nur Musik triebt; achte Cavaliererziehung!' [These few words alone hold the whole key: the son can play, drink, fight, swear, quarrel, visit brothels, so long as he pursues his music; behold the portrait of a Cavalier]. F. Th. Vischer, 'Die realistische Shakespeare-Kritik und Hamlet,' in *Jahrbuch der deutschen Shakespeare Gesellschaft*, vol. ii, p. 149 (author's note).

15   W. Oehlmann, *Jahrbuch der Deutschen Shakespeare-Gesellschaft*, vol. iii, p. 211 (author's note).

smiling Claudius is a villain, can put that fact beyond the reach of doubt or vicissitude; for subjective impressions, Hamlet is too well aware, do not retain the certitude which during one vivid moment seemed to characterise them. He will henceforth remember nothing but the ghost, and to assure himself of *that*, he sets down his father's parting words, 'Adieu, adieu! remember me.' That is to say, 'he puts a knot upon his handkerchief'.[16] He is conscious that he is not made for the world of action; that the fact is always in process of gliding away from him and being replaced by an idea. And he is resolved to guard against this in the present instance.

It is now in a sudden inspiration of excited feeling that Hamlet conceives the possibility of his assuming an antic disposition. What is Hamlet's purpose in this? He finds that he is involuntarily conducting himself in a wild and unintelligible fashion. He has escaped 'from his own feelings of the overwhelming and supernatural by a wild transition to the ludicrous,—a sort of cunning bravado, bordering on the flights of delirium.' His mind struggles 'to resume its accustomed course, and effect a dominion over the awful shapes and sounds that have usurped its sovereignty.'[17] He assumes madness as a means of concealing his actual disturbance of mind. His over-excitability may betray him; but if it be a received opinion that his mind is unhinged, such an access of over-excitement will pass unobserved and unstudied. At this moment Hamlet's immediate need is to calm himself, to escape into solitude, there to recover self-mastery, and come to a clear understanding of the altered state of things. In the light of the court he is persecuted by the eyes of the curious and the suspicious; he is 'too much i' the sun'. To be in presence of all, and yet to be hidden,—to be intelligible to himself, and a perplexity

---

16 Hebler, *Aufsätze über Shakespeare* (Bern, 1865), p. 138 (author's note).

17 The first quotation is from S.T. Coleridge; the second from an essay by Hartley Coleridge, 'On the Character of Hamlet.' *Essays and Marginalia*, vol. i, pp. 151–71. An earlier writer than S. T. Coleridge had well said, 'Hamlet was fully sensible how strange those involuntary improprieties must appear to others: he was conscious that he could not suppress them: he knew he was surrounded with spies; and he was justly apprehensive lest his suspicions or purposes should be discovered. But how are these consequences to be prevented? By counterfeiting an insanity which in part exists.'—Richardson's *Essays upon Shakespeare's Dramatic Characters* 1786), p. 163. (Author's note) For the first two extracts see *CRH*, ii, 74 and 197.

to others, to be within reach of every one, and to be himself inaccessible, that would be an enviable position! Madness possesses exquisite immunities and privileges. From the safe vantage of unintelligiblity he can delight himself by uttering his whole mind and sending forth his words among the words of others, with their meaning disguised, as he himself must be, clothed in antic garb of parable, dark sayings which speak the truth in a mystery.

Hamlet does not assume madness to conceal any plan of revenge. He possesses no such plan. And as far as his active powers are concerned, the assumed madness is a misfortune. Instead of assisting him to achieve anything, it is one of the causes which tend to retard his action. For now, instead of forcing himself upon the world, and compelling it to accept a mandate of his will, he can enjoy the delight of a mere observer and critic; an observer and critic of both himself and of others. He can understand and mock; whereas he ought to set himself sternly to his piece of work. He utters himself henceforth at large, because he is unintelligible. He does not aim at producing any effect with his speech, except in the instance of his appeal to Gertrude's conscience. His words are not deeds. They are uttered self-indulgently to please the intellectual or artistic part of him, or to gratify his passing mood of melancholy, of irritation, or of scorn. He bewilders Polonius with mockery, which effects nothing, but which bitterly delights Hamlet by its subtlety and cleverness. He speaks with singular openness to his courtier friends, because they, filled with thoughts of worldly advancement and ambition, read all his meanings upside down, and the heart of his mystery is absolutely inaccessible to their shallow wits. When he describes to them his melancholy he is in truth speaking in solitude to himself. Nothing is easier than to throw them off the scent. 'A knavish speech sleeps in a foolish ear'. The exquisite cleverness of his mimetics and his mockery is some compensation to Hamlet for his inaction; this intellectual versatility, this agility flatters his consciousness; and it is only on occasions that he is compelled to observe into what a swoon or syncope his will has fallen.

Yet it has been truly said that only one who feels Hamlet's strength should venture to speak of Hamlet's weakness. That in spite of difficulties without, and inward difficulties, he still clings to his terrible duty,—letting it go indeed for a time, but returning to it again, and in the end accomplishing it—implies strength. He is not incapable of vigorous action,—if only he be allowed no chance of thinking the fact away into an idea. He is the first to board the pirate; he stabs Polonius through the arras; he suddenly alters the sealed commission, and sends his schoolfellows to the English headsman; he finally executes justice upon the king. But all his action is sudden and fragmentary; it is not continuous and coherent. His violent excitability exhausts him; after the night of encounter with the ghost a fit of abject despondency, we may be certain, ensued, which had begun to set in when the words were uttered,—

> The time is out of joint; O, cursed spite
> That ever I was born to set it right.
>
> (I, v, 189–90)

After he has slain Polonius, he weeps; after his struggle with Laertes in Ophelia's grave a mood of depression ensues:—

> Thus awhile the fit will work on him,
> Anon as patient as the female dove,
> When that her golden couplets are disclosed,
> His silence will sit drooping.
>
> (V, i, 282–5)

His feelings are not under control. They quickly fatigue themselves, like a dog who now hurries before his master, and now drops behind, but will not advance steadily.[18]

At the moment when Polonius has dismissed Reynaldo, Ophelia comes running to her father, 'Alas, my lord, I have been so affrighted!' Such is the piteously inadequate response of Ophelia to Hamlet's mute confession of his sorrow. His letters have been repelled; her presence has been denied to him. Hamlet resolves that he will see her, and hear her speak. He goes, profoundly agitated, in the disordered attire which is now nothing unusual with him, and which constitutes part of Hamlet's 'transformation.' He is not in the mood to consider very attentively particulars of the toilet. He discovers Ophelia sewing in her closet. He stands unable to speak, holding her hand, gazing in her face, trying to discover if there be in her

---

18 The illustration is Hebler's (author's note).

any virtue or strength, anything which can give a shadow of hope that the widening gulf between them is not quite impassable. He endeavours to make a new study of her soul through her eyes. And in her eyes he reads—*fright*. The most piteous part of the incident is that Ophelia is wholly blameless. She is shocked, bewildered, alarmed, anxious to run away, and get under the protection of her father. No wonder Hamlet cannot utter a word! No wonder that his gesture expresses absolute confirmation of his unhappy fears, utter despair of finding virtue in her! A sigh rises from the depths of his spirit. He feels that all is over. He knows how strange and remote his voice would sound. And as Hamlet can feel nothing without generalising, he recognises in this failure of heart to answer heart a type of one great sorrow of the world.

Polonius receives from the docile Ophelia the letters of Hamlet. She does not shrink from betraying the secrets of his weakness and his melancholy confided to her. The oddest of the letters, that which seemed most incoherent, is carried off to be read aloud to the king,—Ophelia consenting. What is the purport of this letter? Was it meant as a kind of test? Did Hamlet wish to ascertain whether Ophelia would be puzzled by the superficial oddity of it, or would penetrate to the grief and the love which lay beneath it? 'He that hath ears to hear let him hear'—upon this principle Hamlet constantly acts. He is content that the feeble-hearted and dull witted should find him a puzzle and an offence.

The Prince comes by reading. Polonius accosts him, assuming that Hamlet is downright mad. Hamlet's irony here consists in his adoption and exaggeration of the ideas of Polonius. 'You have immured your daughter; you have repelled my letters, and denied me sight of her; O wise old man! for woman's virtue is the frailest of things, and there is no male creature who is not a corrupter of virtue. If the most glorious and vivifying thing in the universe, the sun, will breed maggots out of carrion, truly Prince Hamlet may be suspected! Beware of your daughter; Friend look to't.' And then, in more direct fashion, Hamlet breaks forth into a satire on old men with their weak hams and most plentiful lack of wit. Polonius retires bewildered, and two new persecutors appear.

In Goethe's novel, *Wilhelm Meister*, the hero, when adapting the play of Hamlet to the German stage, alters it in certain particulars. Serlo, the manager of the theatre, suggests that Rosencrantz and Guildenstern should be 'compressed into one'. "''Heaven keep me from all such curtailments,'' exclaims Wilhelm; "they destroy at once the sense and the effect. What these two persons are and do, it is impossible to represent by one. In such small matters we discover Shakespeare's greatness. These soft approaches, this smirking and bowing, this assenting, wheedling, flattering, this whisking agility, this wagging of the tail, this allness and emptiness, this legal knavery, this ineptitude and insipidity, how can they be expressed by a single man? There ought to be at least a dozen of these people if they could be had; for it is only in society that they are anything; they *are* society itself, and Shakspere showed no little wisdom and discernment in bringing in a pair of them' ".[19] What Goethe admirably expresses, Shakspere 'der Schalk'[20], has perhaps hinted in the address of the king and queen to the pair of courtiers:

> *King.* Thanks, Rosencrantz and gentle Guildenstern.
> *Queen.* Thanks, Guildenstern and gentle Rosencrantz.
>
> (II, ii, 32–3)

That is, 'six to one, and half a dozen to the other'. With no tie of friendship, or capacity for true human comradeship, the companions hunt in a couple; and they go with the same indistinguishable smirking and bowing to their fate in England. There is a grim irony in this ending of the courtiers' history. 'They were lovely, and pleasant in their lives', after the taste of Claudius' court, 'and in their death they were not divided'.[21]

In the first scene of the third act Ophelia is stationed as a decoy to expose to her father and the king, the disease of the man she loves. It will assist, she is assured, to bring about Hamlet's restoration; and Ophelia is docile, and does not question her instructors. A book of devotions is placed in her hands. [Polonius (giving the book), says:-

---

19 *Wilhelm Meister's Apprenticeship*, book 5, chap. 5. See *CRH*, ii, 34. (Dowden is quoting from the Carlyle translation.)
20 The joker. The epithet used by Vischer. See p. 329 above.
21 II Samuel, i, 23.

> Read on this book;
> That show of such an *exercise* may colour
> Your loneliness. We are oft to blame in this,-
> 'Tis too much proved—that with devotion's visage,
> And pious action, we do sugar o'er
> The devil himself.
>
> (III, i, 46–51)

Hamlet seeing her at prayer exclaims,

> Nymph, in thy *orisons*
> Be all my sins remembered.][22]

Hamlet comes by, brooding upon suicide, upon the manifold ills of the world, and his own weakness. He sees Ophelia, so lovely, so child-like, so innocent, praying. She is for a moment something better and more beautiful than woman, something 'afar from the sphere of his sorrow'[23]; and he involuntarily exclaims,

> Nymph, in thy orisons
> Be all my sins remembered.

But Ophelia plays her part with a manner that betrays her. Observe the four rhymed lines, ending with the little set sentence (which looks as if prepared beforehand)

> For to the noble mind
> Rich gifts wax poor when givers prove unkind.

And then, upon the spot, the Prince's presents are produced. How could Hamlet, endowed with swift penetration as he is, fail to detect the fraud? He had unmasked Rosencrantz and Guildenstern, and thereby his suspicions had been quickened. And as for a moment he had been touched and exalted by the presence of Ophelia's innocence and piety, he is now proportionately indignant.

22 Passage in square brackets presented as author's note.
23 Adapted from lines 15–16 of P. B. Shelley's 'One word is too often profaned.' Dowden repeats this on p. 348 below.

One of the deepest characteristics of Hamlet's nature, is a longing for sincerity, for truth in mind and manners, an aversion from all that is false, affected or exaggerated.[24] Ophelia is joined with the rest of them; she is an impostor, a spy; incapable of truth, of honour, of love. Have they desired to observe an outbreak of his insanity? He will give it to them with a vengeance. With an almost savage zeal, which is underneath nothing but bitter pain, he pounces on Ophelia's deceit. 'Ha, ha, are you honest?' His cruelty is that of an idealist, who cannot precisely measure the effect of his words upon his hearer, but who requires to liberate his mind. And again Hamlet plays bitterly at approving of the principles and conduct of Polonius in the matter of his relations with Ophelia: 'You have been secluded from that dangerous corrupter of youth, Prince Hamlet; you love to devote yourself to prayer and solitude. Most wise and right! I am all that your father has represented me, and worse—very proud, revengeful, ambitious' (all that Hamlet was *not*). 'And yet there *is* in the world such a thing as calumny; it may happen to touch yourself some day. You who are so fair and frail, so pious in appearance, so false in deed, do you look on us *men* as dangerous to virtue? *I* have heard a little of women's doings too; keep your precious virtue, if you can, and let us male monsters be. Get thee to a nunnery!' And to complete the startling effect of this outbreak of insanity, solicited by his persecutors, he sends a shaft after the Chamberlain, and a shaft after the King:-

> *Ham.* Where's your father?
> *Oph.* [*coming out with her docile little lie*]
>   At home, my lord.
> *Ham.* Let the doors be shut upon him, that he may play the fool nowhere but in's own house.
>
> (III, i, 132–5)

This for Polonius; and for the King with menacing emphasis the words are uttered, 'I say we will have no more marriages: those that are married already, all but one, shall live; the rest shall keep as they are. To a nunnery, go!'

---

24 False, as the bearing of Rosencrantz and Guildenstern; affected, as the manner of Osric; exaggerated, as Laertes' theatrical rant in Ophelia's grave (author's note).

Hamlet bursts out of the lobby with a triumphant and yet bitter sense of having turned the tables upon his tormentors. He has thrown into sudden confusion the ranks of the enemy. Ophelia remains to weep. In the pauses of Hamlet's cruel invective, she had uttered her piteous, little appeals to heaven: 'Heavenly powers, restore him!' 'O help him, you sweet heavens!' When he abruptly departs, the poor girl's sorrow overflows. In her lament, Hamlet's noble reason, which is overthrown, somehow gets mixed up with the elegance of his costume, which has suffered equal ruin. He who was the 'glass of fashion', noticed by everyone, 'the observed of all observers', is a hopeless lunatic. She has no bitter thought about her lover. She is 'of ladies most deject and wretched;' all her emotion is helpless tenderness and sorrow. Her grief is as deep as her soul is deep.

Hamlet now binds himself more closely than ever to Horatio. This friend and fellow-scholar is the one sterling thing in the rotten state of Denmark. There is a touching devotion shown by Hamlet to Horatio in the meeting which follows the scene in the lobby with Ophelia; a devotion which is the overflow of gratitude for the comfort and refuge he finds with his friend after the recent proof of the incapacity and want of integrity in the woman he had loved. Horatio's equanimity, his evennness of temper, is like solid land to Hamlet after the tossings and tumults of his own heart. The Prince apologises with beautiful delicacy for seeming to flatter Horatio. It is not flattery; what can he expect from a man so poor? It is genuine delight in the sanity, the strength, the constancy of Horatio's character. Yet all the while Shakspere compels us to feel that it is Hamlet with his manifold weakness, and ill-commingled blood and judgment, who is the rarer nature of the two; and that Horatio is made to be his helpmate, recognising in service his highest duty.

There is no Friar Laurence in this play. To him the Catholic children of Verona carried their troubles, and received from their father comfort and counsel. Hamlet is hardly the man to seek for wisdom or for succour from a priest. Let them resolve his doubts about the soul, about immortality, about God first. But Shakspere has taken care to show us in the effete society of Denmark, where everything needs renewing, what religion is. To Ophelia's funeral the Church reluctantly sends her representative. All that the occasion suggests of harsh, formal, and essentially inhuman dogmatics, is uttered by the Priest. The distracted girl has by untimely accident met her death; and therefore, instead of charitable prayers,

> Shards, flints, and pebbles should be thrown on her.

These are the sacred words of truth, of peace, of consolation which Religion has to whisper to wounded hearts!

> We should profane the service of the dead,
> To sing a requiem and such rest to her
> As to peace-parted souls.
>
> (V, i, 231–3)

This is the religion that helps to make Claudius a palterer with his conscience, and Hamlet an aimless wanderer after truth. Better consort in Denmark with players than with priests![25]

When the play is about to be enacted Hamlet declines a seat near his mother, because he wishes to occupy a position from which he can scrutinise the king's countenance. He is now fully roused, every nerve high-strung. Just at present Ophelia is nothing to him. If he say anything to her it will be for the sake of staying his own heart in its tremulous intensity, and getting through the eager moments of suspense. It will be something issuing from the bitter upper surface of his soul—a bitter jest most likely. Hamlet derives an acrid pleasure from perplexing and embarrassing Polonius, and Rosencrantz and Guildenstern. Now it pleases him to embarrass Ophelia with half-ambiguous obscenities. These are the electrical sparks which scintillate and snap while the current is streaming to its receptacle. With Ophelia, who cherished the proprieties as though they constituted the moral law, Hamlet finds himself tempted to be intolerably improper. Ophelia understands his words, and ventures to deliver a gentle reprimand. 'You are naught, you are naught; I'll mark the play.' But Hamlet continues his persecution. All this comes from the superficial part of Hamlet; as one toys with some trifle while a doom is

---

25   H. A. Werner. *Jahrbuch der Deutschen Shakespeare-Gesellschaft*, vol. v, p. 56 (author's note).

impending. His passion is concentrated in watching the countenance of the king.[26]

This is the night of Hamlet's triumph. The king's guilt is unkennelled; Hamlet disposes of one after another of his tormentors; he has superabundant energy; he takes each in turn, and is equal to all. And yet Hamlet is for ever walking over ice; his power of self-control is never quite to be trusted. The success of his device of ascertaining the guilt of Claudius is followed by the same mood of wild excitement which followed the encounter with his father's spirit; again he seems incoherently, extravagantly gay; again his words are 'wild and whirling words.'[27] And as on that occasion Hamlet had felt the need of calming himself, and in his somewhat fantastic way had expressed that need, 'For my own poor part, look you, I'll go pray', so now he calls for music, 'Come, some music; come the recorders!' But he is haunted by the irrepressible Rosencrantz and Guildenstern. With them Hamlet is now severely and imperiously courteous, now enigmatical, now ironical. At last, when he advances to interpret his parable of the recorders, he becomes terribly direct and frank. The courtiers are silenced; they have not the spirit even to mutter a lie. And having disposed of them, Hamlet takes in hand Polonius. He is assuming the offensive with his foes. He steps forward to assist the old chamberlain to expose his folly; he lends him a hand to render himself contemptible. Next Hamlet hastens to his mother's closet.[28] He has words that must be spoken. He has a great essay to make towards the deliverance

---

26 On the speech of 'some dozen or sixteen lines' which Hamlet inserts in the play, see a note by F. J. Furnivall.—*The Academy*, Jan. 3, 1874, pp. 12–13 (author's note in the first edition; in the third edition Dowden substitutes for the reference to Furnivall 'see the discussion by Prof. Seeley, Mr Malleson and others, *New Shak. Soc. Trans.* 1874').

27 On the line 'A very, very—pajock,' see the article on Shakspere in *Edinburgh Review*, October 1872, pp. 361–2.

28 Of the speech in presence of the praying Claudius, Richardson had said what S. T. Coleridge, in other words, repeated, 'I venture to affirm that these are not Hamlet's real sentiments.' Notice that the ghost appears precisely at the point where Hamlet's words respecting Claudius are most vituperative. Hamlet is immediately sensible that he is weakening his heart with words, and has neglected deeds. The air, which had been so heated, seems to grow icy, and the temperature of Hamlet's passion suddenly falls—to rise again by-and-by (author's note).

of a human soul from the bondage of corruption. The slaughter of Polonius seems to him a trivial incident by the way; it does not affect him until he has spent his powers in the effort to uplift his mother's weak soul, and breathe into it strength and courage and constancy. Then in the exhaustion which succeeds his effort, his tears flow fast.

In the dawn of the following morning Hamlet is despatched to England. From this time forward he acts, if not with continuity, and with a plan, at least with energy. He has fallen in love with action; but the action is sudden, convulsive, and interrupted. He is abandoning himself more than previously to his chances of achieving things; and thinks less of forming any consistent scheme. The death of Polonius was accidental, and Hamlet recognized, or tried to recognize in it (since in his own will the deed had no origin) the pleasure of heaven:

> I do repent: but heaven hath pleased it so,
> To punish me with this, and this with me,
> That I must be their scourge and minister.
>
> (III, iv, 157–9)

When about to depart for England, Hamlet accepts the necessity with as resolute a spirit as may be, believing, or trying to believe, that he and his concerns are in the hand of God.

> *Ham.* For England!
> *King.* Ay, Hamlet.
> *Ham.* Good.
> *King.* So it is, if thou knew'st our purposes.
> *Ham. I see a cherub that sees them.*
>
> (IV, iii, 46–50)

That is, My times are in God's hand. Again, when he reflects that acting upon a sudden impulse, in which there was nothing voluntary (for the deed was accomplished before he had conceived what it was), he had sent his two schoolfellows to death, Hamlet's thoughts go on to discover the divine purpose in the event:

> Let us know
> Our indiscretion sometimes serves us well,

>   When our deep plots do pall; and that should teach us
>   There's a divinity that shapes our ends,
>   Rough-hew them how we will.
>   *Horatio.* That is most certain.
>
>   (V, ii, 7–12)

Once more, when Horatio bids the prince yield to the secret misgivings which troubled his heart before he went to the trial of skill with Laertes, Hamlet puts aside his friend's advice with the words, 'We defy augury; there's a special providence in the fall of a sparrow. If it be now, 'tis not to come; if it be not now, yet it will come; the readiness is all' (V, ii, 165–8).

Does Shakspere accept the interpretation of events which Hamlet is led to adopt? No; the providence in which Shakspere believed is a moral order which includes man's highest exercise of foresight, energy, and resolution. The disposition of Hamlet to reduce to a minimum the share which man's conscious will and foresight have in the disposing of events, and to enlarge the sphere of the action of powers outside the will has a dramatic, not a theological significance. Helena, who clearly sees what she resolves to do, and accomplishes neither less nor more than she has resolved, professes a different creed:

>   Our remedies oft in ourselves do lie,
>   Which we ascribe to heaven; the fated sky
>   Gives us free scope, only doth backward pull
>   Our slow designs when we ourselves are dull.[29]

Horatio, a believer in the 'divinity that shapes our ends', by his promised explanation of events, delivers us from the transcendental optimism of Hamlet, and restores the purely human way of viewing things:

>   Give order that these bodies
>   High on a stage be placed to the view;
>   And let me speak to the yet unknowing world
>   How these things came about: so shall you hear
>   Of carnal, bloody, and unnatural acts,

---

29 *All's Well That Ends Well*, act i sc.1 [lines 212–15] (author's note). This is a misreading of Helena's lines, as a glance at their context in her soliloquy makes clear.

> Of deaths put on by cunning and forced cause,
> And in this upshot purposes mistook,
> Fall'n on the inventors' heads: all this can I
> Truly deliver.
>
> (V, ii, 331–40)

The arrival of Fortinbras contributes also to the restoration of a practical and positive feeling. With none of the rare qualities of the Danish Prince, he excels him in the plain grasp of ordinary fact. Shakspere knows that the success of these men who are limited, definite, positive, will do no dishonour to the failure of the rarer natures, to whom the problem of living is more embarrassing, and for whom the tests of the world are stricter and more delicate. Shakspere 'beats triumphant' marches not for successful persons alone, but also 'for conquered and slain persons.'

Does Hamlet finally attain deliverance from his disease of will? Shakspere has left the answer to that question doubtful. Probably if anything could supply the link which was wanting between the purpose and the deed, it was the achievement of some supreme action. The last moments of Hamlet's life are well spent, and for energy and foresight are the noblest moments of his existence; he snatches the poisoned bowl from Horatio, and saves his friend; he gives his dying voice for Fortinbras, and saves his country. The rest is silence:

> Had I but time—as this fell sergeant, death,
> Is strict in his arrest—O, I could tell you.
>
> (V, ii, 288–9)

But he has not told. Let us not too readily assume that we 'know the stops' of Hamlet, that we can 'pluck out the heart of his mystery.'

One thing, however, we *do* know—that the man who wrote the play of Hamlet had obtained a thorough comprehension of Hamlet's malady. And assured, as we are by abundant evidence, that Shakspere transformed with energetic will his knowledge into fact, we may be confident that when Hamlet was written, Shakspere had gained a further stage in his culture of self-control, and that he had become not only adult as an author, but had entered upon the full maturity of his manhood.[30]

---

30 I believe my study of the play is indebted chiefly to the article by H.A. Werner in *Jarhbuch der Deutschen Shakespeare-Gesellschaft,* vol. v., and to an essay by my

b) From the introduction to the edition of *Hamlet*, 1899.

The duration of the action in the play presents difficulties. It opens at midnight with the change of sentinels. Next day Horatio and Marcellus, with Bernardo, inform Hamlet of the appearance of the Ghost; it cannot be the forenoon, for Hamlet salutes Bernardo with 'Good even, sir'. On the night of this day Hamlet watches and meets his father's ghost. The season of the year is perhaps March; the nights are bitter cold. The second Act occupies part of one day; Polonius despatches Reynaldo to Paris, Ophelia enters alarmed by Hamlet's letter, the players arrive; and, when Hamlet parts from them, his words are, 'I'll leave you till to-night'. But before this day arrives two months have elapsed since Hamlet was enjoined to revenge the murder—it was two months since his father's death when the play opened, and now it is 'twice two months'. Next day Hamlet utters his soliloquy, 'To be, or not to be', encounters Ophelia as arranged by Polonius, gives his advice to the players, is present at the performance

---

friend, J. Todhunter, M.D., read before the Dublin University Shakspere Society. The doctors of the insane have been studious of the state of Hamlet's mind—Doctors Ray, Kellogg, Conolly, Maudsley, Bucknill. They are unanimous in wishing to put Hamlet under judicious medical treatment; but they find it harder than Polonius did to hit upon a definition of madness:-

For to define true madness
What is't but to be nothing else but mad

The critics are nearly equally divided in their estimates of Ophelia. Flathe is extravagantly hostile to the Polonius family. Mr Ruskin (*Sesame and Lilies*) may be mentioned among the English writers as forming no favourable estimate of Ophelia; and against Mrs Jameson's authority, we may set the authority of a lady writer in *Jahrbuch der Deutschen Shakespeare-Gesellschaft,* vol. ii., pp. 16–36. Vischer chivalrously defends Ophelia, and Hebler coincides. The study of Hamlet by Benno Tschischwitz, is learned and ingenious. H. von Friesen's 'Briefe über Shakespeare's Hamlet' contains much more than its name implies, and is indeed a study of the entire development of Shakspere. Sir Edward Strachey's 'Shakespeare's Hamlet,' 1848, interprets the play throughout in a different sense from the interpretation attempted in this chapter. See especially what is called 'Hamlet's final discovery,' pp. 91–3 (Author's note).

Werder's 'Vorlesungen über Shakespeares Hamlet' 1875, presents with remarkable force the view that Hamlet's was *not* a weak nature. Mr Frank Marshall's 'A Study of Hamlet' if less brilliant is ... more sound. Last must be mentioned Mr Furness's magnificent Variorum edn. of the play in two volumes 1877. (Further note added to the third edition.)

of the play; and, night having come, he pleads with his mother, and again sees his father's spirit. Here the third Act closes, but the action proceeds without interruption; the King inquires for the body of Polonius, and tells Hamlet that the bark is ready to bear him to England. We must suppose it is morning when Hamlet meets the troops of Fortinbras. Two days previously the ambassadors from Norway had returned, with a request that Claudius would permit Fortinbras to march through Denmark against the Poles; Fortinbras himself must have arrived almost as soon as the ambassadors, and obtained the Danish King's permission. In IV, v, Ophelia appears distracted, and Laertes has returned from Paris to be revenged for Polonius's death. An interval of time must have passed since Hamlet sailed for England—an interval sufficient to permit Laertes to receive tidings of the death of Polonius and to reach Elsinore. In the next scene letters arrive announcing that Hamlet is again in Denmark; before he was two days at sea, he became the pirates' prisoner. On the day of the arrival of letters Ophelia is drowned. Her flowers indicate that the time is early June. Ophelia's burial and Hamlet's death take place on the next day. Yet the time has been sufficient for Fortinbras to win his Polish victory and be again at Elsinore, and for ambassadors to return from England announcing the execution of Rosencrantz and Guildenstern. We might obligingly imagine that the pirate ship conveying Hamlet to Denmark was delayed by baffling winds; but his letters are written after he has landed, and they describe his companions as holding their course for England. The truth is, as stated by Professor Hall Griffin (whose record of the notes of time has aided me here), 'Shakespeare is at fault'; 'he did not trouble himself to reconcile . . . inconsistencies which practical experience as an actor would tell him do not trouble the spectator' . . .

Hamlet is not the exponent of a philosophy; he has, it is true, a remarkable power of reflection and a tendency to generalise, but he is not a philosophical thinker who seeks to co-ordinate his ideas in a coherent system. Perhaps Ulysses, perhaps Prospero approaches nearer to the philosopher[31], but neither Ulysses nor Prospero is a wit; and Hamlet is a wit inspired by melancholy. He is swift, ingenious, versatile, penetrative; and he is also sad. And when Shakespeare proceeded to follow the story in

---

31 Ulysses, in *Troilus and Cressida*, Prospero in *The Tempest*.

the main as he had probably received it from Kyd[32], it turned out that such subtlety overreached itself—which Shakespeare recognised as wholly right, and true to the facts of life. Hamlet's madness is not deliberately assumed; an antic disposition is, as it were, imposed upon him by the almost hysterical excitement which follows his interview with the Ghost, and he ingeniously justifies it to himself by discovering that it may hereafter serve a purpose. But in truth his subtlety does not produce direct and effective action. Hamlet is neither a boisterous Laertes, who with small resources almost effects a rebellion in revenge for a murdered father, nor a resolute Fortinbras, who, mindful of his dead father's honour, can march through danger to victory. Hamlet's intellectual subtlety sees every side of every question, thinks too precisely on the event, considers all things too curiously, studies anew every conviction, doubts the past, interrogates the future; it delights in ironically adopting the mental attitudes of other minds; it refines contempt into an ingenious art; it puts on and puts off a disguise; it assumes and lays aside the antic disposition; it can even use frankness as a veil,—for sometimes display is a concealment, as happened with Edgar Poe's purloined letter. Hamlet the subtle is pre-eminently a critic—a critic of art, a critic of character, a critic of society, a critic of life, a critic of himself.

The intellectual dexterity and versatility of Hamlet are united with a moral nature essentially honest. He will not hire a couple of assassins to despatch his father's murderer. He will not himself take action until he has evidence of the King's guilt. Like the Amleth of Saxo, he is a lover of truth concealed in craft. His emotional nature, though deeply disturbed by his mother's lapse from loyalty, and liable to passionate fluctuations, is sound at heart. He reverences the memory of his great father, a man of action, whom Hamlet resembles as little as he resembles Hercules. He is bound to Horatio by ties of the deepest esteem and affection. He is kind to the poor actors. He expends his utmost energy in an effort to uplift and redeem his mother's faltering spirit. He is over-generous in his estimate of Laertes. He has loved Ophelia as a vision of beauty and innocence, and is proportionately embittered when he supposes that he

---

32   Earlier Dowden had accepted the conjecture that a lost play of *Hamlet* was by the playwright Thomas Kyd. The matter is still the subject of controversy.

has deceived himself and been deceived. But all his inclinations are toward those who are unlike himself. He is complex and self-tormenting; Ophelia seems all simplicity and innocence; he is oppressed by melancholy thought; she is 'something afar from the sphere of his sorrow'. Horatio is a man whose blood and judgment, unlike Hamlet's own, are well commingled; one who can see the evil of the world, yet not grow world-weary; more of the antique Roman Stoic than a Dane. For Fortinbras Hamlet has the admiration which the man of ideas feels for the man of resolute action. In Claudius he might have perceived some of his own intellectual subtlety and reflective habit, but conjoined with grosser senses and an evil moral nature; and him Hamlet loathes with an impatient aversion.

Together with such an intellectual and such a moral nature, Hamlet has in him something dangerous—a will capable of being roused to sudden and desperate activity. It is a will which is determined to action by the flash and flame of an excitable temperament, or by those sudden impulses or inspirations, leaping forth from a sub-conscious self, which come almost like the revelation and the decree of Providence. It is thus that he suddenly conceives the possibility of unmasking the King's guilt, on the accidental arrival of the players, and proceeds without delay to put the matter to the test, suddenly overwhelms Ophelia with the reproaches of womanhood, suddenly stabs the eavesdropper behind the arras, suddenly, as if under some irresistible inspiration, sends his companions on shipboard to their death, suddenly boards the pirate, suddenly grapples with Laertes in the grave, suddenly does execution on the guilty King, plucks the poison from Horatio's hand, and gives his dying voice for a successor to the throne.

Hamlet's love for Ophelia is the wonder and delight in a celestial vision; she is hardly a creature of earth, and he has poured into her ear almost all the holy vows of heaven. The ruin of an ideal leaves him cruelly unjust to the creature of flesh and blood. It is the strangest love-story on record. Never throughout the play is there one simple and sincere word uttered by lover to lover. The only true meeting of Hamlet and Ophelia is the speechless interview in which he reads her soul, despairs and takes a silent and final farewell. Even in the letter, written prior to the terrible announcements of the Ghost, there is a conventional address, and a baffling conclusion. After the silent parting, no true word, except when passion carries him away to undeserved reproach, is uttered by Hamlet to Ophelia. His love has for the first time its outbreak at her grave, when the pity of it for the moment restores his lost ideal. Never to Horatio, never to himself in soliloquy, does he utter the name of Ophelia.

23. Frank Marshall

1875

Francis Albert Marshall (1840–1889), born in London, was one of the most successful popular playwrights of the Victorian period. His successes included an adaptation of Byron's *Werner* as a vehicle for Henry Irving, whom he greatly admired and whose biography he wrote (published in 1883). He was for a time drama critic of the *London Figaro* and the principal editor of the Henry Irving edition of Shakespeare. His *Study of Hamlet*, from which the following excerpts are taken began its life as two lectures addressed to the Catholic Young Men's Association.

From the Preface:
'What! another book on *Hamlet!*' I seem to hear many, both critics and students of Shakespeare, exclaim with somewhat of a jaded air. 'What can you have that is new to say about *Hamlet*?' they ask—not unreasonably. My answer is that I hope I have something to say which is worth hearing, whether it be quite new, or whether it be old truths presented in a new guise; though I must confess I have not hazarded any theories, or indulged in any criticisms, simply because I thought they were new. To those who seek for abstruse verbal commentaries, or for ingenious, but, to my mind, paltry attempts to nibble away our greatest poet's reputation, this book will not be welcome. I leave to others the task of treating our author like a prisoner arrested for felony, of turning his pockets inside out, and stripping him to the skin, in order to see if they can discover a rag or two which might have belonged to some one else.

Those I would fain have as my readers are those who love Shakespeare as one who has added to the beauty and happiness of life; who reverence his mind as one of those precious gifts of God to this world, whence beings, born of Fancy indeed, but none the less real in their nobleness and purity, may spring, to gladden the hearts of those whose earthly lot it is to find few friends save in the realms of imagination. These persons will grudge neither time nor trouble if, by their own efforts, or by the aid of others, they can gain a clearer insight into the beauties of Shakespeare's creations . . .

I have made frequent allusions to the acting of three of the most distinguished representatives of Hamlet on the stage that I have had the pleasure of seeing—namely, Tommaso Salvini, Ernesto Rossi, and Henry Irving. I had intended to have entered into a somewhat elaborate comparison of their respective interpretations of the character; but for many reasons, some of which I will mention, I thought it better not to do so . . . The charming grace, and melodious elocution, of Signor Salvini could not be obscured by the fact that he was under the disadvantage of speaking a language, with which but very few of his audience were familiar: he has, by his performance of Othello and Hamlet, won a position among Englishmen, as an interpreter of Shakespeare, which few of our own countrymen have gained. Ernesto Rossi, whose style is totally different from that of Salvini[1], though he is in grace and talent his most worthy rival, will be sure of a generous welcome: his appearance amongst us will stimulate that revived interest in Shakespeare's plays which has been such a marked feature of the last year. As far as regards the Hamlet of the three great actors I have named, I should say that Salvini's interpretation was the most tender, Rossi's the most passionate, and Irving's the most intellectual.

Now that it has been proved that the plays of Shakespeare can be made to bring money as well as glory to the managers, I live in the hopes of seeing some performances of our greatest dramatist's masterpieces worthy of the honour in which we hold him. I do not mean as regards scenery and dresses, but as regards the representation of the characters themselves; one good actor cannot make an efficient cast; and unless the minor characters in Shakespeare's plays are adequately represented, it is

---

[1] A writer in the *Times*, speaking of Rossi's Othello, as given in Paris, said that the two great Italian actors were as similar in style as Phelps and Macready. I never saw Macready, but I am sure that all who have seen Rossi and Salvini in the part will admit that there could scarcely be two more dissimilar interpretations of Hamlet (author's footnote).

impossible to form any just conception of the excellence of his work. This can only be effected by actors, managers, and audiences, uniting together in making greater sacrifices to Art than they have hitherto seemed willing to do.

Part 1. *Hamlet* is perhaps the most popular of all Shakespeare's plays. Nearly all people have either read it, or seen it upon the stage, more than once. I will not say that it is the one most often quoted, yet perhaps the quotations taken from it are the best known of any of those lines of Shakespeare which have become household words. I do not think it is difficult to understand the universal popularity of this play; if we do not all agree in considering it Shakespeare's greatest work, it certainly is his most human; though less pathetic than *Othello*, less sublime than *Macbeth*, less touching than *Lear*, it is certainly of all his tragedies the one which appeals most widely to human sympathy; because the character of Hamlet has more in common with all mankind than any other hero. His very weakness, which has been so severely censured by some critics, is greatly the cause of this; for most tragic heroes are endowed with such gigantic intellect, and monstrous passions, as to place them beyond both the understanding and the sympathy of ordinary mortals. Deeply as we are moved by the agonising jealousy of Othello, freely as we weep with Lear over the body of the loving Cordelia, instinctively as we shudder with Macbeth at the unearthly apparitions which so mysteriously control his fate, few of us ever feel that Othello, or Lear, or Macbeth, might be our very own self; but when Hamlet speaks, it seems as if thoughts and feelings, long pent up in us, had found their most natural utterance: the least philosophical comprehends his philosophy; the least melancholy muses sadly with him over the mysteries of life; the least humorous of us smiles with him as odd fancies and playful satire break forth from him in the midst of the most tragic surroundings.

No doubt the question of suicide might be debated more learnedly, certainly more sensationally, than in the celebrated soliloquy of Hamlet: but if philosophers and novelists were to try their very utmost, they never could express more clearly, more vividly, certainly not more beautifully, than Shakespeare has in those few lines, the struggles of a mind weighed down by the sense that the burden imposed upon it was too heavy to bear.

The popularity of *Hamlet* is the more remarkable when we consider how subordinate in it is what we commonly call the '*love* interest'. Few plays except Shakespeare's have retained their hold upon the popular mind either on the stage or in the study, the principal motive of which has not been, in some form or other, the love of man for woman, or of woman for man. In Hamlet the chief motive is filial affection; one which I hope will always inspire the deepest and most general sympathy; but which it would be idle to deny, exercises a less powerful charm over the vulgar mind than that more selfish, and intrinsically less noble affection which sometimes threatens to monopolise the name of Love. If for no other reason, I should be deeply grieved to see the character of Hamlet losing any of its hold upon the minds of my contemporaries, and especially of the young; for if there is any one of the natural affections which the rapidly advancing steam-engine of improvement seems likely to improve off the face of the earth, it is that most holy, unselfish, and noble affection—an affection rooted in humility, and in a single-minded sense of duty; incompatible alike with intellectual pride, or with enervating self-indulgence—the affection of a son for his father. No one can ever hope to appreciate Hamlet who does not cherish unsullied within his soul, in youth, in maturity, and in old age, that reverential love of parents which is the foundation-stone of all social virtue.

The intense love and worship which Hamlet feels for the memory of his father, mark him out, on his very first entrance, as alone in the crowd of courtiers around him; alone, too, even in the presence of those who should have loved and revered that memory as highly, if not more highly, than Hamlet himself. The noble excess of his love tends, hardly less than the inherent weakness of his character, to paralyse his capacity for action when it is most needed: of this I shall have to speak more fully, and I will now pass on to notice briefly those other points in the character of Hamlet which ensure him the sympathy of mankind.

As I have said before, the very weakness of Hamlet makes us love him the more, because it brings him nearer to our own level. Who has not known what it is to feel life, with its glorious opportunities, slipping away from us day by day, without bringing us any nearer the fulfilment of some great duty, or the execution of some noble purpose, to which either the example, or the exhortation, of others, or the voice of our own conscience has called us? It may be by the death-bed of some very dear one; it may be in the wearying discipline of some long illness; it may be in the close and earnest contemplation of the evils around us, that we hear the first sound of the voice that calls us to sacrifice our ease, and our pleasures, for the sake of righting some wrong, or destroying some abuse, to the full heinousness of which our minds have been roused. Perhaps, like Hamlet, we sit down and contemplate the horrid features of the monster, till the very acuteness of the pain and disgust, which such a contemplation inspires, obtaining complete mastery over our feelings, and occupying our thoughts to the exclusion of almost any other subject, gradually wears away our energies, without their finding vent in that prompt and decided action which alone, as we know, can accomplish the great end we have set before us. In this state of mind, the *desire* to act is never lost; it is only the *power* to do so which is swallowed up in excess of feeling. Another state is when we simply content ourselves with exclaiming against the injustice and wickedness of the world in general, or of some persons in particular, but weakly decline to act, from despair at the magnitude of the labour involved in any attempt to remedy the evils to which we cannot blind ourselves. In such a state of mind we might slightly alter the words of Hamlet—

> The world is out of joint, oh cursed spite!
> *But I* was never born to set it right.

To this canker of cowardice, which blights the lives of so many in whom great sensibility is coupled with indolence, and in whom the reflective part of the mind is morbidly developed at the expense of the executive part—it is to this that Hamlet alludes in the words—

> That craven scruple
> Of thinking too precisely on the event,
> A thought which quartered hath but one part wisdom,
> And ever three parts coward.
> (Q2, IV, iv, 40–3, Additional passage J)

This weakness may be developed into a worse form, till it assumes the most repulsive of all shapes, that impotent snarling cynicism, which yaps like a cur at the heels of every wrong-doer, but never attempts to help the wronged.

One feature in the character of Hamlet, which most attracts us, is his keen sympathy with all that is good, his contempt for what is mean and evil; this he shows without regard of place or person; and it is more admirable in a prince, whose temptations to acquiesce in things as they are, and to accept the world's standard of right and wrong, are greater than those of one in a lower station of life.

The fidelity which Hamlet shows to his friends, few indeed, but chosen for their merit alone; as well as the dignified courtesy, with which he treats all but those whom he knows to be practising some treachery towards him, add to the affection with which we regard him . . .

Briefly then, I would attribute the popularity of this play not only to the inherent interest of the story and the dramatic skill with which, in spite of many blemishes of construction, it is developed; but even more to the sympathetic character of Hamlet himself: sympathetic, because he has more in common with mankind than any other tragic hero; because the motives of his conduct, the idiosyncrasies of his nature, the very blemishes which mar his virtues, his strength of feeling, his weakness in action, all alike endear his character to us. The creation of the poet is imbued with the very essence of human nature, while it is beautified by the infusion of so lovable and noble a spirit, that what we instinctively admire we are also able to comprehend. This is the chief difference between real greatness and mere excellence, whether in poet, sculptor, painter, or actor. The great poet appeals not only to the intellect which some men possess, but to the heart which all possess; everyone feels the meaning of his words, though everyone cannot explain it. I do not deny that the most exquisitely finished style in poetry, or in any other art, is perfectly compatible with greatness; but in work that is not only clever, but great, the style is subordinate to the matter; regularity of metre and precision of detail are sacrificed to nobility of thought and beauty of subject. The most faultless poems and pictures are rarely the noblest. Genius is impatient of restriction, seeking truth in great, rather than accuracy in little things; and so it happens that talent often exceeds genius in beauty of form, but never in grandeur of imagination . . .

The number of commentaries and essays which have been written on the tragedy of *Hamlet* is so great that time will not allow me to do more than mention a very few of those which are best worth your attention. Goethe and Coleridge have both exercised their powers of psychological analysis on the character of Hamlet; I need scarcely say that every one, wishing to study this play critically, should read every word which those two intellectual giants have written on the subject. The commentaries of Johnson, Steevens, and Malone are very unequal[2]; whatever is valuable in their annotations will be found in later editions of Shakespeare, especially in that published by Routledge, edited by Staunton. Professor Richardson's essay on *Hamlet*[3] shows more correct appreciation of the beauties of the character than any other that I have come across, always excepting Coleridge's lecture . . . If I were asked to mention the best criticism, on the whole, which has been written of Shakespeare, I am afraid I should have to give you no English name, but that of a German, Schlegel. [I have said the best criticism *on the whole*; I do not mean to say that there are not many criticisms on individual plays, which are better than those of Schlegel. The work of Professor Gervinus, in two volumes, which has been translated into English, is one of the most valuable additions to the Shakespearian literature of modern times; it was originally published in 1850, and the English translation in 1863; I have alluded more fully to this author's essay on *Hamlet* in another part of this work. Ulrici also merits the warmest praise, from every lover of Shakespeare, for his volume of delightful and learned essays on our great poet's dramatic genius. In assigning to Schlegel the first place among the critics of Shakespeare, I do not wish to be guilty of any injustice to the numerous English and German writers who have made our author the subject of so many valuable essays: I do not pretend to express anything more than my opinion, which is that, for practical purposes, Schlegel's estimate of Shakespeare's plays, is *on the whole*, the best guide to any would-be student of our greatest dramatist.[4]] This is something humiliating to our national vanity; but I do not think we need fear, now Germany

---

2   I do not mean to disparage Malone's labors as an annotator; but as an aesthetic critic of Shakespeare I think he has committed outrages on good taste and good sense which can never be forgiven. Steevens is worse (author's note).

3   London: Samuel Bagster. 1818 (author's note). For illustrations of the critics mentioned see *CRH*, i and ii.

4   Passage in brackets presented as the author's additional note 1. For Gervinus and Ulrici see *CRH*, iii.

has been swallowed up in Prussia, that Schlegel, any more than Goethe and Schiller, will find any successor. A nation which allows itself to be turned into one large barrack must be content with so glorious an achievement; it can well afford to leave more humanizing studies to those who have the leisure to follow them.

When Hamlet first enters, it is in company with the King (his uncle), the Queen (his mother), and their Court. Gertrude, Hamlet's mother, has married, within the short space of a month after her husband's death, Claudius, his brother and successor . . . The figure of Hamlet, dressed in black, his eyes cast on the ground, his whole appearance betraying the utmost dejection, the only mourner in the brilliant Court, at once arrests the attention. We cannot wonder at his melancholy when we consider the position in which he found himself. The news of his father's sudden death would have reached him at the University of Wittenburg: it is most probable that the first parting between him and his father had taken place when he went to that town to complete his education. He hurried back on hearing the dreadful news, and naturally the first person he would seek in his sorrow was his mother. We can imagine what a terrible shock it must have been to his feelings when he found her preparing for her wedding with her late husband's brother, almost before that husband's funeral rites were over; the revolting features of such an union were intensified by the indecent haste with which it was completed. It is probable that the revulsion of feeling, which such an outrage on his father's memory would cause in a nature like Hamlet's, prevented him from dwelling on the mortification which he must have suffered on finding himself ousted from the throne by his incestuous uncle. It is natural that Hamlet should at once have suspected that the death of his father was no accident of nature . . .

Claudius, very plausibly and with an assumption of fatherly affection, greets Hamlet as his son and future successor. As to the suspicion which Hamlet entertained of foul play, he could take no immediate action thereon without some evidence; and his generous nature would be hampered in any such attempt by the consciousness that such a suspicion might spring as much from wounded vanity, on account of his being deprived of his rights, as from affection for his father. The very first words that he speaks in reply to the King, who has addressed him as—'My son'

> -a little more than kin and less than kind,

words probably intended to be spoken half aside, show how impossible was any reconciliation between stepfather and stepson. It is to be remarked that Hamlet only once addresses the King during this first scene, and that in the sarcastic answer to—

> King. How is it that the clouds still hang on you?
> Hamlet. Not so, my lord, I am too much i'the sun.

The very fact that the King does not dare to rebuke Hamlet for the marked manner in which he ignores his advice, tendered as it is with affected kindness, shows that he was conscious of his guilt. Short as the scene is which precedes Hamlet's first soliloquy, nothing can be more admirable than the skill with which Shakespeare at once strikes the key-note of his hero's character, and seizes hold of the attention of his hearers. It is to be noted that while rebuking his mother, Hamlet never forgets the respect due to her in presence of the Court; it is not till he is alone that his pent up feelings, the passionate indignation that he has been forced to conceal, burst forth in this magnificent soliloquy:

[Marshall quotes the whole of the soliloquy: 'O, that this too, too solid flesh would melt . . .]

[**I, v**] The very few words that Hamlet utters during his interview with his father's spirit not only serve to intensify the dramatic effect of the scene, but also to illustrate his character in the most incisive manner; they are just like those few magic strokes of a great artist's pencil which make a face that one knows live before one. He echoes the word 'murder' in a tone half of horror, half of painful astonishment at the justification of his suspicions. The next speech, the longest by which he interrupts the ghost, is most remarkable:-

> Haste me to know't, that I, with wings as swift
> As meditation or the thoughts of love,
> May sweep to my revenge.
>
> (I, v, 29–31)

Shakespeare employs here—not by accident, I think—as illustrations of that swiftness of action, the want of which becomes afterwards the most prominent defect in Hamlet's character, those two very distinctive features of his disposition which so frequently retarded the execution of the ghost's commands, 'meditation' and 'the thoughts of love': an overindulgence in meditating on the innumerable aspects of the wrong which he had to revenge, and an imperfect power of wiping out of his life that love which had been the sweetest part of it, were, undoubtedly, the two main obstacles in the fulfilment of that purpose which the solemn interview with his father's spirit had made, as he believed, the one motive of his life. The only other words he speaks, 'Oh, my prophetic soul, my uncle', may be regarded less as the expression of gratified vanity, or malice, at finding that he had at once instinctively detected the murderer of his father, than as a sigh of relief from a generous heart, rejoiced to find that he had not wronged one who had given him the greatest cause for resentment.

The echo of the spirit's sad farewell, 'Adieu, adieu, adieu; remember me', has scarcely died away before the tension of nerves from which Hamlet has suffered during that most pathetic address is relieved by that outburst of passionate emotion, which, singular to state, most of the representatives of Shakespeare's Hamlet, on the stage, have either omitted to a great extent, or have deformed into a mere interjection:

[Quotes whole of Hamlet's speech 'O all you host of heaven! O earth! What else?—I, v, 92–113.]

Here we have at once the evidence of Hamlet's titanic strength of feeling, and the foreshadowing of that convulsion of the mind which renders his simulation of madness almost a necessity. He seems to feel that the task imposed upon him is so terrible that he can find no room in his life for any other pursuit, affection, or passion.

Study, speculation, philosophy, love, must all yield to this one great purpose; and there is no doubt that had the guilty Claudius entered at that moment, the murder of King Hamlet would have been instantly avenged. But while his mind is still surging with the agitation into which the ghost's narrative has plunged it, the voices of his friends are suddenly heard; and the necessity for concealment at once engrosses his faculties, causing him to check himself, when he is on the very point of bestowing upon them that confidence which alone could have relieved his overcharged heart. The conclusion of this scene has been more misunderstood by the exponents of Hamlet in the theatre, and by students of his character in the closet, than any other portion of the tragedy, except one—the scene with Ophelia.

Coleridge has expressed in one sentence what seems to me the whole gist of the scene: 'For you may perhaps observe that Hamlet's wildness is but half false; he plays that subtle trick of pretending to act only when he is very near really being what he acts'. I cannot agree with Coleridge that the subterranean speeches of the ghost 'are nearly indefensible'; they seem to me to be absolutely necessary, in order to bring out that feverish anxiety to conceal from all others the solemn revelation which he has received; an anxiety which induces Hamlet to hurry Horatio and Marcellus away from each spot whence the voice seems to come, forgetting that he alone can hear it; and gives him time for maturing hastily, but effectually, that scheme, by which alone he perceives that he can preserve his freedom of action, and give to his over-taxed mind that relief which is absolutely necessary, if it is not utterly to lose its balance. However strange or odd he may bear himself in future, these two trustworthy friends, at least, are secure to him as allies; for they will not be surprised at those 'antic dispositions'; but will accept, wholly and sincerely, as an assumption that which may be assumed indeed at some times, but at others will be only the inevitable indulgence of a mind filled with so terrible a purpose, that the relief of eccentricity becomes absolutely necessary to its healthy existence.

Nothing can be more affecting than the mixture here presented—the forced employment of a cunning most repulsive to his own over-frank character, and those touching appeals to the affection of his friends which would be the natural relief of his sensitive nature—

> So, gentlemen,
> With all my love I do commend me to you:
> And what so poor a man as Hamlet is
> May do, to express his love and friending to you,
> God willing, shall not lack. Let us go in together;
> And still your fingers on your lips, I pray.
> The time is out of joint: O cursed spite!
> That ever I was born to set it right!
> Nay, come, let's go together.
>
> (I, v, 183–91)

Between the first and second acts an interval of time occurs, the exact length of which we have no means of ascertaining; but that it consisted of several days, at least, is evident from the fact that the ambassadors to Norway had time to fulfil their mission, and to return; also that the King and Queen had time, after having observed Hamlet's altered demeanour, to procure the presence of Rosencrantz and Guildenstern, most probably from Wittenburg. How Hamlet employed this interval is to us the important question; he seems to have taken no step towards the fulfilment of the ghost's charge, except the consistent assumption of that eccentricity and humorous melancholy, by which he hoped to gain a character for harmless oddity; for we can hardly use such a strong term as madness, though Polonius most wisely expounds the reasons why he is mad. The ingenious Mr. Malone says that nothing could be more foolish than Hamlet's assumption of madness, because that was the very way to provoke the King to place him under restraint, and so prevent his doing anything to revenge his father's death. If Hamlet had counterfeited what doctors call the homicidal mania, this remark would have been a very sensible one; for Mr. Malone, whose only eccentricity took the perfectly innocent form of very dull criticism, would probably regard such an odd character as Hamlet as a dangerous lunatic; but King Claudius was not so sensitive on this point as Mr. Malone, and when he saw that his nephew was by turns melancholy and satirical, that he courted solitude and shrank from taking part in any of the Court festivities, but that he never attempted to injure himself or anybody else, he could have no pretext for depriving him of his liberty. He was naturally anxious to conciliate Hamlet, because, after all, the young prince was loved by the people, and Claudius dared not show any open animosity against him (see IV, iii, 3–4f., also IV, vii, 18–24)[5]; it was his object to conceal his crime, which was, as he believed, known only to himself; though he instinctively felt that the son of his murdered brother suspected him.

The most important step which Hamlet had taken was the resolution to break off his affectionate relations with Ophelia. The struggle must have been a very severe one. The meddlesome officiousness of Polonius in compelling his daughter to cease all correspondence with the young

5   As author's footnote.

prince, as being above her sphere, was a piece of diplomacy by which he hoped to obtain an explicit proposal for her hand; the shallow meanness of which device Hamlet most probably saw through. This forcible severance of all communication between Ophelia and himself seemed a plausible reason enough for Hamlet's melancholy; but we know it had little or nothing to do with it; and we may be sure it had less to do with his abandonment of his love-suit. On the day on which the second act commences we have Ophelia's vivid and beautiful description of the last interview, if we may call it so, that took place between them:-

[Quotes II, i, 78–87.]

Ophelia's modest expression of her belief contrasts beautifully with the pompous assurance of Polonius. She goes on:-

[Quotes II, i, 88–101.]

Now, the question is, what was in Hamlet's mind when he gave way to this violent agitation? It has been said by some commentators that he behaved in this extraordinary manner in order to impress upon Ophelia's simple nature the belief that he was mad; I cannot but think that Shakespeare meant something more than this. Since his interviews with the Ghost, Hamlet's mind had been dwelling upon his father's sad fate, and upon his mother's atrocious infidelity. What a fearful shock it must have been to his affectionate nature to know that the mother whom he had so loved and revered had been false to a husband so noble, so gentle, so loving, that the most abandoned woman might have shrunk from dishonouring him! The revelation of such a hideous fact might have forced a far stronger nature than Hamlet's to abandon all faith in womankind. During those days of mental agony, when he might have looked for the gentle consolation of her he loved, he was left to suffer alone, uncheered, save by the occasional company and the heartfelt sympathy of one true friend, Horatio. At such a time the horrid idea must have been present to his mind that the pure and innocent girl to whom he had given his first and only love might possibly grow up to become—most horrible thought!—what his mother was. Doubtless, his father had often told him of the perfect joy and happiness which he had known when he first married his young and virtuous bride; she had been no less innocent and no less pure, no less single-minded in her devotion to her betrothed than Ophelia; and yet what had she become? No wonder that with such a terrible thought haunting him, Hamlet forgot to carry out the command which his father's spirit had enjoined. When he escaped from this mental torture, another difficulty stared him in the face; he knew his weakness, no one better; could he pursue the sweet course of love and obey the Ghost as well? Could he ask Ophelia to link herself with a life so insecure, with a heart and mind so preoccupied, with a nature crushed under the weight of such a terrible responsibility? He struggled, and not unsuccessfully, against those hideous forebodings as to what Ophelia might become; he flung away all suspicion of her perfect purity; but one of the two must be given up, his love or his task of vengeance. While the struggle is going on within him, while his heart-strings are snapping asunder, pale and trembling beneath the tempest of emotion, he bursts into the chamber of his love, like the apparition of some terrible transformation of himself; he holds her by the wrist; he gazes into her eyes, as though he would read the very depth of her nature, as if he would know the full beauty of that heart which he is giving up for ever; he cannot trust himself to speak; his frame is convulsed with a sigh so piteous and profound that it seemed to shatter his very body, a sigh which was the cry of a breaking heart; without removing his gaze from her, whom he was never to look on again with the eyes of love, he vanishes from the room, unable to utter the awful sentence of death to his love which his heart had pronounced.

    I must here allude to a question which it would be more pleasant to pass over altogether, were such a course not capable of misconstruction; some people have held, and others hold still, the monstrous opinion that Hamlet was guilty of the ruin of Ophelia. This accusation, which betrays ignorance of this play itself, and an utter inability to comprehend Shakespeare's mode of working, is easily refuted. It rests upon the verses of some idle song, caught up, probably, from her nurse, which Ophelia innocently sings in her madness. Nobody can examine the scenes between Polonius and Ophelia, Laertes and his sister, or that between her and Hamlet, without seeing at once that this accusation is utterly groundless. Shakespeare would not have wantonly introduced such a foul stain upon

Hamlet's character without using it for some dramatic purpose. The suggestion of vice is a delicacy of modern date. Hamlet's love for Ophelia was pure and honourable; and any one who thinks the contrary is not to be envied. For my own part, whatever objection may be taken to the song alluded to, I cannot but think that it is one of Shakespeare's most delicate touches in the sweetly innocent character of Ophelia, that when her unhappy mind is so distraught with grief for her father, and her reason is overthrown, she should repeat, with such simple child-like ignorance of their meaning, the verses which probably she had never heard since she was being dandled on her nurse's knee, and which, in her right senses, she might never have remembered.

As I am now treating of the relations between Hamlet and Ophelia, it would be better to go at once to that scene at the beginning of the third act, which has caused so many difficulties both to actors and critics. It is very necessary for the right understanding of this scene that we should carefully observe what has gone before. Polonius, having come to the conclusion from what Ophelia has told him, and from letters of Hamlet's to her which he has found, that the cause of Hamlet's madness is simply love for his daughter, proposes that Ophelia should place herself in the gallery, or lobby, in which Hamlet is accustomed to walk for hours together; and that the King and he should conceal themselves behind the arras and watch the result; 'if', Polonius says, 'he love her not',

> And be not from his reason fall'n thereon,
> Let me be no assistant for a state,
> But keep a farm and carters.
>
> (II, ii, 167–9)

This proposal is carried out; Ophelia is given a book and told to read it—

> That show of such an exercise may colour
> Your loneliness.
>
> (III, i, 47–8)

In fact she is made a party, a direct and conscious party to the trap set for her lover.

Hamlet enters, debating with himself the question of suicide in that well-known soliloquy, 'To be or not to be', etc., at the end of which he turns and sees Ophelia seemingly in prayer. I think it extremely probable that Ophelia is intended really to be praying for the unhappy prince, whose agitation during the soliloquy she cannot fail to have observed. Hamlet accosts her with serious but kindly courtesy—

> Nymph, in thy orisons
> Be all my sins remember'd.

Ophelia answers—

> Good, my lord,
> How does your honour for this many a day?

Except in that awful interview which she has described to Polonius, during which, as you remember, Hamlet never spoke, Ophelia has not seen him for some time. Hamlet answers as if wishing to check any inquiry into the cause of his apparent illness, 'I humbly thank you: well'.

> Ophelia. My lord, I have remembrances of yours,
> That I have longed long to re-deliver;
> I pray you, now receive them.

She had probably been instructed by her father to return Hamlet's presents. Hamlet determined to avoid the discussion of a very painful question, perhaps also to ignore the fearful state of agitation in which he had been when he last saw Ophelia, and shrinking from definitely breaking off all affectionate relations between them, denies having given these gifts to Ophelia—

> No, not I;
> I never gave you aught.
> Ophelia. My honour'd lord, you know right well you did;
> And with them words of so sweet breath composed;
> As made the things more rich: their perfume lost,
> Take these again; for to the noble mind
> Rich gifts wax poor when givers prove unkind.
> There, my lord.

At this point, just as Ophelia is going to force back on Hamlet the sweet remembrances of his love, the fussy old Polonius, who has been fidgeting behind the arras, anxious to see the result of his most notable advice, pops his head out, and in so doing drops his chamberlain's staff: Hamlet hears the noise, and instantly suspects the truth, that he is being made the object of an artfully devised scheme to entrap him into some confession of his secret. His suspicions had been already aroused by the manifest constraint of Ophelia's manner; at the same time his heart had been deeply touched at the equally manifest emotion under which she laboured. True, she was acting a part; but she was speaking from her own heart when she alluded to the sweet words of love which accompanied Hamlet's presents, when she recalled the happy hours she had spent with him before this mysterious shadow had fallen on his life. We may imagine that, but for his worst suspicions being aroused by the evidence that he was being watched, he would have spoken to Ophelia with the greatest affection; now, however, it is with a rude revulsion of feeling that he treats her as a party to, indeed as the chief agent of, the deception contrived against him: all that follows is couched in half enigmatical satire, the sting of which is fully to be comprehended only by the guilty Claudius. Hamlet, who guesses he is one of the parties concealed, speaks at the King, as it were, the threats he dare not utter to his face: at the same time there is a wild incoherence about Hamlet's words which can only serve to bewilder the hearers as to the real cause of his condition.

After warning Ophelia against believing any man, thereby conveying a delicate rebuke of her deceitfulness, Hamlet is about to leave her with the words—

>Go thy ways to a nunnery.

He is crossing the stage, when his eye falls on that part of the arras whence the noise had proceeded, and he is instantly struck by some such thoughts as these:—'Have I been right in suspecting this innocent maiden of being, knowingly, a party to such a contemptible trick? Can she, whose pure and open nature I so loved, be capable of such paltry disingenuous conduct? No! before I condemn her I will put her to the plain proof.'

He turns round and holds out his hands towards her; she, forgetting her part, thinking, poor girl, he is going to take her to his breast and forgive her, flies across to him; he checks her with his outstretched hand, and holding hers, he looks straight into her eyes, as only one who loves her has a right to look into a maiden's eyes, and he solemnly asks her the question, 'Where is your father?' What can she answer? Once committed to deceit there is no escape from it. She would fain tell the truth, but she dares not; she thinks it would be disobedience to her father, and unkindness to her poor distracted lover, were she to do so. With downcast eyes and blushing cheek, with hands relaxing their grasp, escaping from the touch of him she loves so well, she falters out her first lie, 'At home, my lord'. There is a little pause; then with a sigh, as his last hope in the truthfulness of one woman at least dies in him, he drops her hand, saying with solemn sternness—

> Let the doors be shut upon him, that he may play the fool nowhere but in's own house. Farewell.

Ophelia, who sees in this strange answer nothing but the sign of a noble mind o'erthrown, utters the simple prayer—

> O, help him, you sweet heavens!

But now indignation has taken the place of sorrow with Hamlet, and he bursts into a bitter denunciation of the follies and petty deceits of women; lashing those very faults from which Ophelia seemed, and was indeed, freest; so that she can feel no pain and anger on her own account, all that she can feel is the agony of grief at seeing her sweetest hope for ever ended, her worst fears too fully confirmed.

Whether the view of this scene which I have ventured to put forward is, or is not, the correct one, it is at any rate a more consistent one than that which would see in these speeches of Hamlet nothing but brutal outrages on the feelings of her whom, as he afterwards tells us, 'he loved', so that

> —forty thousand brothers
> Could not, with all their quantity of love,
> Make up my sum.
>
> (V, i, 266–8)

[In the course of this passage on Ophelia's relationship with Hamlet Marshall points to an appendix (D) that he has added 'On the Character of Ophelia', in which he discusses Goethe's and Gervinus's views on her character in greater detail, and further defends her purity. He again excuses the bawdy song 'By Gis, and by Saint Charity' by elaborating on Jameson's view—unacknowledged—that Ophelia is remembering a song sung to her in her infancy by a nurse. Here is Marshall's discussion of Hamlet's conversation with Ophelia as they watch the play to illustrate Marshall's defence of her character]:

Hamlet's nerves are strung to the highest pitch, and the eccentricities in which he indulges are but the safety-valves for an excitement which, if totally suppressed, might overpower his senses. His resentment against Ophelia for what he considers her duplicity towards him, which is still working in his mind, coupled with the mischievous pleasure he takes in misleading his uncle, induces him to take his place at her feet. From the first entry of the King, Queen, Polonius, Ophelia and the court, Hamlet has appeared to be in the highest spirits; when he answers to his mother's invitation to sit by her side—

> No, good mother, here's metal more attractive—

at the same time approaching Ophelia with a gay air, it is natural that she should be alarmed at the change which has come over him since she last saw him. He commences in a tone of cruel banter—

> Lady, shall I lie in your lap?

Her answer is in a tone of outraged modesty, but simple as a maiden's should be. He continues in a manner which must have increased her alarm. The belief that he is mad enables her to suppress her indignation; the only resemblance of a reproach that escapes her lips is contained in that pathetic remonstrance—

> You are merry, my lord.

The pleasure of having him near her overcomes her timidity, and she tries to seem at her ease with him. She asks him to explain the dumb show which precedes the play, but Hamlet's answer is so brutally filthy that even his assumed madness can be no excuse for such an outrage on decency. (I should like to be able to prove that some of the most offensive lines were inserted by the players to suit the depraved taste of their audience, but I am afraid that they must be acknowledged to have been permitted, if not approved, by Shakespeare, in common with some equally repulsive passages in other plays. I have no wish to see Shakespeare universally Bowdlerised, but I think the text as published in the Clarendon Press Series, might be generally adopted for the purposes of the library . . . [6]) Ophelia's gentle nature is roused to some show of resentment; for a moment she turns away from him with the simple rebuke—

> You are naught, you are naught: I'll mark the play.

But he does not leave her long to herself:

> Hamlet. Is this a prologue, or a posy of a ring?
> Ophelia.'Tis brief, my lord.
> Hamlet. As woman's love.

This last sentence is spoken looking at the Queen, though undoubtedly Hamlet means it as a satire on the fickleness which he thinks Ophelia has shown towards him. His next observation, after the speech of the Player Queen, in which she vows fidelity to her husband's memory, ought to be addressed to Ophelia . . . but should be spoken aloud at the Queen, on whom, as well as on Claudius, Hamlet's eyes are riveted.

In spite of the cruel insults he has addressed to her, which she excuses to herself on the ground of his distraction, Ophelia cannot refrain from the attempt to win one look of love or one tender word from Hamlet. But he is merciless; to her playful remark—

> You are as good as a chorus, my lord-

he answers only with a morose sarcasm-

> I could interpret between you and your love, if I could see the puppets dallying.

---

6   Passage in brackets presented as author's note.

She cannot conceal her bitter pain; at any other time he must have felt stung by her reproach—

> You are keen, my lord, you are keen.

But his intense excitement makes him like one under a demoniacal possession; his only answer is again a brutal insult: the last words she speaks are these somewhat enigmatical ones—

> Ophelia. Still better, and worse.
> Hamlet. So you must take your husbands.

Thus do these two, who once had been so happy in their mutual loves, virtually take leave of one another: he who was once so gentle and so affectionate to her, so full of tender and refined homage to her beauty and to her virtues, upon the 'honey of whose music vows' her soul had rapturously fed—he will never more speak one word to her—no, not to tell her how harshly he had misjudged her, and to ask her forgiveness. She will hear nothing more of him until she is told that her father died by his hand, and that he is sent away, half in pity, half in punishment, to a distant land; and he, what would he not give to recall these cruel taunts, these ferocious insults, which, in his half-assumed, half-real madness, he has now uttered, when he sees the body of his beloved being lowered into a dishonoured grave?

There is a terrible pathos in this love story of Hamlet and Ophelia, though Shakespeare has only permitted us to snatch a hasty glance at it.

Every word uttered by Ophelia in this scene seems to strengthen the view of her character which I have taken, and to render impossible, except in distorted natures, the slightest suspicion of her purity. Every impure allusion, every foul innuendo, which is aimed at her in this scene, seems to drop harmless from the armour of her spotless chastity. Compare for a moment the rich voluptuousness of Juliet, the reckless banter of Beatrice, the mischievous *double entendres* of Portia, with the crystal simplicity of Ophelia's language, and one cannot fail to see which is the purest creation.

Part II. [Marshall returns to Act II, scene ii to discuss the roles of Rosencrantz and Guildenstern and Hamlet's soliloquies 'O, what a rogue and peasant slave am I' and in the following scene, 'To be or not to be'.] ... There are two things I wish particularly to notice in this scene; one is that Hamlet makes a distinct allusion to the contempt with which he is treated at Court; when both his young friends offer to wait upon him, he replies, 'I will not sort you with the rest of my servants; for, to speak to you like an honest man, I am most dreadfully attended'. (II, ii, 269–71). Another point is, that during the whole of his conversation with them Hamlet does not assume the madman; all that he says is full of humour, of satire, and notably in one instance, the speech in which he accounts for his melancholy, it is full of poetry. He hints to them over and over again that the real cause of his estrangement from all the gaieties of the Court is to be found in the conduct of the King and Queen, but he never gets from them the slightest expression of sympathy; they are consistent courtiers, and the rising sun of to-day blinds them to the glories of the setting one of yesterday. In the last playful speech he addresses to them, before the re-entering of Polonius, he seems to warn them against lending themselves to any system of espionage on the part of the King and Queen:-

> my uncle-father and aunt-mother are deceived.

With an assumption of amiable imbecility, they answer—

> In what, my dear lord?

Hamlet answers—

> I am but mad north-north-west: when the wind is southerly I know a hawk from a handsaw.

Had they taken this kind hint, it would have been better for them.

[Hamlet decides to make use of the visiting actors.] ... suddenly, but clearly, he sees the practical use to which the force of mimic passion may be turned; he sees a chance of testing by natural means the truth of that supernatural visitation which he has suffered. It is not too much to say that, without knowing it, he snatches at another chance of delaying the stern action from which his nature has shrunk; for while he seemed, most plausibly to himself, to be advancing in the task of vengeance which had been set him, he was really delaying to strike that blow which must, in the natural course of things, become more difficult to strike every day; but had Hamlet acted with the decision of a Malone, or the relentless common sense of a Steevens[7], the world would have lost three acts, at least, of this most glorious play; and I am afraid the approbation of these terrible judges, however gratifying to the *manes* of the poet, would scarcely have consoled the world at large for that loss.

The temporary distrust, which Hamlet expresses with regard to the genuineness of the apparition that he has seen, I look upon as of little importance, except as a symptom of that intermittent scepticism which often infects dispositions similar to that of Hamlet. The personality of the devil was a doctrine more generally accepted in Shakespeare's time than it is now. This distrust is not deep-seated in Hamlet's mind; he is but unconsciously employing arguments with himself, apparently suggested by prudence, but, in reality, springing from the inherent weakness of his character, which made him so ready to feel but so unready to act
. . . [Marshall now offers further remarks on the soliloquy 'To be or not to be'.]

Although Shakespeare has not hampered himself by any over-delicate dread of anachronisms, it would have been too glaringly out of place to have represented Hamlet as restrained from suicide by any deep religious feeling. The uncertainty which the narrowest-minded infidel must feel as to the existence of a future state often serves, in the place of a nobler motive, to restrain him from the crime of taking his own life. Sensitive natures like Hamlet's are most exposed to this horrid temptation; but those very natures should be most open to the highest influences of religion, without which nothing, but what I may call an intelligent fear, could keep them, in many cases, from putting an end to that life the troubles and sorrows of which they cannot but feel more keenly than others. But we must not forget that in the case of Hamlet it is no guilty weakness on his own part, no contemptible abandonment to passion, no degraded indulgence of his appetites, that has brought him to feel that strange longing, which many of us at some time may have felt, to 'slit the thin-spun thread of life' and so end all our troubles, at least in this world. It

---

7   For an account of these two eighteenth-century Shakespearean scholars see *CRH*, i.

is in his case an overwhelming sense of the fearful task imposed upon him, of the terribly conflicting affections which agitated him, of the seeming impossibility of revenging his father without cruelty to his mother; it is a noble despair at the apparent triumph of evil over good, not in his own nature but in the world around him; a despair which might well crush the strongest of us, did not faith in a God, not only all-powerful and all-wise, but all-loving, sustain us.

The result of the interview between Hamlet and Ophelia on the King is remarkable; his dread of Hamlet, which had been increasing ever since the night of the ghost's appearance, now suggests to him that he must at any cost rid himself of his nephew's presence.

> He shall with speed to England.

The first hint of that treacherous design which afterwards, as we know, he attempted to carry out with such signal failure. Polonius pleads for one more experiment:—

> Polonius. Let his queen mother all alone entreat him
> To show his grief: let her be round with him;
> And I'll be placed, so please you, in the ear
> Of all their conference. If she find him not,
> To England send him, or confine him where
> Your wisdom best shall think.
> King. It shall be so:
> Madness in great ones must not unwatch'd go.
>   (III, i, 185–91)

One of the most distinctive features of this play is the infinite variety of it; the way in which the sombreness and pathos of tragedy are relieved by scenes not of vulgar farce or forced humour, but by frequent flashes of high comedy, or, as in the case of the gravedigger scene, natural humour. Indeed, it may be said of all Shakespeare's great tragedies, with the sole exception of *Macbeth*—in which the incidents are so many and the interest so intense, that no such relief is wanted—that he is always careful not to be monotonously gloomy, but to be true to nature, even in this point as in all others; for in life we rarely find but that the greatest calamity, or the heaviest sorrow, is relieved either by the presence of some element of beauty, or by a gleam of brightness, which extorts our admiration, or forces from us a smile, even at the supremest moment of fear or grief. This it is which more than anything else distinguishes Shakespeare from all his contemporaries or successors in tragic poetry: the oppressive gloom which crushes us in Ford, Marlowe, or Cyril Tourneur—to mention three of his most formidable rivals—or the tearful tediousness of Otway, Rowe, and their many imitators, never affects us when reading the tragedies of Shakespeare. In accordance with this principle, before we approach the more tragic incidents of this play, Shakespeare affords us a pleasant resting place in the short scene between Hamlet and the players, in which he lays down in most admirable precepts and most perfect language the true principles of acting. This scene bears little upon the character of Hamlet except as it shows the universality of his talents and the liberality of his mind, and helps establish his claim to be called in the beautiful language of Ophelia,'the glass of fashion and the mould of form'.

Polonius, with Rosencrantz and Guildenstern, now enter to announce the consent of the King to be present at the play. Hamlet despatches them all three to hasten the players, in order that he may take Horatio into his confidence more thoroughly, and benefit by his aid in the experiment upon the King's conscience which he is now about to try. In this speech to Horatio Shakespeare has almost exceeded himself; a more beautiful epitome of the character of a true friend does not exist, nor a better guide for those who wish to find this treasure; we have in this speech further evidence of the singular clearness of Hamlet's judgment, and of the marvellous beauty of a character, the strength of whose intellect stands out in bolder relief from the very fact that in action he is so weak and undecided. We have here one note for the actor which he should heed well in the following scene—

> For I mine eyes will rivet to his face.

Were the force of this line more heeded by the representatives of Hamlet on the stage, we should not be tormented by those exhibitions of feline agility with which they seem to think it incumbent to favour us in the celebrated play scene.

King and Court have now arrived. It must be acknowledged that Claudius' overtures to his nephew do not meet with much encouragement. Hamlet replies to the courteous inquiry—

> King. How fares our cousin Hamlet?
> Hamlet. Excellent, i'faith; of the chameleon's dish: I eat the air, promise crammed.
> (III, ii, 89–91)

By which words he means to refer to the fact that his uncle has promised that he should succeed to the throne; a very generous promise, which restored to him his right when the usurper could no longer enjoy it. The demeanour and language of Hamlet to Ophelia in this scene are both repulsive: it is not enough to blame the coarseness of the times for such blemishes in the works of one who, in general, was pure-minded. I think some explanation of Hamlet's revolting language may be found, if we presume that my interpretation of the former scene (Act III, sc. i) was a correct one. Hamlet had ceased to respect Ophelia after detecting her in a deliberate lie; he may exaggerate the disrespect which mortification induced him to show towards her, for the purpose of impressing the King and Queen, and still more the courtiers, with the idea that he was scarcely responsible for his actions; at any rate this short dialogue serves to enhance the sweet purity and innocence of Ophelia's character; and as all the offensive portion of it can be omitted from representation without any injury to the interest of the play, we need not dwell any further upon it.

The course of the play represented before the Court is interrupted by a few short and striking sentences between Hamlet and the King and Queen. The King begins to suspect the gist of the play.

> Is there no offence in't?

he asks of Hamlet, to which he answers—

> No, no, they do but jest, poison in jest.

By a great effort of self-restraint Hamlet preserves the same quiet tone of bitter irony throughout, while his eyes cannot be diverted, even by the beautiful face of Ophelia, from their fixed watchfulness of the King. The poisoner in the play represented is the nephew of the king; this, I think, is no accident; by making the relation the same as between himself and Claudius, Hamlet adds one more to the many strokes of irony directed against his uncle. While the mimic poisoner is in the very act of pouring the poison into the sleeping king's ear on the stage, Hamlet half rises from his recumbent attitude and thus explains the incident:

> He poisons him i' the garden for his estate. His name's
> Gonzago; the story is extant, and written in very choice
> Italian: you shall see anon how the murderer gets the love of Gonzago's wife.
> (III, ii, 249–52)

At this point most of the actors, that I have seen in the part of Hamlet, are wont to execute what I must venture to call the most vulgar piece of melodramatic absurdity which can be conceived. They crawl on their hands and knees from the feet of Ophelia to the King, whilst the poisoner is speaking his short speech on the stage; they then scream, or rant, in the King's ear these words, in such a manner as to justify any respectable and sane member of the Court of Denmark in conducting Hamlet to the nearest dungeon. Tradition, deriving itself from Edmund Kean, is said to justify this astonishing piece of business (technically so called); but not every actor, much less every man, is an Edmund Kean, and what may have appeared natural and effective in him, certainly appears quite the contrary in his imitators. To me it seems an error from the actor's point of view, for surely it would be much more effective, as well as natural, that Hamlet should not abandon himself to the intensity of his excitement until he is alone with Horatio, which he is a few moments afterwards, when he bursts into that wild song of triumph—

> Why, let the stricken deer go weep,
> The hart ungalled play;
> For some must watch, while some must sleep:
> Thus runs the world away.[8]

8   It is a great pity that here, as at the end of the Act I, no representative of Hamlet on the stage ventures to speak the words as they are set down; some omit one portion, some another, while Signor Salvini gets rid of the difficulty by omitting all, and simply falling on Horatio's neck. [Mr. Irving speaks only the lines beginning 'For thou dost know, O Damon dear,' etc., giving a new force to the word 'pajock' or 'peacock,' which Hamlet substitutes for the manifest rhyme 'ass' by looking at

Any licence may be allowed to the actor now; exulting in the success of his scheme, Hamlet gives way to an excitement almost hysterical. His satirical humour shows itself in the midst of this exultation, in fact he uses it here, as in many other instances, partly as a veil to conceal the depth of his feelings; he calls for music because the tension of his nerves is becoming too great to bear; but before the recorders, or small flutes, can be brought, Rosencrantz and Guildenstern re-enter, and Hamlet speedily regains his self-possession in the presence of the two courtiers, whose demeanour is so much changed as to verge almost on insolence. The dignified sarcasm which Hamlet displays in this scene shows that, when he chose, his self-command was as complete as that of the sanest person; although he tells them that his wit is diseased, Rosencrantz and Guildenstern must have felt that the rebuke the prince administers to their disrespectful familiarity proves the disease had not affected its vigour. Plausible as are their professions of love, Hamlet's keen insight into character, a quality which we often find coupled with the eccentricity of intellectual natures, at once divines that they are in reality playing him false. The entry of Polonius gives him an opportunity of indulging in mischievous banter of the unfortunate Lord Chamberlain; his expression—

> They fool me to the top of my bent,

shows how he enjoys the joke. Directly he is alone, he is again serious, proving that, amidst all the wild humour in which he indulges his overburdened mind, he never entirely forgets that great purpose which he has in view; he braces up his nerves for the interview with his mother, and once more he seems on the point of that decisive action which would fulfil the solemn duty that his father's spirit has imposed on him.

We come now to a scene rarely, if ever, represented on the stage, but which forms a foundation for the most plausible attacks that have been

---

the fan of peacock's feathers which he had borrowed from Ophelia, and held in his hand during the representation of the play, as if that had suggested to him the substitution.] The subtlety with which Shakespeare has here portrayed the rapid transitions which characterize nervous excitement in a nature like that of Hamlet's is much obscured and weakened by any omission. From Appendix G, the passage in brackets as footnote.

made on the character of Hamlet. The King informs Rosencrantz and Guildenstern that they must prepare for immediate departure to England in company with Hamlet ... When the King is by himself, he gives expression to that remorse which was secretly preying on his heart. The distinction between repentance and remorse is most clearly and beautifully drawn. [Marshall now quotes from Claudius's confessional soliloquy, III, iii, 51–72.]

While he is kneeling in the agony of prayer which is stifled by the consciousness of its insincerity, Hamlet enters unseen by the King; he then speaks the lines which certainly betray a spirit of diabolical revenge. No doubt commentators have not ransacked contemporary literature of that day in vain for instances of similar ferocity; the desire had been expressed by more than one vindictive nature to kill the soul as well as the body. I need not point out to you how impotent such malice is; man may slay his fellow-man unprepared, or even, as in some instances quoted, with a blasphemous denial of God on his lips, extorted from him through fear of death; but the ultimate fate of the soul is in the hands of God alone. The very extravagance of the idea may have struck Shakespeare, and he may have purposely put these horrible words into Hamlet's mouth to show the excess of vindictiveness to which his thoughts would go, out of defiance, as it were, of the timid inertness of his action. Violence of language is not uncommonly found in highly sensitive natures; but very rarely in such natures, except in the moment of extreme passion, is it supplemented by violent deeds. Complete as his conviction of the King's guilt now must be, in face of the opportunity, in sight of the man himself tortured with the agonies of a guilty conscience, Hamlet shrinks from striking the fatal blow. He knows himself, that deliberate murder—murder committed, not in the heat and fury of passion, but with sufficient leisure to allow of reflection, though justified, ever so strongly, by what we may call the natural laws of vengeance—is an act of which he is incapable. The ghost's solemn exhortation to revenge may be ringing in his ears; in thought he is more than capable, in deed he is incapable of executing it; and so he indulges in this discussion with himself, in which, affecting a bloody-mindedness that he could not really feel, he excuses himself for once more putting off the time of action. The reason which he alleges at the end of his speech probably weighed more strongly with him than he was inclined to allow; he had yet to try and wake his mother's conscience; that was a task much more congenial to his nature, much more within his capacity. I do not go so far as to deny that this speech of Hamlet's is revolting to our feelings; it savours of an age when bloodshed and violence were unhappily familiar; it is consistent with the state of rude and imperfect civilisation which existed in the time of which this play treats; it must be admitted as one of the blemishes inseparable from all human work; but I do venture to assert that Shakespeare did not intend us to believe that these horrid sentiments were entertained with any seriousness by the mind of Hamlet.[9]

We come now to the scene known as the 'closet scene', which concludes the third act, and is, perhaps, for more reasons than one, the most important in the play. The death of Polonius at the hands of Hamlet leads not only to the madness and suicide of Ophelia, but to the final catastrophe of the tragedy. There are three questions involved in this scene which have occasioned much controversy—first, the conduct of Hamlet to his mother; secondly, the amount of guilt with which he is chargeable for the accidental murder of Polonius; and thirdly, how far the Queen was accessory to the murder of her first husband. [Detailed analysis of III, iv omitted.] As regards the first of the three questions involved in this scene, that of Hamlet's conduct to his mother, however lacking in respect it may be, we must remember both the revolting nature of her crime and the utter want of contrition which, hitherto, she had displayed. Hamlet had, until now, refrained from reproaching her; though he was certainly justified in doing so, both in respect of the ordinary duty of a son to a father—a duty which renders any outrage on the father's honour equally an outrage on that of the son—and in respect of the solemn charge imposed upon him by the supernatural visitation which he had received. It is probable, though he does not mention such intention, that Hamlet contemplated producing a strong effect upon his mother's feelings in the play-scene; and when he found that she had sent for him only to rebuke him for his conduct to his uncle, his indignation would very naturally be roused to such an extent as to overpower his courtesy. It is evident, both from the manner and the matter of his speech, that he considers himself,

---

9   In appendix H (noted at this point) Marshall makes a comparison between the F version of Hamlet's speech beginning 'Now might I do it pat' and that of Q1.

in thus vividly representing to Gertrude the nature of her guilt, to be fulfilling a mission with which he had been charged, indirectly, by the Deity. He has previously, in the scene with Ophelia, assumed the same lofty position, in those words—

> I say we will have no more marriages: those that are married already, all but one, shall live; the rest shall keep as they are.
>
> (III, i, 150–2)

This is the language of one who believes himself charged with a power and authority greater than those of an ordinary mortal. But we have a stronger proof of this in the words which he uses in expressing his repentance for the death of Polonius—

> For this same lord (*pointing to Polonius*)
> I do repent: but heaven hath pleased it so,
> To punish me with this, and this with me,
> That I must be their scourge and minister.
>
> (III, iv, 156–9)

It accords with the earnest character of Hamlet, no less than with the nature of such a sacred mission as he claims, to show no scruple or delicacy in laying bare the hideousness of the double crime committed against his father, to one part of which his mother was more than accessory. The utter indifference to all sense of right and wrong exhibited by those who surround Claudius and his Queen; the despicable servility with which they acquiesced in his reaping the fruits of his brother's sudden death—granting they did not suspect him of having caused it—and in her shameless disregard of what, even in that time of imperfect civilisation, may be called the ordinary decencies of conduct, must have exasperated so loving and loyal a son as Hamlet, even had he been of a disposition less sensitive. When we consider, then, the circumstances of the case, and the character of Hamlet, we cannot call his conduct unnatural, because, in his endeavours to wake his mother's torpid conscience to a sense of her guilt, he uses language at once so plain and so vehement that it left no room for prevarication, or affected misunderstanding. There is nothing selfish, or paltry, in Hamlet's indignation; he barely alludes to the usurpation of which he has been the victim; it is the outrage on his father's love and honour that he resents so fiercely, the shameless impenitence of his mother he rebukes so sternly.

With regard to the second question, the amount of guilt incurred by Hamlet through killing Polonius in mistake for the King, there can be no doubt that the mistake was a genuine one; the rash haste, displayed by Hamlet, was the result of that feverish desire for vengeance which was intensified by the consciousness of his inability to execute such vengeance deliberately; therefore, as I have before implied, he snatches at the opportunity, which seems to offer itself, of killing Claudius on the impulse of the moment, and, as it were, in the dark. Nor is the fate of Polonius so undeserved as at first sight it appears; we well might wonder—did not the history of every age and every nation multiply instance upon instance of such selfish cowardice—we well might pronounce incredible and impossible the utter indifference shown by Polonius and the whole court to the crimes of Claudius. We must remember that his usurpation was successful; having stolen the crown, he contrived to keep it, and so long as he kept it, and no longer, would his incestuous marriage, his treachery to his brother, his injustice to his nephew, be alike endorsed and encouraged by those who could profit by his favour, or suffer from his anger. Fidelity to our allegiance is only a virtue as long as he who claims such allegiance is glorified by the sun of prosperity; let rebellion grow to revolution and be crowned by success, and the ruler, before whom all bowed the knee with ready subservience, becomes the object of our derision, if not of our violence; then the adherence to him, or to his descendants, which once was loyalty, deserving of the highest rewards that the State could bestow, becomes the plotting, or the treason which, in the eyes of the successful rebels now exalted into high-minded patriots, merits only the prison or the halter.

Thirdly, as to the question of Gertrude's connivance at, or complicity in, the murder of her first husband, I think we may safely come to the conclusion that she can be charged with neither. Certainly her language in this scene, unless we suppose her to be guilty of almost superhuman hypocrisy, tends most decidedly to acquit her of such a charge, but we have more direct evidence on this point in the 14th scene of the Quarto (1603), no vestige of which is found in the later editions; the Queen, speaking of the King to Horatio, says,

> Then I perceive there's treason in his lookes
> That seem'd to sugar o're his villanie:
> But I will soothe and please him for a time,
> For murderous mindes are always jealous,

and still more strongly in this very scene in the same edition, when the Queen speaks thus, after the disappearance of the ghost,

> But as I have a soule, I sweare by heaven,
> I never knew of this most horride murder.

A little further, in answer to Hamlet's appeal,

> And mother, but assist mee in revenge,
> And in his death your infamy shall die,

The Queen answers—

> Hamlet, I vow by that maiesty,
> That knowes our thoughts, and lookes into our hearts,
> I will conceale, consent, and doe my best,
> What stratagem soe're thou shalt devise.

From these passages, supported as they are by the prose history of Hamlet on which the play was founded, and never contradicted by any passages in the play as afterwards revised by Shakespeare himself, no less than from the character of the Queen as it is developed in the following scenes, we may confidently acquit her alike of guilty knowledge or of wilful ignorance of the vile crime committed by Claudius against his brother's life, though in that against his honour she was the weak and shameless accomplice.

The latter portion of this scene, which is never represented on the stage, is very much expanded from its original form in the Quarto of 1603; I give in the Appendix [Appendix L], side by side, the two versions of this scene from the point of the ghost's entrance, in order that comparison between them may be easier. The passage relating to the body of Polonius—

> This man shall set me packing:

> I'll lug the guts into the neighbour room.
> Mother, good night. Indeed this counsellor
> Is now most still, most secret and most grave,
> Who was in life a foolish prating knave.
> Come, sir, to draw toward an end with you—
>
> (III, iv, 185–90)

has been much censured for its coarseness, and even for the affected brutality with which Hamlet speaks of the corpse of him for whose death he has, a short time before, expressed what seemed to be genuine contrition. I confess I do not understand why Shakespeare thought it necessary to add anything here to what he had originally written[10]; but we must remember, as has been pointed out by the commentators, that the word 'guts' was not in Shakespeare's time the abominable vulgarism that it is now; and that the rude stage appointments, and limited numbers of the company, necessitated the removal of the body by one of the characters on the stage . . .

There are two points of much greater importance which must be noticed: the first is the promise given by the Queen, which I have already quoted [III, iv, 181–3], that she would not betray Hamlet's secret to the King, a promise which she most faithfully kept. The second point is the remarkable language in which Hamlet speaks of his coming journey to England.

> Hamlet. I must to England; you know that?
> Queen. Alack,
>   I had forgot: 'tis so concluded on.
> Hamlet. There's letters seal'd: and my two schoolfellows,
>   Whom I will trust as I will adders fang'd,
>   They bear the mandate; they must sweep my way,
>   And marshal me to knavery. Let it work;
>   For 'tis the sport to have the enginer
>   Hoist with his own petar: and't shall go hard
>   But I will delve one yard below their mines,
>   And blow them at the moon.
>
> (Q2 III, iv, 184–93, Additional passage H)

10   The assumption here is that Q1 is Shakespeare's first draft of *Hamlet*.

It would certainly seem that Hamlet, suspecting that this mission to England concealed some treachery on the part of the King, had already determined to defeat that treachery by cunning; and to visit upon the heads of Rosencrantz and Guildenstern their complicity, conscious or unconscious, in the scheme. The words 'They bear the mandate', would seem to anticipate the discovery which Hamlet afterwards made regarding the nature of the commission with which they were charged; whether we are to take this as an oversight on Shakespeare's part, or whether we should understand Hamlet to be speaking of suspicion as if it were certainty, I cannot myself determine; nor do I find the slightest notice of this passage in any of the numerous commentaries which I have examined. The next words—

> they must sweep my way,
> And marshal me to knavery,

are difficult to interpret. They may mean that Hamlet was so certain that his suspicion of Rosencrantz and Guildenstern was well-founded, that he determined to be revenged upon them; and, by this act of severity, to strengthen his mind for the more important purpose he had in hand, namely the killing of the King. If he could conquer his weakness, and subdue his scruples of conscience sufficiently to work upon these two false-hearted courtiers a most signal act of vengeance; and granting that he should, before doing so, be able to assure himself that Claudius, in sending him to England, was sending him to a treacherous death; he might naturally hope, should he succeed in returning safe to Denmark, to find himself no longer hesitating for one moment to fulfil, to the uttermost point, the ghost's charge of vengeance.

The whole effect of this scene, apart from its intrinsic beauty of language and grandeur of conception, is to raise our interest to a much higher point; and I cannot agree with those who consider that at this point the play ought to have ended; however elaborate may be the episodes, which somewhat check the progress of the main action in the two last acts, our curiosity, as to what is to follow, is so skilfully whetted in this scene, that a more abrupt conclusion to the play would be as ineffective as it would be inartistic.

Part III. The fourth act opens with a short but significant scene: the persons present are the King, the Queen, Rosencrantz and Guildenstern. The Queen has evidently just returned from her interview with Hamlet. In fact, the action at this point in the play is continuous. The King speaks first:—

> King. There's matter in these sighs, these profound heaves:
> You must translate: 'tis fit we understand them.
> Where is your son?
> Queen. Bestow this place on us a little while.
> [*Exeunt* Rosencrantz and Guildenstern]

What the Queen has to reveal is for the King's ears alone; not even the subtle fidelity of the two courtiers entitles them to the privilege of being admitted into the royal confidence. When they are gone the Queen continues:-

> Ah, mine own lord, what have I seen to-night!
> King. What, Gertrude? How does Hamlet?
> Queen. Mad as the sea and wind, when both contend
> Which is the mightier: in his lawless fit,
> Behind the arras hearing something stir,
> Whips out his rapier, cries 'a rat, a rat!'
> And in this brainish apprehension kills
> The unseen good old man.

This speech is certainly, at first sight, a most puzzling one; we have just heard Gertrude give her son the most solemn assurance that she will not reveal to his uncle the fact that his madness is assumed; therefore we must understand that she is now deliberately deceiving Claudius, and affecting to believe in the reality of Hamlet's madness. Otherwise it would seem that the Queen had only pretended to believe her son was not mad, and that she was now giving his uncle fresh cause to put some restraint on him. The meaning of her conduct becomes much more intelligible on reference to the Quarto of 1603.

In that edition a subsequent scene between the Queen and Horatio, to which I have before alluded,[11] makes it clear that the author's intention

---

11   In appendix M. See above pp. 381–2.

was to represent the Queen now as helping Hamlet's counterplots against the treachery of Claudius. In order to do this, she could adopt no better device than to pretend a most thorough belief in the genuineness of her son's madness, knowing, as we have seen, from the latter part of the preceding act, she did, that Hamlet had determined to go to England agreeably to the advice, or rather the command, of Claudius.

As doubts and fears of discovery thicken around the guilty Claudius, his sententious bursts of plausible hypocrisy become more and more specious. He overflows with nice morality. It would seem as if, not content with treacherously robbing his brother of his crown, his Queen, and his life, he had also pilfered his philosophy. Listen to his exquisite and pathetic complaint:-

> Alas, how shall this bloody deed be answer'd!
> It will be laid to us, whose providence
> Should have kept short, restrain'd and out of haunt,
> This mad young man: but so much was our love,
> We would not understand what was most fit,
> But, like the owner of a foul disease,
> To keep it from divulging, let it feed
> Even on the pith of life.
>
> (IV, i, 15–22)

We almost feel inclined to bring out our handkerchiefs and weep for this poor injured uncle, whose impracticable nephew was always trying his angelic patience, till at last even its limit was reached, and it could endure no more. The first actor who has the courage to represent Claudius as the plausible smiling villain he really was, with features so expanded by conviviality that even the pangs he suffered from the ingratitude of his dear brother's son, whom he loved with such a disinterested love, 'could grave no wrinkle there'; who attempts to realise Shakespeare's conception, so exquisitely sarcastic, yet so true to nature, instead of representing the seducer of Gertrude as a beetle-browed villain, on whose brain and shoulders all the melodramas for the last fifty years seem to have left their fearful weight—the first actor who has the courage to effect this innovation will, I venture to predict, create at once a great sensation and a greater success.

The Queen's next speech contains a beautiful touch; in answer to the inquiry of Claudius, where Hamlet is gone, she says:-

> To draw apart the body he has kill'd:
> O'er whom his very madness, like some ore
> Among a mineral of metals base,
> Shows itself pure; he weeps for what is done.
> (IV, i, 23-6)

This shows that Hamlet's affectation of something which seemed like brutality, at the end of the last scene, was not long sustained; and that the suffering of his gentle nature, when the excitement under which he had committed this misdirected deed of violence had passed away, was greater than he cared to show before those whom he wished to believe in his assumption of insanity. Claudius has not yet exhausted his vein of moral indignation—

> this vile deed
> We must, with all our majesty and skill,
> Both countenance and excuse.

The two courtiers are summoned back—'Ho, Guildenstern!' It is a remarkable fact, that the inseparability of these two charming young men is so great, that it is only necessary to call one for both to appear...

It is useless to deny that in the play of *Hamlet* there is not one line that can be fairly said to prove that Rosencrantz and Guildenstern knew what were the contents of the packet committed to their care. Hamlet himself does not say they knew it; he expresses his distrust of them in the strongest language to his mother (see Act III, scene 4, lines 202 to 210 inclusive), but all that he says to Horatio now is—

> Why, man, they did make love to this employment;
>   ... their defeat
> Does by their own insinuation grow;
> (V, ii, 58-60)

and he seems to justify the terrible punishment he had inflicted on them by the very fact that their conduct throughout had been so underhand, and so cunningly false to him as their friend and prince, that although their treachery was undoubted, they had not been openly guilty of any design against his life. Hamlet declares—

> They are not near my conscience;

because he considered that by laying themselves out to serve the King's ends from the very first moment they arrived at Court; by their lack of frankness towards him, their old schoolfellow, at their first meeting; by their steadily blinding their eyes to the state of affairs at Court, and by denying to the griefs of their friend any sympathy; by readily accepting the theory of his madness without trying to account for his melancholy and retirement from Court in any other manner; by accepting an embassy which their own common sense must have told them could not mean any good to Hamlet, they had been so false to the duties of friendship and to the honour of gentlemen, that they deserved the death of traitors. It must be remembered that in Hamlet's character Shakespeare intended to protest against conventionality of all kinds. As to what the world might think right or wrong, Hamlet cared little: public opinion might justify the usurpation and marriage of Claudius; respectable members of the Court might overlook the indecent haste with which that marriage, really incestuous, was concluded; worthy men of the world might hold it honourable as well as expedient to do the bidding of such a man as Claudius, seeing he was a king; these two well-behaved young gentlemen, who passed for his two most intimate friends, might wonder why Hamlet was so odd and so out of spirits, might choose to forget how he loved his father, might assume that he acquiesced in the dishonour of his mother and in his own disinheritance; others might see nothing to blame in their conduct; but this brave, accomplished, eccentric prince was unlike others in this, that he judged conduct by a higher standard than that of courts, or of the fashionable world; he loved good for its own sake, not for what could be got by it; and in his indignation at the despicable weakness of these two courtiers, in the scorn which he felt for their time-serving cowardice, he allowed himself to be hurried into the commission of an act of cruelty, because, at the time, it wore an appearance of an exquisitely ironical punishment. It is possible that Shakespeare meant to mark, as strongly as he could, the hatred of a noble, honest nature for that complicity in crime which is the result of wilful blindness and self-interested negligence. The lesson is one which in this age we may all take to heart; and while we shrink from the cruelty which is inseparable from all acts of vengeance, while we are pained to see the treachery of Claudius retorted on his agents with such terrible exactness, we cannot help feeling how dangerous it is to side with evil against good, however high the wages; to shut our eyes to the truth, however unpleasant; to do wrong because the world cries out loudly it is right, and drowns the voice of conscience in the roar of its applause . . .

Part IV (Act IV, scene 5) The exclamation of Laertes when Ophelia quits the scene is, indeed, so full of simple pathos that our sympathies, chilled, if not alienated, by his bombastic language on his first entry, return to him—

> Do you see this, O God?

Nothing can be more touching than this cry of grief. Laertes is so genuinely affected by the sight of his sister's madness that his passion is moderated into a rational anger; he listens patiently enough to the King's promise to explain the circumstances of Polonius' death, and accepts his well-timed offer to submit the question of his share in it to the arbitration of Laertes' own friends. The language of Claudius is singularly judicious:

> Laertes, I must commune with your grief,
> Or you deny me right. Go but apart,
> Make choice of whom your wisest friends you will,
> And they shall hear and judge 'twixt you and me:
> If by direct or by collateral hand
> They find us touch'd, we will our kingdom give,
> Our crown, our life, and all that we call ours,
> To you in satisfaction; but if not,
> Be you content to lend your patience to us,
> And we shall jointly labour with your soul
> To give it due content.
> (IV, v, 200–10)

Laertes could not but be impressed by such well-assumed generosity; his answer is just and temperate—

> Let this be so;
> His means of death, his obscure funeral,
> No trophy, sword, nor hatchment o'er his bones,
> No noble rite nor formal ostentation,
> Cry to be heard, as 'twere from heaven to earth,
> That I must call't in question.

The omission of all the proper ceremonies, and of the honours usually paid to the noble dead, evidently had much to do with the violent indignation of Laertes. His pride and the honour of his family were touched. This speech is one of the additions in 'the true and perfect coppie' of 1604; in the earlier edition Laertes' speech is very different—

> You have prevail'd my Lord, a while I'le strive,
> To bury griefe within a tombe of wrath,
> Which once unhearsed, then the world shall heare
> Laertes had a father he held deere.

The whole scene between Claudius and Laertes has been much elaborated from the original bald sketch found in the first quarto. Shakespeare seems to have spent great care on the character of the latter; and the mention of the 'obscure funerals' etc., is evidently meant to impress on our minds how much the 'honour' of Laertes was of that conventional and fashionable type, which suffers more from the neglect of that ceremony demanded by etiquette than from the commission of a dishonourable action—provided it is not likely to be found out.

While Claudius is relating to Laertes the way in which Polonius met his death, the stage is occupied by a scene (Act IV, scene vi) replacing that one in the earlier play, between Horatio and the Queen, which I have transcribed in the appendix[12]. Horatio is visited by some sailors, who bring him letters from Hamlet, announcing his capture by the pirates, etc. There are two or three points to notice in this scene. Horatio says:-

> I do not know from what part of the world
> I should be greeted, if not from Lord Hamlet.
>
> (IV, vi, 4–5)

---

12 See Appendix M (author's footnote).

This passage seems to imply, what the rest of the play confirms, that Horatio's was a singularly lonely position. Who or what he was we can only conjecture: all we know is that he was a fellow-student of Hamlet's, but of what rank in life we are not told. His fortune, we know from Hamlet's own words, was very small—

> For what advancement may I hope from thee,
> That no revenue hast but thy good spirits,
> To feed and clothe thee?
>
> (III, ii, 55–7)

and it would seem that he was equally poor in friends, since he knew of no one who was likely to send any letter to him but Hamlet. This very loneliness was probably one of the causes which first drew the young prince towards Horatio.

Another point in this scene worth noticing is that the sailor who delivers the letters alludes to Hamlet as

> The ambassador that was bound for England;

which shows that Hamlet had preserved his *incognito* to all but the chiefs of the pirates, perhaps even to them; though he must have told them he was a person of great influence at Court, as they treated him well because he was 'to do a good turn for them'. It is not difficult to believe that Hamlet fraternised with these rough sailors just as he did with the actors, and probably enjoyed his stay among them well enough.

Horatio loses no time in setting out with the sailors to join Hamlet, whereby he would be prevented from hearing of Ophelia's death till, in company with his friend, he witnesses the 'maimed rites' of her burial.

In the next scene (Act IV, scene 7) we find that the King has completely satisfied Laertes not only that he was innocent of Polonius' death, but that he stood in great danger himself from the violence of Hamlet. What was the exact account which Claudius gave of the affair we do not know; but probably he contented himself with very much the same account as that given by the Queen (Act IV, scene i, lines 7–11):

> in his lawless fit,
> Behind the arras hearing something stir,

> Whips out his rapier, cries 'a rat, a rat!'
> And in his brainish apprehension kills
> The unseen good old man.

It will be remembered that then he expressed his fears for his own life. It had been so with us, had we been there:

but the story is incomplete in one very important point—Claudius, naturally, withholds Hamlet's reason for seeking his life from Laertes—an omission which makes him ask with much reason:

> but tell me
> Why you proceeded not against these feats,
> So crimeful and so capital in nature,
> As by your safety, wisdom, all things else,
> You mainly were stirr'd up.
>
> (IV, vii, 5–9)

The King's answer is plausible enough; his devotion to the Queen made him unwilling to punish the son whom she loved so much, and Hamlet's popularity was so great that any public proceedings against him would have been likely to have led to a revolution. Laertes is obliged to accept this explanation; 'but', he adds,

> my revenge will come.
> King. Break not your sleeps for that; you must not think
> That we are made of stuff so flat and dull
> That we can let our beard be shook with danger
> And think it pastime. You shortly shall hear more:
> I loved your father, and we love ourself;
> And that, I hope, will teach you to imagine—

It is evident that Claudius refers to the letter he had sent, by Rosencrantz and Guildenstern, to England ordering the instant execution of Hamlet; indeed, he probably would have given Laertes a very broad hint as to what was the revenge he might speedily expect, had he not been interrupted by the entry of the messenger bringing letters from Hamlet himself, announcing his 'sudden and more strange return'. One is rather apt to overlook the dramatic nature of this situation (to use a technical term) when one finds fault with the construction of the last two acts of this play. A more complete surprise, as far as Claudius was concerned, could scarcely have been devised, or one which more thoroughly defeated all his plans.

That Claudius is thoroughly puzzled at the strange turn of events, and that, at first, he is quite at a loss what to do, his words show. He even appeals to Laertes for advice—

> Can you advise me?

and his next speech is, as it stands in the text, hopelessly obscure; though it is clear enough that he is unable to account satisfactorily to himself for this sudden return of Hamlet, and that his mind is harassed by the possible dangers to himself that such a return suggests. Laertes, on the contrary, rejoices at the idea of meeting Hamlet—

> It warms the very sickness of my heart,
> That I shall live and tell him to his teeth,
> 'Thus didest thou'.

He has the advantage over the King of being single-minded in his purpose; he needs no tortuous means to his end, though, ultimately, he weakly consents to use such. It would have been well for his own honour had he adhered to the frank declaration of vengeance which he here makes, had he reproached Hamlet to his face, and openly challenged him to fight.

But to the wily mind of Claudius any straightforward revenge, such as could be obtained by a fair fight between Laertes and Hamlet, was utterly distasteful; besides, such a revenge would be at best uncertain, and might fail in the end to rid him of his hated nephew. Once embarked upon the ocean of crime, one must sail on through all the rocks and quicksands; a straight course is impossible. Already in his fertile brain and treacherous heart a scheme of cruel and underhand vengeance is being planned; his only doubt is whether this generous, and seemingly noble-minded, youth will consent to be his instrument in carrying it out. So much more tractable is Laertes now than when, but a little while since, he rudely burst in upon the royal presence at the head of a riotous mob, that he consents to be ruled by the King so long as he does not 'overrule' him 'to a peace'. The scheme, which in so short a time has grown 'ripe' in the 'device' of Claudius, answers every end required—it is sure, it is safe, involving no danger or blame to those who execute it:

> But even his mother shall uncharge the practice,
> And call it accident.

Laertes gives the other his cue when he says—

> My lord, I will be ruled;
> The rather, if you could devise it so
> That I might be the organ.
> King. It falls right.
> You have been talk'd of since your travel much,
> And that in Hamlet's hearing, for a quality
> Wherein, they say, you shine: your sum of parts,
> Did not together pluck such envy from him,
> As did that one, and that in my regard
> Of the unworthiest siege.
>
> (Q2 IV, vii, 67–75, Additional passage K)

Observe the cunning with which Claudius manages his flattery; Laertes has so many good qualities, and of these the 'least worthy', according to this good King's thinking, has excited Hamlet's envy; but this quality is depreciated by the artful tempter only to be extolled the next moment as

> A very riband in the cap of youth,

then, after tantalising him with some laboured and sententious phrases, he lets him know that this high report of his qualities comes from one, himself a pattern of manly skill and courage, for whose opinion, as Claudius probably knew, Laertes had the utmost respect, and to be praised by whom was alone enough to excite his vanity in the highest degree. At last it turns out that the quality, so especially praised by this great authority, was skill at fencing; the very art in which Hamlet and Laertes had doubtless, in their early youth, been friendly but keen rivals . . .

I have dwelt thus at length upon this scene both because it is of the greatest importance to follow it carefully before attempting to form any judgment of the character of Laertes, and because I believe it to be one of the most carefully elaborated scenes, as far as Shakespeare is concerned, in the whole play. The bare skeleton of it in the Quarto of 1603 shows us what great pains he has taken in the revision of it; and there is one important alteration which I cannot but think shows, more than anything else, what judgment Shakespeare intended us to form of Laertes. In the older version the King makes his proposal thus:

> When you are hot in midst of all your play,
> Among the foyles shall a keene rapier lie,
> Steeped in a mixture of deadly poyson,
> That if it draws but the least dramme of blood,
> In any part of him, he cannot live;

so that the idea of the poison does not come from Laertes, a circumstance which lessens his guilt in no little degree.

As a psychological study, I think this scene, as it now stands, one of Shakespeare's greatest efforts. The contrast between the two natures is admirable. On the one side we have the older and hardened criminal, an adept at treachery, and incapable of denying himself the pleasure of doling out his stores of iniquity slowly, and with subtle relish of their super-excellent quality; so enamoured of hypocrisy that he must smother every word of his murderous proposal with a pile of moral platitudes; so inured to juggling with his conscience that it comes natural to him to regale the youth, whom he is inviting to a vile crime, with unctuous lectures on the heavenly nature of filial love, and of 'goodness' in general. Opposed to this highly polished gem of villainy, we have the passionate, violent, unreflecting youth, full of generous impulses and high courage; naturally averse to any but the directest road to whatever might be his object; ready to 'cut his enemy's throat in the church' without a thought of the consequences; who would have fought by the hour, and as long as he could hold a sword, if anyone had dared to call him a coward; and yet was so devoid of any true and stable principle of courage or honour, that he could listen to a proposal to stab an unarmed man under cover of a friendly trial of skill, and could aggravate such a proposal by the addition of a subtle and deadly poison to the weapon of assassination. This contrast, so skilfully preserved in all the finest details, ceasing only when, in accordance with the great moral truth which the poet is instilling, their perfect resemblance is shown in their common want of that vigilant and incorruptible virtue which is the result of fixed and unalterable principles, and alone can preserve us from crime—such a study of character shows the hand of a master who knew human nature, not by the reading of books, but by the observation of mankind, less from laboured research than from that instinctive knowledge which is only given to the few who are born to the imperishable heritage of genius . . .

The fifth act commences with the well-known scene between the 'Clowns', or 'Grave-diggers'. This scene has been much censured by some critics, on the ground that its broad humour is out of place in a tragic work. But here is the very excellence of Shakespeare's genius—that he does not shrink from mingling the humorous with the pathetic; in fact, he does not shrink from portraying human life as it really is. He knew mankind in general as well as he knew that portion of it which forms the audience of a theatre; he knew that if his plays were to attract spectators they must be varied, and not monotonous: we may admire such tragedies as Voltaire's in the closet, but on the stage they crush us under their massive weight of lugubriousness. But this system of brightening up tragedy, by the infusion of the comic element, is contrary to all the canons of foreign criticism. Any one who has seen *Hamlet* played on the Italian stage will have observed the preternatural gravity of Polonius, for instance, and generally how careful all the actors were, including even Hamlet himself, to divest the play as much as possible of any taint of humour. In this very scene we are now considering, when I saw it played at Naples, there was only one grave-digger (he was necessary for Hamlet), and he sang quite a pretty little song in place of the humorous ballad of which 'The First Clown' in Shakespeare gives us such an odd version . . .

The malignant way in which Steevens has misrepresented Hamlet's conduct in this scene is pretty well known, chiefly from the indignant remonstrances it has called forth. But it may be as well to give the passage here:—

> He interrupts the funeral designed in honour of this lady (Ophelia), at which both the King and Queen were present; and by such an outrage to decency, renders it still more necessary for the usurper to lay a second stratagem for his life, though the first had proved abortive. He insults the brother of the dead, and boasts of an

affection for his sister, which before he had denied to her face, and yet at this very time must be considered as desirous of supporting the character of a madman, so that the openness of his confession is not to be imputed to him as a virtue.[13]

Poor Hamlet! Had you been standing in the Old Bailey dock, and George Steevens counsel for the prosecution, you would have scarce escaped hanging! For good taste and veracity this venomous indictment reminds one of the Old Bailey in its worst days. It was, perhaps, well for Mr. Steevens that no usurper was at hand to punish outrages to decency, on the part of critics, in his day with the same sternness which Claudius found necessary in Hamlet's case. Seriously speaking, it is hard to believe that the man who wrote the above criticism had ever read Shakespeare's *Hamlet*. One would think it referred to the conduct of some misguided young man who had rudely interrupted the funeral 'designed in honour' of some distinguished person in Westminster Abbey. The whole circumstances of the case, the character, situation, and calamities of Hamlet—in fact, all that has happened, or has been told us, in the former part of the play, is ignored. It is sufficient to observe here that when Hamlet told Ophelia 'he loved her not', he was speaking in the character of a madman; while in this case, it is real passion which completely overcomes his self-control.

Maddened as Hamlet is by the sight of Laertes' grief, he still retains sufficient command of himself to remonstrate with him. Immediately on his leaping into the grave, Laertes seizes him by the throat, exclaiming—

> The devil take thy soul!

Hamlet forbears, at first, to repel violence with violence. There is dignity as well as self-command in his answer—

> Thou pray'st not well.
> I prithee, take thy fingers from my throat;
> For, though I am not splenitive and rash,
> Yet have I in me something dangerous,
> Which let thy wisdom fear. Hold off thy hand.
>
> (V, i, 256–60)

---

13   For an account of Steevens and his views on *Hamlet* see *CRH*, i, 218ff.

He does not forget that Laertes is, after all, her brother; he does not at first struggle with him; he begs him to take his hand off him; for though he is not prone to violence, he has 'something dangerous' in him now. It would seem that Laertes, forgetting all but his hatred of Hamlet, would then and there have taken his revenge. The latter is driven to defend himself, and some of the courtiers are obliged to part the two. Hamlet's blood is now up, and he flings away all concealment:

> Hamlet. Why, I will fight with him upon this theme
>   Until my eyelids will no longer wag.
> Queen. O my son, what theme?
> Hamlet. I loved Ophelia: forty thousand brothers
>   Could not, with all their quantity of love,
>   Make up my sum.

It is impossible for me to describe the effect which that cry of agony, 'I loved Ophelia', has upon me. I never heard it yet spoken on the stage with one-thousandth part of the force that rightly belongs to it. Is it not the key to much of the mystery which Hamlet has been to all around him, and, in some degree, even to himself? It is the cry of a love which has been cruelly beaten down, which has been kept, as it were, chained and gagged in the farthest corner of his sorrow-darkened heart; it has never ceased to struggle against its fetters; and now at last, in the anguish of death, its bonds are burst and its voice can be stifled no longer. Whatever the consequences, in the presence even of his uncle, before whom he would have shrunk from showing any glimpse of his real feelings, Hamlet is obliged to lay bare his heart's wounds. Precisely in proportion to the sincerity and depth of his love for Ophelia has been the difficulty which he experienced in fulfilling a task involving the abandonment of that love. Much of his bitterness to her and others is now explained; for he was trying to kill an affection which would not die.

It is remarkable that in his fury Hamlet makes action the test of sincerity:

> What wilt thou do for her?

And again:

> Hamlet. 'Swounds, show me what thou'lt do;
> Woo't weep? woo't fight? woo't fast? woo't tear thyself?
> Woo't drink up eisel? eat a crocodile?
> I'll do't. Dost thou come here to whine?
> To outface me with leaping in her grave?
> Be buried quick with her, and so will I:
> And, if thou prate of mountains, let them throw
> Millions of acres on us, till our ground,
> Singeing his pate against the burning zone
> Make Ossa like a wart! Nay an thou'lt mouth,
> I'll rant as well as thou.

It is evident that Hamlet speaks these words with the utmost vehemence; he is in that state of excitement in which such temperaments as his crave the outlet of action; *at this moment* he would do any of the things he mentions. Whether, finding himself carried away by his rage into a declaration of his love for Ophelia, he has sufficient presence of mind to exaggerate his language wilfully, in order that he may lessen the importance of such a confession, may be a matter for conjecture. I believe myself that this outburst is one of those uncontrollable paroxysms of excitement which persons who, like Hamlet, are on the verge of madness, must occasionally suffer if they are to preserve their reason at all. It is possible that Hamlet's fury was aggravated by the recollection that he, like Laertes, was prone to threaten much and to perform comparatively little. For Laertes is by no means the man of action that he at first sight appears to be. The catastrophe which overtook Ophelia might have been prevented, had he, instead of discussing schemes of vengeance with Claudius, have followed his sister out, when he saw her unhappy condition, and not have left her until he had placed her in some trustworthy hands. It was in more than one respect that Hamlet might have seen in the circumstances of Laertes some reflection of his own; for in both of them strong feeling and enthusiasm were wrongly directed.

The Queen's description of Hamlet's mental condition is very beautiful, and no doubt it is also true; in fact, this is one of the speeches which, like that in which she describes her son's grief over the body of Polonius, is intended to admit us behind the scenes, and to reveal to us those phases of Hamlet's character which could not be exhibited on the stage:

> This is mere madness:
> And thus awhile the fit will work on him;
> Anon, as patient as the female dove
> When that her golden couplets are disclosed,
> His silence will sit drooping.

Hamlet almost justifies this description by the sudden change in his tone from passionate invective to gentle expostulation—

> Hear you, sir;
> What is the reason that you use me thus?
> I loved you ever.

Had he been able to restrain himself and to argue calmly with Laertes, he might well have asked him why he execrated the friend of his youth for an act which was committed unintentionally, and which had been bitterly repented, without giving that friend any chance of explaining his conduct. It seems as if Hamlet now felt the effects of reaction after his vehement outburst of rage, and was inclined to yield to that spirit of fatalism which every now and then got possession of him. This is the only explanation which I can see of the somewhat enigmatical words with which he concludes this speech—

> but it is no matter;
> Let Hercules himself do what he may,
> The cat will mew, and dog will have his day. *Exit*

The commentators have not exerted their ingenuity on this passage, which is rather unintelligible: the meaning would seem to be, 'Not even the strength of Hercules can change the disposition which Nature implants in us; it is not in your nature to understand my motives; and do whatever I will, you will persist in misunderstanding them.'

Hamlet goes away in such a state of agitation that he forgets the presence of Horatio, whom the King wisely bids to wait on him. The last three lines that Claudius speaks are addressed to Laertes, and the speech should thus be marked:

> (To Laertes) Strengthen your patience in our last night's speech;
> We'll put the matter to the present push.

Critical Responses to Hamlet 401

(To the Queen) Good Gertrude, set some watch over your son.
(To Laertes) This grave shall have a living monument:
    An hour of quiet shortly shall we see;
    Till then, in patience our proceedings be.

By 'a living monument' Claudius means that a living man shall be sacrificed to the memory of the dead. Laertes could not but be confirmed in his purpose by what had passed; everything is most ingeniously contrived by Shakespeare to fan the flame of his resentment against Hamlet . . .

The next scene [between Hamlet and Osric] is one of the most charming pieces of high comedy which Shakespeare has left us; and those are very superficial critics who talk of the slovenliness of the last act, for the elaborate finish of this scene, at least, cannot be denied. It barely exists in the first version of 1603. Shakespeare was too great an artist not to know that any interruption to the action at this point would not be tolerated, unless it were of so interesting a nature as to reconcile the audience to the delay. Some pause is necessary before the scheme of the King and Laertes can be carried out. Nowhere is the irony, which pervades this great work, more remarkable than in the contrivance of introducing what the spectators know is a treacherous design to assassinate Hamlet with a genuinely comic prelude. Affectation was never more happily ridiculed than it is in this mincing periphrastic courtier; nor was satire ever more effective and good-humoured than is that of Hamlet, whose wit shines now with greater brilliancy than ever, though he is heavy at heart and is standing unconsciously on the brink of his own grave . . .

Osric has left them but a very short time when 'a Lord' enters with a message from the King, who sends to know if it be Hamlet's pleasure to play with Laertes at once, or if he prefers to wait. The first sentence of Hamlet's answer sounds oddly in his mouth:

Hamlet. I am constant to my purposes; they follow the
King's pleasure: if his fitness speaks, mine is ready; now or whensoever, provided
I be so able as now.

How different the tone of this answer to that in which he replied to Rosencrantz and Guildenstern when they were acting as the King's ambassadors (Act IV, scene ii, lines 24–30). Hamlet seems to be anxious to atone for his outbreak of temper at Ophelia's grave in every way; and it is as much from this motive, as from the spirit of emulation which was strong in him, that he accepts Laertes' challenge. All his answers are courteous, and even submissive:

> Lord. The king and queen and all are coming down.
> Hamlet. In happy time.
> Lord. The queen desires you to use some gentle
>   entertainment to Laertes before you fall to play.
> Hamlet. She well instructs me.

There is no bitterness, no affectation of madness; no rebellion against his mother's authority. He is confident of winning the wager; yet about his heart 'all is ill'. Horatio tries to persuade him to abandon the match, even at the last moment, but he will not listen to his suggestions; the very misgivings that he feels only serve to strengthen his resolution; a strange fitful obstinacy, not uncommon in those whose indecision is the result of over-much reflection. Such persons seem often to find a kind of relief in acting on sudden impulses, or in spite of strong forebodings. Hamlet's last speech to Horatio points to the fact that his fatalism has been growing upon him until it has entirely usurped the place of any other faith. True that it is not a pagan fatalism, but neither is it the resignation of a Christian, in spite of the allusion to the New Testament. It is at best the negative courage of a conscientious doubter, who knows that death must come, but is content to leave the hereafter in uncertainty:

> we defy augury: there is a special providence in the fall of a sparrow. If it be now, 'tis not to come; if it be to come, it will be now; if it be not now, yet it will come: the readiness is all; since no man has aught of what he leaves, what is't to leave betimes? Let be.
>
>   (V, ii, 165–70)

On the stage a change of scene now occurs, but it appears that originally there was none, the conversation with Horatio and Osric taking place in the same hall in which the fencing match occurs. The King, Queen, Laertes, and Court enter, the flagons of wine are set on the table, and the first part of the treacherous plot against Hamlet's life commences with the placing of Laertes' hand in Hamlet's by his pious Majesty King Claudius. What must be the feelings of Laertes at this moment, as he suffers himself to go through this monstrous hypocrisy? He has need of a courage such as few murderers have ever shown, if he is not to tremble as he takes, in solemn reconciliation, the hand of the man whom he is about to assassinate in the most perfidious manner.

I transcribe the whole of Hamlet's speech here, as it has been made the grounds for an attack on his good faith and truthfulness by Johnson, whose note on the passage is—

> I wish Hamlet had made some other defence; it is unsuitable to the character of a good or a brave man, to shelter himself in falsehood.[14]

Of course, Steevens greedily seizes on this accusation, and adds it to his long list of charges against Hamlet; but I believe it to be utterly unjust, and founded on a total misconception of this particular passage, and of Hamlet's character. Let us see what it is that Hamlet says, and under what circumstances he says it:—
[Marshall quotes the whole of Hamlet's speech, V, ii, 172–90.]

Now this apology, and I maintain that it is a most generous and frank apology, has to be made in the presence of Claudius, and of the courtiers before whom Hamlet had, for his own purposes, assumed madness. He could not have ignored this assumption; he could not have said—'The King and Queen and all about the court have thought me mad, but I am not mad at all; I have been only pretending to be so; I killed your father by mistake', etc. etc., entering, in fact, into a long explanation of that which it was imperatively necessary he should keep concealed. The madness which he alleges, as his excuse, before Claudius and the others is the madness which he had assumed; but there was another madness, the 'sore distraction' into which the tragic calamities that had darkened his young life had driven him, the terrible anguish of mind which he felt on hearing with such awful suddenness of his beloved Ophelia's death. It was not untruthful of him to say that he had killed Polonius, and had raved against Laertes by the side of his sister's grave, when in such a state of mental agitation as might well be held to excuse him from any guilty intention. I do not see how Hamlet could possibly make a more open confession, under the circumstances, than he does in the last four

---

14 See *CRH*, i, 191.

lines. It was such a confession as might have induced Laertes to question him further when alone; but it was not a deliberate piece of falsehood, nor was it so wanting in thoroughness and magnanimity but it should have forced the most relentless spirit, however greatly wronged, to pause in its work of vengeance . . .

Hamlet is full of gracious courtesy and elegant compliment, as if endeavouring to efface from the minds of all who had witnessed it his violent behaviour in the churchyard. Even for Claudius he has a gentle and polite answer:

> Very well, my lord;
> Your grace has laid the odds o'the weaker side.

There is a wonderful skill and power in the tragic touches of this last scene which we, who know what is going to happen, are apt to overlook. What can be more pathetic than to see this noble-hearted, generous, youth falling with such unsuspicious readiness into the treacherous plot, and by his very fairness and courtesy making the guilt of his murderers appear so much greater? As unconsciously he goes to his death all that is most amiable in his nature seems to put forth itself: the grating irony, the savage vindictiveness of language, the bitter contempt for the inferior natures around him, have all disappeared in the Hamlet we have now before us; and as we contrast him with the Hamlet of the grave scene, we are forcibly reminded of the Queen's beautiful description . . . (Act V, scene i, lines 283–5[15])

Laertes would really seem to deserve the playful reproach of Hamlet—

> you but dally;
> I pray you, pass with your best violence;
> I am afeard you make a wanton of me—

for he scruples, now it is in his hand, to use the treacherous weapon. It may be, if he had not committed himself so deeply with Claudius, in whose presence he felt an ignoble shame at the idea of seeming to flinch

---

15 This speech is given to the Queen in Q2, to Claudius in F. Most modern editors follow F.

from his deadly purpose, Laertes' better feelings might even now have prevailed. But it is too late: he rouses himself to action, attacks his antagonist with the utmost vigour, meeting with a more obstinate and skilful defence than he had anticipated. At last he breaks down Hamlet's guard and wounds him; both had already become somewhat heated in the struggle, and the slight pain which Hamlet would feel, though he does not notice it, would serve to aggravate his excitement: their play becomes wild, and in the scuffle Hamlet changes foils with Laertes and wounds him in turn. So completely absorbed is he in this trial of skill that he seems to have forgotten for the moment everything else, and does not even feel the wound, or see the blood to which Horatio draws attention. But he is soon back to a horrible consciousness of his tragic surroundings, no less than of his own fate. His mother falls on the ground in agony: Hamlet's first anxiety is for her; he does not even answer Horatio's inquiry as to himself. The Titanic hypocrisy of Claudius does not even now fail him; he cannot resist the temptation to lie, however useless it may be:

> King. She swounds to see them bleed.

Perhaps he thought Gertrude's love would even now be stronger than aught else, and that she would with her dying breath seek to conceal his infamy. But he is mistaken:

> Queen. No, no, the drink, the drink,—O my dear Hamlet,-
> The drink, the drink! I am poison'd.

It is fit that the first denunciation of his treachery, which was his death-warrant, should come from her who was at once the cause, and the victim, of his heaviest crime.

Laertes makes all the atonement now in his power, and it is remarkable that against him Hamlet neither expresses, nor feels, any resentment. In the few moments that are left to him of life he is all action; the excitement sustains his strength, even under the deadly effects of the poison, sufficiently to enable him to stab the King, and, heedless of the cry of 'treason' and the appeal for help which the wounded wretch makes, to pour the poison, 'temper'd by himself', down the murderer's throat. The entreaty of Laertes—

> Exchange forgiveness with me, noble Hamlet:
> Mine and my father's death come not upon thee,
> Nor thine on me!

is frankly and generously answered. It may be observed that Laertes makes no allusion to Ophelia, and that Hamlet does not stop to consider the difference in degree of their respective guilt before he exchanges forgiveness with his assassin. Though life is fast ebbing away, he yet has strength to snatch the poisoned cup from Horatio, who could not bear the idea of being parted from his friend even in death, and to charge him with the solemn duty of vindicating his good name; the well-known lines in which with touching anxiety he makes this last request are so beautiful that I cannot refrain from quoting them:—

> O good Horatio, what a wounded name,
> Things standing thus unknown, shall live behind me!
> If thou didst ever hold me in thy heart,
> Absent thee from felicity awhile,
> And in this harsh world draw thy breath in pain,
> To tell my story.

The approach of the victorious Fortinbras, the sight of whose energetic action had so keenly rebuked Hamlet's indolent procrastination, and the arrival of the ambassadors from England with the news of the success of his deadly stratagem against Rosencrantz and Guildenstern, add to the dramatic force of this closing scene.

Almost the last syllables he can utter are devoted to practical ends: there is no moralising now; anxious as he is to hear the fate of those false friends on whom he had taken so terrible a revenge, he leaves the subject to urge with his dying voice the claim of Fortinbras to the crown that should have been his own. Death overmasters him before he can complete his directions to Horatio, and he expires with the strange and pithy dogma in which his doubting creed is summed up—

> The rest is silence.

Neither hope, nor despair, as to the future, possesses his departing soul: his religion is a resigned uncertainty—better than a fretful doubt, but infinitely below the sweet hope, and humble trust, of a true Christian.

With the death of Hamlet the play virtually ends. Horatio's farewell—

> Good night, sweet prince,
> And flights of angels sing thee to thy rest!

recalls Hamlet's own words, 'to die, to sleep'. The entry of Fortinbras and the ambassadors is necessary merely to complete the story. We may, perhaps, regret that Shakespeare never felt impelled to write the speech of Horatio over the bodies of Hamlet and the others. Had he done so, it would have formed a splendid parallel to that of Antony over the body of Caesar.

'The rest is silence'. These are the very words that rise to our lips as we look back upon the mighty work which we have thus followed, step by step, from its solemn beginning to its tragical end. Through what scenes of infinite variety have we travelled; what marvellous insight into human nature have we attained! Admiration may well be dumb, for such creative power as that which called these characters into existence seems to us almost more than human. The mind may well ponder in silence on the great problems which the history of Hamlet presents; the soul may well lie hushed in awe as she contemplates those mysteries which have wrung this noble heart with such agony of incertitude. The contest between doubt and faith is finished; and in the boundless ocean of eternity this storm-tossed spirit, let us trust, has found rest and peace at last.

We have traced his faltering steps from the day when the eager energy, and hungry love, of his youth were paralysed and blighted by the crime which robbed one parent of life, and the other of that sacred right to love and honour, without which a mother's name is to her son but a terrible inheritance of infamy. We have seen him, while scarcely able to sustain the burden of this great sorrow, yet laden in addition with a charge of vengeance, which he gladly embraces as a sacred duty, but perpetually scruples to fulfil. In spite of his constant hesitation, of his overstrained conscientiousness, of his fitful and fruitless energy, of his misplaced tenderness and his equally misplaced bitterness—in spite of the painful contrast between the vigour of his words and the feebleness of his actions, we have seen so much that is noble, and generous, and grand in his character, that, in spite of all his weakness, we honour him as much as we love him. When we analyse this feeling, we find that our admiration for Hamlet is chiefly excited by the strong love of virtue and hatred of vice which never fail to distinguish him, and from the excess of which his very worst faults arise. Nor is his standard of right and wrong based on that comfortable compromise with Heaven, which is the foundation of the world's morality. Every character in the play, with the exception of Horatio and Ophelia, represents some type of such morality, from the plausible murderer, Claudius, to the harmless but ridiculous 'waterfly', Osric. With all these Hamlet is in a state of antagonism. It matters nothing that we ourselves may not have the courage to do anything but swim with the stream, and bow our heads gracefully before the wind of popular opinion; our own pliability in no way interferes with the admiration that we feel for the uncompromising scorn with which Hamlet ridicules, exposes, and denounces, the falseness and baseness of those around him.

What, then, is the chief moral defect of Hamlet's character? 'L'Amleto c'è il dubbio', says Signor Salvini, in his musical voice, and with that charming manner which almost carries conviction with it. [In a conversation which I had the privilege of enjoying with the great Italian actor, he drew an eloquent comparison between Hamlet and Orestes, whose circumstances present so much similarity, while their characters form so great a contrast. It would be interesting to know if reading the story of Orestes suggested to Shakespeare the creation of Hamlet's character. Horatio, the 'Pylades' of Hamlet, has no parallel in the old history of Saxo Grammaticus.[16]] 'Doubt' or 'hesitation' is certainly one main characteristic of Hamlet's nature, and it may arise, in great part, from his over-reflective habit of mind. But the 'diagnosis', so to speak, of this mental disease of 'hesitation' it is difficult to determine. It seems to me that the principal flaw in Hamlet's character is the want of humility, and consequently of faith. I do not mean that humility which is the brightest jewel in the martyr's crown, that patient and cheerful submission to every provocation, that glorious self-abasement which our Saviour first taught and practised; but rather that humility which is the backbone of enthusiasm, which consists of a complete subordination of one's own prejudices and desires and will to some great purpose, and of a belief, so thorough and unquestioning in the justice of that purpose, as to render any hesitation, in one's efforts to accomplish it, impossible. Had Hamlet possessed

---

16 Passage in brackets, as author's footnote.

this humility he would never have doubted for one moment that the Ghost's charge of vengeance was to be fulfilled at any cost; he would never have thought of the consequences to his body or to his soul; but would have openly slain Claudius, and would have stood before the people with the blood fresh on his hands, indifferent as to their judgment and fearless of their punishment. Such humility does not always lend itself to the accomplishment of great or good ends; the fanatic shares it with the enthusiast, the assassin with the liberator.

The want of faith in Hamlet's character is very remarkable. It is true he believes the Ghost at first, the more readily because its revelation confirms his suspicion; but he puts off acting on his belief from day to day, and ultimately reveals the fact that he has been harassed by doubts as to the identity of the Spirit which assumed his 'noble father's person'; not being content until he had confirmed its statement by a device of his own contrivance, sufficiently ingenious, but not infallible, and which any one, who had real faith in the supernatural messenger, would have thought it neither necessary, nor becoming, to employ. In many other instances does Hamlet show how little certainty there was in his faith even on the most solemn subjects; he does not disbelieve, but neither does he believe; he wishes to do so, but his mind cannot refrain from questioning everything which is not capable of absolute proof. I do not for one moment believe that Shakespeare intended to represent Hamlet as an infidel, but rather as one of those men, whom we meet not unfrequently in real life, who are deficient in that intellectual humility which is content to receive supernatural truths on some grounds other than natural evidence. The moral natures of such men are frequently of the noblest and purest type; but their practical power for good, in this world, is fettered by a constant tendency to doubt the principles of their faith just at the very moment when that prompt action, which can only spring from perfect trust and entire conviction, is necessary.

The metaphysical theories which have been put forward as explanations of the problem which Hamlet's character presents are numberless. Some of them are ridiculously far-fetched, while others are evolved more from the writer's own mind than from the text of Shakespeare. I do not wish to wrest a moral from this play, which its contents do not justify, merely because it may accord with my own moral or religious opinions.

But I think an unprejudiced mind cannot fail to be struck by the coincidence that this wonderful psychological work, which seems to bear more strongly than any the impress of the author's own mind, should have been written at a time when this country had just broken away from the old Faith, and had abandoned unquestioning obedience to the Church's authority for a partial submission to private judgment. The Catholic religion still represented, to many who had separated from Rome, all that was definite in their faith; their hearts still yearned towards that communion, and they were trying to reconcile their consciences to a compromise which was morally impossible. They could not see, or they would not acknowledge, that imperfection is a necessary quality of humanity; and therefore that abuses and scandals must exist as long as the ministers and disciples of religion are men; but that the way to get rid of these evils was not to break away from the Church, but to conform more rigidly to her Divine precepts. These men wished to preserve most of the dogmas of Catholicism, while they reserved to themselves the right to reject the authority on which their dogmas rested. The consequence was that they involved themselves in a moral dilemma; they began by asserting that each individual was bound to question the grounds of his faith by the aid of his own reason, and that thus he would arrive at truth; but having once admitted this power of questioning what claimed to be revelation, it was impossible to limit the exercise of that power; so that many minds were tossed about upon a fathomless sea of doubt, hopelessly uncertain which way to steer, no longer believing in their compass, and distrustful of the very stars by which otherwise they might have directed their course. Truth after truth, which men had long cherished as Divine, was condemned before a self-constituted court of human judges, till to some minds nothing in this world seemed certain or secure; and the very foundations of Christianity were shaken beyond repair by the same storm that had shattered the pinnacles of the edifice.

Of such minds Hamlet is a striking type, and the creation of his character might well be the outcome of an intellect perplexed and agitated by such doubts as I have described, with a yearning desire to be convinced, but with its powers of conviction hopelessly debilitated.

PR
2807
.C75